A NOT-SO-STILL LIFE

A NOT-SO-STILL LIFE

A child
of Europe's
pre-World War II
art world and
his remarkable
homecoming to
America.

by
jimmy ernst

Pushcart Press

Many of the photographs reproduced in this book were preserved in trust by Maja Aretz in Cologne, longtime member of the Lou Straus-Ernst household. Others were preserved as twentieth-century documents by various cultural institutions in Europe and the United States.

Every effort has been made to locate the copyright holders of the illustrations reproduced in this book. Omissions brought to our attention will be corrected in subsequent printings.

Design by Mina Greenstein

Library of Congress Cataloging in Publication Data

Ernst, Jimmy, 1920–
    A not-so-still life.

    "A St. Martin's / Marek book."
    Includes index.
    1. Ernst, Jimmy, 1920–   2. Painters—United
States—Biography.   3. Avant-garde—Europe—History—20th
century.   I. Title.
ND237.E7A2   1984   759.13 [B]   83-21088

ISBN 0-916366-81-2

To Dallas,
Amy Louise and Eric Max—
what is owed to them
exceeds the pages of a book

CONTENTS

ACKNOWLEDGMENTS

As the manuscript pages accumulated into this book, an irreplaceable friend from my life in America was never far from my thoughts. I can still see him in 1947, sitting in a corner of the room while I painted late into the night, writing down, on whatever scraps of paper I had not used for drawing, images from my young life as they emerged in our conversation. Robert Alan Aurthur even had a title for our collaboration, based on our mutual enthusiasm for New Orleans and Chicago Jazz, the classic "That Dada Strain." The only copy of this sensitively crafted bit of personal history was irretrievably lost by a well-meaning friend shortly after Bob and I decided to let the matter rest until our lives had aged a bit more.

Bob Aurthur was the unobtrusive brother–friend whose hand was never far from mine when either one of us faced a mountain to be scaled or found ourselves in a moonless night that called for some light. When he died unexpectedly in 1978, I had just responded to his earlier encouragements to "paint the book" on my own. I wish I could have sent him the galleys. He, of all friends, should have seen them. But no authority has as yet been able to give me the correct zip code to where he is now.

In a 1968 interview for *Art in America*, then edited by Jean Lippman, Francine du Plessix Gray brilliantly transformed some of my personal recollections into an image of the world in which I grew up. Some years later Thomas M. Messer removed my remaining doubts about anecdotal material by pointing out to me that much of history, and indeed art history, gets its initial impetus from such individual retrospection. By that time the brilliant and sensitive historian Matthew Josephson had confirmed some of my early childhood impressions of the Dada days in the Tirol and rounded out for me his observances from his unique book *Life Among the Surrealists*.

I was fortunate that Maja Aretz, who brought me up, had saved many of my mother's letters and articles as well as a treasure of photographs. I had completely forgotten the haunting photograph of my mother and me by the great August Sander until it reentered my life when the world began to give him his due through many publications not too many years ago. I thank his grandson Gerd Sander and Michael Hofman, editor of *Aperture*, for the opportunity to bring it back into the immediate context of my life.

Beyond that I was in much need of help from a wide range of sources and individuals to assist me in my recall. Particularly where it concerned proper chronology. The material that Serge Klarsfeld compiled into the moving, but terrifying, document "Le Memorial de la Deportation des Juifs de France" clarified facts that had become shrouded for me in clouds of nightmares. The same can be said of a telephone conversation with Robert O. Paxton, co-author with Michael R. Murrys of an essential history *Vichy France and the Jews.* Barbara Goldsmith provided me with some of the writing of Jane Bowles to refresh my memory of that puzzling but extraordinary woman. I regained some clarity about the Art Gallery scene of the nineteen forties in New York from Julien Levy's *Memoir of an Art Gallery.* Margaret Barr, with her uncanny perception of the time she shared with her husband Alfred H. Barr, Jr., removed a number of obscurity-threatened gaps. As did Russell Lynes' brilliant *Good Old Modern* and Rudi Blesh's very human *Modern Art U.S.A.* The writings on Max Ernst by John Russell, Werner Spies, Patrick Waldberg, and Diane Waldman became important touchstones for my own recollections.

I knew better than to take for granted the biographical data compiled by my father as they appeared in successive publications and catalogues. I was both amused by and in turn understanding of events and facts glossed over, expanded or contracted, depending on some intangible changes in temperature. Much, but not all of it was the result of an extremely personal sense of humor. Except that once in a while a smile could freeze into an icicle.

My deep love and compassion for Peggy Guggenheim enabled me to disregard the unfortunate self-destructive tone in her autobiographical writings. I got to know a few of the real images hidden by those self-portraits. But I suppose not much of the self-damage can be undone.

Ethel Baziotes brought back to life so much that I remembered about her and Bill Baziotes from the glowing days that I spent in their presence.

I knew it to be essential that I speak openly to a wide range of individuals whose judgment, fairness, and sense of history I could trust in matters of objectivity, the craft of writing, and particular views of a world we share from varying vantage points of disparate biographies. They are, with deep apologies for slippages of the mind: Abe Ajai, James Brooks, Milton and Blanche Brown, Sidney Cohn, Morris Dorsky, Jean-Charles Gateau, Rust Hills, Joseph Kaufman, Arthur Kleiner, Mary Mothersill, Dorothy Norman, Gabe Perle, Bob and Wanda Ramsey, Gil and Anne Rose, Bryant and Liz Rollins, Irving Sandler, Harry Scordo, David Shaw, Hein and Eva Stünke, Joe Wilder, Joe and Bobbie Weinstein, Bill Woolfenden, and Mahonri Young.

On innumerable occasions I was able to turn for guidance to Herbert Schutz, Wilfred Sheed, Budd Schulberg, Eloise Spaeth, and Alden Whitman.

Much valuable research was provided by Judith R. Wolfe and Patricia Estes.

I will remain in awe of Carol E. W. Edwards' patience with this neophyte writer who is still bewildered by the patently impossible transformation into a book of a manuscript that resembled Central Park Meadow after a rock concert. When I was Andy Carpenter's age, the legendary Joan Kahn, now with St. Martin's Press, trusted me, a young painter, with a cover for a mystery. Now this young artist has shown me how it should have been done. In designing this book, he has deeply impressed me with his style and sensitivity.

Syd and Annie Solomon, as well as Sidney and Rita Adler, were among the many who helped me wrestle with the title. Conrad Marca-Relli's title suggestion "From Fatherland to Disneyland" would have been perfect for a book of a different complexion.

I found much sustenance, as I have over many years, in the magic visions of contemporary poets. With them the artists of our time walk the picketline for civilization. I treasure in particular a profound personal relationship with Louis Simpson, whose own life history is not dissimilar to mine.

I still owe John Hammond the $2.50 that I did not pay when I sneaked into Carnegie Hall in 1938 to hear and see "From Spirituals to Swing."

The reality of this book is owed by me to the existence of two superb human beings, Joyce Engelson and Gloria Safier. Because of them my words were allowed to touch upon a dimension beyond the mere re-creation of a past.

But finally all of the above and everything that follows could not even have been a fugitive dream if it had not been for Hans Augustin. He saved my life and beyond that he made it possible for me to live it in America.

Jimmy Ernst
East Hampton, N. Y.
1983

An Echo Etched in Smoke

THE forbidding silence was stone-colored against the barely budding trees above the streets of tombs in Paris' Père Lachaise Cemetery on this second day of April 1976. The crowns of this stand of woods mute the traffic noises from the Boulevard de Menilmontant while its roots caress what remains of Colette and Daumier. Balzac and Oscar Wilde are here forever, as are Rossini, Molière, Delacroix, Chopin, Proust, Modigliani, Apollinaire, Gertrude Stein, Seurat, Bizet, Corot, La Fontaine and Paul Éluard, Max Ernst's closest friend. Here, 143 Communards were shot by a firing squad in the late spring of 1871 at the Wall of the Fédérés.

Had it not been for that somber gray sky over the cobbled courtyard behind the crematorium, I could have been standing in the middle of an early Giorgio de Chirico painting like his 1916 *The Enigma of a Departure*. One towering chimney stood as a gateway for a muted road that led toward an infinite horizon. This solitary finger, sternly pointing toward eternity, was the guardian of arcaded cloisters that, moving away from each other, embraced the space outside the chapel. Under the arches successive railed walkways led past row upon row of small, but opaque, windows of the columbaria of vaults. These were openings not to be looked through from either side. It was a many-tiered prison with cells the size of large post-office boxes, for messages that arrived at a final destination without the need of a forwarding address.

Only eight of us had been allowed to come here. The gloom of the chapel with its canned music had driven us outdoors, and we were but a few forlorn solitary figures in this strange setting. Paris can be merciless in its beauty, demanding tears for each stone that contributed to its grandeur. Each breath of air unlocks a door to memories, both tragic and exhilarating. Very soon there would be blossoms on the trees and children would again sail their toy boats on the pond in Parc Luxembourg, observed and envied by those who, like me, could recall how little it sometimes took to be happy.

I stood on the edge of a knife, with fifty-five years littering the cobblestones and beyond in a bewildering lack of sequence. Stepping to safety into a life with new ghosts, without taking the residue with me, was patently impossible. I saw no safe bridge from here to there, no stepping-stones into the alien water of tomorrow. Like the other lone figures, I was waiting for the clock to start moving again.

It started as a rumble under my feet. Only fire could make that kind of noise. The furnace chamber was below me. The sound traveled past me. I thought I heard a gritty sigh in the tall chimney and saw a dense plume of smoke belch toward the low clouds. Undisturbed on this windless moment, the straight black column stood in the sky over Paris like an enormous exclamation mark. My father, Max Ernst, was now ashes.

A sudden thought was almost audible to me. It was of an image I had never seen. More than thirty years ago and many days by cattle car, to the east from here, my mother had also risen in smoke, namelessly joining the vapor of other burned ciphers. I did not even know if the sun had been shining when Lou Straus-Ernst became a statistic of Hitler's "Final Solution."

In 1965 my father and I had watched on French television the state funeral for the architect Le Corbusier replete with a long procession of official mourners and the mounted Garde Républicain. Max had expressed apprehension then that, because he had accepted the Légion d'honneur, his own death would occasion a similar spectacle. He had left strict orders that his own end go by without any notice. Of his relatives only his present wife, Dorothea Tanning Ernst, one of her nieces and a niece of Max, I and my wife Dallas were to be present, plus his lawyer and wife, and the art historian Werner Spies, who had gained the master's absolute trust. Spies had, in fact, asked my permission to take my place as the official witness to the actual cremation in the crypt. He reassured Dorothea that he had indeed seen the coffin actually being moved into the furnace. There could be no question whose ashes would be interred. But I had not been particularly eager to go down into the crypt to observe the burning.

The aura of a melancholy late Paris afternoon was tangible when a procession of four men emerged from the crematorium carrying, suspended from steel rods, the still hot ashes in a purple cloth-covered casing. Dorothea and I faced an opened cubicle on the ground floor of the columbarium as the anonymous canister, still emitting wisps of smoke, was gently placed into the recess. A mason sealed the opening with brick and mortar. One of the attendants approached us and asked our preference for a proper marking, without neglecting to quote the cost of each possibility. Spies' suggestion of the master's signature in relief somehow seemed out of place. Instead there was to be a black marble plaque with the gold-engraved inscription: MAX ERNST—1891–1976 . . . and again there was that sudden search for an image and a place: Where are my mother's ashes?

Max Ernst had died on April 1, 1976, just a few hours short of his eighty-fifth birthday, in the rue de Lille apartment where he had lain, incapacitated by a stroke, for a year. Two days later small clusters of callers filled the first-floor living area—some of them not quite sure how welcome they were and others still in shock that no exceptions had been made to the privacy-dictum for the funeral itself, even for old friends who, after traveling clear across France, found themselves barred at Père Lachaise. It was not just the passage of time or death that had me looking in vain for some familiar faces on that early Paris evening. During my father's last fragile years an inevitable inner circle had somehow isolated him from a number of dedicated friends and admirers. I experienced a curious sense of both fascination and detachment as I observed the first stirrings in the evolution of a new pecking order, now that the King of the Birds was dead. A small group had sequestered themselves around a table examining parts of a projected portfolio of poetry and lithographs, proposed by Louis Aragon in honor of Max Ernst. Judgments were already in the air about the relative importance of each one of the contributors and their proper order within the volume. The scene struck me as a bit ill-timed, with my own thoughts centered on whether the linens were still on the deathbed upstairs or had been turned to ashes with the body. In the fifty-five years of my existence I had never felt up to the kind of sophistication that I saw at play here again, but I now sensed with relief that it was this very failing which had prevented me from seeking room in that particular edifice of my father's world. With a stab of discomfort I heard a question directed to me from the other murmurs: ". . . all of the beautiful things on the walls here. . . . Many of them are going to belong to you. What are you going to do with them?" I was afraid that I would get drunk if I remained here. Later, my wife Dallas and I walked the streets of Paris. It was dark by then and the lights were diffused by a frigid haze.

The black smoke, the purple-covered box, the hands and trowel of the mason and the rumble of the furnace underground had joined the other ectoplasmic images in my cage of nightmares, there to mingle with their predecessors of a lifetime, and to emerge, night or day at their own bidding, from that amorphous enclosure that has followed me everywhere, devoid of physical weight or space. Not all of them have remained specters of fear as they transmute themselves behind my eyes from a vision-blocking flora and fauna into a giant plate of glass through which I stare, watching the past beyond and behind me, as my face of the present is reflected on its surface.

For three days now the cage of nightmares had pulsed with the in-and-out movement of its contents. Even my alcoholic haze, which followed the death message from a wire service, had not dimmed the clarity and details of the competing imagery. In defiance of chronology the past crowded in on me, hard-edged particles of a dust storm, raising a silent clamor of old questions that had outlived the fog of years. And now there were the new arrivals circling the eye of the storm. A blank. A void, created by the final disappearance of a smoke-plume over Père Lachaise, left me incapable of knowing whether I was grieving for a dead father or for the passing of a great artist whose magic had exploded the scope of functions for the eyes and minds of generations to come.

For the most part the early obituaries and announcements in the press and on television alluded as much to his personal life of numerous marriages as to the momentous body of work in painting, sculpture and collage, now a familiar part of any museum collection in the world. Even in the rich cast of twentieth-century creative geniuses, he had been unique, in all of his ways defying classification in his life both as an artist and as a human being. Most of this life would remain an enigma not just to the outside world but even to those who had been close to him.

Before they had taken the body away that morning, I had stood alone by his deathbed. In the all-too-common reaction when facing a corpse, I fully expected his eyes to flutter and then open, showing no surprise that the room had begun to fill with the chimeras that had come into being in his paintings and collages. Among the persistent Ernst themes: predatory nightingales posing for monuments; living forests reaching with petrified arms toward the moon; an evasive creature, Loplop, making erotic offerings; a carnivorous flower, Nymph Echo, waiting for prey; Napoleon rotting in a wilderness; bat-winged Courbet nudes with cloven hooves; a giant, daisy-nippled, breasts standing nonchalantly on trousered legs; vulture-headed dandies absconding with shrouded bodies; eerie herons devouring snakes in a Bosch landscape. I imagined his very bed becoming engulfed in a tidal wave of the sea. But the room remained very still and silver-gray, like the now translucent skin drawn tightly against the armature of his face, devoid at last of expectant curiosity or fervor. At this moment the apparitions were mine alone, but he had seen them before anyone else, and I had to expect that their presence, from now on, would be more than hallucinatory.

A
Cage of
Nightmares

Memory is a deserted midnight village,
Full of ancient surprises hoping for sleep.

ANONYMOUS

IMMOBILIZED as he had been that final year, Max Ernst must have fought the enforced languor of his body by letting his extraordinary creatures, who retained the suggestion of a smile even as they screamed or hissed or roared in alien elements, mate and battle with each other in the infinite spaces of his mind. I had the strange feeling that this ironic scoffer at popular credos knew where he was going after all of this. He had more friends in that other world than in this one, and none were casual acquaintances. His alter-ego, his enduring image, Loplop, the King of the Birds, had commuted to that fabulous landscape since April 2, 1891. Who knows? At this point he may have been looking forward to the adventure because he suspected that Loplop had not told him everything. A lifelong heretic, he once mused aloud to his trusted friend, historian Werner Spies, about a mysterious family of fish, lantern-fish, who, living in the blackest depth of the ocean, have been provided with light-emitting tentacles, as if to concede with some awe the possible existence of a cosmic Surrealist.

It seemed probable that during the new phase of his voyage he would travel exclusively in the company of the strange creatures and forces created by the obsessions of a lifetime. It would no longer be necessary to tolerate intimate human diversion; people were often so unreasonable when the newness of a relationship had worn off a bit and they were no longer so unique to him. The human population (often victims) in Max Ernst's *Lanterna Magica* had never properly understood that they were in fact only aspects of a magic slide show, likely to be discarded at the brightest moment. It was the chimeras and gorgons that dominated his life as friends and lovers. He seemed always apprehensive that the end result of emotional involvements was a detestable prison. "Why *not* eat the dessert first? I might not be hungry afterward," he once told Lou in the early days of their marriage.

There was about this man, my father Max Ernst, an almost unreasonably magic combination of physical beauty and intellectual sparkle, a magnet for which there seemed no defense. Yet, as a son I had experienced some of the terror that others, most particularly women, must have felt at the unexplained appearance of an impenetrable barrier that would freeze attempts to approach the inner person.

As I grew up, I got to know many of my father's companions who suffered these painful rejections, while being unable to explain to anyone, not even to themselves, the rational reasons for the change. Yet I rarely saw any bitterness in the extraordinary women who found themselves in his bewildering world. Immature as I was, I could not help but feel genuine compassion for most of them.

His self-absorbed behavior, as well as his early separation from my mother, had constantly raised new barriers to any possible rapport between us. I was far too young to know how much valuable time I was wasting in setting up standards of personal conduct for my father that were quite normal in their breach all around me. It is, of course, much easier now to look back at and understand Europe, and particularly the Paris of the decades that followed World War I. The intellectuals, artists and poets of that period were involved in a revolution that made no allowances for anything "normal" in personal relationships. Unlike our own time, which knows the term "revolution" as a much-used advertising slogan, these small bands of individuals were surrounded by massive hostility. Dedicated supporters or friendly patrons were practically nonexistent. Small interdependent knots of poets, artists and composers were at war with other groups whose aesthetic and political goals had to be opposed with vigor and vitriol. The perpetual battles of that era, including the constant specter of hunger and personal economic disaster, dictated an, at times, total disregard of what complacent minds choose to label "decency" or "human values." I would be hard pressed if I were asked to single out, in retrospect, individuals of that generation who, in one way or another, could not be called "monsters."

I spent the first seventeen years of my life openly declaring that I wanted to have nothing to do with art. I observed everything in sight with great curiosity, but I always managed to pretend that I found it totally irrelevant to my daily life. Painting could indeed be fascinating, particularly when it offered glimpses into the mysteries of sex. But it was an eccentricity, an invasion of privacy and at best a luxurious amusement. I could live with those who adored it, but I rejected their devotion to it. Lou Straus-Ernst endured many a teenage diatribe from her son on this subject, knowing full well that he was venting his anger and confusion against an absent father. She received these tirades with tolerant silence, perhaps a patient smile and sometimes with a few words: "Maybe you will feel differently when you grow up."

I am a painter now, but it was not until the onset of maturity that I surrendered my last resistance against that which is now my reason for existence. Since then I have discovered a great many things that, instead of hostility, deserve not merely respect but also unreserved love. I can even perceive some positive aspects to the terrors and upheavals that caused the quixotic and migratory personal history of my younger years. Had it been more tranquil, I might well have become saddled with the luxury of a "properly furnished mind."

There are many fragments of my personal history that I continue to find corroborated in documents, photographs, critiques and other writings about the personalities and ideas that began to see daylight almost coincidentally with my birth. Some of these accounts have been romanticized, cleaned up, but also scandalized over the span of decades. I cannot deny a perverse pleasure in my speculations about the motivations for such truth-bending. A lot of this material gives me very little room for conjecture about my own remembrances. It can be disconcerting to discover important events in one's life thus chronicled, but it also serves to remove doubts about their actuality.

The authenticity of my very first remembered graphic image was confirmed for me in an unpublished autobiography by my mother. The precious document came into my possession in 1948 via Switzerland, from Ella Picard, an old friend to whom Lou must have sent it for possible publication in 1941 or 1942. There were other witnesses as well: the American biographer and social historian Matthew Josephson recalled it, and Paul Éluard spoke to me about the same scene in 1937, and so did my father before his death. I recall it mainly as a possible portent for a life-long dilemma.

The memory and the "reality" are this: For the second consecutive year a number of Dadaist poets and artists were spending the summer of 1922 in some run-down buildings of a farm near Tarrenz in the Austrian Alps. Max and Louise Ernst, myself age 2 and my devoted nanny Maja Aretz were joined by the French poets Paul Éluard and Tristan Tzara, the Swiss sculptor Hans Arp, and a trickle of visitors, including Matthew Josephson and his wife. Éluard was accompanied by his wife Gala, (Mrs. Salvador Dali in a later marriage). On one particular late August day the entire colony spent the day at a *déjeuner sur l'herbe* on a nearby mountain lake not unlike Bluebells above Aspen. In the warm afternoon everyone went swimming in the nude. My mother was holding me in her arms, letting the mysterious water cover my legs. Suddenly the mirrorlike surface ahead of me was broken. A head and then a torso rose up from beneath. Max was laughing as the water streamed from his face. He raised his arms to me, and Lou was lifting me toward him. I became aware of innumerable long-legged, water-skating insects on the glassy surface surrounding Max's body, and I began to scream and struggled against being handed over. Max's face went dark and angry; he turned and swam away.

On the way back to the farm I was being carried piggyback on Arp's shoulders through a dark pine forest. Max and Lou walked by themselves ahead of everyone. Lou's manuscript recalls the conversations and circumstances of that day and what had preceded it.

One day we went swimming in the lake. Jimmy became scared of the waterbugs or perhaps of Max. He would not let Max carry him in his arms in the water. I don't know why. He was too small to know anything about our problems. In any case, it is one of Jimmy's earliest memories.

As we walked back through the forest, the sadness on my face must have made some kind of impression on Max. It had been a foregone conclusion that he would follow Gala to Paris. "For a while," he had said. For several weeks now he had not only shared the Éluards' rooms across the hall but also Gala with Paul.

Max seemed embarrassed by my dejection. "You know," he said, "you don't have any need for a husband anymore. You are twenty-eight years old. You know all about love; you have a son. . . . What more do you want? Your life with the child will be a very happy one."

It was a strange attempt to cheer me up. I could certainly not foresee what my life would be from now on, and even though I tried to be understanding, I was hurt by his cruel words.

"Do you know what you are talking about?" I asked him with amazement. "I am still young! I am only twenty-eight and I want to live."

He seemed not to understand me, and the thought must have been, indeed, an uncomfortable one for him.

On the eve of his departure we both looked at Jimmy, innocently asleep in his bed. We both cried.

Lou did not tell Max that she was pregnant again, and I did not know of it until some forty years later. She went to Innsbruck for an abortion and, after her recovery, made the long voyage with me back to Cologne, back to the same apartment on the Kaiser-Wilhelm-Ring where she had lived with Max and where I was born in 1920.

She returned without a husband and with no prospects for any kind of livelihood. Art historians were not in demand in that early Weimar where those who had jobs brought their salaries home in large paper bags filled with worthless currency. Little, if any, help was forthcoming from her father, who wanted to teach his daughter a lesson for marrying not only a non-Jew but a good-for-nothing artist to boot. Max's devoutly Catholic family was equally distant because their son had married the daughter of a Jewish hat manufacturer. Only Max's sister Emmi and brother Karl had attended the civil marriage ceremony.

Lou had met Max at the University of Bonn early in 1913. Her field of study was art history, whereas his interests ranged somewhat wider, leaning toward an interest in psychology. They had known each other casually for about a year when Lou's professor insisted that all his students should know something about the craft and techniques of their subjects. Attending a mandatory weekly life drawing class, Max chose to sit next to her and, noticing her complete inability to draw, surreptitiously took her pad and in a few minutes completed her assignment. In return, Lou felt obliged to allow this handsome, blue-eyed friend to escort her to the door of her dormitory on these weekly occasions. Sunday strolls along the majestic Rhine followed as a consequence. They often sat quietly on the bank of the river while he sketched. He also practiced his personal charms on her. She discovered that his intentions were more than student camaraderie when he said to her on one occasion, "Fräulein Straus, I can show you a place where this river actually flows upstream." It was a long walk to a quiet spot beyond the city limits of Bonn where a long stone jetty caused a gigantic whirlpool, and the water, indeed, flowed upstream. The relationship grew closer, but it remained a very proper one until Max enlisted the aid of one of his closest friends. As Lou tells about it:

> "Don't hold on so tightly to your little wreath," . . . Hans Arp whispered to me in his soft and singing voice, as he, Max and I sat together in the bulrushes on the banks of the Rhine. The three of us had shared an evening meal of sardines, sausage, bread and wine. I was cradled in Max's arm under a clear night sky lit up by a full moon. It seemed so light that I would have been able to read the time on my wristwatch, but I did not even try. . . . Hans Arp told me a few years later that on that evening, watching Max and me embracing tenderly and with him feeling a little bit lost, he had for a short time fallen in love with me.
>
> "Don't hold on so tightly to your little wreath." Yes, indeed, I had been holding on to it very firmly. It occurred to me years later that Max must have been really deeply in love with me to have been content with being my constant escort and nothing more for three quarters of a year. When he had first sensed my anxious passivity, he had assured me that he would make no attempt to take me by storm. I had promised that someday I would come to him on my own.
>
> But did I really want to do that? I still lived under the impression that the man to whom I would give this could only be my husband. A marriage to such an unconventional individual as Max seemed out of the question.

Lou Straus as well as her family had taken it for granted that she would marry Otto Keller, the son of a wealthy family prominent in Cologne's Jewish community.

That I would love Max forever dawned on me now very forcefully, but, naturally, I would marry Otto. He knew it, my mother hoped for it, and I had no doubt that I would be very happy and secure with him.

Marriage . . . it was, after all, a very bourgeois, a conventional formality that should not interfere with something as uncomplicated as total love. I tried to convince Max of my point of view, but he rejected it. He said that I was far too intelligent and vivacious to allow myself to be buried in the mediocrity of that way of life. There was, he said, no amount of money or any kind of security in the world that could compensate for love itself. And if I thought that it was possible to compromise by marrying one man while continuing to love another, he, Max, would have no part of it.

I do not know if I had really ever considered that combination, but obviously my thinking would have resulted in such an arrangement. (It turned out, in a typical joke of the Fates, that almost exactly eight years later this very situation did develop, but in reverse.) At that moment I had to admit that Max's point of view was the only clean and ethical one. I gave up any thought of a comfortable solution with Otto and prepared to face any future consequences of a life with Max with whatever courage would be needed.

Lou's decision came none too soon. World War I began and Max was drafted into the artillery of the Kaiser. For four years there were almost daily letters from the western front and occasional short furloughs to Cologne. Some months after one of these visits in 1916 Lou created a major crisis at home when she had to tell her family of missing several of her periods. Throughout the screaming and recriminations she steadfastly asserted that Max would get special furlough and face the family as well as the situation. Her mother kept repeating: "You'll see; he won't come. He will never, never see you again. And we won't be able to show our faces in Cologne. . . . The shame of it all . . ." One day, while she waited for the mailman with a possible letter from the front, Max emerged from the little park across from the house in full formal uniform, including the helmet that officers would traditionally wear for a marriage ceremony. He had come after all. The pregnancy crisis had been a false alarm, and they decided to wait for the end of the war.

Whatever opinions they might have held about marriage as an institution did not prevail. The hostility of both families was so great that Max and Lou agreed to the bourgeois formality after Max's return. He had led his company of soldiers, prior to the armistice, out of the front lines across France and Belgium to the other side of the Rhine, where he dismissed them and told them to go home. He refused to accept his Iron Cross First-Class, which was to be his reward for his two injuries. A captured Belgian horse had kicked him while his men were trying to shoe it, and he had been hit by the recoil of a supposedly cleaned artillery piece while inspecting it, with the result that his face blew up into a gigantic balloon every time he blew his nose. But there appeared to be other scars from that war experience, which began to manifest themselves after marriage. Recurring moods of introversion and withdrawal alternated with the erstwhile animation and sparkle. There would be severe reproaches because his slippers were not in their accustomed place or a special teacup from which only he was to drink had been used and broken by one of Lou's friends.

It is strange that the spirit of rebellion against the mores of the hated bourgeoisie did not penetrate very deeply into the private lives of nonconformists like Max Ernst and his fellow Dadaists. Most of the male prerogatives of home life, including a different code of morality for men and women, remained pretty much in place. And for all of the verbal attacks on the hypocrisy of sexual convention, these revolutionaries drew a silent line on homosexuality—an attitude that changed little after Dada had evolved into Surrealism.

Quite apart from such ambiguities, however, the provocative gestures and actions of that loose international coalition called Dada were meant to put the torch to worldwide spiritual atrophy, exemplified by the loathsome battlefields of Verdun, where by perverse coincidence Paul Éluard and his closest friend-to-be, Max Ernst, had been shooting at each other.

Dada shriveled when it acclaimed itself as a movement and died when some of its creators as well as its victims accepted it as art. But while it lived it was a fever that broke out in disparate places of the world without the benefit of instant communication. The high temperature warned of a rampant disease; World War I was only one of its more visible sores. Degenerate royal houses disposed of their subjects, almost playfully, by the millions. A managerial class, braying patriotism, divided spheres of profit across supposedly hostile borders. Academies, under the mantle of respectability, made it their mission to abort the birth of any new thought.

The Dadaists painted the true portrait of their time by dipping the tail of a donkey in a bucket of paint and honoring the resulting image on the stable wall as "art." They took the growing perversion of language to its logical conclusion by writing and reciting totally incomprehensible poetry. The rubbish of the gutter became valid components for all kinds of imagery. The unspeakable was transformed into howls of derision. Leonardo's *La Gioconda* grew a mustache, and who was to say that a urinal, signed R. MUTT, did not deserve to be called sculpture? Sacrilege was the only potent answer to sanctimony.

Dada in Cologne managed to equal, if not surpass, the decible count of Zurich-Dada's cabaret-literati and the more numerous Paris group under the

often divided leadership of André Breton and Tristan Tzara. The Cologne Da-
daists, unlike the Berlin activists, who included George Grosz, Otto Dix and
Raoul Housemann, were closely identified with the organized political left. (The
"bourgeois" Kurt Schwitters lived with his *Merz*-world alone in Hanover.) Under
the not-always-benign watch of Cologne's Lord Mayor Konrad Adenauer and the
World War I British occupation forces, Max Ernst and close friend Johannes
Baargeld, with the periodical involvement of artists Heinrich Davringhausen,
Franz Seiwert, Anton Raederscheidt, Heinrich Hoerle and Otto Freundlich,
staged outrageous anti-art exhibitions and published tracts derisive of state,
church and culture. Never a very amiable cooperative, its activities were punctuated by incessant counterrevolutions within its midst. It was the Weimar
Republic in miniature and similar, as Max was to remark later, to watching
amoeba split and multiply under a microscope.

Heresy was nothing new in Cologne. From its earliest days as a Roman
outpost, Colonia Agrippina, it had been the setting for a curious blend of Teutonic mysticism and Gallic sophistication. Albertus Magnus, more scientist-
magician than devout monk, was said to have constructed a talking and mobile
mechanical man in a corner of his cell, which a frightened functionary of the
hierarchy chopped to pieces as the work of Satan. The Church of St. Ursula had
apses resplendent with the golden-blond likenesses of an alleged eleven hundred
virgins martyred by the Huns, whose pagan deities they refused to worship. The
altar nave of St. Gereon, where I carried the train of Max's sister Loni on her
wedding, was studded with the gilded skulls and other relics of the Theban
legionnaires who had rebelled against Emperor Maximian Herculius. Throughout
its history the city had provided refuge for political and religious dissenters of all
stripes. Cologne's citizens always resented the inclusion of the Rhineland into the
alien state of Prussia. After 1918, many of them, including Max Ernst, joined a
militant movement for secession from the German Reich as an independent state
under French hegemony. The annual three days of carnival were always an
astounding display of unbridled hedonism that thumbed its nose at the stiff-
necked prudery of the German *Spiessbürger* (philistine).

Max and Lou Ernst lived on the top floor of a four-story town house on
Kaiser-Wilhelm-Ring that was otherwise occupied by its owner, a wealthy dentist
with a saber-scarred face from his student days, who resented the bohemian
rabble climbing his stairs and staying up all night, obviously formulating the next
step in turning the Fatherland over to the Reds. The living room and the adjacent
smaller studio became the hub for Cologne Dada as well as visiting artists, writers,
critics and poets, sometimes of more detached persuasions but still friendly
enough to be welcomed. Kaiser-Wilhelm-Ring became an annex of the railroad
station opposite the *Dom* (cathedral). On a given morning there might be

sleeping figures in the apartment wherever they had found room to curl up. The most frequent visitors were Hans Arp and Sophie Tauber, Paul Klee, Jankel Adler, Lyonel Feininger, Tristan Tzara and, staying for extended periods, Paul Éluard and his wife Gala. Occasionally, alert art dealers like Karl and Joseph Nierendorf, Andreas Becker or Berlin's Alfred Flechtheim would come to take a look but failed to be supportive. In contrast, the legendary Mutter Ei (Mother Egg), from Düsseldorf, had transferred all of her maternal instincts from a drunken brewmaster and twelve children to embattled avant-garde artists wherever she could find them. She was of enormous size, and when she walked, everything shook, including herself. I remember the friendly twinkle in her eyes behind steel-rimmed glasses, and many of the artists of that time remembered the princely sums in inflation marks she paid for their works, which meant at least another bag of groceries or even the rent. Nobody could understand how she could be so well fed from an art business that consisted of buying, but rarely being able to sell, the works of such relative unknowns as Klee, Adler, Dix, Barlach, Nolde, Rohlfs, Kandinsky, Kokoschka, Jawlensky and Ernst.

I also remember from those days that there was something about Gala Éluard that I did not like. I would not let the lady with the intense eyes touch me. Paul Éluard, in contrast, could have been Rumpelstiltskin in repose. He was the gentle imp who moved in the casually elegant manner of an athlete who knows his body well. He held his head high as if looking for the North Star at dusk.

Lou was cast in the role of providing the hospitality and ambience and had to make her peace with her husband's total immersion in the affairs of Dada. Occasionally she managed to find a typing job or sold hosiery at the Tietz Department Store, whose owner was a patron of the arts. It may well have been that there were days on which I was the only one in the house with something to eat. If not, Maja, a nanny of all work who rarely ever saw a salary, would descend on Max and Lou with a fury they had learned to fear.

Nevertheless, Lou managed to participate in the Dada activity by creating occasional collages for which she used the Dada name "Armanda Geduldged-alzen." Max conferred on her the title "The Rosa Bonheur of Dada."

Some of her collages were part of Cologne's first Dada exhibition, arranged by Ernst, Baargeld and Arp in a glass-roofed enclosure behind a Brauhaus-restaurant. The only access to the exhibit was through the men's urinal. It featured, along with provocative collages, drawings and paintings, a young girl in a white communion dress reciting obscene poetry, and a wooden sculpture from which hung a hatchet inviting visitors to destroy it. The show was promptly closed by the police, but reopened in triumph when no law could be found to justify the prohibition. It also caused severe family reaction. Max had found some

Hebraic type at the printer and included them in the announcement, causing a rage from Grandfather Jacob Straus. Grandfather Philipp Ernst seethed at his son's sacrilege in using the communion-dress girl. It added fuel to the anger of both patriarchs directed at Max and Lou as well as at each other. Total hostility from both sides affected me until I was about thirteen and abated only slightly when I left Germany at age eighteen. In that early spring of 1920, the two patriarchs were only grandfathers-to-be. I attended the rebellious exhibition in the Schildergasse as my mother's guest in her seventh month of pregnancy. She claimed that I had kicked inside her as much on that night as when she and Max had gone to the circus and the band had played for the prancing horses.

Lou Straus wrote about her marriage at that particular stage as having become an all-out effort to mold her own life completely to Max's needs. She understood quickly that Max hated to be observed while painting. No questions could be asked about work in progress. She dropped friends whom Max did not like, she stopped playing her violin, read only books that he liked and, all in all, tried to become an extension to his life. She sensed very soon, however, that

> . . . the greatest secret of two people living together is a certain measure of distance and discretion . . . that in spite of all the togetherness one remains basically unique and alone in the end. But I was not ready to admit this to myself.

I was born in June of that difficult year, and my arrival obviously did not solve any of these intangible problems.

> The child, however, which in conventional or bourgeois marriages would certainly have become a force that binds, instead created more of a gap between us. We both loved him and we had wanted him, but in a very mysterious way, which I have never completely understood, he failed to create the hoped-for new cohesion between the two of us. Perhaps the unity of two, which we both had tried to create, had been split by this third being and forced us into a new direction.
>
> At times, I think that the responsibilities with which this son entered our lives, disturbed and frightened Max. He loved his personal independence above anything else, as he was to prove in his life, later, time and again.

The two made a brave effort to hold together what they had gained in their respective battles against their families as well as the stiff-necked mores of the German bourgeois society. From all accounts they enjoyed their son and allowed him to be part of everything that happened in that lively household. I was pampered and free to roam among guests and friends, free to sit on any available lap no matter how serious or fiery the conversation. Manifestos, protests and theories were in formulation while someone around the table bottle-fed me. Lou Straus-Ernst was given a belated lesson in how to diaper me properly by Paul Klee, who demonstrated the procedure on the dining table. Max christened me "Jimmy, *Dadafax minimus, le plus grand Anti-Philosophe du Monde.*" Everyone, it seems, also agreed that my real name, "Hans-Ulrich," was far too Teutonic. Max liberated me from that name in front of the nearby fountain of nymphs and sea gods, the Hildebrand Brunnen. It became "Jimmy" when a group of "Jimmies," the common nickname for the popular British soldiers then occupying the Rhineland, crowded around the perambulator and complimented a beaming father. Twenty-odd years later a federal judge, objecting to the use of diminutive names, swore me into American citizenship as "James U."

The threatening cloud appeared early in the insecure atmosphere of the marriage, with the first visit of Paul and Gala Éluard. Ernst's and Baargeld's activities had aroused increasing interest in Paris and the French poet Éluard found a spiritual brother in the magical artist. Gala developed an interest of a different complexion. Lou Straus-Ernst called her

> that Russian female . . . that slithering, glittering creature with dark falling hair, vaguely oriental and luminant black eyes and small delicate bones, who had to remind one of a panther. This almost silent, avaricious woman, who, having failed to entice her husband into an affair with me in order to get Max, finally decided to keep both men, with Éluard's loving consent.

Still Lou decided that merely to put the blame on "this third person" was far too simplistic; she remained hopeful that the very perverseness of the situation would bring Max back to his senses. But the presence of the Éluards was pervasive, and it was on the last vacation trip to Tyrol that Lou recognized the depth of the involvement.

> One rainy day we were all together in the living room. Max was working with Gala on the translation of one of his books and in his arguments about some nuance of language became very sharp and insulting. Meaning to tease her amicably, I remarked, "Why do you allow him to scream at you like this? That is something he has never dared with me." Max looked up briefly and replied, "Yes, I also never loved you as passionately as I do her."

> Éluard's consenting solution to the problem was: ". . . You must understand that I love Max Ernst much more than Gala. . . . You don't know what it is like

to be married to a Russian female." Tristan Tzara saw the situation as a further complication in his aesthetic differences with André Breton, telling Matthew Josephson: "Of course we don't give a damn what they do, or who sleeps with whom. But why must that Gala Éluard make it such a Dostoevski drama? It's boring, it's insufferable, unheard of!" Lou was thus not unprepared for the final episode on the way home from the picnic by the lake. Not too long before Max had tried, gently, to explain: "I would like very much to be just happily married to you. But it just is not working."

The affair with Gala was merely the trigger for the inevitable change that Max Ernst had to make. Free spirits the world over searched to breathe an air that was not contaminated by provincial convention. There was really no place for Max Ernst in the Germany of 1922, which provided an arena for rebellion but not, then, the climate to bring ideas into bloom. The answer and goal was Paris, a most powerful magnet of civilization and the only city with the right to call itself international.

Xenophobia was as common a national trait in France as it was in other European nations at that time, and yet Paris prided itself on its willingness to harbor the dissidents of the world. They were expected not to make any trouble, become public charges or enter the labor force. They were looked upon with a certain condescension and pity, each group keeping pretty much to itself, perusing its little emigré newspapers seizing on any minor rumor from the homeland that a change or overthrow was imminent, stimulating them to grab their baggage, symbolically always packed, from under their beds in dingy hotel rooms for a return to the past. Disenchanted by the travesty of World War I, a wave of intellectuals from all parts of the world made their way to this cultural capital of the world. Unlike other refugee groups, these found ready acceptance by their French peers. Paris seemed to have little fear of aesthetic ideologies even though they might spill over into the political area or create some occasional public scandal. Republican France was more mature and tolerant than those countries that were still struggling with recently abandoned monarchies in a political and cultural morass already the fertile breeding ground for new tyrannies. The France of 1922 did not extend its tolerance to Germans, however, particularly those who, like Max, had only recently fought them in the trenches of Marne and Verdun. Penniless, Max arrived in Paris illegally. He lived with the Éluards in their house in Eaumont near Paris, working, again illegally, in a factory producing trinkets for tourists. In that environment he created some of those momentous early paintings that now mark the birth of Surrealism in painting. Among them is the imagined group portrait of every friend *Au Rendez-Vous des Amis,* in which the sole woman is Gala. The impact of Dadaism had come to an impasse when it began to be perceived as an art movement. If Dada had been the debris-cleansing storm, Surrealism lit up the sky as a fireworks of the mind. Fed by the essence of its short-lived forerunner, it was to reveal the marvelous and the magic that had lain hidden in the recesses of human consciousness by confronting that incomplete power with its essential counterpart, the dream, the subconscious. The result of that far-seeing concept was an avalanche of ideas and images so powerful and so liberating that its tremors remain strong enough, even today, to effect new earthquakes in the human imagination.

Jacob Straus, wealthy hat manufacturer and pillar of his temple on Rathenau Platz, did nothing to conceal his glee at having his worst expectations confirmed. This goy with pretensions to being an artist had turned out to be a disastrous husband. Furthermore, there was now a child whose circumcision had been for medical reasons only and who could therefore not even be considered a Jew. Jacob's house was open to Lou and me on certain holy days, but there could be no help for his daughter's desperate financial situation until, at least, the ritualistic formalities of circumcision were brought up to date. It was one of the conditions laid down by Leah Straus, the former nurse who had attended my grandmother on her deathbed and whom Jacob married two weeks after the funeral. It was, of course, rejected on principle. Steadfast Maja, that outspoken and robust Catholic peasant woman—holding together the family she had adopted when the man she called *der Schweinehund Max*, had abandoned it— took it on herself to berate the obdurate Jacob with random citations from the Old Testament, thus securing occasional amounts of money when there was no bread or milk for her *Jung* (boy). Maja was loved and feared not just by Lou and me but also by Lou's circle of friends. It was Maja who provided the domestic stability that enabled Lou to build her own life and career. Maja dressed, loved, scolded and spoiled me. When at the age of five or six I expressed a Christmas wish for a roasted swan, because "they are so beautiful," she somehow procured a large goose and put it on the table as my swan. She was the protector of the enclave and the family until the events of 1933 put an end to our warm and lively community.

When I was five, during a particularly difficult period of Lou's efforts to earn a living, Maja took me to the country, where we stayed with her mother and sisters. Across the road was a walled-in abbey of monks who had dedicated themselves to the care of the mentally disturbed. From my window I could see the strange people in that garden. I began going into the lovely chapel almost daily and then, regularly, to vespers and Sunday masses. I sat among the inmates and tried my best to follow the rites and responses. I had long talks with the monks while they were tending the gardens. I kept asking them if it was all right for me to go there even though I was only half Catholic, and the other half Jewish. They treated me kindly and assured me that I was welcome. One of the brothers gave me a rosary and instructed me on its purpose and use. Maja, who had watched the behavior of *der heilige Jung*, (the holy boy) thought I had gone a bit too far. She took me by the hand and together we returned the rosary to the monk, who got a gentle dressing-down for trying to convert such a young child.

Maja never thought much of Lou's abilities in the kitchen and would never leave the house until my meals had been prepared. Once Lou gave Maja tickets for a matinee performance of *Pagliacci* and *Cavalleria Rusticana*. Maja at first refused because she would not be home for my noon meal. At last she relented, preparing a pan of roulades, with strict instructions to Lou when and how to cook them. We spent the better part of the morning in the kitchen. An important phone call came and during that interval the meat burned to a crisp. Lou quickly prepared a bowl of cream of wheat with raisins, and we promised each other not to tell what had happened. Maja returned from the opera, stepped into the kitchen, sniffed the air, found the burned roulades and lit into Lou. "I knew it, I knew it. I can't leave you alone for a minute. *Der Jung* is going to starve if I leave things to you."

There was no love lost between Maja and Max. She had witnessed everything and never forgave him what he had done to Lou and *der Jung*. Many years later, in the late sixties, I was with Max in Cologne and told him that I had found Maja, then in her seventies, living with her sister in very modest circumstances and not at all well. He reached in his pocket and gave me several thousand-mark banknotes to give to her when I saw her again. Maja was amazed by the large sum but finally concluded that this was really my money and I was merely making it all up.

If there was scarcity of money, food or clothes in our little enclave, I was certainly well shielded from it. There was always something to eat for me, and often my clothing was changed as much as four times daily. This lasted well into my kindergarten years and my enrollment in the public school in 1926. Perhaps it was the grayness and shabbiness that was all too common to Germany during those inflation-burdened years that conditioned me to the absence of things I could not have. Lou's meager earnings as a bookkeeper, secretary at an art gallery, pieceworker in a lace factory, and a succession of equally insecure jobs were brought home in amounts of billions of marks in brown paper bags, to be converted, as quickly as possible, into whatever was available at the grocery store. The milk that I was sent for with a tin pail was in no danger of turning sour during the long trek from the store. Its color was a steely blue from all the water that had been added to it. Once a week the three of us would walk to another part of the city where the farmers from the outlying areas were offering their somewhat cheaper goods. I derived tremendous pleasure from gathering carrots, beans, cabbage leaves and other greens that had fallen off the handcarts, and proudly presented my contribution to Maja, who would sniff with disapproval but quickly throw them into the net shopping bag. It was always a double triumph for me because the competition from other children was fierce. Later I was allowed to watch Maja convert my collection into a soup on the large coal stove that dominated the kitchen. It was during the height of the inflation period that Grandfather Straus, in a rare gesture, decided to settle on his daughter a good part of her inheritance to "help her along." He gave it to her in cash, and after three days the amount was barely enough for a tram ride.

I was only vaguely aware of my mother's struggles. When I visited her at her various places of employment, her respective bosses would pat me on the head and tell me what a courageous and ever-optimistic mother I had in *unserer kleinen Lou* (our little Lou). After work she often took me along to museum libraries, where she would spend the hour before closing on research for possible freelance articles on Gothic architecture, the work of medieval artisans and painters or some aspect of the Roman heritage in a small corner of Cologne that had escaped other historians. On those occasions we received respectful and friendly treatment from librarians and museum personnel because they were aware of her scholarship and her Ph.D. thesis on medieval goldsmiths of the Rhineland, which had gained her a summa cum laude. Sometimes she would encounter colleagues from her university days whom she would bring home for dinner. Maja would sniff, walk huffily into the kitchen, and somehow there would be enough food on the table, plus a bottle of wine contributed by one of the friends. After dinner, friends or not, Lou would disappear to take a short nap and then would type her articles till deep into the night in her incredibly cluttered study. Maja would spend that time altering and repairing Lou's modest wardrobe. "You can't run around in the same dress day after day." Items beyond repair were made into pillows or little napkins, and once I found myself being dressed for the Sunday morning stroll in a suit (short pants and jacket) made of beige raw silk.

Those Sunday walks along the broad circular avenue of Cologne called the Ring was a weekly ritual of all burghers when the weather allowed it. Before turning back, if there was a little extra money, we'd make a stop in a coffeehouse, where I was treated to an enormous slab of fruit tart with mountains of whipped cream. Lou, who all of her life fought a tendency toward stoutness, would surreptitiously take a scoop or two from my plate, which I resented because, as I told her, "It doesn't look nice, and besides, you'll gain weight." On one occasion she responded, "A lot of people like me a little round." When I asked her if she meant "men," she said, "Yes . . . why not?" Again I was scandalized and protested that it was not proper for men to look at my mother's figure.

On those Sunday strolls we'd also occasionally see small flag-waving parades of political organizations. Most of the marchers carried the colors of the old monarchy, and the men wore the dress uniform from the time of Kaiser Wilhelm, some with all the decorations that a chest can bear, which they had earned in the service of the Reich during the war of 1914–1918. After explaining to me the mentality and aims of these paraders, Lou and I automatically would turn our backs on the men who were singing about their lost and heroically fallen comrades.

One Sunday morning, however, was not quite as simple. Across the avenue, on top of an old five-story building, was a gigantic sign: THE JEWS ARE OUR MISFORTUNE *(Die Juden Sind Unser Unglück)*. Flags featuring a strange cross hung from the windows, and the sidewalk in front of the house was a solid block of brown-uniformed men standing stiffly at attention, then breaking into a song that somewhere contained the phrase ". . . we shall kill and win revenge for comrades murdered by Jew betrayers." It was Cologne's first Nazi headquarters, a "Braun-Haus" (Brown House), as they called it. It was not a good day, that Sunday. We quickly turned to get back to our apartment. Our landlord, the dentist, who made no secret of the fact that he would love to see us move out, greeted us at the door, gold teeth grinning out of his saber-scarred face: *"Fabelhaft, wunderbar . . . nicht wahr?"*

"Mosquitoes . . . just a small bunch of flies . . . annoying, perhaps . . . Hindenburg will protect the Republic . . . yes, but the sign . . . that dreadful sign . . . it shouldn't be allowed . . . maybe Adenauer will do something. . . ." Lou spent the afternoon on the telephone, seeking assurance from friends as well as acquaintances with political connections. It was the first time I saw genuine fear in her face. She told me that there were indeed people in Germany, as well as in other places, who hated Jews, but there really was nothing to be disturbed about. We were, after all, she said, "Germans like everybody else," and there was a constitution that would not allow any harm to come to us.

Later that afternoon I left the house under the pretext of wanting to look again at an amazing new American invention in a store window on the Ring: an icebox called Frigidaire, powered by electricity. Instead I walked over to the Braun-Haus. The number of uniformed people had increased. The men, with their swastika armbands, had spilled beyond the sidewalk into the street, completely halting traffic in one direction. They were arranging themselves into military formations. Large red flags, with the black swastika on a round white field, were being carried out of the building to the applause of women on the sidewalk who sported swastika brooches and necklaces. The storm troopers raised their right arms stiffly as the banners were carried to the front of the columns. The shout of "Heil Hitler" was followed by a command to march. Almost everybody broke into a martial song about a raised flag . . . comrades who had died and were marching with them in spirit. It was their anthem, "The Horst Wessel Song." I stood in the midst of all this, somewhat scared because I was not singing along. I turned my face to a large glass-covered bulletin board and saw the pages of a newspaper called *Der Stürmer*, with grotesque caricatures of evil-looking, hook-nosed men tearing at the clothes of a young woman. A few blocks up the avenue the marchers were approaching a line of policemen blocking their way. Screaming and yelling, as if in joy at an approaching battle, the women and other bystanders rushed to the scene. I stood almost alone in front of the building. A cry of triumph went up as the police line dissolved before contact had been made. I walked home with a lot of questions on my mind. Few, if any, were ever going to be answered.

Konrad Adenauer, Lord Mayor of Cologne, forced the offending sign to be removed that very night. Lou, who had been very angry about my excursion, said, "Well, that is over," and then, in an unguarded afterthought, "Or is it?"

Politics, indeed, began to enter into our lives with more frequency and insistence. As Lou established herself as an art and theater critic and a journalist for some major newspapers, her circle of friends broadened and changed somewhat from the days of Dada. Now there were actors, playwrights, composers who enlivened the apartment almost constantly. The theater people and writers, in particular, were those of the left. Kurt Weill, Hanns Eisler, Bertolt Brecht, and many others would drop in when their productions brought them to Cologne. According to Lou, Brecht laughed off my dislike of his body odor. "That kid is used only to Cologne sweat; mine is from Berlin." One evening several policemen came to arrest a number of actors who that evening during a performance had stepped to the front of the stage to denounce Cologne's chief of police. A call to Adenauer's press secretary, an intimate friend of Lou's, solved that little problem. The mood during some of these gatherings was often belligerent, sometimes gloomy, with denunciations of everyone from President Hindenburg and whoever was Reich Chancellor to intellectuals and former friends in the arts who had "sold out" and were now mere *Spiessbürger* again. The fear of Hitler grew, but I can recall few, if any, solutions being voiced. I retain to this day an image of a group that was always badly splintered. I remember the sarcastic and scathing outbursts around the dinner table, mostly hostile in tone only. They were loud enough for me to hear from my bedroom. The idea of hope was constantly drowned out by a call for solidarity from one group or another and then rejoinders to the effect that the people were cattle and deserved to die on the wrong side of the barricades. Friends would leave the house as bitter antagonists, only to return a few days later for afternoon coffee and cake as if nothing had happened. Or, more likely, some new problem had arisen and they all needed each other to solve it by tearing each other apart again. Of course it was not a consistently grim scene. These were people just as capable of humor, though, sometimes, even that quality was a bit too biting for me. The poet Joachim Ringelnatz, an ex-sailor who composed and performed sardonic verse from the stages of cabarets in a perpetually inebriated state, overheard me asking Maja if she was absolutely certain that my eggs had been cooked long enough to be very hard. He took the eggs, opened the window and threw them four floors to the street, then turned to me and advised me to go downstairs to check on their hardness.

In all of this diversity the physical absence of a father manifested itself for me only when, on rainy days, I played with school chums in their homes or when Lou took me with her to long-lasting noontime meals with the families of her friends. There was no dearth of surrogate fathers. Even after Max had left, Arp would visit and take me on steamer trips up the Rhine. On long walks through forests and fields he became as excited as I with the discovery of unusual insects, rare wild flowers and strangely formed tree branches, the configurations of which would set off a contest as to what imagery they suggested. Tristan Tzara plied me with whipped-cream fruit tarts and cocoa in fancy pastry shops as I speculated whether he wore that monocle while asleep. Paul Klee, even after he had joined the Bauhaus in Dessau, stopped over a few times in Cologne on his way to see his early patron and friend Mutter Ei in Düsseldorf. He and I had a common passion, the age-old Hänneschen Puppet Theater. If it was summertime, we went to see it in the park, and in winter, in the old section of Cologne near the river. The plot was always the same: Hänneschen fighting off ogres and villains with a cardboard stick, always coming close to annihilation but overcoming the enemy at the last second, with loud cries of support from children and Klee. This is a memory almost always evoked for me in the subject matter of Klee's marvelous works.

As the name of Lou Straus-Ernst became a respected by-line, my mother's circle of friends grew correspondingly, and so did the number of father substitutes. How many of them acted out of opportunism and how many of them may, in fact, have been intimate friends and lovers, I shall never know. Lou writes in her book with great glee of her discovery that her life as a woman had not ended with the departure of Max. She freely admits that some of her lovers may well have had ulterior motives. She describes, indeed, one situation during her later emigré days in Paris when she woke up in the middle of the night and felt with absolute certainty that the tender and loving man in her bed was an agent for the secret German police, who, like many others, had been sent to infiltrate the intellectual exile circles. Whatever motivation she may have suspected in some of her relationships, she did not hesitate to use her growing influence in the cultural life of Germany. She arranged exhibitions and solicited support from important collectors and dealers for heretofore unknown artists. Struggling poets found their work accepted by prestigious publications. Out-of-work actors knew where to go for a decent meal and, if there was any, even a little money to tide them over. Among her "mistakes" she mentions a young sculptor, Arno Breker, who for a while was in constant attendance and showered me with gifts such as hand-knitted ties. Breker went on to become one of Hitler's favorite sculptors as well as the recipient of many contracts for the design of public buildings. Lou passed these and other disappointments off with an almost humorous shrug of the shoulder, as if to say that such slips of judgment were a small price to pay for living a full and productive life as a woman. She wrote many articles and some unpublished novels dealing with the problems and joys of single women in a society that had a very low opinion of such an existence. She was indeed a singular woman who enjoyed her personal and professional success without pretension. The fact that she managed to stand on her own feet, support a child and a happy household, be considered a peer among her mostly male colleagues and maintain the respectful attention of the intellectual community was a source of great pride to her. "It was," she wrote, "a life full of color, full of changes, full of responsibilities and full of surprises."

The knowledge that I had a father had about it an aura of abstraction. His name came up frequently in conversations and comments by visitors in the presence of the paintings that hung all over the apartment. Every now and then my questions concerning him resulted in lengthy and gentle attempts by my mother to explain not only the man but also the situation that his absence had brought about. He was an unusual man, she would say, to whom the ordinary rules of life and behavior were less important than his work; they had loved each other very much, and my very existence was proof of that. More often than not, I refused to let her finish her explanations, turning away in anger because I could not understand her tolerance and objectivity, or because I could not comprehend that there was anything more important than me, my mother and Maja. Maja, on the other hand, responded immediately to such questions with a diatribe: "What that terrible man did to your mother and to you. . . . There was nothing to eat for you when he left. . . . He has no heart. . . . He thinks he is so handsome and so important. . . . Why, even when he was here, he . . . well, you are too young to hear about such things yet . . . but you will find out when you grow up." These responses were also almost always cut short by me because I suddenly felt that no one should talk about my father that way. Sometimes it was Lou who stopped Maja by telling her that she was overdoing it. She punctuated most of these exchanges by telling me that what had happened was something purely between her and Max and that, most of all, it had not been an act hostile to me. I would have my chance to get to know him better and then I would understand. I had been intrigued by her equation of my existence with love, and I asked her what she had meant. She tried to explain to me the physical process of conception in very clinical terms, adding again that this had been the culmination of love between her and Max, as it was with all men and women. It must have been the starkness of detail, involving a man I hardly knew, that caused me never to raise the question again. I do recall very vividly the setting and the verbiage of that occasion, as well as my inability to understand or to accept the logic of love coexisting with the sexual act. I did, however, feel quite superior to my school-mates when the "forbidden" subject was discussed with wild fantasies on our long treks home from school. Obviously no other parent had gone so far as mine in sharing such important confidences with them. I was certain that I had a very special relationship with my mother and managed to get into many a fistfight with my pals when I made fun of their ignorance.

Nor had this been the only instance where Lou had made an effort to let me share in her life, her experiences, her enthusiasm and her views. From an early age on I knew of the existence of various religious disciplines and of the fact that she was Jewish whereas Max was Christian, but that they had both decided not to commit me to either belief, leaving the choice, if any, for me to make when the time came. I became familiar with tenets and rituals, their histories and their respective humanistic and cultural importance. In this way she tried to make me understand why Grandfather Jacob acted the way he did and why I had yet to meet Max's parents. She took me to seders at her father's home and to temple, but we also went to many of Cologne's beautiful churches to hear musical masses or to see the wonder of stained-glass windows and altarpieces by the Rhenish masters. The church bells, particularly those of Cologne's pride, the majestic Dom, became as much part of my life as was the voice of the cantor. Lou took me along on several occasions to see the Isenheim altarpiece by Matthias Grüne-wald in Colmar, and read to me what poets and essayists had written about that masterpiece. My response to art, in particular to painting, was negative and would remain so for a long time, but something about the Grünewald remained with me. What especially intrigued me was the mysterious chamberpot next to the Virgin Mary's bed with its Hebrew characters. I still don't know about that little pot and the letters on it. It has become a humorous tentacle to my awe and love of this haunting, most sublime, work of art.

Despite my stubborn aversion to painting, Lou took me along to art open-ings and exhibitions at museums and galleries as well as on her visits to various artists' studios, where she constantly attempted to change my outlook.

Poetry was an important part of her conversations with me, particularly before going to sleep. "Listen to what I have just found in Goethe. It has to do with what we were talking about yesterday at the zoo." Or she would put on a record of the Brecht/Weill *Dreigroschen Oper (Threepenny Opera)*, sometimes calling attention to the lyrics and drawing some parallel to a topical event in German politics. I was able to read a newspaper before I entered school, and Lou would explain in detail anything I had read without understanding it.

As a result I was a pretty good student at school, but I recall that not all of the teachers responded favorably to my precocity. I must have been about nine or ten years old when I attended a "dissident" school, one of a system of public institutions that coexisted, as a compromise by the Weimar Republic, with state-supported parochial schools. One of my teachers was a lady named Otto. Fraülein Otto was a forbidding figure. With her mannish hair combed straight back, she was always dressed, as if in a uniform, in stern black with a double-breasted jacket. Apart from teaching she held an elected seat as a Communist deputy to Cologne's city council, where her actions were as severe and aggressive as her looks. Lou often told me at dinner about Fraülein Otto's latest diatribe at a public council meeting. It usually concerned Fraülein Otto's pet bête noire, Lord Mayor Konrad Adenauer—particularly if he happened to be presiding. To her he was a symbol of the forces in Germany that prevented "the downtrodden from achieving their human rights." Adenauer was a *Kapitalist Bonze* (a capitalist big-wig), who, with the connivance of the Thyssens and the Krupps, aimed to deprive the proletariat of its bread and dignity. Her speeches were always punctuated by ". . . but the people, the poor and the unwashed, will remember when their time comes."

In my classroom was a boy by the name of Adamovski. He was the son of a Russian ex-prisoner of war who had returned to Minsk, leaving his family temporarily behind until the revolution's inevitable success would reunite them. Adamovski lived in a lean-to shed in the mud flats that separated the inner city from the immediate suburbs. His onion-shaped face seemed to be the only clean thing about him. He was periodically sent from class to the school infirmary for a thorough delousing. His study performance was way below average. His classmates, including me, all from liberal, if not left-wing, backgrounds, avoided him during and after school. He was not even allowed to join in our rest-period brawls against the pupils of the parochial school who shared the building with us.

One day, as happened so many times, Adamovski had great difficulty in responding to a question from Fraülein Otto. She wasted little time bringing him to the front of the entire class, castigating him for his mediocre Slavic mind, sloppy habits, and filthy appearance. He made no effort, she said, to emulate his far neater and more studious classmates. Adamovski merely shrugged as if to say, "I don't care," or, more probably, "I can't help it." For this gesture he was to be punished. Adamovski obediently leaned over the front desk and Fraülein Otto's bamboo stick was fetched from the corner of the room. Some instinct, perhaps learned at the dinner table, made me leap to my feet. I blurted out my knowledge of Fräulein Otto's public pronouncements at the city council. Here, I postured, surely was a living example of the people whom she pretended to champion. There probably was no soap in Adamovski's home, I said, and daily food was more important than clothes. What good were her speeches, I asked; people like that should receive sympathy, not ridicule. Fräulein Otto's stick remained in midair as she screamed at me that personal and mental hygiene had nothing to do with politics. "And furthermore, this is something that your mother put you up to. I have read her articles. She is a typical representative of the lying, dirty, capitalist press." The school bell rang and the bamboo rod was returned, unused, to its corner.

To my chagrin, Adamovski clung to me as a newfound friend. He walked home with me from school, and I had to invite him to the apartment to share my noon-time meal. He rang the bell in the morning to escort me to school. Maja was appalled by my choice of friends, and Lou, sensing my confusion and discomfort, grinned from ear to ear, remarking that these were, sometimes, the consequences of heroic acts, and it was now up to me to solve the problem.

A few days later Adamovski took me to his shack. There were already about ten kids seated around the table, all having come from similar abodes on the mud flats. It was a communal meal presided over by a young woman, with short hair combed straight back, and dressed in a double-breasted black jacket and matching skirt just like Fräulein Otto. As we ate our soup, we were told what a heaven Germany would become after the coming socialist revolution. The woman took me aside and asked about my background. She told me that the newspapers for which my mother wrote were hostile to the proletariat, and she doubted that my association with any members of her after-school group was at all desirable. That solved my problem. Lou and I agreed, however, that we should leave some of my clothes and some soap at Adamovski's hut. The package was returned to my school desk by him without comment.

Max, after having resolved the legitimacy of his presence in France (he had been vouched for by the French painter Marie Laurencin), came to Cologne on a series of visits. The first was sometime around 1925, when I was five years old. He had come to settle the costs of his divorce from Lou. He sold a stack of paintings to Mutter Ei in Dusseldorf for approximately $20 per canvas. One of them, *Au Rendez-Vous des Amis,* was bought in the early nineteen sixties by a German museum for about $250,000.

I recall that visit quite well. I was sitting on the couch listening through earphones to a newly acquired miracle, a crystal radio set, and I was annoyed by the sudden appearance in our living room of a blond man carrying a suitcase. He stood there for a long moment as we stared at each other. It occurred to me that this could be my father. Lou came in from her room and embraced him, and Maja, passing by, merely sniffed very audibly. It all fit. This was my father. He sat down and asked me about school. I told him that I had not started yet. He was trying to make more small talk and I was not helping him one bit. There were long silences, with Lou desperately trying to get something going. As final proof I demanded if, in fact, he was a real artist. I pointed to a magazine cover that featured a prominent German movie star and asked him if he could do as well as that. He opened his suitcase, took out a drawing pad and pencil and in short order produced a striking facsimile of the image. That broke the ice somewhat and I offered to share my earphones with him.

He stayed at the apartment for about two weeks. Old friends dropped in, the evenings were lively. He took me for walks in the park and as a special treat to a fancy new movie palace on the Ring. I was glad to see that there was no hostility between him and my mother, and even Maja broke down once in a while to address a civil word to him. I don't know if it occurred to me that he might have come back to stay.

After several days he seemed to get somewhat restless. He walked around the apartment, looking intently at the paintings he had left behind. Finally he took a large one off the wall and, carrying it, took me along for a visit to the studio of the painter Anton Raederscheidt, just around the corner. I was familiar with Raederscheidt's work because his son was one of my playmates. Raederscheidt, much to my secret delight, had been painting an endless series of full-length portraits of his wife, showing her in the nude, exercising on parallel bars, horses, ropes, rings and other gymnastic equipment. After some polite conversation, Max began to make some very complimentary remarks about Raederscheidt's paintings and offered to make an even exchange with him for the one that he "just happened" to have with him. Raederscheidt accepted readily.

As soon as we got back to the apartment, Max asked me to help him unpack the cardboard box in which Lou had stored all of his art materials. Much to my chagrin, Max began to cover the exciting nude form of Mrs. Raederscheidt with his own paint. When I asked him why he was doing that, he told me that he felt like painting and canvas was very expensive. When I said that he could have painted over his own, he merely snorted in reply. He worked for several days, on the dining table and on the floor, since there was no easel. Once, late during the night, I crept out of my bed and peeked through the living room door. Max was sitting in a high-backed chair, studying his just completed painting. The sensuous body of Mrs. Raederscheidt had become a petrified-forest landscape with a yellow-ringed moon floating in a gray-blue night sky.

A few days later I got into a nasty quarrel with Raederscheidt's son while we were playing in the street. When our wrestling and punching had ended I called out in frustration: *"Njae-njae, njae-njae,* my father painted right over your father's painting!" The answer was immediate: *"Njae-njae, njae-njae,* so did mine, so did mine!"

About two years later Max returned to Cologne again for another short visit. This time he came with his new French wife, Marie-Berthe, a lovely, somewhat frail-looking young woman. She reminded me of the exotic waterbirds I had seen at the zoo. Her green eyes were quick, yet gentle, and her hair was a pompadour of innumerable reddish-gold ringlets punctuated by wispy bangs on her forehead. That hair must have intrigued me. As Lou, Max and Marie-Berthe were still awkwardly standing around exchanging polite greetings, I climbed up on the high-backed chair, reached out for those curls and pulled with all of my might. Marie-Berthe cried out in pain, and Max, in one swift motion, turned and delivered a hard slap on my face. I was astounded and began to bawl. Marie-Berthe immediately cradled me in her arms, in spite of Max's command not to do that. She held me as she chirped something in French to Max and Lou, then sat down and rocked me on her lap, which encouraged me to force out some more tears. Max left the room, slamming the door angrily. Lou sat down next to Marie-Berthe, and while they took turns embracing me began to talk to each other quietly in French. Lou finally must have lost patience with my tactics; she put me down with an admonition that I was too old for such theatrics. I calmly sat down opposite them and watched with fascination as the two women continued to get acquainted. In the years to come there grew a bond and understanding between them that went beyond having shared and finally lost the same man. There was an almost saintly quality about Marie-Berthe. She deserved better than her eventual sad fate, and I cannot think of her, even today, without a deep feeling of compassion and love.

In 1928 Lou felt financially secure enough to move to a modern apartment in the suburb of Sülz. She felt that her son needed more fresh air and that the growing political strife in Germany's inner cities might be less visible there. We were also rid of the hostile landlord and the increasing traffic that she and Maja felt was hazardous on my long walk to school and when I was playing in the streets. Sülz was near the city's greenbelt, and I wasted little time on things other than flying kites and playing soccer with my new schoolmates. Homework was a snap for me, and after lunch I was gone for the rest of the day.

When the giant *Graf Zeppelin* was about to fly over the city, a school holiday was proclaimed. I rose long before dawn, took my kite and watched the monstrous airship from a hill on the large sheepmeadow as it majestically moved across the sky, illuminated by the rising sun. The zeppelin was a subject of national pride second to none. Yes, we had heard of, or seen in newsreels, the American blimps, but "*our* Zeppelin" was superior and was always cited in the press and in school as the symbol of a nation that could exceed every other in whatever area it chose to compete. The flying of kites, once the ship had disappeared, by the thousands who had come out for the event, was in celebration of this well-publicized boast.

Maja would be furious that I had waited to spend my two groschen on two greasy potato pancakes that one could buy from a stand just around the corner from the apartment.

Standing there while eating gave me a chance to observe the street activity at dusk. People were out for their evening stroll. Some gathered in bunches to read the glass-encased pages of the evening edition of the *Kölnische Zeitung*. I felt tempted to explain to them that the by-line on page 5, "Lou Straus-Ernst," was my mother, and that she lived right around the corner on Emma Strasse. As people finished their evening's reading, they formed small groups discussing the events of the day. In some instances the arguments became vehement and noisy. I clearly remember one voice, rising above others: ". . . to us Social Democrats, it's the Communists and not the Nazis who are the real enemy." I would have to ask my mother about that strange remark. The groups fell silent as a number of brown-shirted storm troopers came up the street. Everybody knew that the wearing of uniforms by political organizations was against the law, and anyone who did so was always ready for a fight. Indeed, a group of men on the corner, identifiable by the red ties they wore, casually positioned themselves in such a way that the Nazis would have difficulty not bumping into them. The street emptied quickly; I grabbed my kite and string and ran for home. There was nothing unusual about this. Vicious street fights were a common occurrence, particularly at the end of the day, and this general retreat was merely a conditioned reflex. That night, as happened frequently, Maja slapped my behind vigorously for exposing myself to such danger and for eating the potato pancakes. She scrubbed the grime off me in a hot bath and sent me to bed without supper. But less than an hour later she turned on my light and set a tray on my bed, explaining that she had not forgiven me but that if I did not get enough to eat I might get sick and that would mean more work for her.

The move to Sülz had not been as easy as I had thought. Lou told me that she had underestimated the costs involved. As she was packing and sorting out her papers, books and paintings in her perpetually cluttered study, she realized that there was absolutely no money to pay for the moving van. With her usual optimism she kept right on filling the cardboard boxes. She was also, she said, afraid of a severe scolding from Maja, who was really running the household. She was finally down to a stack of papers that included some of my drawings from school. One of them was titled, "The Easter Bunny hides the eggs on the night before," which was nothing more than a large blot of black ink with the tips of rabbit ears protruding on top. On the bottom of the pile was a fairly large watercolor by Paul Klee, whose work had begun to sell a little by now. A gift that she had forgotten or mislaid. She promptly rolled it up and went to see Karl Nierendorf, who with his brother had a gallery in Cologne. Coming back in triumph with the exact amount needed for the movers, she confessed all to Maja, who screamed at her for not getting at least enough additional money to buy the first week of groceries at the new place. "And the *Jung* needs a bigger bed."

The new apartment was cheerful, with a balcony overlooking the street. What was even better, I now had my own room. I had always worried, at times thrown tantrums, when I noticed, at the old place, that my mother's bed had not been slept in. Maja sometimes explained that Lou was on a trip doing a magazine article. But I would point to the unused suitcase and demand a better excuse. On one occasion I woke up on Ash Wednesday morning, the end of carnival time, and realized that Lou had not yet returned from a masked ball. I was under the impression that anyone caught in carnival regalia after the stroke of midnight would be automatically arrested by the police and thrown in jail. Like all German kids, in fact like most Germans, the mere sight of a policeman filled me with terror.

My room became a fortress, a world unto itself. The center was usually taken up by some fantastic and precariously balanced high structure that I had built with wooden blocks or a constantly expanding erector set. The top of my dresser contained my precious collection of primitive carvings from various parts of the world that were gifts from Lou's museum friends. The walls were covered with drawings and small paintings from the artists of her circle, most of them dedicated to me and therefore more than just "Art," which I otherwise continued to view with hostility. The fact, however, that images could take the place of writing and therefore remain private in nature appealed to me. And I began a diary which, I was certain, no one else could decipher because all the pages appeared to be nothing more than scribbles. In it I fantasized about Indians and cowboys, inspired no doubt by two of my most prized possessions, a movie poster of Tom Mix and a full-feathered Indian head on a Sarasani Circus poster. I wrote about my triumphs as the center forward of my favorite soccer team, Sülz 07. The real center forward was a slightly built Austrian by the name of Ferdl Swatosh, who ran a tobacco shop a few blocks away, and I recall my shock and anger when I learned that he and the left wing forward, Ulrich, were in fact no amateurs at all. The tobacco shop had been given to Swatosh by the club. He ceased being my hero, and I wrote a dirge.

I also wrote long letters, legible, however, to Max about my daily life, particularly about my great preoccupation, sports. Max's rare answers were not entirely satisfying because he did not seem to share my enthusiams. My fervently expressed hope that Germany would soon produce a long-distance runner better than Paavo Nurmi received the answer that he couldn't care less about the nationality of any individual and that if I wished for better Germans it should be replacements for the likes of Stresemann, Hindenburg, Hugenberg or Hitler. I told him in return that I did not like Pierre Laval's face or Aristide Briand's physical posture and that France's national soccer team had a far way to go to find a goalkeeper as good as Spain's Zamora.

There must have been some correspondence between Max and Lou. She told me that he had invited me to spend the 1930 spring vacation with him in Paris. I am not certain that I looked forward to seeing him, but I was very excited about my first long train ride by myself, and beyond the borders of Germany at that. The stumbling block regarding the high cost of the train fare was resolved by Lou's footing the bill one way and Max the other. I spent most of the long trip standing by an open window in the train's corridor watching the landscape, the passing villages and cities, fully expecting to see dramatic changes as the train entered first Belgium and then France. I could detect no change except for the names on the railroad stations. It was not until the train began to enter Paris and I saw Sacré Coeur above me and the Tour Eiffel in the distance that I realized that some foreign places can indeed be radically different from home. At the Gare du Nord Max was very annoyed because my face was black with soot. How could he take me in such a state to an elegant restaurant before going to the apartment? Marie-Berthe took me to the *toilettes* to clean me up. To my horror I noticed the sign on the door, which said DAMES.

Lou had cautioned me to forgo my finicky eating habits and I bravely ate my first bowl of French onion soup with its long trails of melted cheese as one spooned it. I asked what *escargots* were only after I had eaten them. Marie-Berthe chattered happily as Max acted, somewhat gruffly, as translator whenever my French failed. It appeared that he was doing quite well. He owned a small convertible automobile and after dinner we zipped around Paris for some sight-seeing. I had never seen a city like this and it was a heady experience. On the train ride I had accumulated a pocketful of small French coins, which much to Max's annoyance I jiggled constantly and during dinner repeatedly put on the table to count them. As we were driving over one of the bridges of the Seine, Marie-Berthe asked me to give her all of it. I did so, and she stood up in the moving car and, with a triumphant giggle, threw my precious coins with both hands into the river. Max explained, in a somewhat pedagogical manner, that this was what they thought about money or of people who were unduly possessive about it. As I recall, my reaction at the time was one of resentment that my father, who had not been part of my life, was hasty in reprimanding me like this. This was certainly not a good beginning for my visit, and I was apprehensive about the weeks to come. I need not have worried, even though there were isolated instances of paternal posturing.

Max and Marie-Berthe lived in a spacious apartment on boulevard Saint-Germain just off the corner of rue des Saints Pères. Since the second bedroom was Max's studio, I slept on the couch, which meant that I had the privilege of staying up very late, particularly when, as frequently happened, friends stayed late into the evening, playing chess or talking animatedly. Some of the visitors were familiar from the Cologne Dada days, such as Arp, Éluard, Tzara and Peret. But there were many new faces now. And the atmosphere seemed to be quieter, the tone contemplative rather than contentious, the behavior and gestures more reserved. There was no lack of vehemence, but the flames seemed more controlled, as if these artists and poets felt themselves to be keepers of a common fire.

Dada was no more. It had become palatable now for its inevitable imitators. Some of its characteristics, its impudence and its reliance on the laws of chance had been absorbed into its successor: Surrealism. That was just about all they ever talked about, particularly on the few occasions when André Breton was present. Obviously this was an ideology that was meant to encompass human thought and behavior far beyond paintings and graphics and poetry. I had been hearing French around me for years now, but my understanding of it was obviously not adequate to follow the complicated philosophical turns of conversation. I did discern a certain rising of tension at the mention of Marx, Lenin, Stalin and Trotsky, but for the most part there were long discourses on Hegel, Lautréamont, Flournoy and Apollinaire. Éluard and Breton had visited Sigmund Freud in Vienna as early as September of 1921, and his name floated about constantly. Then there were tirades with words like "traitor," "arriviste," "counterrevolutionary," the names always changing, but I remember one in particular: Giorgio de Chirico, who was pointed out to me by Max as we walked with Man Ray on the rue Bonaparte. "Watch what he does when he sees me." And sure enough, the hurrying figure, bent as if against an imaginary wind, abruptly defied traffic and crossed the street to avoid his Surrealist enemies. Denunciation and banishment from the movement, for violating some intangible rule, seemed an ever-present peril. I had heard from Lou about Ernst's and Joan Miró's "excommunication" in 1926 by André Breton because they had collaborated on the set-design for Diaghilev's *Romeo and Juliet* ballet. Éluard had finally smoothed over *le scandale*, but Max's attitude toward Breton, after that, remained merely "correct," and his relationship to the Surrealists as a group was marked by a bridgeable but distinct gap. As a result I remember seeing André Breton only a few times during that period, but my initial impressions were profound. I cannot compare him to any other man in the aura of dignity that was his at all times. Handsome, so erect in stature as to make him appear larger, he was the ideal of what one could imagine as the perfect blending of poet-philosopher-royalty. His mien never seemed receptive to inconsequential thought. When he spoke, one listened, not as an act of obeisance but out of deep respect. The proud carriage of his head and profile never suggested a pose. It was that of an elder and sage angel, but nevertheless an angel who now and then would carefully look over his shoulder in apprehension that some dust motes might have settled on his wings.

As a nine-year-old I was obviously bewildered by what I saw and heard in the studios of my father and his friends. He tried to explain the ideas as best he could, but still with some impatience for having to simplify a very profound matter. "It is just what it says in French: beyond, or above, realism. When you go to sleep, you don't stop thinking at all. Your mind is wide awake. You have dreams. People think that dreams are somewhere far away and that they are evil." He went on to describe dreams as the ultimate enemy of insane prohibitions and laws invented by "the idiots who run the world." The Surrealists, with their painting and their poetry, were really doing nothing more than sailing to a new territory, "the continent of the mind . . . just like Columbus did."

Some of the "sailors" on that ship, whom I remember from the apartment and the sidewalk cafés on St. Germain, were Giacometti, Man Ray, Brauner, Miró, Jacques Prevert, Louis Aragon, Masson, René Clair, Mareel Jean, Roland Penrose, Philippe Soupault and Yves Tanguy. On at least two occasions I recall the young Spaniard Salvador Dali, who came with filmmaker Luis Buñuel. This represented a somewhat delicate situation because Gala Éluard, this time without the consent of her husband, was now living with Dali. Max told me, with great glee, about the visit to Dali, in Cadaques, by the Éluards and René Magritte, where it had all happened very quickly. I did not find it amusing. I could not understand why anyone would prefer this small, almost skeletal apparition with big intense eye-pupils in a chalk-white face, and the pencil mustache that would have gone well with the caricature of a gigolo, to Éluard or Max. Dali did seem shy and friendly, though. Max said, "I hope she doesn't tear him into little pieces."

I felt particularly drawn to Alberto Giacometti. This gaunt and moody man was as close to Max personally as was Arp. He made a special effort to be attentive to me, probably because of his devotion to Max. Man Ray kindly played several games of chess with me. Not being able to speak English or enough French, I tried my Latin during our games, and Giacometti attempted to use his limited knowledge of that dead language to act as interpreter. Man Ray was very patient with me. My ineptitude as a chess player must have bored him terribly. At times

Max showed some resentment about all the fuss that was being made over me. There was little he could do, except to scowl, because I could not be sent to bed until everybody had left.

To my delight breakfast was taken across the street in a *brasserie*. There Max and I would sit in the morning with our croissants and café au lait. Marie-Berthe never joined us because she liked to sleep late. After Max got through with his newspaper we would usually have a little talk. He wanted to know more about my life and possible ambitions. I asked about his friends and what their work was like. During those mornings I learned a great deal, and I began to have a feeling of these obviously unique artists and poets in the Paris of that time. Sometimes I learned more than I wanted to know.

I brought Max up to date on Lou, her work and her friends. He did not approve of many of them, but he spoke warmly of her, her courage and her talent. Sometimes I sensed that he was close to explaining why he was not living with us any longer and had married again, but he seemed to be unable to find the right words facing his son. I cannot even say that I was waiting for such an explanation. I tried to act out the worldliness and comprehension with which my mother had characterized the situation. One of my ways was to be very open in my affection for Marie-Berthe. It had not taken me very long to discover that the financial situation in that household was pretty much like a roller coaster. As soon as some money came in, it went out again just as quickly. We still went out for dinner quite frequently, but often Max would ask the *propriétaire* to put the meal on the cuff, explaining that he was entertaining his son. A few times Max suggested that I walk a bit around the streets while he was waiting for the bill in a restaurant where he had probably exceeded his credit. I recall that on at least one occasion Max brought a drawing of his to a restaurant where we had eaten the previous night. Marie-Berthe, as I discovered much later, paid off grocery bills and other debts by surreptitiously taking paintings from Max's studio and successfully offering them in exchange for relatively small amounts of money owed. It was thus, for example, that Max's portrait of Dominique De Menil, who with her husband Jean had been one of Max's early and steadfast patrons, was rediscovered, many years later, in the display window of a small frame shop. Marie-Berthe occasionally managed to supplement the income by knitting dresses for Elsa Schiaparelli or, in really dire circumstances, asking for help from her well-to-do family, the Aurenches, who as conservative upper-class Catholics had bitterly opposed their daughter's marriage to a German, renegade Catholic, who was divorced and penniless. Marie-Berthe adored Max and lived her precarious existence as Max's wife without complaint. Her problems were not financial ones alone. I noticed very soon the way Max scrutinized every good-looking woman in sight, and he did little to hide his involvements with the many women who appeared at the apartment or joined us in the Deux Magots for coffee in the late afternoons. While the artists' coffeehouse had been the Dôme in Montparnasse for a long time, the center now was Deux Magots and later would become the Flore next door.

These afternoons on the sidewalk opposite the church of St. Germain-des-Prés were a ritual that started very modestly with three or four people, but it always grew as more and more friends dropped by. I recall one afternoon when Picasso joined the group. The small round tables first became a circle of five and finally a cluster of ten. Picasso was not a member of the Surrealist group but he was always welcome in their midst, and there were times when hopes were voiced that he might become one of them. He was a close friend of Éluard and his new wife Nuche. As the conversation flowed, with an occasional contribution from him, he kept his hands busy creating a construction out of empty matchboxes. When he ran out of empty ones he ordered more from the waiter, disposed of the matches and continued building his many-faceted tower. Nobody paid much attention to him except the tourists, who perhaps did not recognize Giacometti, Man Ray or Arp but knew who this master was even in those days. As time neared for dinner, the social gathering broke up and all of us, including Picasso, left for Brasserie Lipp. The people at the surrounding tables were ready to pounce on the "sculpture" that had been left behind, but halfway out, Picasso stopped, returned to the table. He picked up his creation, crushing the matchboxes with both hands and stuffing the wreckage into his coat pockets.

Inevitably, be it at breakfast or at dinner, the topic would be turned by me to my favorite subject: sports. Max was obviously bored by all of it and repeatedly asked what I hoped to achieve in that field. It was, after all, an occupation for the young only, and there were no financial gains to be made. I reeled off names like Max Schmeling, Johnny Weissmuller and Bill Tilden, among others, and expressed the hope eventually to become some kind of manager or coach. Oh . . . to coach the German national soccer team, now there was a dream.

One afternoon Max came home with a lot of packages for me. They contained boxing gloves, a punching bag on a stand, gym shoes and boxer shorts. The punching bag was set up in the apartment's foyer and Max told me to begin working out because good athletes, like ballerinas, had to start early. He also asked me, please, not to bring the subject of sports up anymore. I discovered that hitting the bag for hours at a time was a tremendous bore, but I kept it up for appearance's sake. After a few days Max, doubtlessly disturbed by the incessant noise, told me that my persistence was not necessary, that all athletes took long, long rest periods, and he suggested that I take the equipment home with me and set it up in our Cologne apartment.

He called me into his studio to show me where and how he worked. On the

easel was a painting of the backside of a reclining nude in a very strange landscape. I asked him who that was and he said it was Marie-Berthe. When I told
him that it was hardly proper for him to show me such a picture, he said that
I was a pain in the neck. A few days later he called me in again. The nude had
disappeared from the landscape and in its place were a number of white seashell
forms. He said quite formally, "I hope that this will meet with your approval.
Now leave me alone, I am quite busy." I really was fascinated and curious about
his activities and sneaked into the studio whenever he was not at home. The
painting on the easel containing the floating oyster-shell forms was not the only
one of its kind. He seemed to be working on a series of them. There were also
a few larger works showing strangely intertwined linear birds within an oval, or
egg, form. They reminded me of the medical drawings depicting the human
embryo that Lou had shown me. Max returned home unexpectedly one day and
found me standing in the middle of the studio. He said nothing and did not seem
angry. He went over to a large table where he began to rummage among a mass
of steel engravings, some of them cut up, and began to shift heads, arms, legs,
animals, furniture and other elements from one area of white cardboard to
another. He glued the head of a lion to the body of a man and placed the head
of some ogre into the window of a room so that it looked as if the beast were
staring in from the outside. He seemed so engrossed that I felt it to be safe to
steal silently out of the studio. Without turning, he said, "You can stay if you
want to." From then on I spent a lot of time there, knowing, however, when it
was time to leave him alone. The shell forms, I discovered, came into existence
on top of other colors when Max squeezed white paint onto certain areas, which
he then spread, or partially removed, by palette knife with an undulant circular
motion of the arm and hand. "Looks very simple, doesn't it?" he remarked once
and I must admit that I thought, at the time, there surely must be more to
painting than that.

Max often took me along when he went to see different dealers at their
galleries; he told me that they had to be kept amused but in reality he was
checking and hoping that there might have been a nibble or perhaps even a sale.
He usually had nothing good to say when we were out on the street again. I knew
that he had had solo exhibitions in Berlin and Brussels as well as Paris, and during
my stay there was a steady stream of collectors, gallery owners and museum
directors passing through his studio. The results were spotty because as a constant
innovator he made placement into some category, so beloved by the art world
even then, very difficult. His lithograph portfolio *Histoire Naturelle* (rubbing-
derived flora and fauna) was so unique and visually encompassing that it deterred
the utilization of its frottage technique by possible emulators for a long time after
its publication. Here again, so much originality, unimitated, was far too adventur-

ous for all but a few eyes of that time. The volumes were stacked high in his studio, and I am glad that the two copies he gave me then, for Lou and me, are still in my possession.

His principal supporters, during those years, appear to have been the art dealer Jeanne Bucher and the now legendary Caresse Crosby, who, through her publishing imprint Black Sun Press, brought the art and literature of the Surrealists and other aesthetic groundbreakers of the time to public attention. Her peripatetic parties and dinners all over Paris and at her mill-estate in the country, to many of which Max took me while I was there, hosted a cross-section of Paris' intellectual and political life. A typical gathering might consist of Harriet Monroe, Ernest Hemingway, Scott Fitzgerald, Ford Madox Ford, Georges Auric, Elliot Paul, Aleksandr Archipenko, Edgard Varèse, Amédée Ozenfant, Sylvia Beach, and Alexander Calder. There were always people present to whom Max would not speak or on whom he would brusquely turn his back. And he always gave me the reasons. Archipenko, for example, had barred him and his fellow Dadaists from exhibiting at the Paris Section d'Or in 1920.

Caresse Crosby's daughter, Polly Peabody, was everything I had ever imagined an American heiress to be, from what I had read about these beautiful and carefree young women who traveled the continents at will, with innumerable young men at their feet. I developed a hopeless crush on her, to the point of seething with resentment every time somebody flirted with her, and I was particularly incensed when I saw my father doing it. I had to admit even then that he was a master at it.

Toward the end of my visit Max took me to a private screening of the as yet unedited Buñuel film L'Âge d'Or. I had obviously much to learn about Surrealism because I was mystified by the fantasy of seemingly unrelated sequences that pictured, among other scenes, human skeletons, wearing bishop miters on their skulls, conducting their rites while seated atop rocky crags in a desert landscape. Max played the small part of a desperado or outlaw, and I was very much impressed by the fact that my father was now also a film star.

What was less pleasant was his undisguised anger and embarrassment when the problem of my return train fare arose. For several days we walked around Paris and various art galleries, where Max was trying to borrow enough money for the ticket. At one point his anger turned toward me. He asked me why Lou hadn't bought a round-trip ticket, and rather than resent his attitude I recognized how awkward it must have been for him to have his son see him so helpless. I am quite certain that I felt real compassion toward him for the first time because this was a circumstance with which I was all too familiar. It also destroyed my delusion that Max lived a magic life untouched by everyday problems. And worse than that, he could raise only a small amount and I suggested that we write to Lou for the money, which made him even angrier. In the end Marie-Berthe borrowed the rest from her father. Just before my departure Max, Marie-Berthe and I were invited for Easter to the country home of the French minister of culture. He had been helpful, some years ago, in getting Max his *carte d'identité*, which allowed him to live in France, though as an alien. He had remained interested in Max's activities and the two had developed a friendship. In my honor an Easter-egg hunt was hastily organized in the garden just before dusk, and for dinner there was roast goose and plum pudding served with flaming brandy. It was only the second time that I had tasted this bird, and this time I knew that it was not a swan. It was a festive occasion and I could see that Max was pleased to have provided this impressive event as a going-away present for me. At the train station, with the boxing gloves and punching bag as additional baggage, Max raised the hope that I would find a more interesting preoccupation than sports.

At the German border in Aachen (Aix-la-Chapelle), two custom inspectors took a very long look at the volumes of *Histoire Naturelle* and then engaged in a dialogue over the content of *La Femme 100 Têtes*, the collage novel that Max had given me for Lou. They argued with each other whether the pictures weren't just a bit too erotic to allow into Germany. I told them that they were the work of a world-famous artist, who was also my father. They relented, even though one of them remarked that this was a strange character to have as a father. The boxing paraphernalia, however, was confiscated because I didn't have the money to pay the duty on it. It was a symbolic loss that I shall never regret.

There was little I could tell my mother about the visit to my father. She dismissed, as superficial, many of my complaints. She saw nothing wrong in Max's looking at pretty women on the street and dismissed as exaggeration my amplification that Max was not only looking but also undressing them with his eyes. She did not press me for details about his life or his work and waited patiently for me to volunteer my impressions, which I did, but gradually. My Latin teacher from *Gymnasium* was not at all pleased. He had asked me to have Max symbolize, in some artistic way, his concept of "Teacher." When I handed him the stick of wood that Max had given me as his answer, he came close to hitting me with it.

The strongest impression that I had come away with was something that I could not put into words at the time. I had become fascinated with Max's face. Those blue eyes that could change, in a split second, from gentle amusement to piercing hardness, without any apparent provocation. His moods that opened and closed his face almost audibly like a slamming door. His biting and precise reply to some vague question as opposed to his almost humorous reaction to some external adversity. I was certain that he was totally absorbed by his paintings, collages and constructions at every waking, if not sleeping, moment. Everything outside of that was a delicious dessert to be tasted and then dismissed. Somehow I don't recall ever being frightened by his anger or intimidated by his sarcasm. I had seen enough of both the radiance of his smile and the intensity provoked by things others could not see to fear these clouds of harshness. This was obviously not the case with many of those who became friends or managed to get close to him. About six or seven years before his death the art dealer Pierre-André Weill and his wife Lucy had a birthday party for Patrick Waldberg at their apartment in Paris. Max, Dorothea and I were invited. Patrick, that extraordinarily marvelous poet and writer, considered his very special friendship with Max to be of major importance in his life. Beginning to reminisce on that birthday over some drinks, Patrick recalled his first encounter with Max. He described his trepidation when he rang Max's doorbell, a feeling that persisted not only during that first meeting but through their entire relationship. "I must honestly say, Max, that I have always been a little afraid of you. Even after all of these years. I love you and I think I know how you feel about me, but some anxiety, in your presence, has never left me." Max seemed to enjoy this admission hugely—liking the idea of someone fearing him—but he, obviously, did not take Patrick's confession very seriously.

I couldn't resist turning to Max and saying, "I guess that makes me one of the few people who were never afraid of you." His face took on one of his sudden changes to severity and, shaking his finger close to my face, he retorted, "And I have never been afraid of you, either."

The few years on Emma Strasse in Cologne-Sülz can, perhaps, be best characterized as having had the form of a sparkling gem. Most of its facets reflect a very happy boyhood in which the only disturbing elements were the daily agonies of Latin and math in school. I excelled on the school's swimming team and I was not bad at tennis. There were the endless street games, not too dissimilar to stickball, sidewalk hockey on roller skates and, yes, hopscotch and rope-skipping, the latter two, in particular, introducing a new element into the life of a boy my age: girls. There had, to be sure, been an earlier encounter for me with that gender. It appears that during that last Dada summer in Tyrol, I had induced the farmer's daughter (we were both about two at the time) to follow my example and take off all her clothes, after which we proceeded to cover each other from head to toe with a thick layer of axle grease. We responded to the call for dinner by appearing in this state at the communal table presided over by the farmer on one end and by Max on the other. The response was predictably mixed; Max and Arp roared with laughter while the "Father of the Bride" threatened to evict the "whole bunch of immoral intellectuals" from the house that they had rented from him.

This time the "affair" was much more sedate and proper. The best way to tell it is in the form of a short story by Lou Straus-Ernst written and published in 1931.

Two Women, an Encounter.

Lately I have observed something new and strange in my son's daily behavior. Just about every half hour or so he climbs four stories to the apartment from play in the street to wash his hands and polish his shoes. For a ten-year-old boy, who has a severe contempt for anything that smacks of such "affectations" as excessive neatness, clean fingernails and combed hair, such behavior is thought-provoking. Initially, my questions about this phenomenon are met with a slightly embarrassed mumble, but then, with an equal mixture of pride and nonchalance, comes the answer: "Well, I have a girl-friend."

Having conditioned myself, for a long time now, not to show even a hint of surprise about anything that he may have to confide or discuss with me, I ask in a matter-of-fact way: "Well, what is she like? Do I know her?"

But I have already gone too far. The only answer I get is: "That's not a matter for grown-ups. They don't understand anything about such things." Good enough, I can wait.

Sure enough, on the very next day he reports proudly during dinner time: "Guess what? Today I walked all the way to Grandfather's house and back instead of taking the trolley. Can I keep the carfare that I've saved?" Yes, he may. "Oh, that's good. Now I have at least something for my girl."

"What do you intend to buy for her?"

"I don't know yet. If she feels like it she can have a potato pancake from that little stand around the corner. Or else, I'll buy her a bar of chocolate. She is already twelve years old, you know."

On the following day I watch from the balcony. He is standing amid a group of boys and girls in energetic conversation, his cap rakishly aslant on his head, the belt over his sweater pulled much too tight, which is meant to convey a sportlike elegance. Later, as I come out of the house, he immediately breaks away from his peers and runs over to me. He doesn't want the other children to overhear our conversation. Mothers, after all, are bound to say things that result in embarrassments. But I take care to go through some mere facial motions as indifferently as possible, except to murmur: "Which one is it?" He hardly moves his lips, eyes rolling upward; "The one in the red dress . . . and for heaven's sake, don't be too obvious when you walk past her."

"She" is intensively engaged in skipping rope at the moment. A sturdy, self-assured little individual. The dress, very red and very short, allows a generous view of a pair of sun-tanned, long and well-turned legs. A copper-red mass of curls frames a sensitive face with a jaunty turned-up nose and very large, light-blue eyes. Eyes that at this very moment are looking directly into mine with the alert and thoughtful expression of a fully matured little female.

"Well, well," I say to myself, "you are the first one to take away a small piece of my little son's heart. There are going to be others, plenty of them, but in any case, you will have been the first. I must admit, you are pretty, he certainly has good taste. I just wonder if you are a kind person. But then, basically, I guess, that is something of minor interest to men, and to that extent my young boy is already a man. . . . What would you think if you knew that your manly soccer-playing boy-friend takes his almost hairless one-eared teddy-bear to bed with him every night? That he sews aprons and clothes for this bear that he has slept with since the age of two? But that is none of your business. That is something only for me to know and for me, alone, to keep." The girl, with more than casual curiosity, takes the measure of this stranger, the mother of her boy-friend, who now remembers that she must get to the trolley-car station. As she hurries away she is aware of the looks that follow her. She is pleased that today, of all days, she is well and elegantly dressed and has passed the critical appraisal of the girl who, even now, energetically continues to skip rope with her quick feet and shapely limbs.

The romance did not last very long. In order to show off in front of her, I provoked a fistfight with another boy, which I lost decisively. In my humiliation I deliberately avoided the girl for a few weeks, and when I condescended to approach her again she had already found someone else to buy potato pancakes for her. This one even had enough money to treat her to ice cream from the street vendor. Even so, the matter did not quite end there. Some months later, to my chagrin, Lou's short story appeared in the Sunday literary section of a Cologne newspaper. I believed my mother's almost tearful explanation that the editor had ignored or forgotten her request not to use her by-line. Whenever I saw the girl after that, I had a strong suspicion that there was the hint of a smile around her lips.

There was also a certain opacity to the time. All of my life up until that time had had the constant background of political unrest and violence. I remember riding a full trolley car in 1931 with people smiling over the headline news that President Herbert Hoover had proposed a one-year moratorium on the German war debt. Surely this would bring some peace to the streets, and the thousands of unemployed who gathered every day in front of state buildings waiting for the dole or a job would diminish. No more mass meetings by uniformed bigots denouncing the Jews for the "betrayal" at Versailles, no longer the red flag or the swastika. Nothing, however, changed. The noise, the ugliness and the national paranoia not only continued but seemed to grow. I felt the approaching darkness as one experiences the days getting shorter and winds blowing colder when winter nears. And yet so inured had we all become that any disastrous climax could not be imagined. Never mind that there were constant encounters with terror. During the time of a Reichstag election campaign I was on my way home from my grandfather's house in the center of the city. The National Socialists, Hitler's party, had peaked in a prior election, and a mood of ugly uncertainty prevailed in the streets. On a corner I was suddenly pushed against the wall by three beefy men in the feared brown uniform of the S.A. They went through my pockets and triumphantly tore up some Social Democrat leaflets that I had found and was bringing home in triumph to my mother. They pushed me around and began to beat me, and one of them yelled: "I bet he's a Jew." They tore open the front of my short school pants as well as my underwear. "I thought so," one of them triumphed, "I can recognize them when they are a kilometer away." They threw me to the ground and began to kick me. They must have seen the policeman on the next corner, who was watching all this without making a move. But they stopped. "We'll let you go this time, but don't you dare to stick that thing into a German girl, because then we'll have to cut it off." Holding my pants together awkwardly, I managed to get home, where I bravely announced that I had stood up against three storm troopers but that they had somehow torn my pants. I gave my mother a leaflet that had remained in my pocket and held it up for Maja and my mother to see. They saw my bruises and cuts but controlled their fear and agony and told me always to cross the street if I saw anyone in that brown uniform. But this and similar experiences surely were aberrations. The Germans were a civilized people after all. The Kaiser and militarism had been dealt with before I was born, and the blood and assassinations that had followed the war were faint stories that largely were ignored by our history teachers. There was always Field Marshal Hindenburg, the President, a father figure if ever there was one, for whom it would obviously be a matter of personal honor to preserve the tranquillity of his people, after the hunger and humiliation that had really been caused by the munition makers. Such, anyway, was the talk in our home when there was news of another outrage caused by political unrest. Often, before going to sleep, I heard the gunfire from an adjoining suburb that consisted of crowded tenements and was considered a "workers' quarter." It was not unusual to see ambulances and hearses removing the bodies from the night's carnage found in a children's playground that was a shortcut on my way to school. There was concern, but "good sense will prevail; we are not a nation of monsters."

Christmas was the time for Engelbert Humperdinck's *Hänsel und Gretel* at the opera house; a children's party at the Rathaus given by Lord Mayor Adenauer, whose face always suggested that his lineage went all the way back to one of the three wise men from the Far East; and almost as a ritual, Lou Straus-Ernst discussing with her son the meaning and origin of all the tribal and religious festivities that coincided with the shortest days of the year. The Christmas tree was always a real pine, with real candles and several buckets of water ready for safety's sake. Blustery Saint Nicholaus came in person on the eve of December 6 to fill the stockings for "good" children. It was the Christkind, Christmas Child, who came, unseen, on the very night of his birth, and I was called from my bed to see the tree and to open my presents. I remember that inner glow generated by the flickering candles, and I also recall that my mother and Maja cried at that magic moment. At least, I remember it, in particular, during those last few years, before it all came to an end. I was taken several times to midnight mass in the Dom, our gigantic cathedral, and also to my grandfather's synagogue on Walter Rathenau Platz for the final evening of Hanukkah. Not having been brought up in any specific faith, these experiences have left me with a sense of awe and respect not just for the ritual but for the very idea of belief itself. It is now quite clear to me that Lou Straus-Ernst, in the very face of ever-growing and obvious brutality in the land and in the minds of its inhabitants, made a determined effort to induce in her son a feeling about the basic goodness in human beings, to value the private or religious convictions of others without necessarily being unduly influenced by them. She talked constantly about the spirit of humanity and its glorification by poets, artists, composers, philosophers and historians. The rose window at Chartres or the Grünewald altarpiece came out of the same well as the carved figures of an African tribe, as did the diverse visions of Rembrandt, Van Gogh, Klee or Max Ernst. The music of the people deserved the same attention as Bach's great organ works. The poet and writer spoke not only of beauty and love but also, in holding up a mirror to reality, often succeeded in creating a determination in a people to rid itself of ugliness and terror. She even tried to explain or rationalize the misdirected anger of those who strutted through the street with hate on their lips and faces. It was as if she sensed the growing darkness and, more often than not, she seemed to be talking to herself as much as to me. Her optimism never waned, and yet there were, at times, undertones of desperation, as if our happy life together were to be the last act of a play and that its message might be lost on the way out of the theater. Much of these matters came up in conversations as we walked along the banks of the Rhine, in parks, museums, concert halls and on streets filled with thousands watching political parades. A memorable ritual occurred early every afternoon in her workroom as Maja woke Lou from her nap by bringing in a glass coffee maker. The three of us watched an alcohol-fed wick flame heat the water, forcing it from the lower round glass ball into an identical upper one that held the coffee and the filter. The observation of this little miracle usually took place in silence, giving Lou a chance to wake up completely, and as the coffee slowly dripped back down, our conversation began. The topics ranged from trifles to tragedy. The séance was casual and intimate, as if we were the only three people in the world; I recall these hours vividly as periods of insight, learning, togetherness and, particularly, as moments of peaceful contentment and a sense of belonging.

My favorite sport was soccer. I don't think that I was very good at it. It seems that I lacked the necessary aggressive instinct to get the ball past the goalkeeper for a score. But I had one advantage. I kicked with my left foot, and that always opened the position of left-wing forward for me for school and pick-up games. My manual activities had been exclusively left from the very beginning, and my schoolteachers had merely succeeded in making me ambidextrous rather than driving my left-handedness completely out of me. Since I was perfectly willing to dribble the ball up the left side of the field and feed it there to another forward looking for the glory of achieving a goal, I played almost every day somewhere out in the greenbelt. There were other games in the street for me, including roller skating. The little park behind a nearby church became the equivalent of the Wild West for my playmates and me. Always on the lookout for humorless policemen, we re-enacted scenes from stories about American Indians among its very proper plantings and flower beds. Without exception we would fantasize about "Amerika." Not just about cowboys, trappers and Indians but using whatever little information had made its way into the illustrated press. America was a faraway place and it was so big. Its citizens were rich, their jaws moved with chewing gum; they drove cars like the Essex Super-Six, Cord, Packard and Nash. They didn't have to get their milk every day at the store. It was delivered to them in waxed cardboard containers, and they kept it fresh, with the red California apples and hamburger meat, in that fabulous electric icebox. They could go to a theater and watch women undress down to nothing, for an entire evening, sometimes several "strippers" at a time. And, would you believe it, in the end they would be all naked? Wow! We outdid each other with exaggerated stories about gang warfare in Chicago and New York, the outlandish salaries of movie stars like Al Jolson and the cowboy Tom Mix, and reenacted scenes from the *Hunchback of Notre Dame* by screwing up our faces and bodies to resemble Lon Chaney. We nonchalantly dropped names like Bill Tilden, Johnny Weissmuller and Jim Thorpe as if we knew what they actually did. Everyone had a different story about a mysterious game called baseball and its hero Babe Ruth. Every time there was an aborted flight across the Atlantic, our respect for Charles Lindbergh grew . . . and it was a good thing that Legs Diamond had been recognized at the border in Aachen and been denied admission to German soil. He might have been killed by a rival gangster on the Hohe Strasse, right here, instead of some street in the Bronx. A man named Franklin Roosevelt had been elected in place of Herbert Hoover. That was too bad because Hoover really had tried hard to help Europe recover from the big war. But Roosevelt had allowed the Americans to drink alcohol again. Can you imagine telling a whole country what it can or cannot drink?

Sometimes our little "Wild West" park was invaded by a group of brown-shirted Nazis, listening to denunciations, by one of their own, of the sinister "Bolshevik Jews" who had teamed up with that foul chimpanzee Aristide Briand and the treacherous Georges Clemenceau, "the Tiger," debasing the *Vaterland* with the shame of Versailles. Those same "Izzies," one of them screamed, who had really kidnapped and killed the Lindbergh baby and were now succeeding in railroading a hard-working German carpenter, Bruno Hauptmann, to take a fall for them. My friends and I knew better. Lumber that had been used for the kidnap ladder and stacks of ransom money had been found in Hauptmann's garage. The American police knew their business. They had caught their man much faster than ours had when the notorious "Düsseldorf Murderer" had made a joke of them by scattering the corpses of his female victims up and down the banks of the Rhine, seemingly at will, for an almost endless stretch of time.

Among my playmates I was the acknowledged expert on American movies. They thought of me as a walking encyclopedia of Hollywood. Not only could I talk about George Bancroft and Hoot Gibson, Charles Chaplin, Buster Keaton, Richard Barthelmess, the Barrymores, Warner Baxter, John Gilbert, Ann Dvorak, Myrna Loy, Sidney Blackmer, Kay Francis and Greta Garbo, but I even knew the names of directors like Mack Sennett, Cecil B. De Mille, Michael Curtiz, Roy Del Ruth, D.W. Griffith, George Cukor and William Dieterle. Without substantiation I might even enlarge on my "expertise" by claiming to know the difference between different cinematographers.

On Saturday afternoons I was allowed to go to the *Kino* (movies) and sometimes even on Sundays, if it rained and I could not go to watch a soccer game. My preference was always American films. Often the seats were hard, uncomfortable benches and the prints might be so old that everything seemed to be taking place during a rainstorm. There were the movies about cowboys and Indians, or gangsters and star reporters and detectives, or big musicals or comedies about elegant people in posh settings. Most films were dubbed into German, but I was always fascinated by films that had subtitles. I could not understand how people were able to speak while hardly moving their lips. Before the main feature was shown, there were, of course, cartoons and a newsreel. The latter was always something of a shock to me. I recall seeing thousands of Americans taking part in a protest march because they were over fifty and could not find work, and a segment showing a man traversing the Mississippi on a cable and wheel while suspended by his hair. I saw Governor Lehman dedicating a tunnel under a river, all the while calmly smoking his pipe, and there had been the "bonus march" rout of war veterans with a close-up of two smartly uniformed officers, MacArthur and Eisenhower, their jaws resolutely set for action. The last name sounded very German to me, but I was not too surprised because illustrated magazines and weekend newspapers ran with some regularity stories of how close the United States had come at its inception to deciding on German as its official language. On special occasions my mother or Maja took me to one of the fancier movie palaces downtown to see films like *Trader Horn, Rasputin* or *All Quiet on the Western Front.* I recall that as we came out of the latter film the police forced us back into the theater because they and the Nazis, who like other militarists had tried to prevent the showing, were engaged in a pitched battle. I was frightened by the sound of breaking glass and the screaming of people. Some Nazis had found their way into the theater and provoked fistfights with people in the audience. My mother explained that there were a lot of people in Germany who hated any expression of the tragedy and futility of war. *All Quiet on the Western Front,* by Erich Maria Remarque, a German novelist, had been made into a film in America, and that was all the more galling. It became the focal point for violent demonstrations wherever it was shown, and if any local police commander refused to provide protection to a cinema, it would be pulled from the program. It got so bad that the film would open without advance advertising and people would go to it as if to a secret meeting.

My very favorite film star was Rin-Tin-Tin. I inevitably cried when in the last reel it looked as if he had been killed by the villains. But he always survived. The Northwest Mountie kneeling beside his inert body, bravely fighting back his tears, suddenly found himself miraculously touched by the dog's paw. Rin-Tin-Tin would live. The Mountie walked off into the sunset or through the snow, followed by his limping friend.

Naturally I read all about Indians. My father had left behind a beautifully illustrated book from the turn of the century depicting different tribes—the way they danced and decorated their bodies and how they lived and hunted. I read German translations of James Fenimore Cooper and, most of all, Karl May, a very popular writer who spoke with such authority in his tales about the red man that his descriptions were taken as gospel. The main protagonists were a powerful and extraordinarily intelligent Indian chief named Winnetou and his white friend, the equally imposing and rugged Old Shatterhand, who could shoot out one eye of a fly on a distant tree and whose fists were the terror of the Plains. Winnetou, in studying the footprints left in the tall grass by a potential adversary to his tribe, was able to tell the man's height and weight, what he had eaten for breakfast, what he was wearing and if he was armed, as well as how fast, and where, he was going. Between these two blood brothers few words were needed and no enemy was ever safe. Every German knew Winnetou and Old Shatterhand. What was not generally known was that Karl May had never set foot on American soil, had in fact never traveled outside Germany at all. My geography teacher in Gymnasium, a priest named Kaese, told my class that he and some friends, as students, had written to Karl May wanting some reassurance about these terrible rumors. They had received by mail a glass vial containing a long black strand of hair from "Winnetou's" head. They tested it in the laboratory and determined that the hair had come from a horse's tail. A lot of my schoolmates thought that it was scandalous for Monsignor Kaese, a Roman Catholic priest, to be calling our great Karl May a liar and a fake.

May's popularity persists to this very day, and many social groups, then as now, spend their weekends deep in some forest dressed up in the regalia replete with warpaint, feather headpieces, loincloths and tomahawks, and engage in the hunts and war games as described by Karl May. I shall never forget when, in 1965, I drove from Malmédy in Belgium across the border into Germany and had to stop my car in order to allow hundreds of painted and costumed men, women and children to cross the highway. They were running and screaming and I found out why they were in such a hurry. Before I proceeded, an equally large group broke through the pines in hot pursuit of the fleeing "enemy tribe."

Other intriguing aspects of America for me were its entertainers and its music. Max and Marie-Berthe had taken me once to a Paris music hall where Lucienne Boyer had been the only white performer. The rest of the bill was black, featuring "Bojangles" Robinson and a small jazz combo, with Fats Waller sitting in, that night, as a guest. American jazz, until that night, had meant Paul Whiteman, symphonic sounds with occasional solos by Bix Beiderbecke, Joe Venuti and the crooning of the "Rhythm Boys," but I had never heard anything as exciting as that small group and the amazing keyboard-runs of Waller. I was astounded by the absence of sheet music and the intuitive interplay by the individual musicians.

Black entertainers *(les nègres américains)* were of course all the rage in France, and I regretted that I was too young to be allowed to see Josephine Baker clad only in some banana peels. Such entertainment in pre-Hitler Germany was rare. In fact, the very first black people I saw, in the late twenties, were in the Cologne zoo, whose enterprising director had imported, for a summer, an entire tribe from Africa. There they were observed by large crowds in their compound of grass huts, cooking on open fires, presenting their semi-nude bodies once every hour in an orgiastic dance to the sounds of drums. The special feature of this particular tribe was their lips, which had been artificially expanded by progressively larger pieces of wood, depending on the age of the individual. Lou Straus-Ernst protested loudly to the Cologne authorities for making a spectacle of people whose culture, though different, deserved respect and not ridicule by showing them like freaks adjacent to wild animals in cages. The "Herr Stadt-Direktor für Kultur" haughtily rejected her opinion, saying that the city needed the revenue and, besides, that the tribe would go back to Africa after their tour of Germany with an improved standard of living. Lou did not let it rest there and wrote a stinging article for her newspaper in which she said that she was ashamed of inadvertently having allowed her son to witness this cruelty. She became even more infuriated when, as a result of her story, attendance at the zoo doubled. She promptly took me to the UFA Film Palace, where King Vidor's *Halleluja* had just opened, but warned me afterward that blacks in America did not, as a rule, appear in white robes singing mighty spirituals with arms stretched heavenward. In answer to my questions about blacks living in America as well as Africa, she described as best she could their role as ex-slaves, how they had been brutally shipped, in closely packed conditions, to provide forced labor for large cotton plantations in the Southern states. She described them as a minority in America and that they were still mistreated and poor, even though some of them were popular entertainers. She warned me that the Jews in Europe, and particularly in Germany and Poland, were also a minority who had never been fully accepted in the places where they lived. True enough, they had contributed to their societies as writers, doctors, lawyers, composers and other academic and professional people, and for that very reason alone had become subject to hatred and ostracism. It was not just Hitler and his Brownshirts who were racist. This was a sickness carried by many others in all walks of life and the disease was growing.

I wanted to know more. Was I a Jew . . . or what? She told me, as she had before on several occasions, that she and Max had decided, at my birth, that the choice was to be mine when I grew up. Max, she said, was a Catholic who had absolutely no use for that religion. (It had been a source of glee for Max in 1926 when Cologne's archbishop had scathingly denounced him in public for his painting *The Virgin Spanks the Jesus-Child in Front of Three Witnesses: André Breton, Paul Éluard and the Painter*. It shows a seated Mary administering a sound beating to the rosy behind of her little blond son, whose halo has fallen on the floor while hers remains sedately in place. The three friends watch through a small window. He told me that he got the idea from watching Maja disciplining me in Tyrol. My mother used the apparent ex-communication as a way out from continuing to pay church taxes for her absent Catholic husband.) She was born a Jew, and even though she did not observe the ritual and had grave reservations about organized religion, she would always be considered a Jew and I, probably, would be too. She held that no group had the right to call themselves "the Chosen People," but she was proud of her heritage nevertheless.

Lou Straus-Ernst, her friends, colleagues and peers had lived too long with political and economic uncertainties to allow themselves to be panicked into anticipating a return of medieval terror to Western Europe. They hoped that what they were observing was an uncomfortably laborious birth of German democracy. There was plenty of time. Kaiser Wilhelm lived, safely removed, in Doorn, Holland, and it would take perhaps one or, at most, two more generations for the majority of Germans to outgrow their stiff-necked air of superiority, their love of uniforms, boots, side arms and, most of all, their masochistic enjoyment of being a nation, though "unbeaten," betrayed into surrender in war. A lot of other things should be allowed to wither away as well.

I was aware of all this and, as a youngster, of a great deal more. I recall all too clearly one of my schoolmates saying to me once during recess, "I would gladly go to war and die for Germany." I had seen several of my teachers at the Gymnasium surreptitiously put a swastika pin on their lapel as they left the schoolgrounds. Through the open doors of workers' pubs, I had heard drunken voices: "Brothers, listen for the signals, get ready for the last battle. The internationale will win your human rights." At a nearby park behind a church, I had observed men and women stand in a circle, arms upraised, singing the "Horst Wessel Song." During their proper Sunday promenades, or at the zoo, fairs, exhibitions, on excursion buses, trains and steamboats, each family seemed like a separate armed camp. The suspicion that one sat perhaps next to Nazis, Communists, Catholics, Protestants, dissidents or even Jews hung in the air constantly. The latter could of course be easily recognized because everybody had seen Semitic characteristics in political cartoons. Children playing with each other on such outings were often summarily called back by their parents and forbidden to continue their games with strangers.

I watched it all from the safety of a warm and enlightened home on the fourth floor of Emma Strasse. I read about it as avidly as I did about soccer, track and other sports. Politics and its personalities were as fascinating as movie stars and American gangsters. At one time I knew the name of every one of the thirty-two splinter parties who were on the ballot for the next Reichstag election. The Nazis' *Völkische Beobachter* and Streicher's *Der Stürmer* could be read in their entirety in long rows of glassed display boxes outside any party headquarters. The only difficulty was that the glass was likely to be shattered by flying rocks. The same was true of the Communists' *Die Rote Fahne (The Red Flag)*. I collated that material as carefully in my mind as I did long articles about a proposed change in the game tactics for the upcoming soccer match between the national teams of Germany and Austria.

Both political extremes expressed astonishing similarities, chief among them being their love for the German worker and their contempt for free-thinking intellectuals. They spoke of Germany's rebirth, one through nationalism and racial purity and the other through a "worker's paradise and the internationale." Both of them would publish glowing portraits of honored leaders almost constantly and, as if in tandem, would suddenly drop their names altogether. In the *Völkischer Beobacter* Gregor Strasser was suddenly gone, as was Trotsky in *Die Rote Fahne.* There were differences. The *Beobachter* and *Der Stürmer* reviled all Jews anywhere, the *Fahne* swore that there was absolutely no anti-Semitism in the USSR but claimed a large segment of Germany Jewry was making a deplorable mistake in supporting the political center rather than joining the Communist party's battle for total equality. The rich *Bonzen* would pay dearly, be they Jewish or not, once the proletariat took power in its hands.

Joseph Goebbels reminded the masses of the poison of the Versailles Treaty with the scream of a cheerleader, and Hitler shrieked about the coming "Third Reich" and all the due bills that would then be collected. Communist Ernst Thälemann quoted Marx and promised victory under the red banner of "Dialectic Materialism." Very little was said by either side about the shame of hunger and the agony of hatred, two related epidemics that seemed secondary to political victory.

Both sides needed heroes for the masses to admire. The Nazis manufactured a martyr out of a pimp who had been killed by a professional competitor. Horst Wessel, they said, became the National Socialist missionary among the "misguided" Communist workers only to lose his life at the hands of those whose political purity he had tried to save. This well-constructed mannequin became more successful than the long-gone Rosa Luxemburg and Karl Liebknecht of the left. Mass demonstrations, organized with military march-time-music precision, uniforms, shiny boots and gold-tasseled flags symbolized that much-longed-for sense of order far more effectively than the shuffling feet of thousands as they moved in uncoordinated parades under the homemade banners of the Communists or the Social Democrats. The shallow splendor of Hitler's marching columns was obviously more appealing to those millions who had been watching from the sidelines. The social justice and equality advocated by the left was viewed with growing suspicion. Would Germany's honor, stolen on the battlefields of Verdun and the Marne, be restored by securing human rights for everyone? And who were those intellectuals, speaking as they were of Germany's culture, the beauty of its soul and the rich rewards of humility and moderation? They were outsiders not worthy of citizenship in a proud nation. They were an elite, most of them Jews, of course, who pretended to understand these insane paintings, unreadable poetry, music without melody and similar cultural outrages.

The anger in the air became almost palpable. It seemed, at times, like a steely vise, and yet its potential victims, millions of them, spoke of a coming explosion almost as if in hope that it would sweep away these bad dreams of barbarity and insanity. On their horizon stood the ultimate bulwark, our President, protector of the Weimar Constitution, the ultimate guardian of the black-red-gold national flag: our much-honored Field Marshal Hindenburg. It was he who received a delegation, headed by Franz von Papen of the Catholic Center party, as he sought advice for the solution of the political crisis. And it was that towering symbol of Germany's rectitude, who, in his dotage and in return for his heirs' exemption from inheritance taxes, elevated Adolf Hitler, "that miserable *Feldwebel*" (corporal), whom he had sworn never to receive in his office, to the chancellorship on January 30, 1933.

My mother and I were listening to music from the Cologne radio station of the Deutsche Rundfunk when the program was interrupted to make the announcement. "Nothing to be scared of," Lou said. "Hindenburg did it only because he knows Hitler will fail in the next Reichstag elections. These fanatics will be thrown out on the street. That's where they came from and that is where they belong."

I still don't understand why I was not frightened. In the months that followed we watched, with disbelief, the usurpation of police powers and other "constitutional aberrations" to which few took exception. Policemen sported the swastika armband. My teachers wore their swastika lapel pins openly as they taught us Latin; the Nazi flag was hoisted on the Gymnasium tower during a hastily called recess. My art teacher said to me, "Aside from the fact that you are Jewish, your father is also a degenerate artist, and I am not surprised that you are such a bad student."

My mother described another jarring experience in her 1942 autobiographic account of the events:

Cologne without its carnival is unthinkable. We think of it as the "grandest festival of the year." It is difficult, in fact, to imagine a more unrestrained and joyful, week-long, day-and-night celebration. Everything comes to a standstill. Very few in this city can think of anything other than dancing, singing and drinking. During the day the streets are filled with celebrants wearing funny masks and costumes. Night is the time for elaborate masquerade balls that continue well past dawn.

The carnival of 1933 turned out to be a dance of death. We had all seen it coming, but none of us had been willing to take the danger seriously. When it came, we were totally unprepared.

I had never been actively involved in politics and read the newspapers only superficially. The constant turnovers in government leadership presented little in the way of change with each succession. The innumerable splinter parties that sprang up with each new election presented a confusing picture that I found much too disconcerting. I was vitally interested only in my work, which concerned itself mainly with literature and the arts.

During the preceding summer a journalist friend on a visit from Berlin had expressed amazement about our lack of concern. "You seem so disinterested in what is happening in Berlin," he said. "When 'they' take over, it probably will not be for very long. But in a relatively short time they can create a great deal of havoc."

As he talked to me under the shady trees along the Rhine, I dismissed his words as exaggeration. To the contrary, however, his apprehensions had not been pessimistic enough. A short while later the Nazis gained a frightening majority in the Reichstag elections.

We felt the growing peril, but still nothing changed very much in our part of the country. The Rhineland with its predominantly Catholic population had relatively fewer Nazi adherents, and anti-Semitism seemed less overt than elsewhere. Sometimes, somewhere in the suburbs, there might be gunfights between Nazis and Communists, but our tranquillity was hardly disturbed. Berlin and Munich were known for tumult and chaos, but that, obviously, had nothing to do with us.

Naturally I was quite scared when, on January 30, 1933, the German Radio news referred, almost grotesquely, to Adolf Hitler as "Reichskanzler Hitler."

"As long as we have our Adenauer, nothing can happen to us," was the common expression. Adenauer was Lord Mayor of Cologne, a personality known far beyond the limits of the city for his liberal initiative and independent ideas. Through his additional position as chairman of the Prussian State Council, he had considerable political power. He was often referred to as "the Uncrowned King of Prussia." I knew him fairly well, having written many of his speeches that concerned cultural affairs. No . . . as long as we had him, nothing could happen to our city, and we journalists would be free to do our work under his protection. But . . . how securely did he really hold his seat?

Carnival came as it did each year, in February, and it was celebrated as if nothing had ever happened. One of its most brilliant galas was, always, a masked ball called "Der Paradiesvogel" (Bird of Paradise). Since this event was to be held in the grandiose halls of the Cologne zoo, I had decided to choose an appropriate costume. My friends always compared my body with Renoir's models, so I chose a long black pleated chiffon skirt, a small, tight-fitting, very low-cut blouse, and a tiny flowery hat that I wore askew, on my upswept hair.

I danced, danced and laughed for many hours in the crush of a colorful mass of revelers. Sometime during the night, on my way to repair my makeup, a friend from one of the city's museums said: "Do you realize that in three weeks we will have elections for all city officials?"

At this moment, surrounded by laughing and colorful celebrants, amidst the blare of music and the communal singing, it suddenly dawned on me that everything might be over. A change in the individuals who had been administering this gay and beautiful city might well result in an alien way of life that could never resemble the one we had led. It could mean the end of my work, my loves, of the home with Jimmy and Maja, the end of all of that.

One week later was Rose Monday, the apex of carnival. The unusually hectic electioneering was suspended. This was a holiday. No one wanted to be disturbed by politics in such a fun-loving city. All commercial activity came to a halt, schools were closed until Wednesday, and from early morning on, a multi-colored costumed and masked crowd moved through the narrow streets of the old city with only one thought: to find the best vantage point from which to view the gigantic carnival parade.

Late that afternoon I left Jimmy and Maja to amuse themselves and went to the old city hall. It was, more or less, a professional duty for all newspaper people to watch the parade from there. But it was also a lot of fun to be with so many jovial colleagues, to drink with them marvelous Rhine wine that was served in the beautiful Rococo-Hall and from there to look down on the *Alte Markt* to watch a rainbow-hued spectacle of outlandish plumed headdresses, long red, blue or green wigs, torn umbrellas with glittering bands waving from their naked ribs. There would be loud applause for a unique mask, an inventive or risqué costume, or, perhaps, for a monstrously large masked figure pushing a gaudy baby carriage containing a diapered midget. The noise of kettle drums and other noisemakers provided the rhythm for the flower field of heads and bodies below us. Somewhere there would be a sudden opening in the crowd where a couple had decided to embrace and kiss each other. They were surrounded immediately by a ring of dancing revelers urging them on and finally emulating their lack of inhibition.

The small medieval houses looked down on this annual frolic while on the other side stood the solemn tower of the Church of St. Martin.

Every now and then a shadow came between me and what I was looking at. Didn't anyone there have a sense about what was really happening? Was there no foreboding that that relaxed and festive amusement might soon transform itself into terror? . . . And yet, how could one expect those simple people down there to have any such worries, when we, the "informed ones," refused to acknowledge the seriousness of the situation?

"Hitler and Göring are said to be visiting Krupp in Essen today," a usually well-informed colleague whispered to a few of us. *"Ach,"* came the rejoinder, "they are right here in Cologne, hidden behind funny masks, enjoying the carnival."

At home that evening Jimmy watched with great amusement, from his room, as I prepared my makeup and costume for the big Rose Monday Ball.

Was I especially tired that evening? Or were the shadows more frequent? Here I was again with the same masked people, the same songs, the same swells of laughter escalating into loud screams and foot-stamping. . . . At the same time it somehow seemed to be so strange to me. The people here were, after all, not a faceless crowd, but artists, intellectuals and enlightened politicians who knew, as much as anyone could, about what was going on in the rest of the country. How many of them would dance here again next year? . . . Tonight they were dancing on top of a volcano . . . and many of them must have known it.

I didn't feel much like joining the crowd and remained with a few friends in a corner, away from the dance floor. Shortly after the midnight unmasking a young man, his dark eyes blazing, shouted across the table: "The Reichstag is burning. . . ."

The news traveled around the huge hall. There were pockets of silence, whispering heads moved closer to each other around some tables, but, after a while, the merry noises swelled up again and continued. The ball went on and, if anything, the frenzy seemed to increase. Without saying good-bye to anyone, I left to go home. For me, the festival had come to an end.

On February 28, the next day, claiming that the burning of the Reichstag was to have been a signal for a Communist uprising, Hitler obtained Hindenburg's signature on a decree that allowed his various ministries to curtail individual civil rights, freedom of the press, freedom of expression, freedom of assembly and other rights guaranteed under the Weimar Constitution. It was to permit them to monitor all postal and telephone communications. The decree also constituted an unlimited warrant for the arrest of political criminals as well as house searches and seizure of possibly incriminating documents.

Two nights later, around 3 A.M., three SS men demanded access to the apartment. Lou, Maja and I stood in the foyer as they went through my mother's papers and her wardrobe. They threw my books and artifacts around and searched the drawers containing my underwear. They lifted the mattresses on the beds and and finally left with Lou Straus-Ernst's passport. The following day she gave notice to the landlord for the termination of her lease as of June 1. After standing in line for seven hours, she finally regained possession of her passport.

Still no final decisions were made. The whole thing might blow over and we would merely move to a new apartment, but to see the large FOR RENT sign across our windows every time I returned from school was always a moment of terrible fear for me.

For some weeks there were moments of illusion that Lou could continue to function. Her articles were still being accepted for publication but with diminishing frequency. I think that any notions that she might have had about staying in Germany became untenable when, in response to a formal invitation, she took me along to tea at the home of one of her university classmates, now the director of one of Cologne's most important museums. The occasion was stiff and formal, and there was just small talk as the more than twenty guests sat uncomfortably sipping from their cups. My mother whispered to me, "It's all very strange. Everyone here, except the host and his wife, is Jewish." The tall, friendly man, whom I had known all my life, stood up and cleared his throat politely to ask for quiet: "I have asked you to come here because I think of you all as friends and colleagues of long standing. My feelings will never change, and I hope that you will not forget our common past, working together or breaking bread at your tables and mine. As a scholar and administrator of a great institution, I consider it my duty to work for the goals of our new Germany. This small gathering is my way of saying "Adieu" to you personally in preference to the option of informing you about the end of our mutual relationship by formal letter. . . ." The exit of all was in stunned silence. Lou and I walked home, past the little park where she had watched me on cold winter afternoons skating without letup on the tree-lined pond. She cried and said not a word.

The hysteria engendered by the Reichstag fire made the results of a respective federal and municipal election a foregone conclusion. Communists and a number of other left-wing deputies were arbitrarily arrested, and whatever opposition remained was mere cosmetics. Konrad Adenauer was forced to resign before the vote in Cologne had become final. He was subsequently put under house arrest and later confined in a camp. A new Lord Mayor, a Nazi by the name of Riesen, was put in his place and his appointment rubber-stamped by a docile city council. I wondered briefly about the fate of Fräulein Otto.

The melancholy task of preparing our possessions for storage was eased somewhat by the conviction that all this was to be for a short time only. Lou was going to Paris to prepare the way for us to join her soon. She had gotten a promise from her father that he would assist her financially in opening a small art gallery. I would live with him and his family to continue my education until the time for reunion came.

A few weeks before her departure she received a frantic phone call from the city hall press office. It seems that the hold-over chief of the bureau, an old colleague, and for the last few years her lover, had not shown up for work since the installation of the new Lord Mayor. His Honor was due to make his first public speech on the next day at the Kunstverein (Art Society), where an exhibition of contemporary Italian art was to open. No speech had been written, and unless one was produced by the next morning, Lou's friend would lose his job. She knew his whereabouts. He had reacted to the recent political upheavals by going on an extended drunken binge. Two nights ago, he had shown up at our apartment and was now sleeping it off. Lou reassured his secretary about the speech and also instructed her to notify his wife that her husband would be home soon. Then she did some quick research on the forthcoming exhibition, worked through the night and sent the finished speech to city hall, by messenger, that very morning. She took time out from packing her belongings that afternoon and sat in the audience as Oberbürgermeister Riesen, dressed in his brown uniform with the swastika armband, delivered the speech, his first official one—and it had been written by a Jew. Her quiet amusement at this bizarre occasion eased her depression. She had taken the opportunity while downtown to make her final travel arrangements. As she listened to her own words falling from the lips of a Nazi, the railroad ticket to Paris was in her handbag.

On a sunny Sunday late in May of 1933, Maja, I and a small number of friends stood on the platform of Cologne's enormous glass-roofed railroad station. Lou stood at the open window of her compartment, her arms filled with flowers. There was not much to say except, perhaps, "It's only for a little while. . . . We'll be here when you come back, and there will be more flowers then. . . ." The familiar huge bells from the nearby Dom joined all the other Cologne churchbells to announce the end of morning mass. The mighty sound, which had awed us in the city for all our lives, commanded our silence. Tears accented our forced smiles. Imperceptibly the train began to move. I tried to keep pace with it. A kiss was thrown and then a flower. I didn't pick it up. At the end of the platform I watched the waving handkerchief until the curve of the rails obscured everything.

Back at the apartment Maja prepared our lunch, which we ate among the packing boxes. She stuffed some money into my hand and told me that I could go to a movie. The film I saw was about two rival gangsters in Chicago. The eventual victor of the warfare hit upon the ingenious idea of smuggling machine guns to his headquarters in a truck shipment of pianos. The trucks were temporarily blocked by the other gang, which started shooting at the pianos, each round of ammunition causing a cacophony of music as the keys were hit. The delivery was made and the ensuing battle produced a satisfactory number of bullet-riddled bodies and an infinite variety of dying.

As I came out into the late afternoon sunlit street, a column of brown-shirted storm troopers marched with military precision past the movie house. They sang, in tempo with their steps: ". . . and when from our knives spurts the Jews' blood, it will make us feel twice as good."

When I got home, Maja was not crying but I could see that her eyes were very red. She was not going to upset her *Jung*. I was allowed the ultimate luxury, reserved only for those occasions when I had been an especially *guter Jung*—dinner in bed, dressed for sleep, with my teddy bear.

My room was now bare except for the furniture. I tried to remember what was in those packed and closed cardboard boxes in the corner. There were my books: Grimm's *Fairy Tales, Der Struwwelpeter, Max und Moritz*, E.T.A. Hoffmann, Karl May, Jack London, a Bible, a *Cahiers d'Art* special Max Ernst edition and bound volumes of illustrated German sports magazines. There was a copy of Alfred Flechtheim's magazine *Omnibus* that contained, much to my annoyance when it was published, a photograph of me, stark naked, about to run into the Baltic Sea. The caption read: "Max Ernst, his son Jimmy, 1931." There were other mementos. A Javanese marionette, given to me long ago by Paul Éluard. A number of twigs, interwoven and glued to resemble a running man, that Arp had fashioned for me after a walk through the park. A bird with flapping wings that Tristan Tzara had made for me out of a sheet of typewriter paper. A handwritten poem with a self-caricature from Joachim Ringelnatz. Letters from Max to me with alternating drawings and words. A small paper kite on which Jankel Adler had painted the face of a benign monster. A small drawing of a chess piece that Giacometti had made for me as a consolation prize after Man Ray had checkmated me. There were also my indecipherable diaries, letters to sports heroes that I never mailed and all of the sculpture—my prized collection of small African, Oriental and Pacific carvings. All of this was to go into storage because there would be no room for these things in my grandfather's home. And, after all, why unpack them? Lou, Maja and I would set up a new, cozy apartment in a very short time. My clothes had already been brought to my temporary home, and all I needed for tomorrow were my schoolbooks and the clothes I had worn on Sunday. "After all," Maja said, "I want my *Jung* to be dressed well on his first day at Grandfather Jacob's house."

At school that Monday, in my worry at not having done my Latin homework, I almost forgot the image of the train moving out of sight. During choir practice of Beethoven's *Choral Symphony*, I was thinking that by now my mother had probably finished her first breakfast in a Paris sidewalk café. The Kappell-meister (band master) interrupted us after Schiller's line "All men shall become brothers" to point out that "brotherhood" could apply only to the superior races of mankind. Through the window I could see the upperclassmen, in brown uniforms, going through a military drill in the school's courtyard.

As usual, I joined my gang of friends for the way home. We all stopped for that forbidden ice cream cone and I waved good-bye to them when I came to my street. I raced upstairs, taking my customary two steps at a time. There seemed to be a lot of movement behind the apartment door. After I rang, the door was opened by a man I did not know. Somewhat out of breath, I looked beyond him and saw several people moving furniture. The man asked me what I wanted. I couldn't answer. A woman appeared behind him and, speaking over his shoulder, said, "Is your name Ernst?" I nodded. The man began to close the door, and the last thing I heard was "You don't live here anymore."

Tante Leah, my step-grandmother, scolded me severely for having dawdled on my way from school. It was two hours after lunch, but she would make an exception this time, she said. If it happened again, I would have to wait for my meal until the evening. "Oh, and another thing," she added, "they found your uncle Richard on a park bench two days ago. He committed suicide. Took an overdose of his epilepsy pills. You won't have to sleep on the living room sofa after all. You'll have his room."

Life on Emma Strasse was over.

Darkness
Über Alles

The strong men, the masters, regain the pure conscience of a beast of prey.

FRIEDRICH WILHELM NIETZSCHE

M y ready acceptance, without preparation, of the almost overnight switch from one track of existence onto the spur of a totally different environment is a good example of the capacity of human adaptability. In retrospect, the next five years seem a bit like swimming under water without really knowing the next opportunity to come up for air. I had perhaps been spoiled in my assumption that the elements of cold and anger existed only in the streets. Part of the learning process that led to the creation of a protective shield was my growing appreciation of my parents' "wrong marriage" and the fact that I was now its most exposed living symbol. Understanding why I was met with hostile attitudes made the treatment more bearable but still consistently unpleasant. Very few civil words were addressed to me by Grandfather Jacob or his family, which included two daughters younger than I, technically my aunts. Every month I signed a financial statement, carefully compiled by Tante Leah, consisting of all expenses such as room and board, railroad fare for long-negotiated visits to my mother, school tuition, laundry and room cleaning and other costs, down to the last *Pfennig*. All of it was to be charged to what might accrue to Lou's benefit in Jacob's last will. On seders other than the Sabbath I was sent across town to spend the time with Maja, now employed elsewhere, in her furnished room with the tram fare duly noted. I was a very lonely young boy in that house, and I was never left in doubt about the reasons for it. I could perhaps get used to disdain for me on the street and in school for my Jewish blood, but I had difficulty with the thought that, at my grandfather's house, I did not seem to have enough of it. Could religious rigidity really go to such extremes? This was not my image of credos, and I had to wonder what life must have been like for Jacob's daughter in an air of prejudice as light-forbidding as the heavy drapery and massive furniture.

I had never been to the Ernst house in Brühl to see what kind of an atmosphere young Max had broken away from. That side too needed some urging to acknowledge my existence, and that was done by Max's youngest sister Loni, very much akin to her brother in spirit, who in her art-historical researches at Cologne's museums had found a good friend and colleague in Lou.

A few months after I had moved in with the Straus family, the two grandfathers negotiated regular visits for me to my father's place of birth, all expenses, of course, to be borne by the Ernsts. I found reasons to look forward to these monthly weekends. If there was any animus, it is was not against me. Rather, it seemed to me, there hung over that devout Catholic family always the unanswered question: What mortal sin could it have been for which God had punished them? The small city of Brühl, the pride of which was its Rococo castle and elaborate park, once country residence of Cologne's archbishops, was only an hour's train ride away. It was the same railroad that had intrigued Max at a very early age when he had sneaked out of the house one evening, already in his white nightshirt, in order to discover the place where the overhead telegraph lines and the rails would finally meet on the horizon. He was discovered at the next station by a group of pilgrims returning from some holy shrine. The white-robed figure with the long blond hair and that angelical smile impressed some of the group as the very image of the young Jesus. It was because of the good measure of reverence with which they returned him to his home that Philipp Ernst was forced to conceal his anger and Grandmother Luise joined the pilgrims at the nearby cloister for a prayer of thanks.

The Ernsts were a prominent family in Brühl. Philipp was the principal of a state-run school for deaf-mutes, but his real passion was painting. Apart from commissioned portraits, he produced very beautiful landscapes and skilled copies of sacred paintings, particularly those from the Vatican. In a copy of Raphael's *Disputa* Ernst Senior is said to have substituted faces of friends and fellow Catholics on Christ's right and those of Protestants and "non-believing" friends on his left. Philipp Ernst, as a result of the adventure with the pilgrims, used Max as model for a painting of the young Jesus.

Grandmother Luise was gentle, rosy-cheeked, attractive; her eyes were turned heavenward more often than not, as if to ask forgiveness for whatever sinful thought might be in the air. I found it difficult to imagine her in the act of procreation. Aunt Emmi, one year older than Max, who also taught at the deaf-mute school, hid behind her piety some very worldly and humanistic impulses that in later years came to the fore in such a positive and gentle way that I still think of her as the very personification of an angel. Another sister, Luise, had taken the eternal vows and was teaching biology in a convent near Düsseldorf. One of her erstwhile classmates was my biology teacher at the Gymnasium. We all called him the "Bee" because he had taken it on himself to explain the miracle of sex to all of his classes by using that insect as the object lesson. He was also a self-proclaimed expert on racial purity. In one of his semi-annual lectures to the entire school he declared that, without any doubt, "young Ernst in the Quinta (grade), with his blond hair, egg-shaped skull, blue eyes and aquiline nose" was the most perfect example of a pure Aryan within the entire student body. Uncle Karl was a prominent Cologne surgeon whom I remember mostly for that moment when we stepped out of his father's house together and he promptly pinned the heretofore hidden swastika party emblem on his lapel. Aunt Loni, the youngest, was gay and bright. She was also very beautiful and somewhat more irreverent than the rest of the family.

Philipp Ernst was a curious mixture of humor and rectitude. He would tell me, with amusement, about some of Max's pranks as a youngster, such as the time when Max, during a long-lasting school assembly, drew scathing caricatures of most of his teachers and handed them around to his classmates. Philipp had to seek out every one of the offended subjects to save his son from being expelled. And how, at his first Holy Communion, Max had complained to the priest about the bland taste of the wafer. Very little was said to me about his having married out of his faith. There was no hostility toward Lou. Perhaps enough time had passed for a softer judgment, and as my visits continued, I heard praise for her academic and professional achievements as well as for her optimism and courage. Emmi and Loni, in particular, as it turned out, had always liked my mother very much.

After a while I was asked to move my arrival in Brühl up from Sundays to Saturday afternoon in order to accompany the family to early mass. Initially this created some tension. I didn't know when to stand or kneel, how to cross myself properly after dipping my fingers in the holy water and where to find the proper hymn in the prayer book. Emmi very patiently helped me, but Grandfather was embarrassed. On one occasion Emmi and I were seated in the Ernst pew, very close to the altar. I was amazed and pleased to hear the priest in his sermon attack the bestial German practice of ultra-nationalist students who engaged in saber duels that produced highly desired facial slash-scars denoting "courage and honor." At the end of the sermon the congregation was asked to remain and file past the altar to receive a special blessing of Saint Blasius as a protection against a current epidemic of sore throats in the community. Emmi, knowing that I might not know the proper procedure, decided to leave the church before the blessing. In my hurry to get out, I bumped into the priest who was returning to the altar with his chalice, almost upsetting his balance. There was consternation in the Ernst house. The grandparents anticipated week-long penances for the misdeed of their grandson. Emmi tried vainly to put in a good word for me. It was not until the late afternoon, when the priest from the cloister made a special courtesy call, patted me on the head and laughed the whole thing off, that they forgave themselves and me. I have always suspected that the cleric's visit was instigated by Emmi. On leaving, the good father took my face in his hands and somewhat sternly expressed his hope of my eventually becoming a good Catholic.

I still remember walking with pupils from Aunt Emmi's school as part of a touching Saint Martin's Day (November 11) children's procession with our

Japanese lanterns casting a glow on the snow. The narrow streets of Brühl were filled with young singing voices recounting the miracle experienced by Martin of Tours, a Roman cavalry soldier, who, descending from his horse at the gate to Amiens, had cut his rich cloak in half to warm a naked beggar in the snow. The poor creature appeared to him the next night, still wearing the gift, but also revealing himself to have been an angel all along. It felt strange, being the only one in my group who could hear a spectator's explanation: "They can't sing. They are deaf-mutes."

During those uncomfortable years these monthly trips were a welcome change from the ill-concealed hostility of the Straus family, even though I felt like a stranger in both houses. The fact that the living room wall in Brühl displayed a large Man Ray photograph of Max and Marie-Berthe instead of one with Lou Straus always jarred me a little. On the other hand, the corner of the Straus apartment that was covered with photos of every imaginable relative was also devoid of any pictorial reference to Jacob's daughter or her son. Both grandfathers forcefully displayed their inflexibility. In Philipp Ernst I did, however, discover a man with a marvelous sense of the bizarre by whom I was nevertheless always a bit intimidated because he displayed the same sudden changes of mood I had seen in Max. I found that somewhat disconcerting because Philipp's outlook on life was diametrically opposed to my father's. But my grandfather managed to make a joke even about that. Talking about Max, he said that he found his work very interesting but totally lacking in reverence. This was certainly no way to paint, and he could not understand how his son expected to make a respectable living out of it. To be an artist at all promised, at best, a very precarious existence. "In my time," he said, "mothers watching their children playing outdoors might suddenly yell at them from the open window: 'Hey, kids, hide your sandwiches, there's an artist coming up the street.' " He hoped to God that his son, my father, would not become that kind of bohemian. Then he began very seriously to discuss with me a plan that would prevent the water in the four circular pools in the gardens of the Brühl Palace from becoming scummy without the wasteful use of electrically powered circulation pumps. In his second-floor studio we drew up elaborate mazes of underground, gravity-fed pipes that would circulate the water from one basin to the other. As it became time for supper, he threw up his hands. "This will never work. . . . If you and I were to solve this problem, we could change the world because we would have invented the impossible: a perpetual-motion machine. Our Lord in heaven has not yet given us that power."

On one Sunday Loni took me to the annual fair, which was being held in the large square in the center of town. At the shooting gallery I became the proud possessor of four goldfish, which we carried home in a metal fruit-preserve can.

We had been told that the fish needed oxygen and that some holes in the lid would do the trick, so I asked Grandmother Luise for a hammer and nail. But before I even got started, Grandfather Philipp, his face as stern as I had ever seen, took the hammer away from me. "This is Sunday, the day of the Lord's rest. There will be no hammering or any other such noise in this house." I remonstrated that my fish, also "God's creatures," would suffocate before I got them back to Grandfather Jacob. Philipp, now really angry, retorted: "Would you be allowed to do this in your Jewish home on a Friday night or on Saturday? . . . Well, here it can't be done on a Sunday." I tried to reason with him by voicing my confusion over being subject to a double discipline and that in any case the sanctity of life surely should take precedent over rules of any religion. He turned away from me and warned me that one more word from me would mean that I would not be asked to come to Brühl again. He then scolded his wife, who had been working hard on the evening meal, for having given me the tools. She blew some strands of hair from her sweaty forehead, rolled her eyes toward heaven and shook her head.

I tried to imagine what kind of battles might have taken place in that house when Max was fifteen.

Barbara Tuchman, in her book *The Proud Tower*, masterfully explains the peculiar contradictions within the more intelligent segments of Germany's upper middle class at the turn of the century. She cites a very telling example of this concerning Philipp Ernst. He had painted a picture of his little walled back garden and had omitted a peach tree because it disturbed the composition. In order to make the garden conform to the finished painting, he is said to have cut the offending tree down. The version of this story as told to me by Emmi Ernst is, if anything, an even more disturbing account of Philipp Ernst the painter, who disciplines reality as a means of forcing conformity to his concept of proper composition. It seems that, as he was painting this particular picture, he was fully aware of the fact that the peach tree was hopelessly diseased, would not be part of his garden much longer and therefore had lost its place in the painting as well.

The issue of the respective religion in each household surfaced again when Grandfather Philipp began to give me a shiny ten-mark piece for spending money at the end of each weekend. This represented a lot of ice cream cones, candy and other little things that were *verboten*. It did not take Tante Leah very long to discover my riches when she searched my clothes after I had gone to bed. It was her habit to make surprise inspections at night, swiftly pulling back my blanket to check whether I was masturbating. When she accused me of having taken the money from her purse, I had to admit where it had actually come from. She insisted that, since she and Grandfather Jacob were providing me with bed and board, the money belonged to them, and that I would have to surrender it each time I came back from Brühl. Sure enough, Jacob Straus was sitting in the entrance foyer as I returned from another trip. He silently stuck out his hand, into which I deposited the ten-mark piece. Not a word was spoken.

On the next occasion I told Grandfather Philipp that there was no use giving me the money, since Grandfather Jacob would take it away from me. "Those damn Jews . . . well, what can you expect from them? They are all the same. . . . We'll fix him." He gave me two five-mark coins, told me to find a good hiding place for one and hand the other one over. He assured me that God would forgive this lie. That night Grandfather Jacob, way past his bedtime, was waiting for me in his accustomed chair. I gave him the five marks. He looked at me angrily. "Where is the rest?" I told him that Grandfather Philipp had reduced my spending money. "Those cheap damn goyim," he mumbled, "they are all the same."

By the middle of 1934 it had become obvious that there was no future for me in Germany. The hopes that Maja, Lou and I could somehow be together again in Germany or in France seemed to grow more and more remote. The solution was eventual emigration, perhaps to the United States, and that was a very faraway dream. My mother, though still optimistic, felt that I should be prepared for such a move by learning a craft, something I could do with my hands to support myself. My education up to that point certainly would hardly serve that purpose. Since our little family had broken up, my grades in Gymnasium had declined steadily. When they got so bad that I failed to be promoted into the next class, a decision was made to attempt, instead, to find an apprenticeship for me in a practical field. The state authorities whose function it was to find such placements showed little interest in assisting a "non-Aryan." I tried all kinds of factories, textile mills and mechanics shops but found all doors closed after filling out questionnaires and applications.

My mother, in Paris, discussed the problem with a close friend, Hans Augustin, whose family owned a large and prestigious printing plant in Glück-stadt near Hamburg. He arranged to have me accepted by the firm as an apprentice compositor. It was a most fortunate solution for the present and, as it turned out, even more so for my future. The most immediate benefit was that I would be living by myself, far away from Cologne. A hurdle presented itself when Lou asked both grandparents to make a very small, but necessary, contribution for my room and board. Max offered to help whenever he could, and understandably I could not rely on that. Both parties were agreeable . . . under one condition. I would have to adopt their religion. From Brühl came the demand that I was to take instruction toward becoming a churchgoing Catholic. A priest in Glückstadt was to report on my progress, including my visits to the confessional. Jacob Straus insisted on my becoming a full-fledged Jew. While my mother engaged in lengthy correspondence with both sides, I had almost daily sessions with Jacob's rabbi and on weekends attended mass with the Ernsts and saw the priest in his residence during the afternoon. Perversely, I enjoyed being the object of so much attention. I felt no hostility toward either religion but simply could not imagine ever becoming a true disciple of any ritual. The priest allowed my contention that Jesus had been a Jew but insisted that the Church was the true vessel of his teachings and his heritage while the Jews had remained a closed ethnic sect that did not concern itself with the salvation of the soul. He tried to convince me that the betrayal of Christ by Judas had not been used by Catholics as a catalyst for anti-Semitism. The rabbi spent most of his time describing the many important Jewish holidays and the elaborate feasts that were a part of them. He elaborated extensively on Yom Kippur, the Day of Atonement. It reminded me, I said, a great deal of the Christians' Good Friday, and I was curious about the similarity of many Jewish and Christian holidays. He acknowledged that there was indeed a close relationship, and that many of the observances had been originally derived from the Jewish religion and that practicing Christians were not excluded from the ultimate benevolence of the Creator. That, however, was no reason to condone intermarriage. He had known my mother as a lovely girl and intelligent young woman, but through this particular mistake she had made her family very unhappy.

In Paris, during one of my twice-a-year visits, Lou and I discussed the dilemma. She repeated that, as before, I was completely free to make a choice. We agreed, however, that to do this in exchange for money was totally immoral. We talked to Max about it, who promptly wrote a scathing letter to his father, pointing out that the buying of souls by the Church had come to an end with the Reformation. Philipp Ernst surrendered, giving Jacob Straus little choice but to go along.

My visits to my mother in Paris were always happy occasions as well as inevitably profound experiences in my young years and those confusing times. Often I would sleep at my father's apartment because Lou did not always have the means of getting a small hotel room for me or finding one that a friend was not currently using.

Max did his very best during those years to act the part of the caring and responsible father. I got to see again many of his old friends from the Dada days in Cologne, as well as many new ones. Attending a large party with him where Alexander Calder performed his *Circus* was a special treat and delight, only slightly marred by Max's remark that he had seen it too often, wouldn't have gone if it hadn't been for me and that, though it was all very inventive, these were, after all, merely toys. Max and Marie-Berthe had, by this time, moved into a large modern apartment on the rue des Plantes with a marvelous terrace overlooking

Paris. There were a few times when Max, needing privacy with a visitor, had suggested, "Jimmy, why don't you go out on the terrace for a while and play with the Giacomettis. Be careful not to break anything, though." I enjoyed sitting there and seeing the breathtaking skyline through the static ballet of sculpture that Alberto had stored there because his studio was too small. The studio was not far away, and sometimes he took me over there or I dropped in with Max. His brother Diego was always there working on a variety of Alberto's pieces. However, the later legend that most of Giacometti's work had come from Diego's hands alone is exaggerated.

Marie-Berthe entertained Lou and me for tea and lunch at the new apartment with glee and warmth. The relationship of the two women, begun some ten years before, was growing into a genuine friendship. Lou told me in later years that Marie-Berthe, without guile, had sought her advice on how to hold on to Max or how to handle some domestic problem that had arisen. Whenever I stayed at the rue des Plantes, Marie-Berthe always waited up for me, embraced me as if I were her own child and wanted to know everything that Lou and I had done together on that day. We patiently consulted German-French dictionaries to make ourselves understood to each other. My school-taught French improved tremendously. One evening I found that she had very thoughtfully placed a very explicit, illustrated sex manual, printed in both languages, next to my bed. Lou was delighted when I told her about it. "I think that I have kept you well informed about this subject, but Marie-Berthe's approach is probably far more effective because there may very well be things that had not occurred to me." More often than not, when I came to the apartment at night, Max was not there and I also did not see him the next morning.

Lou Straus-Ernst was living in the Quartier Latin near the Sorbonne in an old rabbit warren of a hotel, its tiny rooms inhabited by emigrés and exiles from all over Europe. For one of my Christmas visits Lou prevailed on the management to let me use one barely furnished room, once occupied by the German poet Rainer Maria Rilke. It was a depressing little cubicle, and the fact that throughout my stay there I suffered from a terrible toothache negated any awe of sleeping in the great man's bed. I have since read several of his letters from that address, and I am not at all surprised about the melancholy inherent in his writing. But then I also have to acknowledge the historical fact that Germany had covered the world with homesick exiles many generations before the advent of Hitler.

Hundreds of hotels like Lou's on rue Toullier were filled with those who had found a haven in Paris and were hoping to go home again. Some of them had been waiting for a long time. They had formed little groups among themselves and sat in the cafés eagerly reading their exile newspapers, gravely discussing this or that bit of information that would permit them to resume their interrupted lives. The Czar would come back or, perhaps, Aleksandr Kerenski. Mussolini was about to make his final blunder. Next week Admiral Horthy would be gone from Hungary, Moscicki from Poland, King Carol from Romania, King Peter from Yugoslavia and, of course, Hitler and his gangsters from Germany.

In the meantime they eked out a living selling underwear, native sausages, notions and books, dragging heavy suitcases from door to door. They took on illegal employment, running a constant risk of losing their invaluable *carte d'identité*. They pretended not to notice the chalk graffiti on walls and sidewalks: à BAS LES JUIFS, LES ÉTRANGERS DEHORS.

Symbolically, Lou's suitcase was also never fully unpacked. She had been fortunate in banding together with a group of friends who countered the uncertainties of every day with a brave show of optimism. They loved Paris and, had it not been for the severe working restrictions, could have considered their life in that beautiful city a great adventure. Meals were prepared ingeniously in a rather precarious cooking corner in the room of her close and irrepressible friend Fritz Neugass, who constantly complained that Lou had never learned how to butter a piece of bread properly. At eating time neighbors and friends "just happened" to drop in. Somehow there was always enough to go around. Christmas and New Year were celebrated in that room and, for my sake, there was always a little tree.

Lou, never having gotten the promised support from her father to start her little antique shop, gave German lessons to university students and businessmen. She conducted museum tours for German-speaking tourists, wrote articles for Swiss newspapers and occasionally took on an illegal position such as bookkeeping or secretarial work. Wanda Landowska, who had graciously consented to several lengthy interviews for publication, befriended her and helped with recommendations and referrals to other celebrities of the music world. Sometimes my continuing presence in Germany presented difficulties. New friends who appeared as if from nowhere might well be agents of Himmler's secret police. Why the Germans thought it necessary to infiltrate the circles of these harmless and impoverished exiles begs for an explanation. In the presence of such newcomers conversation became guarded, and suspicion took a long time to wear off. Lou had somehow come into possession of a list naming hundreds of German intellectuals who perished at the time of the so-called Röhm Putsch, which Hitler had used as an excuse to wipe out whatever opposition he could imagine existed against him. Lou could have placed an article about this important list in several publications for a good sum of money. She refrained from releasing the story, lest she be discovered to be the author and thereby endanger me.

For Max Ernst, Paris was not exactly home either, but it was certainly the only place for someone like him to exist at all. The France of that time was, as for so many others, his reluctant host. Animosity toward Germans, even fifteen years after the Treaty of Versailles, was slow in abating. Max had tasted this hostility when the family of Marie-Berthe Aurenche tried, by whatever means possible, to prevent the marriage of their daughter to a German. Citizenship for aliens was virtually unheard of, even for artists of Ernst's growing prominence, even for those with French spouses. Paris did take great pride in being the cultural capital of the world, but the artists, the poets, composers, musicians, writers, philosophers, scholars and journalists, whose constant inflow from other parts of the world provided a perpetual rejuvenation of its spiritual and aesthetic core, lived even there with a sense of being guests only. Xenophobia was not absent.

Still, it was Paris, and France, rather than Gala Éluard, that had been Max Ernst's song of the siren. With the possible exception of those few treasured, though terribly difficult, years in Sedona, Arizona, in the late 1940s it was in Paris that his dreams found their fewest obstacles. There he had felt safest from the blighting chauvinism that claims ideas as a national property.

Had I better understood then that the measure of his world could never be limited by its mere social conventions, many valuable moments between my father and me would not have been lost. The curtains of distance and separation lifted gradually as we began to see more of each other after 1933, though not all of the respective discoveries proved to be flawless. It must have been galling, for example, for my father to confront a smaller physical edition of himself, but whose brain still needed exorcism of petit-bourgeois dust. At no point can I recall his having tried to mask his personality, modify an expressed attitude, or misrepresent the purpose of his actions, past or present, in order to shield himself from my scrutiny. Such honesty was, of course, tailor-made for a young boy unaware of how much hostility he still felt for his father and only too ready to apply preconceived judgments. I believe it was Max's restraint in the face of my poorly disguised attempts at provocation that led to a change of my stance to grudging admiration. The fact that he did not deny himself the pleasure of a very occasional razor-sharp sarcasm, to put me in my place, may well have accelerated the process. For the first time my mother's long-standing attempts at reasoning had begun to sink in. The change was not to be without its setbacks, but I had to admit that many of my reservations toward my father had been an artificially prolonged pose.

Though I was still disinclined to surrender my personal notions about painting, I began to accept Max's unique status in that world and I was impressed by his matter-of-fact acceptance of constant economic insecurity, though he was obviously perfectly capable of producing works to turn that situation around. He did not seem to care to make any accommodations whatsoever. What I saw, of course, and comprehended only later, was Max Ernst, a spirit totally resistant to external dicta and always above the need for a coterie of flatterers. During his entire lifetime his leapfrogging discoveries and images created obvious difficulties for ambitious literary gymnasts and self-appointed tastemakers. Not being able to hold him in their sights, they were unable to classify him. His was dangerous territory to traverse for imitators or dilettantes. In those years when I really first got to know him, critical acclaim for him was quite select and his circle of dedicated admirers relatively small. At the same time he was far from being ignored. I noted with filial pride the display of his graphics and collage-work in bookstore windows all over Paris. A stack of posters, casually stored in a corner of his studio, documented his various exhibitions in many parts of Europe. On some occasions he did not even seem to mind my watching him in the studio. Once, I meant to compliment him on the astounding skill of his hands at work. Stepping back from his painting, but still looking at it, he remarked, "Asking 'how' it's done is for mechanics. It's the 'why' that makes the difference . . . and that is a question for philosophers . . . some of them, anyway." That lesson also took me a few years to digest. When he gave me a copy, in 1937, of the special *Cahiers d'Art* edition, *Max Ernst,* he inscribed the flyleaf with a repeat of the title he had given to the 1920 collage of me: *Jimmy, Dadafex minimus, le plus grand Anti-Philosophe du monde.*

Max's candor with me about himself extended deep into his private life. I was well aware that Lou had not led a celibate life in Cologne nor in Paris, but she had always been quite discreet about her liaisons. One day, for example, a handsome man sat down at our table in a café on boulevard Saint-Michel. He and Lou seemed to know each other very well, judging from their lively conversation. At one point he covered her hand with his; she withdrew hers and, almost too casually, said to him, "I am going to be very busy while Jimmy is here. Give me a call in three weeks." I asked her who this was. "Oh, he's just a friend. Very interesting man, by the way. He is a *pompier.*" Some years later she confided to me that she had always felt a strong physical attraction for firemen. Max, on the other hand, apparently gave me credit for far more sophistication than I deserved. On several occasions when he took me out for dinner, there would be a woman whom he seemed to have expected to join us. His women friends were invariably beautiful, bright and amusing, but the only one I had known before was Merret Oppenheim, who created *Object,* the fur-lined teacup. At the end of the meal Max would tell me that it was getting late and that he still had things to do, and he'd give me money for a taxi back to rue des Plantes. Marie-Berthe never asked me where I had been with Max, and I was too uncomfortable to volunteer anything. I was also often quite embarrassed when the subject of "women" entered into our conversation. Max rarely masked his words in describing their physical characteristics. I remarked once that Hitler had instituted a bonus to families for producing male offspring who would be useful to Germany in the future, no doubt for cannon fodder. "That is nonsense," he replied. "Every woman has millions of eggs inside her, and if she is impregnated often enough, she will certainly have many boys. Daughters are therefore just as valuable." His 1933 painting *Le Coq Qui Rit* strikes me as an almost exact illustration of that remark. It shows a somewhat grotesque, winged, seated female. Her body below her breasts is composed of limpid organic forms, including what seems to be large embryonic sacs of eggs. A long visceral plant with the head of a rooster intrudes into the body and appears about to be enfolded by one of the wings. It is a beautiful painting, but I can never look at it without being reminded of Max's disturbing observation.

As a very special treat, one evening, Max took me and his friend Lotte Lenya to Montmartre for an elegant dinner and a movie. I was impressed to be in her presence, since I had treasured the fragile shellac-records of the *Dreigroschen Oper*, starring her, that Max had once given me. The film we saw was *Viva Villa*, with Wallace Beery and, I believe, Stu Erwin. During the rousing movie, we enjoyed a box of fancy pralines from a very exclusive chocolatier. As we drove home, I noticed Lenya's hand stroking Max's knee and bringing her mouth up to his ear to stage-whisper some kind of endearment. I asked to be let out at the nearest Métro station, slamming the car door as I left. Back at the apartment, I found Marie-Berthe huddled next to a radiator munching an apple. She explained that there was no food in the house and that the fruit plus the heat were quite adequate in place of supper. I asked her why Max was home so seldom. "Well," she explained, "we have very little money right now, and Max is being taken to dinner by rich ladies. . . . Of course, I can't do that. But I am very happy that Max could have this special evening with you. My father gave us the money for that dinner."

When I talked to Lou about this the next day, she did not exactly scold me for being so critical, but she did tell me not to be prejudiced and jump to conclusions about all the things I seemed to find fault with in my father. "If you want to look for shortcomings, you can always easily find them. Your father leads a very complicated life. Perhaps some of the so-called rules should not apply to him. But if you insist on them, in spite of your age, you should at least be sure of all the causes that bring about certain situations. What happens between a man and a woman, in marriage or out of it, is never a simple question of right or wrong. One thing must be clear to you by now: Max has never lied to you and that is rare in this world."

On one of my visits to Paris I became ill from something that I had eaten. Lou had come from her place to the hotel room she had secured for me from a vacationing friend, and she was trying to bring my high fever down. When she called Max to ask him for the name of a doctor, Max brought over Theodore Fraenkel, one of his friends from the Cologne Dada days, who had set up practice as a physician in Montmarte. He diagnosed my problem as stemming from a kidney stew of a few days before. Max and Lou sat near my bed in casual conversation, and in my feverish state I had the strong impression that I was a small child again and the place was the apartment on the Kaiser-Wilhelm-Ring in Cologne. Before Max left, he handed me "something for you to read." It was his collage-novel, *Une Semaine de Bonté*. Lou and I pored over the thin, varied-colored volumes, each apparently representing a different day and element. I began to interpret the images aloud, narrating the strangely frightening activities being enacted by eerie monsterlike humans in opulent bedrooms and overstuffed railroad compartments. In my fever I began to hallucinate that the events depicted were really taking place, even that I myself was physically involved, and I was terrified by the serpentine monsters and the headless female torso guarding the entrance to *la cour du dragon*. Lou decided that this was not the best way to reduce my temperature and took the books away. After my illness had abated, she brought them out again and, page by page, recounted my reactions and ravings. I tried to pass it all off by saying that I had dreams like that all the time, particularly when I had fevers. She gave me a long look, held up the books and merely remarked on their justification, "Well . . . ?"

At the time the French had succeeded in organizing, at the Orangerie, as complete an exhibition as was possible of Pieter Brueghel. We went there early one morning to avoid the crowds. I vividly recall *Hunters in the Snow*, experiencing again those childhood inner glows of watching December do its work of covering sleeping hills with the ultimate of all colors: white. I remembered sleigh rides in the foothills of the Eifel near Cologne, the sun setting early in the afternoon accentuating the silently linear clumps of trees amid the gentle rise and fall of that familiar snowscape around the lower regions of the Rhine. One painting after the other had left a door open somewhere for me to enter into it: the awesome absurdity of *The Tower of Babel*, the frightening reality of *The Triumph of Death* with its slender and innocent cross standing slightly aside and all alone among the carnage, the obese prone bodies of *The Land of Cockaigne*. All of these images were very real, and yet, for all of their objectivity, pulsed with hidden threats and seemed reminiscent of that sardonic smile in the corners of my father's lips.

I was only half listening to Lou's comments about the Rhenish and Flemish painters and the close affinity of some Surrealists to Brueghel, Bosch and Grüne-wald. I was beginning to experience a distinct sense of disquiet as we moved through the exhibition. Almost at the end of the main gallery hung *The Fall of Icarus*.

I was only too familiar with the theme. For my upright, wax-faced teachers in Gymnasium, Greek mythology had provided conveniently distorted analogies to the cloyingly sick fantasies of Teutonic discipline: Prometheus endured his needless tortures on the rock for the sake of purity and truth, just as his reincarnation, Christ. A singular weakness of Achilles had been betrayed and caused his death in the same manner as Siegried's. The boatmen on the Rhine were brought to ruin by a temptress on a rock, just as Greek mariners were doomed when they listened to the voices of the Sirens. Icarus' destruction was the result of not having obeyed his father's commands to avoid soaring so high the sun would melt the wax that held his wings together, or so low that moisture from the sea would make them heavy. I did not endear myself to my rigid tutors by agreeing that Icarus was indeed at fault, not for disobedience, but for having, in the first place, unquestionably trusted artificial wings fashioned by his father, Daedalus, whose genius had enabled him to entrap the monster Minotaur on Crete.

Faced with Brueghel's version of the tragedy, I saw at first nothing but a deceptively serene promontory overlooking a calm inlet of water. The foreground showed a plowman placidly tilling the soil behind a Belgian horse, a shepherd facing away from the setting sun as well as from his small flock, two frigates, their sails billowing without the merest hint of wind, and a fisherman intently waiting for some action on his line. The only discernible disturbance of the water was caused by two disappearing legs thrashing up some inconsequential spume. In a few seconds everything would be calm as before. Only Daedalus would live to tell the tale.

A strange anger suddenly took possession of me. The ancient dilemma: Should a son make use of wings fashioned by his father? I bolted from the building and delivered myself of a tirade against all painting. I am certain that what I said made no sense at all to my mother. The nature of the crisis that had caused this outburst was something I refused to face. Lou seemed at a loss, as if she had seen in me a bully with an inflexible, narrow mind. She looked past me at a slow-moving barge on the Seine and spoke into that sad tension. "They say that there is going to be a war, a big one, not like any war before. Those who want to make that war are the same ones who want to burn our books, our music, our poetry . . . the paintings, the sculpture, the architecture. They want to kill, once and for all, everything human that somehow survived after they had beaten it into the dust, and that slowly stood up again and was victorious after all. Some of these pictures were painted while Pizarro was wiping out the Incas of Peru, at a time when Bacon and Shakespeare were not even born. They survived destruction even in the Thirty Years' War. Can you imagine, they have existed for over five hundred years? But this time the world may not be so lucky and these paintings will never be seen again together, or by themselves. If I die in the next war, and, you know, that could happen, I want to be sure that I didn't miss loving something that had earned love. I think, I hope, you will regret your tantrums, like this one, in a few years. I don't know how much time there is left."

The depth of what she had said became evident when, not long afterward, I walked with her through the Petit Palais, where André Malraux had arranged an exhibition of Italian masterpieces. I was startled, while standing in front of an Uccello, to see tears welling up in her eyes. For the first time I had some misgivings about my stubbornness.

I told Max, after some hesitation, about my puzzling reaction at the Orangerie. He replied, "Oh, I did that too when I was your age, because I hated that pious father of mine and his Sunday painting. But I don't think I ever picked on a good painter like Brueghel. Maybe you just got angry at that stupid Icarus. That is a very disturbing myth, you know."

Leaving Paris to return to Germany after each visit was very sad, and also frightening because there was never any certainty that there would be a next time. My passport, which I always had to present to the local police for an exit visa, already contained a specific prohibition against travel to countries other than my destination, and there was always the chance that the local chief of police or the Bürgermeister of Glückstadt might arbitrarily prevent me from leaving the country. On my way to Paris, just a few weeks earlier, my train had not proceeded into Belgium. It was put on a railroad siding. For four days nothing moved, a minimum of food was provided, and, with few exceptions, we were allowed only to leave our compartments to take short walks along the train for exercise and fresh air. Hitler, against the provisions of the Locarno Pact, had decided to remilitarize the Rhineland. On March 7, 1936, German troops began moving across the bridges of the river. The next move, according to the gossip among the passengers, was up to the French. If their army moved, we on this train would be like sitting ducks. The crisis itself had not been entirely resolved when the train was finally allowed to proceed, and Lou was happy that I was with her if war were indeed to come. France and her allies, typical for that time, issued some weak diplomatic protests, and that was the end of it.

The departures from the Gare du Nord were always sad, as most such good-byes are, except that this time there was a new face on the platform to see me off.

Having had my own hotel room this time, I was able to have a very welcome and novel personal experience—sex. Early one morning there was a knock on my door. It was not the chambermaid but Lore, a woman friend of my mother; she was holding a tray with breakfast for two. I had seen her in Lou's circle many times and had indeed fantasized about her. She was pert, attractive, and, as it turned out, extremely sensual. I was grateful for having studied Marie-Berthe's sex manual very intently, but now, at the age of sixteen, I discovered, to my delight, that its content was by no means all-encompassing.

Sometime at midmorning there was another knock on the door. I opened the door a crack. There was my mother to pick me up for a planned excursion to Fontainebleau. I'm not sure whether I was able to mutter any kind of rational explanation for not letting her into the room, and she made no move in that direction. With her eyebrows slightly raised and the hint of a smile, she turned to go, saying, "I guess the trip to the country can wait. I will see you around dinnertime . . . if you are not too busy then."

I was indeed kept pretty busy that day, with a leisurely break for lunch in the nearby Russian restaurant Dominique, which gave the maid a chance to put new sheets on the bed and make up the room. I don't know about the legendary effectiveness of oysters, but I am perfectly willing to give them credit for an entrancing, unforgettable, first sexual voyage with constantly changing horizons. Toward late afternoon I was pledged to absolute secrecy. "Whatever you tell Lou, don't let her know that it was me in your room today. We are friends and she will be furious with me."

When I got to Lou's hotel room, she had set out a bottle of wine and two glasses. "You can wipe that all-knowing superior smirk off your face. I know who was with you today. She told me all about it, every bit of it. Let's celebrate the occasion. I am glad it was Lore, not some insensitive German cow in a back alley or the bushes. And don't tell me how it was. From now on you will have your share of secrets from me."

Max's reaction was: "Well, finally . . . perhaps from now on you won't be such a holier-than-thou brat." He hoped that I would introduce this exquisite creature to him. He wanted to thank her for solving at least some of the problems I had been causing him. I told him unequivocally that, knowing him, I would not let her come within ten kilometers of him. This pleased him. It indicated, he said, that I was well on my way to becoming a sensible and normal man.

He did, in fact, meet her when he saw me off on the station platform of the Gare du Nord. Winking at me, he made the Okay sign with his thumb and forefinger. High praise. My relative inexperience manifested itself, however, when I kissed my mother good-bye in the new manner that I had just been taught. She roared with laughter, turned to her friend and said, "Didn't you teach him the difference between mothers and lovers?"

This time the train ride back to Germany was not so depressing. Feeling that I was desperately in love, I had finished two long, passionate letters to my *amour* before I even reached my destination. My great adventure sustained me in the gray and nasty atmosphere that I had come back to. Not one, I was certain, of the thirteen thousand inhabitants of Glückstadt, a small city on the Schleswig-

Holstein peninsula, could possibly ever come close to experiencing the rapture that had been mine. Let them whisper and sneer behind my back about that "Jew," or, worse, that "half-Jew" who would have been run out of town long ago if it hadn't been for the protection of the all-powerful Augustin family.

The firm of J. J. Augustin had been founded in 1632. Its printing plant, except for the Railroad Machine Works, was the largest local employer. Young J. J. Augustin, Hans, had seen to it that my apprenticeship, which began in 1935, ran as smoothly as could discreetly be achieved. When Hans left Germany in 1936 for political reasons and went to New York to establish a publishing branch of the firm, his parents assumed the sometimes difficult task of shielding me from the more obnoxious elements among the townspeople.

Glückstadt, situated on the right bank of the mighty river Elbe near its estuary, had been founded in the fourteenth century by the Danes, who had hoped to develop it into a major seaport. A good number of its initial settlers were Portuguese Jews who were expected to stimulate its commerce. The fronts of houses dating back to that time still lined some of the streets. Denmark's goal, to preempt the importance of upriver Hamburg, was not achieved because a growing sandbank at the mouth of the harbor prevented larger vessels from docking and unloading their freight. One could go for long walks along the river on the massive dikes that protected the low, flat cow pastures stretching as far as the eye could see. With the exception of Saturday night, when most of the young people went dancing at one of two beer halls, or attended the only movie house in town, there was little else to do but walk.

Since I had few friends, I contented myself by reading and listening to my radio. I had found a little bookstore in Hamburg where I could obtain books no longer available in any lending library. I treasured my second complete set of E. T. A. Hoffman, and the poetry of Heinrich Heine, Rilke and Ringelnatz, as well as books by a most frowned-upon author, Franz Kafka. On rare occasions, by some quirk, I could hear broadcasts from Radio Luxembourg and a few times even Radio Moscow with its German-language program. In this manner I managed sometimes to hear of news events that the Nazi censorship withheld from the German press. I particularly recall listening, on a cold wintry night, to a performance of the *Eroica* from Moscow. It was introduced by a commentary that hailed Beethoven as a hero of communism because he had withdrawn its original dedication to Napoleon after "that fascist monster" had shown his true colors by proclaiming himself emperor.

I had to be careful, of course, that my nosy landlady did not discover my listening to forbidden broadcasts. The safest way was to huddle under the bedcovers with the radio. Rumors abounded that there were car patrols that could detect the illegal reception from such foreign radio stations.

In fact, finding room and board remained a constant problem. The Augustins used their influence repeatedly to convince householders to take me in, but sooner or later somebody from the party or the local government succeeded in having that "half-Jew" thrown out, and I had to stay for a while in the local hotel, the owners of which also made no secret of their reluctance to accept me as a guest. My peculiar status and the constant difficulties that it caused convinced me after a while that being a "half-Jew" or "non-Aryan" was far more offensive to this racist society than being a "Jew" because my existence meant that an Aryan had committed an act of despicable miscegenation with a Jew.

In spite of all that, I did not become a complete recluse. Every now and then I would brazenly go to one of those beer halls on a Saturday night and sometimes even find a wallflower to give me one turn around the dance floor.

The craft I was learning was fascinating. It was physically very demanding to stand for nine hours before the open cases assembling type into text, letter after letter and line after line. Apprentices were not allowed to sit down even when there was temporarily nothing to do.

The firm of J. J. Augustin was, among other things, one of the primary printing plants for the German Navy. It issued the only local newspaper and produced thick mail-order catalogs and textbooks. Most interesting of all, it also printed and published the books and papers of many prominent American anthropologists for distribution in the United States. I was unaware, at the time, of the irony that the writings of these scholars were scientific refutation of all Nazi racial theories and that they were being printed on the same presses that produced munition request forms, various technical manuals, as well as instructions on the use of gas masks for Hitler's Navy.

The names Boas, Mead, Reichard, Newcomb, Herskovitz, Bunzel and Weltfish became familiar headings on my worksheets. I hand-set the more complicated parts of their manuscripts and the captions for illustrations of Navaho sand paintings, blankets and baskets, Zuni and Hopi kachinas, silverwork and pottery. I could not read the English text, but I inspected the sheets, after the press run, or looked at the books as they left the bindery and intently studied these facets of a living culture that Karl May had never written about in his tales about American Indians. My favorite book of them all was *Sandpaintings of the Navajo Shooting Chant* by Franc J. Newcomb and Gladys A. Reichard. The oversize book contained thirty-five full-page replicas of the magic images that are created for one day only in this strangely evocative ritual. These illustrations were printed from zinc plates on tan Japan paper with watercolor instead of regular printing inks. I was allowed to help in mixing and matching the proper colors and was made responsible for hanging the moist sheets gingerly from overhead washlines for drying.

The plant had a special department where type was set in living as well as dead languages from all over the world. It was a demanding, but very satisfying, job to stand surrounded by semi-circular type cases of thousands of Chinese characters and to pick out the proper ones, subdivided into geometric units, according to the manuscript. This meant that each single letter had to be looked at as an image all by itself. As a result, I developed a distinct interest in letters and typefaces—in their individual form and design rather than their utilitarian purpose to create words and sentences. Various typefaces became more than mere tools of a craft for me when I began to appreciate the masterful way in which the legendary designers, such as Caslon, Bodoni or Garamond, had succeeded in creating fonts of extreme flexibility without compromising the aesthetics of any individual letter.

One day, it must have been in 1936, Heinrich Augustin brought an exotic-looking, red-haired woman to my corner of the workshop. It was Lou Andreas-Salomé, the great love of Rainer Maria Rilke until his death in 1926. My mother had known her slightly over the years. She had come to Glückstadt to discuss a limited edition of Rilke's poems that she had translated into French. The other compositors, my superiors, were astounded that the big boss himself had brought this somewhat bizarre lady into the shop to meet me. Eyebrows were raised even further when she showed me her manuscript and the dummy for her book and asked me, a mere apprentice, what typeface I could suggest. I seem to remember that my choice was Garamond. Augustin knew that I was far from being an accomplished compositor, but he acceded to Mme. Salomé's wish that I should set the text.

The Salomé-Rilke project, as it was called, caused me some trouble. I had neglected to enter into the worksheet the location where the completed pages were stored. On the day of my regular trip to Hamburg to attend the crafts school, the pressman could not find the set type to proof it. As punishment, on the following Saturday afternoon, after work had stopped at noon, I had to wax and polish every floor of the plant by myself, empty and clean the innumerable spittoons and scour all of the toilet bowls. My fellow apprentices supervised my labor with understandably malicious pleasure.

The Augustins, having become my guardians in every sense but name, continued, as judiciously as the climate of the times would allow them, to do whatever they could to make my life bearable in the community. Heinrich Augustin, a somewhat domineering but eminently civilized and fair-minded giant of a man, and his aristocratic, beautiful wife Hedwig, belonged to that part of the old Germany that would probably have been most comfortable under a benign monarchy. They had no use for Hitler or the bullies who ruled the streets. Their patriotism was unquestioned, as evidenced by Heinrich Augustin's suspending all work in the plant for a moment of respectful silence at the news that Germany's pride and joy, the zeppelin *Hindenburg,* had crashed in Lakehurst, New Jersey. What was not generally known to his workers was that he had canceled his reservation on that flight at the last minute and postponed a contemplated visit to his son in New York. Hans Augustin, better known as J.J., had opened a branch of his father's firm in America to issue the books of the mostly American anthropologists from there. He had for a long time been in serious difficulties with the ruling Nazis of Glückstadt who, through him, hoped to damage his unassailable parents. He escaped imminent arrest by crashing his car through a German border gate into France. Arriving in Paris, a very frightened young man, he knocked on his friend Lou Straus-Ernst's door in the middle of the night. She calmed him down with a cup of tea, held his hand until he fell asleep and then called his parents in Glückstadt to tell them that he was safe. The Augustins never forgot, and it is because of that little gesture that I am now alive in America.

After Grandfather Jacob died early in 1937, Heinrich Augustin took over more responsibilities on my behalf. He became the guardian of my modest cash inheritance. I have the distinct feeling that the financial help for my room and board as well as for my trips to Paris must have come out of his own pocket from that time on, in order to preserve my funds for my eventual emigration to the United States.

It was becoming increasingly clear that any change in Germany in the foreseeable future was out of the question. The occasional news from abroad on my little radio and the atmosphere on the streets left little doubt of that. Since the reimposition of the military draft, young men in uniform seemed to be everywhere, and it was somehow strange and frightening to see them and their officers respectfully make way on the sidewalks for members of the SS in their black regalia, sporting sidearms and death-head insignia. There was talk of German involvement in Spain's civil war. The press openly favored Franco and recounted horror tales of nuns being raped by marauding Loyalists. I heard a drunken *Luftwaffe* lieutenant boast in a beer hall how he and his brothers in the Condor Legion conducted machine-gun target practice from their aircraft on the northwestern coast of Spain by mowing down captured enemies of Franco as they were lined up on the cliff edges overlooking the Atlantic Ocean.

When I went to Paris in June 1937, there was a very specific prohibition in my passport against travel to Spain. Through fragments of news from Radio Luxembourg, I was aware of considerable German involvement in the Spanish War. There was reference, for example, to the total destruction of the Basque town of Guernica by war planes of the Condor Legion.

In Herbesthal, first railroad stop for Belgian passport control, most passengers went to the news kiosk on the station platform to buy whatever French, Belgian or Swiss press journals were available in order to catch up on news events censored by German Press Chief Otto Dietrich. I managed to get the very respectable *Le Temps*. It contained items about the increasing friction between Himmler's SS and the German General Staff, the now almost complete nazification of all aspects of German culture, the absolute control by the party of Germany's educational system, and Hitler's and Mussolini's military assistance to Franco's cause while the Soviet Union, through its agents and commissars, was beginning to be a very powerful element in the internal and military affairs of the Loyalists. And again there was a passing mention of "the tragedy of Guernica" and its implication for the future of warfare.

In the taxi from Gare du Nord to the hotel, I asked my mother for more information about Guernica and what had happened there. Last April 26, she told me, the center of Guernica had been leveled by aircraft of Germany's Condor Legion. The small village of about seven thousand inhabitants was of no particular military importance; it had, however, historically been considered the center of Basque nationalism. It was the seat of the Basque parliament house, and its legendary oak had been the symbol before which Spanish royalty had traditionally sworn an oath to respect the civil rights of the Basque people.

That April day, like every Monday, had been market day. Farmers from the surrounding countryside had put their fruits and vegetables on display in the main square for sale to the villagers. In the late afternoon, the church bells signaled a warning of a possible air raid. There had been intermittent aircraft activity by Franco's Nationalists in the vicinity, but civilians had not been the target. Therefore, few people sought shelter. Ten or fifteen minutes after the warning, five Heinkel planes roared over Guernica, bombing and strafing its main square and the narrow streets. They were followed by the dreaded Junkers that dropped incendiary bombs and high explosives. The fleeing people were systematically machine-gunned. The attacks continued for three hours as the wave of planes repeated their attacks in twenty-minute intervals. The center of the village was in flames. An appalling number of human beings had been killed and the number of injured was close to thousand. Eyewitness accounts were still coming in from survivors as well as journalists who had visited the stricken town. There was no question that the attackers had been German aircraft.

I recall gnashing my teeth in fury and experiencing an entirely new kind of fear in the face of this hideous event. No wonder that even those in Germany who might have known did not dare to discuss it. There had been combat in the air during the World War, and zeppelins had made some very unsuccessful raids on London. During Italy's invasion of Ethiopia in 1935 Mussolini's son, an airman, had likened the effect his bomb had created, in hitting a cluster of tribesmen, to the spectacle of a rose bursting into sudden bloom. But until Guernica, mass death from the sky had still belonged, safely removed from reality, to the pages of science fiction.

A few days after my arrival, I went to see the recently opened World's Fair, using Lou's press pass. Below the Trocadero, the German pavilion faced its twin of the USSR, across the fairway, both structures engaging each other in a meaningless competition of vulgar monumentality. On the other side of the Seine, the Eiffel Tower, built for a similar exposition in 1889, stood like a reluctant referee between the two architectural monstrosities. I entered the smaller and far more tasteful building of the still legitimate government of Spain, designed by José Maria Sert. The entrance to the main exhibit was through a spacious, shaded patio. I never got any farther. In the center stood a fountain, the various levels of which were plateaus of lead slabs. Instead of the expected water, the liquid that gently pearled into a tranquil pool was mercury, a product of Spain. This graceful piece of sculpture had been created by Alexander Calder, the same artist whose Circus I had enjoyed just a few years ago. And on the western wall, at least twenty-six feet long and twelve feet high, was the nightmare that I had just recently become aware of: Picasso's Guernica.

Children consider dreams as their special province, but I was not prepared to encounter so many still elusive images of my private world in one place, and least of all in a painting.

Having lived in close proximity to terror, violence and hatred, I had been aware only of its perpetrators. The personal agony of victims had remained an intangibly private image. In Picasso's mural, the enemy was nowhere to be seen; his dying human and animal prey screamed not so much in pain but in utter disbelief at violent death's last breath.

I had seen enough for one day and walked along the Seine for hours, sensing the presence of the same cruelly dispassionate eye of God that I had seen suspended, as if stationary forever, as a witness to this and all massacres, above the agonized head of the dying horse. Someday this eye might blink and bring soothing darkness to the dead. Right now, it promised nothing more than an endless wait and more horror.

For the next six or seven days I returned to the mural, sometimes twice or three times a day. I was disturbed by the almost magnetic force that drew me to the painting. All of my stubbornly constructed arguments against art were collapsing. I began to admit to myself that many of my prior hostile reactions had been mere shelters, covers for my immature prejudices. I discussed the matter with my mother almost too casually. At seventeen I found my sudden turnabout an embarrassment after all the years of feigned disinterest. Lou offered to come with me for a joint visit to the exposition. I told her that this was something I wanted to do by myself.

The extreme agitation of my initial encounter with *Guernica* had abated, and I tried to look at the work with less reference to the event out of which it had grown. One of my antagonisms had been fed liberally by the art produced for the propagation of purely political ideas. That of the left was for the most part stridently shallow and depressing. Hitler's ideas spawned nothing more than pretentious illustration of false ideals. That a work of art could be an idea independent of external reality had occurred to me, but I had steadfastly refused to contemplate a painting or a sculpture with anything more than my eyes.

It occurred to me that I might have deceived myself, maybe I had actually perceived and understood far more in the past than I had been willing to admit. Suddenly I was not at all certain that painting did not have the potential of transforming an external event or idea into attestation of one human being's universality. After all, Grünewald's Isenheim altarpiece described very specific events and personalities, but it was the painter, and not his subject matter, whose hands and vision had created this phenomenon of consummate magic. The *Guernica* was certainly more than a mere retelling of a given incident of war that propagandized for one side or the other. The innocent victims of the horror were we. This painting, in speaking of atrocity, reaffirmed humanism . . . without preaching. As you stood in its presence, it reached into your own secret well of universal recall regardless of the particular history that had brought it about. The artist, all of him, uninhibited by any preconceived dicta of communication, had engaged in an intense projection of his own private language. The immediacy of his imagery, almost audible, asserted a reality beyond its content.

Here was the artist's elusive miracle. Conscious human knowledge becoming a rope ladder into dark solitude, there to find the blinding flash of ultimate reality, the lightning bolt called the moment of truth. My father's work unreeled like a kaleidoscope somewhere behind my eyes. I was amazed how many of his images had found a permanent place in my memory, in spite of my deliberate resistance.

Max himself had moved to an apartment in one of the old houses on rue Jacob. I had not as yet made an attempt to see him on this visit. I was not quite sure how to tell him about my new experience. Coming back one day, after walking around the Champs de Mars, I took the Métro to St. Germain-des-Prés. When I got to the apartment, I was disappointed not to find him at home. One of the most beautiful women I had ever seen told me in English-accented French that she expected him to be back in about an hour. She made tea, and in the course of conversation told me that she loved Max and that they were living together. Her name was Leonora Carrington, and her dark, glowing beauty so affected me that I found it difficult to talk to her coherently. My unexpected visit must also have been awkward for her, and she broke into one of our mutual silences suddenly: "Look here, it must be strange for you to find me here instead of Max. All of this just happened so recently that you perhaps didn't even know

I existed. Max has told me a great deal about you, and he was a bit apprehensive of your reaction. He loves you very much, and I hope that you and I can become very good friends." She got up, kissed me on both cheeks and graciously left the room. That allowed my hammering heart to return to normal.

Max came in shortly with Paul Éluard and his new wife Nush. "Look who's here; it's Jimmy. We must celebrate." He uncorked a bottle of champagne, quickly followed by a second one. Max and the Éluards had also just been to the Spanish pavilion and were talking about the *Guernica.* Champagne had the effect of loosening my tongue and my inhibitions. I spilled out my entire adventure, rambling on about the things that suddenly had begun to make sense—Brueghel, Guardi, Delacroix, Bosch, Rembrandt, Fra Angelico, Durer, Uccello, Altdorfer, Grünewald, Velázquez, Goya, Raphael, Redon, Zurbarán, Daumier, Ingres, Leonardo da Vinci and David. Max's dry rejoinder, "Nothing more recent than that?" prompted my breathless reply, "Yes, you most of all."

"As your father," he replied into a silence, "I would be expected to say to you now, 'It's time for a long talk between the two of us,' but we better wait before you know how you really feel about me."

"Max," Éluard interjected, "I think you are annoyed because your son may have discovered his way toward you through Picasso. Don't forget what you told me about seeing a Picasso in Cologne in 1912 and how it possibly changed your life."

"But *Guernica?* There's been a lot of supposing about it one way or the other. Is it an important painting or a major political document? The sketches he did before and afterward are in color. Why is the final version in shades of black and white only? . . ."

"But, Max, Jimmy is not a politician, he is trying to reach you, and can you think of any bridge, other than Picasso, that would be more acceptable to you?"

I had been squirming, but Max ended the crisis by saying to no one in particular, "Let's finish the champagne."

I spent a lot of time after that at rue Jacob, mostly late in the afternoon, when Max had finished his work in the studio. Things were not going well with him. After Max had left her, Marie-Berthe's family had made successful efforts to blacken his name in Paris. Paintings dating back several years were now stacked profusely throughout the apartment, unsold. Several versions of *La Ville Entiére, Gobe Avion* and the strange jungles with their malicious animal and plant life were in various stages of completion. He took one of the *Gobe Avion* canvases and, without any preliminary explanation, brushed on its back: "For Jimmy, my son and now my friend." "That's for your birthday. You can't take it with you into Germany, but it is yours and I will send it to you, wherever you are, once this insanity is over." Today that painting lies on the bottom of the Atlantic

Ocean somewhere off Martinique. The French freighter bringing it to me in its hold was torpedoed in the late fall of 1939.

We had not talked too much about my new attitude toward him nor about Picasso's *Guernica*. He must have sensed that I was painfully groping for a self-understanding about the change in my feelings. From his occasional remarks it was clear that he respected Picasso highly and was still grateful for his recommendation of himself and Miró to Diaghilev for the commission of sets and decor for *Romeo and Juliet* in that very difficult year of 1926. Still there was never a complete absence of rivalry among all these giants. I can't believe that it ever went so far as the story of an exchange of paintings between Matisse and Picasso, when Picasso supposedly chose one of the weaker works of Matisse to hang on his walls. Max, every now and then, would get in a dig. He remarked, for example, that just as Picasso had used the art of tribal Africa for an important phase in his work without adding too much personal originality to it, he had, in the same way, appropriated Max's 1927 *Le Baiser* and based an entire series of major paintings on it.

The subject of Guernica came up again the next time that Éluard joined Max, Leonora Carrington and me for tea at rue Jacob. For my sake, he had brought along a large number of photographs about to be published in the magazine *Cahiers d'Art* that Dora Maar, Picasso's mistress of many years, had taken during the progress of *Guernica*. I found the changes and transformations the mural had undergone fascinating and had to ask Max how he really felt about it. Picasso to his mind had created far more important works than this one, but the circumstances of its existence had made it an object of public discussion, obscuring the painting while stressing its subject matter. He was amused, he said, by the awkward discomfort with which the extreme political left had already claimed the mural as its visual manifesto against Franco, even though they might have preferred to have seen the horror of Guernica dealt with by a painter out of their own socialist-realist stable. Yes, it was a very important statement; he could not imagine himself so moved if the more politically doctrinaire George Grosz, Otto Dix or even the admired Käthe Kollwitz had tackled the same subject. How would *L'Humanité* (the Communist Party newspaper), bend the party line if their great poet Louis Aragon were to share with his fellow editors the growing opinion that Picasso, in his agony over Spain, had brought the soul of a great religious masterpiece, Matthias Grünewald's sixteenth-century Isenheim altarpiece, into *Guernica?*

But I was after more answers for myself: Could paintings defeat Franco, stop Hitler or prevent the next war? Éluard replied, "Max probably has not told you that only a few months ago some of us, including Malraux, had to convince him not to volunteer for active field duty against Franco. One of our arguments was that his paintings and collages are far more dangerous to fascism than his bullet-riddled body. I also had to remind him again that both of us may well have been shooting at each other at Verdun in 1916. What if one of us hadn't missed? As for stopping wars, Guernica is a good example of the terrible things that can happen when people who don't want war declare themselves neutral . . . like America."

"Jimmy asked if paintings can stop war," Max stepped in, ". . . I really don't know. But if there is to be a war, he might be safe in America . . . maybe they'll do the right things. Let's hope he gets there in time."

Though they were talking to each other rather than to me, I was deeply touched by the concern that both men seemed to have for my present confusion. It was a further awakening to the sense that my father's very special world, and that of his friends, was of far more import than I had been willing to admit to myself. The accelerated pace of all these new impressions were paralleled by the dilemma of a conflict that was certainly not new but coming into inevitably sharper focus: They were really one and the same individual, the great artist, a man of brilliance, charm and grace, and the flawed, often hermetically cold, human being. Could I ignore the trauma experienced by those who had found themselves evicted from his life and measure him only in his obvious place in the world as a genius? I saw myself less and less as one of the rejected in view of his considerate gestures toward me and his apparent hope that my new understanding of him would make the ways of his life more plausible to me. Whichever way I was going to look at my father, I needed to avoid the extreme example of Picasso's son Paolo, whom I had met several times. Of the same age as I, he had become a street delinquent, a thoroughly demoralized adolescent, in his inability, it was said, to meet the mercurial behavior of his famous father with any alternative other than outright hatred, running in tandem with utter dependence.

Lou watched my progress through the haze of perplexities with satisfaction and encouragement: "Don't be too impatient. It's not going to happen overnight. It's the curse of many a son to want to be like his father but also not wanting to be like him. I don't know what would happen to us art historians if we allowed ourselves to evaluate the works of great masters by using the yardstick of their personal life-conduct."

Max could not resist the temptation to make ironic light about the original impetus of our changing relationship: "This is my son Jimmy, my favorite admirer of Picasso."

I learned other things on this trip as well. It was about time, but it still hurt. There was an end to my romantic notion that my glorious introduction to sex had been tantamount to finding the great love of my life. The shock of finding someone else had taken my place in her bed when I returned to Paris was shattering. The only redeemable feature of the pain was that it did not, after all, center in the heart. I must have appeared a very miserable creature in my despondency, so much so that I brought tears to my mother's eyes. Out of embarrassment I asked her why she was doing that. "I know that pain awfully well," she said. "It's happened to me a lot of times and I wept. Since you are not willing to cry, I am going to do it for you." I can't say that this helped very much at the moment, but I began to have a suspicion that it had been my vanity, more than anything else, that had been hurt.

Max was far less charitable. He was obviously pleased that I was confiding in him man to man, and he apparently decided to shock me back to normalcy. "All women have vaginas, but only in a few of them are they properly connected to their heads. Don't ever confuse vocal chords with brains. . . . Love can be the worst venereal disease of them all." Despite my present state of mind I did not find such wisdom very welcome; it represented a few steps backward in my effort to understand him better. More helpful, but still disturbing, was his confidence to me that the lady, who tearfully waved her handkerchief as my train left Gare du Nord only a few months ago, had propositioned him before they had even left the station platform.

He then took me to dinner at the Cloiserie des Lilas on the corner of boulevard Montparnasse, near the Observatoire, where I got up enough courage to ask him about Marie-Berthe and the end of their marriage. The very intense nature of Max's relationship with Leonora Carrington was manifest every time I saw the two together, and it made me wonder about Marie-Berthe, that fragile, birdlike creature who had shown me so much affection. Lou and I had visited her after she had moved back into her parent's house. Over tea she introduced us to a youngish man whom Lou later described as bearing an uncanny resemblance to Max when he was courting her. The two women had grown very fond of each other. Marie-Berthe had married Max not long after completing her convent schooling, and she had come to Lou for advice when that marriage was beginning to break up. Later she seriously proposed that Lou come and live with her. "Now that we both don't have him anymore, I will take care of you and you will help with some of your courage."

Max was not very anxious to tell me much. Marie-Berthe had, according to him, completely immersed herself in Catholicism again and was even considering entering a convent for life. A few times she had annoyed him and Leonora in some public place and made some uncomfortable scenes. He was relieved at not having to say more by the interruption of a very beautiful woman who joined our table. He introduced her to me as one of Man Ray's favorite models.

Leaving Gare du Nord for Germany again was no longer a voyage of going home. The now familiar landscape of France and Belgium slipped past at a frightening rate, and I thought of what would happen if I simply stepped off the train anywhere before the German border and just disappeared. The railroad carriage and its compartments were filled with drunken German tourists who loudly boasted of what they had done with "those filthy French whores" in the nightclubs and bordellos of Montmarte. They, indeed, were going "home." Home, "where you can tell the difference between women because only the prostitutes wear makeup." "The two I had last night had even painted their bodies and smelled of perfume between their legs." A fight broke out between two men because one told of his friend's erection when one of the girls they had hired for the night turned out to be a transvestite. They quieted down a great deal when the train crossed the border into their homeland. Straightening their ties, with faces shaved and hair brushed, they sat demurely in the compartments, with only an occasional snicker after passport control and customs inspection.

I was relieved that the uniformed men going through my baggage did not discover my contraband. It was a special issue of *Cahiers d'Art* devoted entirely to Max Ernst.

What I saw out of the train window were the same towns, bridges, rivers, mountains and valleys, but I suddenly realized that they no longer belonged to me. For the first time it occurred to me that I might die here because my presence was a stain on the land. I had a long and heart-breaking look at the Dom and the Rhine as the train pulled out of the station after a stop in Cologne. I couldn't get off even here. All of that was gone too. "You don't live here anymore."

Near Hanover the train slowed to a crawl. Both sides of the roadbed were illuminated by searchlights mounted on military vehicles manned by black-uniformed SS troopers. Hundreds of figures in boldly striped prison fatigues were swinging pickaxes and sledgehammers, working on the railroad trestle. Their guards held automatic weapons at the ready. There was a stir among the erstwhile beer-besotted travelers. "Well, well, they're finally doing some honest work with their hands. . . . Didn't think that Jews had any muscles in their arms and legs . . . never worked at anything except being lawyers and doctors. . . . They're not all Jews; they've got all kinds of people in those education camps: Communists, Social Democrats, Gypsies, you name them. . . . Hitler is really using a good German broom. . . . They are being re-educated, God knows what for. . . . Did you know that all Jews sleep with their women stark naked? . . . Filthy . . . isn't it?"

The train seemed to move like a snail, its windows filled with faces, some of the passengers standing on their seats to be better able to see the eerie spectacle. The locomotive blew its whistle, and normal speed resumed as if there had never been a nightmare. "Any beer left? . . . we're getting off soon. Just one more bottle and then it's home. . . . I can't wait."

At a station just before Hamburg, the male elite, of whatever the town, was respectfully embraced by cloche-topped wives and very sleepy children with flowery bouquets of welcome.

I now shared the entire compartment with a gigantic black American who had stared down the German drunks, making me somewhat more comfortable. I don't know who he was except that his ticket, as it was inspected periodically, had Moscow as its final destination. He laughed a lot, spread himself across two seats and told me, in broken German and French, that he was a singer on tour and that, pointing toward the window, "we have road gangs like that in Georgia." He winked at me, and humming some melody, fell asleep, the humming being replaced by loud snoring. I've often wondered whether or not it was Paul Robeson.

The sounds of Europe are punctuated by church bells and train whistles. I bear them as gentle scars even now, over forty years later, and think back to that night, in that speeding train, as one of strange fears. And for the first time I wondered what it must be like to live in a black skin.

The local from Hamburg to Glückstadt, going almost due north, lost its race with the dawn. At every stop the pink, ochre and brown towns with their outlying farm buildings faced the tracks with righteous innocence. Behind those shiny windows with their starchy lace curtains solid burghers were getting ready for a day's work, still another one under the ever impartial disk of the sun. Could all of those neat little houses be infested with evil? I almost wished that I had not gotten to know so much in such a short time of the inexplicable horror that was spreading through the land, perhaps each time a water faucet was opened by hands that needed to be cleansed. Here were the pavements and the soil on which had grown up the men who had burned Guernica and strafed its fleeing inhabitants like monstrous insects, the same shiny-booted humans who had held their weapons on the gaunt men by the railroad tracks, the paunchy louts, smelling of Pilsener and Löwenbräu, who were now reliving their Montmartre escapades under soft, down-filled covers, imagining the breasts, bellies, and thighs of their spouses as perfumed and enhanced with rouge.

Heinrich Augustin told me that his son J.J. was making progress in obtaining the necessary affidavits for an American visa. Under no circumstances was I to tell anyone in town or in the factory about these efforts. Things were getting tighter. Some local Nazi bigwigs had tried to get Augustin's Navy contracts canceled unless I was dismissed as an apprentice. From now on it would be best not to be seen too often in the shop. I was to purchase a railroad pass for unrestricted travel to Hamburg, prepare for my emigration by attending English language classes at Berlitz and make contact with the American Consulate.

The Berlitz classes proved to be an absolute dud and when, at one point,

I was asked to fill out a questionnaire in which I was to explain the purpose of these lessons, I got scared and never went back. The American Consulate took my application, put me on a list, but made it clear that without proper affidavits, a visa was out of the question. Nevertheless, I spent several days of each week in Hamburg, returning each night to Glückstadt. A lot of the time I went to movie houses and tried to see as many American films as I could. It did not help with my language problem because most of them were dubbed into German. Musicals, such as *Broadway Melody of 1936*, I saw several times because the songs and production numbers remained in their original form. There was, indeed, a time when I could sing all of "You are my lucky star . . ." I still think of Eleanor Powell's tap-dancing legs as a supreme aesthetic and sensuous experience.

There was not much to see in Hamburg's museums except perhaps paintings, sculptures, models of ships and old prints about the history of its harbor. Contemporary art was restricted to banal official work. For some reason no one had mustered up the courage to remove a very beautiful memorial to the dead of the last war by Ernst Barlach, a sculptor whose work had been removed from all public institutions. The large brooding column with the relief figure of a mourning woman stood on one of the canals in the fashionable center of the city. Each time I passed it I gave it a nod of respect as a work of art and as a reminder of the cultural life before the advent of the barbarians.

Not far from this place, in an open square, I noticed, on a clammy fall day, a number of trailers with a line of people waiting for admission to them. It was the traveling exhibition of "degenerate art" that had been organized by the Ministry of Culture at the insistence of Hitler to show the Germans what *Kultureller Bolschewismus* was all about. As I entered, I recognized immediately some of the old friends who at one time or another had visited the apartment in Cologne, and others whose works I knew from my mother's library: Klee, Yankel Adler, Chagall, Pechstein, Beckmann, Davringhausen, Hofer, Kandinsky, Franz Marc and, to my secret delight, Max Ernst. His painting hung in a special section entitled "Insults to German Womanhood," and it seemed to be the most crowded room of all. Max's *La Belle Jardinière* had a prominent place between Ernst Kirschner and Otto Dix. It was a magnificent painting from 1923, and strangely enough it is one of the few works from that infamous exhibition that may very well have been burned. Most of the other works surfaced mysteriously in Switzerland shortly before World War II, where they provided the Third Reich with much-needed foreign currency. Ironically, most of them were bought up by New York–based German emigrés, who in turn managed to place them with major American museums, particularly the Detroit Institute of Art and New York's Museum of Modern Art.

The relatively narrow spaces of these converted moving vans made it difficult to stand in front of any one work for more than a minute or so. Paintings that provoked more than the usual interest tended to create a bunching up of people. The officious command to "keep moving" by strategically placed guards was obeyed with reluctant docility. Nobody wanted to run the risk of being called a lover of this *Kultur Bolschewismus*. After all, this event was staged in the manner of a sideshow of freaks at a tawdry carnival. Ernst's *La Belle Jardinière* was one of those works that seemed to create periodical jam-ups, as did other paintings of female nudes. The prominent image of a dove partially shielding the vaginal area of the *Jardinière* caused many a spectator to lean over the restricting rope as if in hope of seeing what the bird was hiding. The pictures by George Grosz and Otto Dix also attracted considerable curiosity. Observing the faces and the bearing of the crowd was not unlike seeing the figures and actions in the works of these and other satirical artists. Surely this must have angered, and fascinated, those who thus saw themselves so candidly mirrored. The price of admission was allegedly for the benefit of the "Winter-Hilfe," a catch-all year-long collection drive to help the hungry and the cold, but it was no secret that all of that money was being funneled into the steel and concrete of Germany's visible remilitarization.

My contribution to that national effort on that gray, dank day was about tenfold. I would wait a while outside and then rejoin the queue for yet another viewing. The fifth or sixth time around I noticed some familiar faces. Other people were doing the same thing. There were some nervous, quick glances and then an almost immediate studied retreat into indifference. Heaven knows what reasons we ascribed to each other for our unusual behavior. Any one of these faces could belong to the Gestapo. When the ticket taker and some of the guards seemed to look at me with a measure of recognition, I thought it best not to go in again for an eleventh time.

I walked across to an arcade building and looked for a while at the long line waiting to get in and at the faces of those emerging. Their expressions for the most part were blank; some mouths were pressed into severe lines. There was no hint of the snickers and leers that had accompanied the shuffling feet inside those vans. It was a strange encounter with my world of the past, and my feelings wavered between pride and fear. Were my father and his contemporaries in there really so feared by the authorities that they had to subject their works to such a funereal circus? I suddenly realized that, as I had been moving in that line, I had been hearing a recording of Hitler's speech at the opening of officially approved German Art, some months ago in Munich, blaring out endlessly from loudspeakers inside each room: ". . . I had sworn that if destiny ever placed me into the position as your leader, I would make short shrift of this degeneracy. The German people deserve to be protected from such diseased minds. The perpetra-

tors of these insults to Beauty and Art will have to be confined in institutions of the criminally insane until they learn how to think like Germans
again. . . ." I guess that the proliferation of loudspeakers on street corners, in
railway stations and other public places had made my ears almost deaf to the
words. I began to feel almost sorry for the people of this land who so willingly
had allowed themselves to be caged in by this madness. They, and not the artists
inside those vans, not only belonged in, but already inhabited, a gigantic ward
for the insane. But past images of bearded Jews scrubbing public sidewalks, the
horror of Guernica, the destruction of my family life, the strutting, faceless men
in their brown and black uniforms and the indecency of that display across the
street put a quick end to my pity.

A large man in a loden coat and a moss-green fedora came up to me to ask
me for a match. As he bent down to light his cigarette from my cupped hands,
he mumbled, "What do you think of that shit in there?" I froze. He stood next
to me dragging on his smoke. "Well, you must be interested. You went in there
often enough during the last few hours."

I felt trapped and scared, but suddenly I heard myself saying with some
pride, but a quaver in my voice, "My father is one of the artists in that show."

As I hurried off blindly, I heard him shout after me: "But that's not your
fault . . . you should be proud of it."

Had this been a challenge to draw me out? Was he one of "them," or did
he really mean what he said? One never knew any longer what consequences a
careless word in a railroad compartment or coffeehouse might have. There must
still be people whose thoughts had not been completely imprisoned by the mass
hypnosis of Hitler or Goebbels. But they were now mere particles floating separately in some vast body of water. They were just as afraid of reaching shore as
they were of the possible fate of drowning. Either friend or stranger might well,
in some sudden motion, manacle your hands and watch as you were being led
away. It was the first time that I had come so close to the face of the dilemma.
And for what? My mother was a Jew and my father created forbidden images.
Fortunately, I found a public comfort station, closed the cubicle door and threw
up.

The thought, "Get out, get out" became almost three-dimensional in its
urgency. I seemed to have a better chance than most, but all of my visits to the
American Consulate ended with the same admonition, "Without your three
affidavits, we cannot even put you on the waiting list . . . and you know that there
is a quota. . . . If it is filled, you'll have to wait another year . . . and even then
it'll be a question of whether you can meet the other parts of our immigration
laws."

Every night I traveled back to that beautiful old town where I would encounter the same stony, hostile faces. The Augustins, wisely, made little outward display of their concern for me. Heinrich Augustin would yell at me with the same force as he did to the other apprentices, even though he knew that bad reports on my work in the plant were, at times, totally manufactured. Usually he would find some private way to let me know his true feelings. "Those swine have put Pastor Martin Niemöller in a concentration camp," he muttered on one occasion, as he was ostensibly scanning a page proof that I had delivered to his office. Niemöller's name was familiar to me from the attacks on him in the German press. This prominent Protestant clergyman had persistently proclaimed the Christian ethic from his pulpit as an answer and indictment of Germany's spiritual and moral degeneration. Heinrich and Hedwig Augustin acted out of an inborn sense of decency and Christianity, but to me they were also a lifeline in the morass of that time.

The small fund set aside for my hoped-for emigration had been reduced to an almost absolute minimum, and so another trip to Paris to spend Christmas with my mother and her friends was not advisable. I had to accept the logic of that decision.

I began to construct a small tree from cut-out cardboard and painted it with cheap poster colors. It was a sad-looking plant. I had planned it as a three-dimensional structure, but the glue or the slots would not hold the awkward branches. After innumerable pieces of tape, paper clips and pins, it held together but looked as if it had been through a severe storm. The paint I applied was very watery and the wind-swept little creature began to curl in on itself. But it finally stood on my night table in Glückstadt, a replacement and illusion for the real event three weeks hence.

A few days later I was summoned to Heinrich Augustin's office. That usually meant trouble and, sure enough, he began to berate me loudly for my inefficiency, laziness and some recent mess I had made of a page of type. Strangely, though, his face was turned partially away from me, and then he leaned backwards to slam the door to his secretary's office. With a barely controlled smile he handed me an envelope. In it was a round-trip ticket to Paris and a healthy bundle of paper money. When I inquired about the advisability of spending any more of the money, he replied with a stern mien, "Young man, I am in charge of your affairs, and I have decided for you to visit your mother. Where the money comes from and how it is to be spent are none of your concern. Now get out of here before I yell at you again. And this time I may mean it."

On my way to Paris I stopped in Cologne to pick up Grandfather Jacob's gold watch. He'd died a short time before. I was to take it across the German border as my own, but in Paris my mother could sell it. Tante Leah was not too eager to give it to me, but this had been one of the provisions in Jacob's will she had not been able to eliminate. I told her that I thought Hitler would start a war pretty soon. She scoffed at the idea. Hitler, she said, had been a soldier himself, been gassed on the western front and knew that the German people would never support another war. Germany would somehow rectify the injustices of the terrible Versailles Treaty. As to anti-Semitism, which had made her and her children pariahs, that too would go away. Good sense demanded it, and further-more it was really directed against "those people from east of the Oder River." Once they had all gone back where they came from, there would no longer be any reason for German Jews to be discriminated against. For her, and so many others, it was admittedly difficult to accept the brutality against them "by a nation that produced Goethe, Heine, Brahms and Beethoven" as "anything more than a passing excess." Her daughters were more realistic. They had, some years before, joined other Jewish youngsters in covert Zionist youth groups.

A somewhat dissimilar, but still rosy, view continued to prevail in those little hotels in Paris. It was terribly simple: Sooner or later Germany's leaders were bound to overreach themselves. The rest of the civilized world, and particularly France, was just waiting for "the proper moment" to restore "our" Germany to "us." Admittedly, I was too young and inexperienced to argue with them. Even Lou Straus-Ernst responded to my fears with a somewhat faraway look in her eyes: "We have logic and morality on our side, and those are stronger than marching boots and hysterical ravings."

Christmas that year was bittersweet for me. A letter from Hans Augustin to Lou had just arrived, informing her and me that he had succeeded in obtaining the precious affidavits for me. Sometime, within six months perhaps, I would be safely with him in New York, and now was the time for her to make the proper applications that should enable her to join me "over here." Lou again voiced those fears about America that I had heard so often from her, her friends and colleagues. "What about the language? . . . people in the movies hardly move their lips . . . who would publish my work? . . . It's a place for young people, it's the impersonal nature of its cities, the high-pitched tempo of daily life . . . and it is so big . . . it is so big. . . . No," she said, "I think I will wait for you here. All of my friends are here. Paris is not Cologne, but it is on the same continent, and sometimes I even forget the differences. If you have to stay there, I may join you someday. By that time you might be famous and successful. That is what America is all about, isn't it? With you there, to make me feel at home, I will be less afraid."

For me, somehow, this particular semi-annual reunion with the only people who had any personal meaning for me and who made the grim isolation for the rest of the year bearable, had lost some of its glowing anticipation from the very outset. For almost five years now I had looked forward to these visits. But maybe this was just idle dreaming. Nobody, I feared, would ever get "home" again. The future, as conjured up by thousands of individual dreams in the shabby little rooms, the sidewalk cafés and the benches in the Luxembourg Gardens, seemed to retreat. At best the temporary accommodations made with life in exile might endure indefinitely. Certainly the White Russian generals who had been lucky enough long ago to exchange their splendid uniforms for the false gold braid and trimmings of elegant doormen must have lowered their expectations of seeing the spires of St. Petersburg again as something possible only for some, as yet unborn, generation.

During our modest, but still festive, Christmas dinner in Chambre 411, a white-haired lawyer from Mannheim, who supported himself with an illegal menial job, collating and stapling briefs in a big law firm, raised his jelly glass of red wine for a toast of good luck to Lou's son, who was soon to have the great adventure of sailing across the ocean to America. "A toast to Jimmy on his last Christmas in Paris," he said, hastily adding, "well, . . . for a few years, anyway."

Lou lowered her head, tears streaming down her cheeks into her glass. "Mother, you are watering your wine. Drink up." But then I cried too. Somewhere behind my eyes, amid the sentiment and melancholia of that moment, came the realization that I was not leaving Europe merely to wait for history to reverse itself in my favor. I was very much aware of the fact that my knowledge of the United States of America was extremely limited, if not superficial, but I was young and so was America. If indeed I got there, I owed it to myself, as well as to the people I would find there, to become a part of it and perhaps even contribute to it. Venerable Europe was being slowly asphyxiated by ideas that emanated from the thirty-seven-year-old grave of the philosopher Friedrich Wilhelm Nietzsche. No . . . I would try not to come to America as a refugee.

The three affidavits had indeed arrived at the American Consulate in Hamburg, and the immigration officer who interviewed me there shortly after my return from Paris seemed quite impressed that in addition to Hans Augustin's voucher, the other two had been signed by the renowned anthropologists Franz Boas and Gladys Reichard. He asked if I knew these people, and I told him that I had been setting the type for several of their books during the past few years. He shoved a sheaf of questionnaires across his desk and demanded detailed responses concerning just about every facet of my family background and personal past. Though a little nervous about having to do some considerable digging in order to come up with information that I did not have at present, I felt somehow reassured that the United States was being extremely careful in its selection of those who would be admitted to its shores. It took me several weeks to collect all the data from both the maternal and paternal side. I brought the results triumphantly to the immigration section of the Consulate, but it was not going to be that easy after all. "Now all of this stuff will go to the Embassy in Berlin and the Department of Labor in Washington. Then we'll see how many quota numbers we'll get for this office, and then you'll be on the waiting list." The officer smiled at me. "Now don't get nervous. Everybody has to go through that. Just keep checking with us. . . . Oh, here is another form; make an appointment with the medical office down the hall for a complete physical exam, and then, if you get your visa, they'll check you out again. After all, you might have caught something that would disqualify you while you were waiting."

The medical went very well. It was a unique experience; my body had never been subjected to such an exhaustive poking, probing and listening to. Unfortunately I could not understand what the physician was dictating to the nurse as he examined me, and for the first time I became really afraid at the thought that my knowledge of English was practically nil. All my fancy schooling in French, Latin and Greek was not going to help me much if I went to any place in New York to apply for a job . . . even as a compositor-typesetter. My panic was alleviated somewhat when the doctor told me in German: "Right now you're healthy enough. But we'll have to see you again . . . if you make it."

All of these proceedings and utterances occurred in a casual and matter-of-fact manner, in welcome contrast to the pompous vindictiveness of German, or even French, bureaucracies. I even got a fleeting, though unthinkable, impression that American officials were not unused to their citizens talking back to them. Still, the feeling that I was involved in some gigantic lottery, with thousands of others like me having bought a chance, was, to say the least, a bit disquieting. Most countries that allowed immigration at all had already decided that they had absorbed just about the limit of their capacity. Individuals in untold numbers were waiting on visitors' visas in Paris, London, Shanghai, Santiago, Rio de Janeiro, Havana, and other temporary havens for their American visa numbers to come up. These, for the most part, were people who could financially afford such travel plans. Getting the life-saving permission to steam into any harbor on either American coast was, indeed, like receiving the Grand Prix. I, like everybody else, was aware that there was considerable opposition in America to enlarging the various immigration quotas. There was still massive unemployment in the United States as a result of the Depression, and there was justifiable fear of having to compete with waves of newcomers for jobs as they became available.

For the next few months I spent at least two days every week in the always crowded waiting room of the Consulate, and my very limited English vocabulary was enriched by the phrase: "Sorry, Mr. Ernst, nothing yet."

In the meantime the pace of European disturbances increased as Hitler, Göring and Goebbels incited the people to superpatriotism and promised them a world of prosperity and peace as soon as their dreams of having all "German-speaking brothers" under the same flag were realized. The Sudenten-Germans of Czechoslovakia continued their terrorism and rioting. Nazis in Austria demonstrated violently against their government, which, in an act of appeasement, had recently allowed them to wear their brown uniforms again. Léon Blum's antifascist coalition, Le Front Populaire, had splintered into little factions when he resigned as France's Premier in June 1937. A parade of smiling and obsequious European statesmen appeared, as if by command, almost weekly at the stately offices of the Reichskanzler and Minister of Foreign Affairs von Ribbentrop, or they were photographed surveying proudly the kill of the hunt with Göring on one of his vast estates.

In early March I found a junior executive from the Augustin firm sitting at his desk with tears of joy streaming down his face. "I never thought I would experience such a glorious day. Our Führer and our great Wehrmacht have made Austria and Germany one nation. Mussolini has just wired his congratulations. I am so fortunate to be living during these historic times. Germany is reborn." . . . The madness was growing, and I felt trapped.

A few days later, Heinrich Augustin relayed a message from his son, J.J., urging me to set up an appointment immediately with a representative of the United States Lines at their Hamburg headquarters.

The man in his glass-partitioned office came right to the point: "We understand that you intend to emigrate to the United States and you have been waiting for your quota number. Have you made arrangements with any steamship lines to get you there?" I told him that I had considered it to be somewhat premature since the outlook was so uncertain and that, furthermore, out of superstition, I had not wanted to press my luck. He scoffed. "Superstition won't get you across the Atlantic." He handed me an order form for a one-way ticket to New York. "If you sign it, we'll try to find out what is holding up your case. I can't promise you anything, but we'll see what we can do here." I signed without hesitation. If I went, I certainly would want to go on an American ship. "We'll have to leave the departure date open. . . . As for pressing your luck, don't be afraid to be lucky. It's not such a rare event." I went directly to the Consulate to check again. "Sorry, Mr. Ernst, nothing yet."

Exactly one week later I was summoned to Hamburg for another medical checkup. "Well, young man, you are still breathing, but your pulse rate is a little fast. Calm down. What are you so excited about? . . . Put your clothes back on. Go down the hall to the waiting room and relax until your name is called."

My pulse rate probably did not go down, and it rose even more when I faced the Consul behind his desk. "Sit down, Mr. Ernst. Let me review your file. . . ." Finally he looked up and said, "Please rise and raise your right hand. Do you swear that the statements made in this application are the truth and nothing but the truth?" I vaguely heard myself responding in the affirmative. He smiled at me. "I think that you will make a fine citizen of the United States. Pick up the processed papers in four days from now, after which you will be free to get on a boat to America. Good luck."

I somehow found my way to the office of my shirt-sleeved angel at the United States Lines and thanked him profusely. He looked at me over his glasses. "Don't thank me, I didn't do a thing. That would be illegal. Maybe I helped a little bit in bringing you the luck you were afraid of. Now let's see . . . the next couple of boats are booked. How about the S.S. *Manhattan,* at the beginning of June? You probably want to see your mother in Paris before you go. I'll book you from Le Havre on June third. Pick up your ticket after you get your documents from the Consulate next week. The *Manhattan* is a fine ship. Have a good trip."

I thought there were tears in Heinrich Augustin's eyes as he wrote out a check for the fare to Paris and for the boat. "Go to the bank with this and be careful with all of that cash. There is more than you need for the trip. You can't go to America wearing the kind of clothes I have seen you in. Now get to work; you are still an apprentice here."

The salesman in the Hamburg men's clothing store must have earned himself a bonus from his boss. He knew all about America, he said; his brother lived in a place called Paterson, New Jersey. He knew exactly what I would need as basic wardrobe "over there"; surely I didn't want to look like a "greenhorn" when I got off the boat. He sold me the most outlandish suits, jackets, shirts and ties. "This is very important, bow ties; that's what the fashionable people wear there." He must have cleaned out his stock of unsalable items, and I was too timid to dispute him. His final coup was to sell me three 1920s gangster-type hats, because: "The rain dropping down from those skyscrapers is very dirty, and you don't want to lose your hair, do you?" I would need three of them, he said, "because it sometimes rains for several weeks without letup." I drew the line at a brown raincoat. I could not believe that Americans were wearing Nazi-brown raincoats.

I did not have a "long last look" at my room in Glückstadt or even at Glückstadt itself, as the Augustin car brought me and my baggage to the small railroad station. This time my ticket to Paris was one-way only. At the various local stations the loudspeakers, when they were not propagandizing, filled in with popular record music. The biggest *Schlager* (hit) in Germany currently was *"Bei Mir Bist Du Schön,"* as sung by the Andrews Sisters. Everybody seemed so proud that America had produced a German song. Somebody in the Ministry of Propaganda was about to lose his swastika armband when the lyrics were discovered to be Yiddish. I enthusiastically joined a bunch of sailors who were traveling to Hamburg's Reeperbahn for a drunken-weekend leave in singing the words with particular emphasis on the recurring *"Wunderbar!"*

The landscape and the cities of my native land rolled past me, as they had for the last five years. It all looked innocent enough, but the clicking of the rails evoked the rhythmic sound of past anxieties. It was an insistent music of misleading lullabies: Humperdinck's *Hänsel and Gretel,* Mozart's *Magic Flute,* Beethoven's *Fidelio,* "The Horst Wessel Song," *"Deutschland Über Alles,"* Christmas carols, Wagner's *Lohengrin,* pieces from Bach cantatas, *"Die Internationale,"* German drinking songs, and bits and pieces that changed as the train slowed down or entered a tunnel. Outside, the landscape recalled the innumerable fears and panics of the past and present. I was not at all certain that my supposedly "happy" childhood had ever been anything but full of apprehensions and disturbances. The sheltered nest on Emma Strasse had been a fool's paradise.

The chimneys of passing houses suddenly reminded me of an early terror. My small bed at Kaiser-Wilhelm-Ring had been fitted into an alcove created by just such a chimney that traversed the entire building. The brick had been concealed by beige wallpaper with a distinctive black linear pattern. The paper had bulged in some places, and in the area just above the headboard an entire piece had been ripped off. The shape thus created became a part of my pre-sleep fantasies that finally became fixed on the appearance of a ferocious monster, perhaps a crocodile. My mother had finally covered the ogre with a sheet of white paper to alleviate my fears. As far as I was concerned, the beast was still there, waiting to escape from its temporary confinement. Memories of past demons succeeded each other without chronological order. As I grew up, some private fears occurred only in feverish dreams, but the new presence of terrors and barbarism perpetrated by human beings upon each other under the guise of one kind of idealism or another had become an almost daily experience. They ran parallel with all the pleasant and warm events of childhood and adolescence. Love and laughter provided a potent antidote, but never immunity, to that ever-present pulse of slithering danger.

It occurred to me that there was no reason to assume I had been singled out for this affliction. Surely, each and every one of the passengers who sat in that third-class compartment from one train stop to another carried his own invisible cage of nightmares with him. For a lot of them the solution to their anxieties was the illusion created by the swastika. They had been told, and they believed, that there was a collective way of unloading their private demons onto others. But I was leaving and they were staying. As the train sped toward the border of this fear-ridden landscape I could, almost physically, feel an old skin, calloused and inured to anxiety, begin to peel off my body. Still, I could not be certain at all that I would not have need of another kind of armor in the life to come to which I was now traveling.

At the border, in Aachen, I got more than the usual attention from the green-uniformed robots who ordered everyone else out of my compartment, to

pore over all of the necessary documents, my passport and the luggage. "Aha
. . . you are emigrating . . . you don't like the Vaterland? . . . you're a Jew, aha,
the great United States of America, that fruit salad over there deserves your kind.
. . . Open your bags . . . all of them. . . . Well, well, at least you are going to
be a very well-dressed *Ausfahrer* (emigrant). . . . We don't have time to inspect
all of that. . . . Only one way to do it . . ." The open suitcases were overturned
and the contents strewn all over the floor and seats of the compartment.

"Everything on the floor . . ." Shiny boots walked over, and probed through,
my belongings. That took care, among other things, of my fancy "American"
hats. . . . "Nothing to declare, hey? . . . some of this stuff seemed brand new
. . . but now most of it looks as if it had been used. . . . You can start packing,
but you'd better hurry, the other passengers will want their seats back." They
smiled at me and at each other, obviously congratulating themselves on a patriotic
job well done.

I stood at an open window of the laboring train's corridor, looking at the
passing thickets of woods leading to the plateau of the Ardennes. I had hiked and
camped in those woods as a youngster, often hearing gunfire from German border
guards who were chasing furtive smugglers of coffee, cigarettes, and other high-
priced import items who had come across the nearby line of Belgium. I was
waiting for that border line, and when it came in the form of a marker near the
railroad track, I closed my eyes and thanked somebody. I was almost disappointed
not to have heard the expected snap of a gigantic trap that had closed just a
second too late. The rails had been silent to me for quite a while now, but
suddenly I hummed along with them a passage from Bach's Cantata 147, "Jesu,
Joy of Man's Desires." I immediately reprimanded myself for such sentimental-
ity. I might just as easily have imagined myself as Tamino in Mozart's opera
bravely playing his flute as he successfully underwent Zarathustra's final test of
fire. Nothing really dramatic had occurred, except perhaps, the image of less than
an hour ago. The contents of my baggage being ground into the dirt had left me
strangely unaffected because the only "declarables" that I was taking with me
were seventeen years of my life. No license for transport across any border has
as yet been defined for the magic valise that holds these permanent possessions.

As I stepped off the train at the Gare du Nord, I realized immediately that
whatever I had hoped to leave behind might confront me wherever I was finally
going to live. Paris, for instance, was engulfed in a gigantic traffic jam on both
sides of the Seine. Adherents of the Croix de Feu and other right-wing organizations had been celebrating their now complete victory over "Le Front Populaire."
Scattered remnants of the massive demonstrations were still roaming the streets
and shouting slogans against foreigners, Jews, Bolshevists and Algerians. Some
groups seemed to be escorted by mounted police, who in two instances that I

witnessed protected and separated them from equally vociferous counterdemonstrators. On that evening very few Parisians sat in sidewalk cafés to enjoy the mild, late spring air of the city.

My mother and the same group of friends whom I had seen on many of my previous visits had taken refuge in Lou Straus-Ernst's hotel room. Somehow this group, like so many others in similar cubicles, had come in from an inclement atmosphere; and Lou, who seemed to wear stripes of optimism on her sleeves, had become their angelic anchor whenever the waters of despair and loneliness rose to threatening heights.

They were still playing their endless rumor games about the day after tomorrow being the end of the bad dream. For the first time I talked back to them and asked them why they were not sitting in their favorite café tonight. Were they afraid of those placards: à BAS LES JUIFS? Had the riots in the streets of their beloved Paris been merely a French affair? To the argument that I had no proof that America lacked potential fascists, I responded that I was equally doubtful that its streets were paved with gold but that I had reasons for optimism about a country where a Jew, Herbert Lehman, had been elected Governor of its most populous state.

Pretending to be very brave, I lectured to them, somewhat theatrically, that I did not want to sit in the same dead tree with them while there was fire all around in the forest. "Hitler, Mussolini, Himmler, Göring, Horthy, and Stalin . . . they are all going to die . . . but not when you want them to. I have been listening to your fantasies for over five years now. You probably talked that way even before, when you were still at home. You were afraid then, but as far as you were concerned, it was all going to change the way you wanted it to." Masking my own uncertainty of what life might be on the other side of the Atlantic, I said, striking a pose, "I'm just not going to wait for any more of your miracles."

Lou scolded me later for what she interpreted as insensitivity toward her friends' problems as well as for my rhetoric, which she characterized as "a bit too pompous for your age and lack of experience." I told her that I had really been addressing myself to her. I was urging her again, I said, and I would keep on doing so, to follow me as soon as possible. She silently shook her head and then began to reiterate all her doubts and fears that I had heard so often before. "Anyway, not right now. Maybe later . . . and probably it won't be necessary at all. . . . It can't last; it will have to go away because . . . well, it just will not be able to continue. It is feeding on itself—"

I stopped her: "No, it is not feeding on itself. Our bodies and our souls are available to them like the vegetables and fruits in the carts and stores on the sidewalks of the rue Mouffetard every Sunday morning."

She looked at me, startled. "You are growing up terribly fast . . . all of a sudden. . . . You used to say things like this only when you had those high fevers as a child. Maybe they weren't just inventions of delirium. You sometimes constructed fables that could only have come out of situations between Max and me that you should have been too young to be aware of." I failed to make my point. There was so much more than an ocean between her world and America.

My father was in the midst of making a very important change in his life. He was turning his back on Paris and had finally completely broken with the Surrealists. He was tired, he told me, that minor squabbles within the group were constantly being blown up into major confrontations with their "conscience" André Breton. "I was a soldier once, and that was more than enough, and also that was in a different life. This is not the Army and, for me, there are no generals . . . and then all those little lieutenants and colonels around him." I guessed that there had been other "banishments" and "reconciliations" like the one in 1926. He filled me in a little bit on the interpersonal schisms among the Surrealists following the profound changes in Moscow. Éluard had refused to emulate Breton's enthusiasm for Trotsky, and his friends were urged to avoid him. He could not have been as doctrinaire or unvarying a follower of Stalin because that might indeed have strained his close relationship with Max, who always disdained commitment to the discipline of any political party. As part of his final break with the Surrealists as a group, Max had decided to move away from Paris. He had acquired a group of abandoned buildings at Saint-Martin d'Ardèche near Avignon and had moved there with Leonora Carrington. He was remodeling the structures with his usual personal whims, using a church and the post office as studios, and embellishing both the interior and exterior walls with reliefs and sculptures made of concrete. Here he hoped to establish for himself and his great love, in his own words, "a little bit of peace." And indeed one of his most powerful works of that period is a large canvas appropriately entitled *Un Peu de Calme*. In the light of this, my suggestions to him concerning his personal safety in Europe evoked nothing more than a slightly quizzical annoyance.

He had come to Paris especially to spend some time with me before my departure. One evening he took me again for dinner at the Cloiserie des Lilas. Somewhat awkwardly he characterized the evening as possibly being "our last supper." It turned out to be a long and memorable occasion. In fact, it was the fulfillment of a dream that eludes so many fathers and sons of almost aimlessly touching on the innumerable facets of a common past, thoughts and ideas concerning the present and the necessarily ambivalent projections into the night to come, a synonym for what is optimistically called "the future."

Initially neither one of us was very comfortable. We were talking about things that, in fact, were over and done with. But now geographical distance was about to be added to the usual distance between us. Perhaps the thought of absolute finality was very much in the air. Max described himself as a "raven's father" who leaves the nest once his young have been hatched. He tried to describe his life and work to me as being incompatible with any accepted norms of family life. "If Lou had allowed our marriage to resume in 1923, everyone involved might well have had a miserable life. She knew it, and we should be glad that it was she who said No to that idea. . . . Cologne and Germany were stifling to me even then and even Paris, where I belong, could not have meant any happiness for you or provided an undisturbed childhood. . . . Don't ever think for a moment, though, that you were an unwanted child."

As he spoke in this manner it occurred to me all of a sudden that my father seemed to be a man who was a stranger to his own personality, or at best a mere observer of it. And again, more forcefully now, I saw him as someone so strongly dominated by a particular reality, alien to most ordinary humans, that accepted norms of judgment could not possibly apply to him. This discovery washed over me with something resembling relief. At that moment I began to understand more completely the nature of his work and the strange detachment with which he had conducted important phases of his personal life. I could sense in him the awkwardness and even embarrassment caused by his attempt to explain himself to me, as an artist and as a father. Until now I had ascribed our tenuous relationship to his obvious fear of excess sentiment, lives separated by time and distance, and my own prejudice-fed immaturity. The fragile bridge between us, which he had thus strengthened, even though it must have been a painful and difficult gesture for him, became an almost physical reality. I crossed it willingly and instinctively stopped him short after he remarked, "You know, I am not entirely without a conscience. . . ." I told him, with just a little lack of inner conviction, that "good" fathers were a dime a dozen, that I had observed them in the homes of my school chums and had found them to be tyrants of whom I wanted no part. "Ah yes," he interjected, "like your grandfathers Philipp and Jacob." I went further by confessing to him that, despite Lou's admonitions to the contrary, I had formed an image of him that had made no allowances for fact and reason.

"Yes, you were pretty impossible with me at times." He grinned. "It could well be something you inherited from me. . . ."

"All the more reason," I replied, "that we did not live under the same roof while I was growing up." He fixed me with a mock severe mien. "Yes, but it might have spared me the embarrassment of being 'discovered' by you via Picasso's *Guernica.* We both laughed at each other openly. The ice was broken.

We engaged in some uninhibited sentimental recall of past vignettes. Perhaps it was the wine but I prefer to think that it was a new atmosphere that released some intimate, if unimportant anecdotes.

Max talked about Lou's brave but often disastrous efforts in the kitchen, which had to be rescued by Maja, who was perfectly willing to feed her and me but not him. "She never approved of me. She disliked me more than did Jacob Straus." He talked of my early willingness to call any man who came to visit or eat with us "Dada," as a result of which he insisted that I call him "Max" while I was learning to distinguish between my real father and merely friends. Strangely enough, he noted, I never had such difficulties with any women who might be in the apartment. Anyway, ever since then it had been "Max," and he felt more comfortable with it than with any variation of "Father." When as a baby I had wetted Paul Éluard's lap, which, according to Max, Paul had tried to characterize as the "human condition," it had infuriated his wife Gala. She had interpreted it as Lou's protest at her presence and this had in fact delighted Lou because Gala was not an altogether welcome guest in our home. The final blame rested with Maja, who had neglected to diaper me at the proper time. Max also remembered that I had a disconcerting habit of offering candy or a piece of cake to anyone who had come for lunch or dinner, only to scream my head off if my offer was taken seriously, as Hans Arp once did. Tzara, allegedly, did not lose his composure for a second when I smeared chocolate mousse all over his face.

My own memories of Max did not, of course, go back quite that far, except perhaps to that important day in Tyrol in 1922 when I was just two years old. I asked him if he remembered, at all, standing in that lake up to his waist and my vociferous refusal to have him hold me? And was it true that it was on that very day he had told Lou that he was leaving to join Gala and Paul Éluard in Paris? Yes, he remembered, but only vaguely until Éluard had recalled it to him. But strangely, I had stopped being a lovable baby almost from the day he had moved across the stairway landing to live, more or less constantly, in their apartment rather than with Lou. It had puzzled him that anyone so small had such a bourgeois reaction to the behavior of his father. After all, he saw me every day and tried to play with me and he was away only while I was asleep. "But then, on the other hand," Max said, "I was very jealous as a child when I was told that my mother had given birth to another daughter. My pet cockatoo died that same day, and I blamed it all on my new sister."

As we left the restaurant, he asked me to come with him to the studio. "There isn't much furniture left, but I have a bottle of champagne and we'll have a drink to celebrate your trip to America." We walked a long way through a warm Paris night, as if we were old pals who had spent a night on the town.

The apartment on rue Jacob was, indeed, quite bare by now. There were just some cots, a few packing cases and a hobby horse on which Max had been photographed by Homer Saint-Gaudens for a *Life* magazine story. Some paintings were still leaning against the walls. I had never seen Leonora Carrington's work. It was quite amazing in its unique Surrealism. Imagined lunar landscapes broken up by deep green waters, peopled with mysterious young women, horses of an unmistakably sensual character. An unfinished double portrait of herself and Max in which he was enveloped in the costume of a gentle rooster and holding an antique lamp.

Carrington, only three years older than I, had defied her very prominent British family in running away with Max. They had never ceased in their efforts to separate the two in any way possible. They had gone so far as to influence British authorities to issue a warrant for Max's arrest, on charges of exhibiting pornographic paintings in London while he was on his way there. It was only with the help of Roland Penrose that he escaped discovery by the police during what had to be a secret stay there.

"All I want now is to leave Paris for a long time and live with Leonora in Ardèche . . . and to love her . . . if the world will only allow it."

We finished the bottle by the dim light of a dismal ceiling fixture, drinking from coffee cups. . . . Yes, he did look like a bird. But not just one particular kind. That night he was all of the birds, except the carrion-eaters. His face and stance became that of an eagle when in anger, a wise raven with the smirk of a joke at the corners of the bill, or a horned owl retreating into watchful silence.

"I didn't really enjoy seeing André Breton punch Ilya Ehrenburg in the nose on some street corner a few years ago," Max said after a while. Breton had reacted to Ehrenburg's calling the Surrealists "a bunch of pederasts" because they had failed to line up in support of Stalin. "I punched Massimo Campigli myself because he liked Mussolini, and I realized right afterward how much I really despise physical violence. Every time you allow yourself to do that, you are in danger of becoming just as despicable as the other guy. Ehrenburg is an untalented hack who had to sell out to that monster Stalin. It was bad enough for him that he could not deliver us to his master. And the world is full of Campiglis, pimps of fascism. I shouldn't have dirtied my hands. Something strange happens when artists sit at the feet of men who can survive only by killing ideas. Poor Dali, he pretends that he is insane and that this entitles him to see mystery in royalty and Franco. And poor Braque, he dreams of the Croix de Feu and keeps painting the *Tricolore*."

Remaining within the Surrealist group right now, he said, would be as bad as attending morning mass, making the sign of the cross or going to confession. He did not want to become an enemy to his friends just because it did not bother them as much as it did him to allow one individual to confer benediction on them. And there was another danger: the word "revolution" was being abused and distorted. Any of the prophets, particularly those on the left, who demanded unquestioning obedience in return for the promise of "a new dawn" were either charlatans or potential traitors to their own ideals. "When Martin Luther posted the ninety-five theses on the church doors in Wittenberg, he started a blood bath that merely replaced one kind of corruption with another."

He was convinced that there were choices other than on which side of a battle line one was to become a cadaver. "But I don't want, and I don't expect, tranquillity. That only happens in sleep without dreams." Much of what I heard that night was known to me only superficially. I was aware, of course, that most intellectuals looked to the left for the only possible antidote to Europe's menacing fascism, but I was only vaguely cognizant of their growing bitter disillusionment, as that hoped-for image of humanism and equal rights became stained and blurred. To demand unquestioning faith in an idea that so far had produced mostly blood and repression became increasingly unacceptable, particularly to painters, poets and philosophers who found their work and opinions impersonally scrutinized by political *fonctionnaires*. The conflicting reactions to these bewildering events would haunt generations to come. Some of these ideological battles are still being reenacted, over and over again, with ever-changing ground rules, perhaps, but with painfully familiar-looking tin soldiers.

The impact of Guernica on me had only been the beginning. I should have realized that the abusive treatment of "degenerate art" in Germany was far more than the excessive behavior of a bunch of strutting psychotics. Listening to my father, it dawned on me that he was not voicing any petty personal complaints. The creation of a work of art, regardless of its final outward appearance, was inevitably also a political act. I have thought of that night often.

In the two weeks that remained in Paris I tried to form an image of what America might look and feel like, from whatever source available.

Europeans, out of wishful thinking perhaps, had looked upon Franklin Roosevelt as America's answer to Adolf Hitler ever since his inauguration, which had taken place ten days before Hitler's coming to power in 1933. The French press limited its reportage from the United States mainly to its President and his efforts to overcome the lingering aftereffects of the Great Depression. Apart from reports of massive sit-down strikes in the automobile industry and the vagaries of the climate in that distant nation—tornadoes in Kansas or terrible floods in California and Ohio—the main concern of the newspapers was with America's foreign policies. There had been dismay when, during the past year, the Neutrality Act had been written into law, seeming to dash all hopes of help from overseas if and when Hitler were to attack in Europe. Roosevelt's decision to remain neutral in Spain's civil war had been depressing, but Roosevelt in his recent statements seemed to be swinging toward a less isolationist attitude vis-à-vis Europe. Former President Hoover had warned against that, and he strongly counseled that under no circumstances should the United States make "alliances" with any openly "anti-fascist" government in Europe and thus take part in another conflict "over there." A congressional resolution, leaving the choice of war or peace to a national referendum in each instance, had failed to be enacted, but the Naval Expansion Act of 1938 provided for a ten-year build-up of America's armed forces.

Culturally, little was reported to the European public. Europe still looked down its nose at American literature and its arts, except for the movies. America produced magnificent athletes such as Joe Louis, Eleanor Holmes, Peter Fick and Donald Budge. The names of Faulkner, Hemingway, Anderson, Steinbeck and Dos Passos were talked of in cafés by cognoscenti, but little was written about them in the popular press. There was very little interest in America's visual arts. Max had noted, for instance, that there had been some interesting paintings done in the nineteenth century by the Hudson River School and that Bouguereau's nudes had drawn big crowds for reasons other than art, but for the most part "civilized" Americans did their social climbing with French Impressionist paintings. There were some brave people. Julien Levy's gallery in New York had shown Max and other Surrealists fairly early. And then there was a very interesting man whom he hoped I would meet—Alfred Barr—who had spent a good deal of time with him, selecting about forty-eight of his works for the "Fantastic Art, Dada and Surrealism" exhibition in 1936 at the Museum of Modern Art.

By coincidence an exhibition organized by that same Museum of Modern Art, "Three Centuries of American Art," had just opened at the Jeu de Paume. The critical response in the press had been devastating. Perhaps the organizers of the show had spread things a bit too thinly in order to accommodate the work of three centuries in painting, sculpture, graphics, architecture, photography and film. The Parisians evidently paid little attention to the show. The galleries were always quite empty when I was there, and I went many times to see that aspect of life in the country where I hoped to make my way. The walls of the Jeu de Paume did indeed seem inhospitable to the mercilessly factual work of Eakins, the restrained elegance of Whistler or a moon-lit Ryder. Of the contemporaries, I recall in particular Edward Hopper's *House by the Railroad Tracks*, an almost frightening juxtaposition of slightly shabby Victorian charm with the industrial age. Joseph Stella's *Brooklyn Bridge* stood out in its poetic tribute to American engineering. Arshile Gorky's strong painting had a distinct European flavor, and Ben Shahn's *Six Witnesses* from the "Sacco and Vanzetti" series seemed to owe a great deal to George Grosz and Otto Dix. I realized, however, that I was making judgments out of ignorance and a predilection to the art that I had grown up with and, in fact, became quite angry when I heard someone remark that Stuart Davis' *Landscape with Garage Light* was nothing more than ". . . a sterile illustration by an artist who doesn't understand Cubism. . . ." The most striking experience for me was the encounter with two totally different paintings, both of which were drawn from contemporary life. One was *Daughters of Revolution* by Grant Wood. I wondered if and where I would ever be in the presence of these three pinch-faced ladies who were raising their teacups with grim prissiness, as if to ward off some unbidden intruder. In direct contrast was a painting by Alexandre Hogue, *Drouth Survivors*. I had read about the catastrophic sandstorms that had blown away the soil on innumerable farms right from under the plows in Kansas and Oklahoma, forcing a sea of bedraggled humanity on a long trek to an inhospitable California. The Hogue painting showed an abandoned tractor half-buried in a mound of sand, the dead vestige of a shrub, a torn barbed-wire fence, a gopher about to disappear into his hole, two emaciated dead cattle, and a gigantic, live rattlesnake sidling up to one of the carcasses. Beyond it, to the horizon, a desert landscape of nothing but sand.

I don't recall if these two paintings were hanging side by side, but they might as well as far as I was concerned. Was this indeed a land of such enormous contrast? Did these two images imply other awesome manifestations of America's vastness and the way of life of its millions?

The section on architecture was fascinating. Skyscrapers such as the Chrysler and Woolworth buildings did not exist on my continent. Any building in Europe that exceeded six or seven stories in height became an immediate tourist attraction. In our cities and towns it was the church steeples that pointed their fingers into the sky, but New York and Chicago resembled the complicated monoliths that I had created out of wood blocks in my room in Cologne with the constant fear that someone would slam a door and the whole structure would collapse as if in an earthquake. In just another three weeks I was going to be right there, and my awe of America's scale kept growing. The section of photography showed me the soaring bridges, the rivers, the Rockies, the deserts, the slums and Park Avenue, the black man and the white man, the Indians, the Chinese, people from the Mediterranean basin, Slavs, proper Bostonians, coal miners, farmers and, yes . . . beggars. How would one live over there without becoming a mere dot on a crowded street during the heat of summertime in New York?

I had pushed the fact that I could not even speak the language into the deep recesses of my consciousness. Things were getting awfully close, and I began to re-experience those almost forgotten fears that had kept me awake on the nights before a crucial Latin exam for which I should have studied. No longer any movies with translated subtitles. Nothing, in fact, was going to have subtitles.

I saw a number of American films at the time that added to the confusing image. A portrait of the slums, *Dead End*, was a sensation in Paris. There were demonstrations outside the theater against social injustice in the United States.

Billy Halop, Leo Gorcey and the other Dead End Kids became the subject of lively café-house conversation. I sat through it three times. *Stand-In* showed Humphrey Bogart, this time joining forces with Leslie Howard and Joan Blondell in trying to save a movie studio on the verge of bankruptcy. A 1933 film, *Man's Castle*, with Spencer Tracy and Loretta Young, described life in a Hooverville on what must have been the banks of the Hudson River around George Washington Bridge. Tracy was eking out a living, walking up and down a crowded nighttime Broadway in top hat and elegant tails, his starched shirtfront flashing advertising messages to the passing crowd. Madcaps Fredric March and Carole Lombard hated and loved each other in *Nothing Sacred*. Mickey Rooney and Spencer Tracy activated the tear glands in a story about abandoned youths in *Boys Town*. Robert Taylor, Judy Garland, George Murphy and Robert Benchley danced, gagged or sang their way through the hard-to-believe glitter of *Broadway Melody 1938*. I absorbed it all hungrily, including the hour-long Disney *Silly Symphonies*, which newsreels theaters had found to be far more acceptable fare than floods, strikes, political melees and visiting statesmen interminably shaking each others' hands. There was the suave and imperturbably witty Melvyn Douglas coping with an unpredictable Irene Dunne in *Theodora Goes Wild*, James Cagney in the *Frisco Kid*, George Raft and Harry Carey in *Souls at Sea* . . . and more. I looked at everything that was being shown—at night, in the afternoon . . . anytime. . . .

Max and Leonora Carrington were having a "good-bye" aperitif with me at the Café Flore. She was trying to teach me some essential English phrases and words. "At least you will be able to find directions to get off your boat in New York. . . ." It became a little party. Some friends, strolling on the boulevard Saint-Germain, joined us—Paul Éluard, Hans Arp, Alberto Giacometti and Man Ray. Max telephoned my mother, and Lou joined us.

Man Ray got into an argument with Leonora. "You are teaching that boy British English. They'll laugh at him all the way down the gangplank. Here is what you're supposed to say . . . and listen to my pronunciation. . . ." Man Ray, a wiry, curly-haired, little bantam rooster of a man, with piercing, but not unfriendly, dark eyes, had come to Paris, a dedicated Dadaist, in the 1920s. He had made his transition to Surrealism with ease but retained in much of his work the spirit of Dada. His Rayograms, a photographic technique that he had developed using no lenses but merely the darkroom itself, were perhaps his major contribution to the Surrealist movement at the time. He was also famous for his fashion and portrait photographs, which appeared in *Vogue* and other elegant publications, but he became quite combative when he was called a "photographer" and even tried to downplay the Rayograms in favor of his paintings and altered found objects. Perhaps he felt a little uncomfortable in being somewhat more financially secure than his friends and peers. He was to become a lifelong friend and mentor, always ready with advice and opinions. Talking slowly so that I could understand his English, he told me: "Listen, kid, I was born in Philadelphia. That's where they say that they pull in the sidewalk at eight o'clock at night. I moved, of all places, to New Jersey . . . New Jersey? . . . Forget it. . . . Well, don't let me scare you. America is just a very, very big place, and you'll be surprised how much room there is for doing things and even thinking about them. You'll find people to whom you can talk. I found Stieglitz, and from then on it was like a pebble dropped into a lake. I didn't want to wait for any more little waves, and I came over here. But I think you'll find more going on there now than when I left. I've gone back a few times, and it's a mess, and you'll have to learn to do some swimming and hold your nose. Just look at what you're leaving behind. If we're still here in ten years, come to visit us."

All of a sudden the table talk stopped. On the sidewalk quite near the tables stood Marie-Berthe, staring at Max and Leonora. Max mumbled, "Oh no, not again. The last time she threw cups and saucers at us . . . another good reason to move away from Paris." Lou and I went over to talk to her. Marie-Berthe was surprised, she had not even noticed us. She began to cry as I kissed her, threw her arms around both of us to hide her face. We walked up and down the street a bit and I told her that I was leaving Europe in a few days. She took my face in her hands and kissed every part of it. "I promise, I will not make any trouble today. Now I am going into St. Germain-des-Prés and pray for your future in America." As she walked away, Lou and I looked at each other, and we were both ready to cry. Back at the café Lou gave Max a look that was a strange mixture of reproach and compassion. He responded with a weak shrug and then said to her, "I hope that this is not the way Jimmy will remember me after he's gone." I believe that I managed to smile and assured him with a slight shake of my head.

As the boat-train for Le Havre slowly pulled out of Gare Saint-Lazare, it was I and not my mother waving from the train window, on a voyage into an uncertain future. The last thing I saw was Max handing his handkerchief to Lou for her tears and draping his arm around her. She buried her face on his chest, continuing to wave as the train went into a curve of the track.

I went back to my seat which, in time-honored European tradition, I had reserved by placing my raincoat on it. The coat and my suitcase had been placed in the corridor outside the compartment. It was filled with American tourists whose tight-lipped expressions did not change when I protested the usurpation of my seat. I complained to the train conductor, who scratched his head and smiled. "Are you emigrating to America?" I nodded. "Well, you better get used to their ways. They wouldn't get up for a ninety-year-old crippled lady. Some of

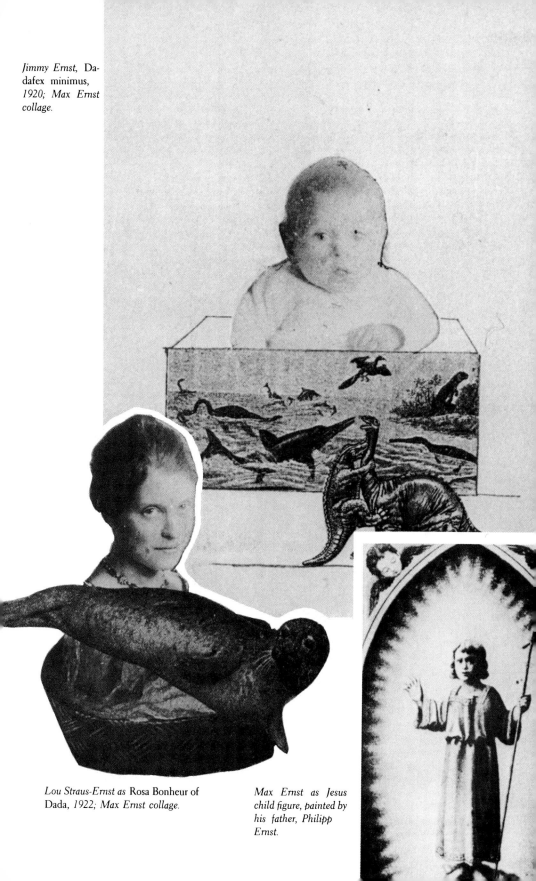

Jimmy Ernst, Dadafex minimus, 1920; Max Ernst collage.

Lou Straus-Ernst as Rosa Bonheur of Dada, *1922; Max Ernst collage.*

Max Ernst as Jesus child figure, painted by his father, Philipp Ernst.

Jimmy, 1922, Cologne.

Lou Straus, daughter of Cologne merchant, 1916.

Lou Straus, art student, 1918.

Max Ernst at 18, Bruhl, Castle Park, 1909.

Below: Hans Arp, Tristan Tzara, and Max Ernst, Tirol, ca. 1921. Roger Segalat.

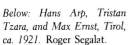

Max Ernst in his World War I uniform, painted by his father Philipp, 1915. Max, while on leave, kept painting out the Iron Cross.

Max, Lou, Uncle Richard Straus, Jimmy and housekeeper Maja, Cologne, 1921.

Lou, Paul and Gala Eluard, Max holding Jimmy, and the Eluards' daughter; Tirol, 1922.

Above: Gala Eluard wearing Max's Iron Cross, Max, Jimmy, Lou, Paul Eluard, Theodor Baargeld, in Max's studio, Cologne, 1921.

Above: Max, Gala and Paul Eluard, Tirol, 1923.
Roger Segalat.

Eluard, Max,
d Gala in Co-
logne, 1921.

Jimmy, Lou, Maja on a Sunday walk, Cologne,
1935.

Lou as a journalist covering Hindenburg's visit to
Coblenz to celebrate the
end of Allied occupation
of the Rhineland.

Lou working as gallery secretary, Cologne,
1927.

Gala Eluard with her daughter and Max when they lived with Paul Eluard in a ménage à trois in Eaubonne near Paris, 1924.

Below: Lou and Jimmy, Cologne, 1926.

Lou and Jimmy, Cologne, 1925.

Right: Jimmy in his cowboy costume, carnival in Cologne, 1925. Cowboys and Indians were among the favorite German myths.

Jimmy on twice-annual visit to Lou in Paris, 1933.

Cousins Karl and Emmi with Jimmy at Aunt Loni Ernst's wedding, Cologne, 1934.

Below: Renowned 1928 portrait by August Sander of Lou and Jimmy, part of the great photographer's life project, a photo portrait of Germany.

Lou and Jimmy on the Seine, Paris, ca. 1935.

Jimmy on a visit to Philipp Ernst in Bruhl, after morning mass, ca. 1934.

The Virgin Chastising the Infant Jesus Before Three Witnesses (Breton, Eluard, and Ernst), 1926. This painting was denounced by the Archbishop of Cologne.

Left: Lou in her Persian lamb hat that had been a collar the year before, a muff before that, a hem to start, Paris, ca. 1936.

Lou with Heinrich Augustin, owner of the German printing plant where Jimmy served as an apprentice, Paris, 1937.

Adolf Hitler, Josef Goebbels, and Professor Ziegler view the exhibition of "degenerate art," Munich 1937. Max Ernst's painting, La Belle Jardinière, second from left, was described in the exhibition catalog as "The German Woman Insulted."

Above: Lou with Otto Keller, Cologne, 1923.

Lou at La Coupole, Paris, 1937.

Max Ernst and his second wife, Marie-Berthe Aurenche, Paris, 1935. Photo by Joseph Breitenbach.

Lou Straus, watching Jimmy sail his boat, Parc Luxembourg, Paris 1937.

*Max Ernst in the 51st Street triplex he shared
with Peggy Guggenheim in New York, 1941.*
Photo by Arnold Newman.

Lou in exile, Paris, ca. 1936.

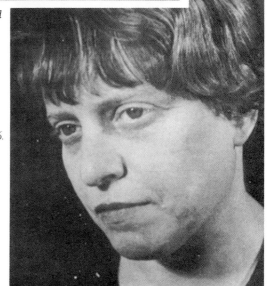

Max with Paul Eluard and Leonora Carrington, Paris, 1937.

Double Portrait *(the artist and Max Ernst) by Leonora Carrington, St. Martin d'Ardeche, 1940.*

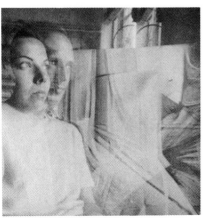

Left: Johannes J. (Hans) Augustin—he was the life raft.

Below: Jimmy working in the Museum of Modern Art Film Library, a still from March of Time, 1939. Photo supplied by Alfred Kleiner.

Double exposure, Jimmy and his future wife, Dallas Brody, with his painting, Dallas Blues, New York, 1947.

Group photo in Ernst-Guggenheim triplex, New York, 1942, Artists in Exile. Courtesy, Philadelphia Museum of Art, collection of Mme. Duchamp. Left to right, first row: *Stanley William Hayter, Leonora Carrington, Frederick Kiesler, Kurt Seligmann.* Second row: *Max Ernst, Amédée Ozenfant, André Breton, Fernand Léger, Berenice Abbot.* Third row: *Jimmy Ernst, Peggy Guggenheim, John Ferren, Marcel Duchamp, Piet Mondrian.*

At the Office of the Emergency Rescue Committee, Marseilles, 1939. Jacqueline and André Breton, André Masson, and Varian Fry arranging for departure to America.

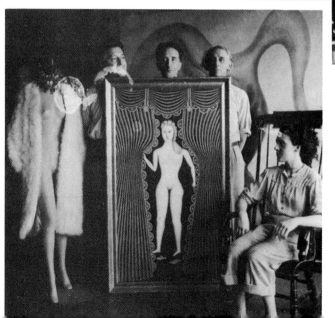

In the Ernst-Guggenheim triplex in New York. Peggy's feather coat on mannequin, André Breton, Marcel Duchamp, Max Ernst, Leonora Carrington seated, with a Morris Hirshfield painting, ca. 1942.

Dorothea Tanning and Max Ernst, Sedona, Arizona, ca. 1947. Photo by Ellinger, courtesy Maria Ellinger.

Dorothea Tanning and Max Ernst with the original of the famed Capricorn *sculpture, Sedona, Arizona, ca. 1948.* Photo: Kasnetis.

Jimmy with Dallas and children, Eric and Amy, with Capricorn, Sedona, Arizona, 1961.

John LaTouche in front of the bathroom mural on Minetta Lane; Jimmy's first commission, 1939.

Group photo of Ernst family, ca. 1909. Max Ernst, Emmi, Louise, another sister, Karl, Louise Kopp Ernst, Loni, and Philipp Ernst.

Salvador Dali garbage can, World's Fair, the Dali Dream of Venus Pavilion, 1938—a Surrealist peep show for the masses.

Pegeen Vail, Peggy's daughter, New Orleans, 1939.

Matisse gallery group photo, School of Paris in New York, 1942, Artists in Exile *by George Platt Lynes.* Photograph courtesy, The Museum of Modern Art, New York. From left to right, first row: *Matta Echaurren, Ossip Zadkine, Yves Tanguy, Max Ernst, Marc Chagall, Fernand Léger;* second row: *André Breton, Piet Mondrian, André Masson, Amédée Ozenfant, Jacques Lipchitz, Eugene Berman;* back row: *Pavel Tchelitchew, Kurt Seligmann*

Au Rendez-vous des amis, *Max Ernst, 1922.* Courtesy,Wallraf-Richartz Museum, Cologne. Left : *1.Rene Crevel 2. Philippe Soupault 3. Hans Arp 4. Max Ernst 5. Max Morise 6. Fedor Dostojewski 7. Rafaele Sanzio 8. Théodore Fraenkel 9. Paul Eluard 10. Jean Paulhan;* right: *11. Benjamin Peret 12. Louis Aragon 13. André Breton 14. Theodor Baargeld 15. Giorgio di Chirico 16. Gala Eluard 17. Robert Desnos*

Jimmy's artist friends, New York School. Nina Leen, Life Magazine © 1951, Time, Inc. *Top row, left to right: Willem de Kooning, Adolf Gottlieb, Ad Reinhardt, Hedda Sterne,* middle row: *Richard Pousette-Dart, William Baziotes, Jackson Pollack, Clifford Still, Robert Motherwell, Bradley Walker Tomlin;* seated: *Theodoros Stamos, Jimmy Ernst, Barnett Newman, James Brooks, Mark Rothko.*

our polite customs are alien to them. You can go in there and raise the roof, but it won't do you much good. You'll just have to sit on your valise at the end of the corridor. They are not bad people; they just feel that what is theirs, they'll keep."

I was in no mood to tilt at windmills and found a place where I could look out a window. I watched the suburbs of Paris trailing away into the broad flat landscape around the Seine. In the late afternoon light of an early June day, the serene green and yellow rectangles of farmland were interrupted occasionally by whitewashed towns or the hint of one where a church steeple protruded above modest hills. Cattle were bunched around water troughs, and farmers were bringing their horse-drawn equipment home. As the train slowed down near a village, I saw a soccer field with youngsters, about my age, in lively action. They shielded their eyes against the sun to watch the train go past. I could still see them from a curve in the trestle, much smaller now, back at play. An aproned woman was removing the day's wash from the line in the backyard of a farmhouse, clothespins in her mouth, oblivious to the clanking bell of the closed gate at the railroad intersection. Puffs of white smoke floated out of chimneys. Family dinners were being prepared. Scarecrows, their arms outstretched, pointed back to Paris and to the Channel beyond the horizon. One of them sported a spiked German helmet from the last war.

As it became darker, I saw not only the outside rolling by but also the reflection of my face in the window glass. It was an almost metaphysical experience, and the present began to be interlaced with images of the past, unreeling behind my eyes. I saw myself on just such a soccerfield as I had seen. But when had that been? I was going to be eighteen in a few weeks. Being a child or a young boy had stopped abruptly some five years ago, when the door to the Emma Strasse apartment had slammed shut in my face. Play and camaraderie with other kids had taken on a different color from then on. Those inhuman, faceless monsters in the streets had stolen my childhood from me.

With rising anger and yet a curious detachment, I looked at my transparent countenance in the glass. How had I managed to live through what I had seen and what had been done to me without becoming a pathetic vegetable of fear and hatred? To be sure, I had shaken with terror and fury at the sight of bearded Hasidim, their women and children, on their knees, scrubbing sidewalks on a Sabbath surrounded by roaring Brownshirts and giggling burghers of Cologne. I had witnessed the burning of the Weimar Republic's flag and large stacks of books in my "Wild West" playground behind the church; I had seen a marching troop of Hitler Youth suddenly breaking rank, overturning and setting fire to the newspaper kiosk of a blind Jew; the smashing of synagogue and church windows in full daylight as traffic and commerce continued at their usual pace and nearby policemen watched with amusement. As it happened, I knew that it was being done to me as well, but if I trembled in fear or resentment I was also curiously aware of not showing it. Was I, like so many others, merely a coward in the face of a lost battle? Would it have been different if some of us had fought back?

Retrospective self-pity suddenly gave way to a towering rage. I pressed my forehead against the windowpane. "Fatherland, dear Fatherland . . . it's not over yet. I will live to see you die, choking on your own slime and stink, even as you strut through the wasteland that once was my home."

It was too dark now to see anything other than my own face and the train corridor behind me. For a moment I thought that I was on one of those trains that had so often taken me back to Germany.

I lowered the window sash. There was a hint of the North Sea as the air rushed past. I was going in a new direction. At the end of this long voyage it would be entirely my own doing to make what I could of my life. I was only a small drop in the large river of human beings who were taking their lives to the same land, for the same reasons. Whatever I had lost would have to be rediscovered in a new context. One thing was certain. I would not awaken each day to face an outcast in the mirror. Everything else was unimportant. Without erasing the past, I would have to cut my ties to it. I had become an alien in the place of my birth. But I was not fleeing into exile; perhaps I was going home.

America

The land is within.
At the end of the open road we come to ourselves.

LOUIS SIMPSON

THE S.S. *Manhattan*, flagship of the United States Lines, was not as large and luxurious as some other liners that competed on the Atlantic run to New York. Boarding it was nevertheless an adventure that, until now, I had only read about in slick magazines or seen in films. Tourist class consisted almost entirely of emigrants, and the English language was rarely heard during the crossing. The menus were printed in German, and the dining room with its white tablecloths, handsomely laid-out cutlery, and a profusion of stewards and waiters presented an elegance that few of the passengers had ever experienced. The crew, mostly German, or German-speaking, seemed surly and contemptuous. From early on we knew what they thought of *diese Auswanderer* (these emigrants) who were so stingy with their tips. The cabin space was also less than glamorous, somewhere deep down in the ship. I shared mine with two men, one a butcher from Breslau going to Chicago, hoping for a job in the stockyards; the other a tailor from Dresden, expecting to work in New York's garment district. The tailor wanted to reserve the cabin for certain hours of each day for himself alone to entertain the many women he hoped to find aboard. The butcher tried to interest me in escorting his two daughters to the movies or the after-dinner games, to give him a chance to visit his wife in another cabin during evenings. My refusal to go along with the wishes did not sit well with my cabin mates.

Initially the mood among the passengers was subdued. The dining room was filled with strangers, all of them with a common purpose and the same destination. Whatever had happened in their lives that had brought them on this voyage seemed to have made them suspicious of everyone except their immediate families. There was much swaggering and bragging by some who apparently refused to acknowledge that they were indeed "in the same boat"—the inevitable little pretensions to social superiority, talk of rich relatives "over there" and feigned annoyance of having to go "tourist" because first class had been filled up. Gradually, however, these masks evaporated. The onset of the meal was held in abeyance out of a heretofore absent respect for those around a given table who wore skullcaps and said their prayers. The open Atlantic was bringing families and individuals into larger groups on the deck and in the lounges. There was talk of quota numbers and how long it had taken to get them, of friends and neighbors left behind, of houses, apartments and furniture representing a lifetime of comfort that now probably belonged to some Nazi. The outrageous German tax on emigrants had left them little more than the amount for the fare and just enough to tide them over for the first few months in America. Very few talked of the country to which they were going. They did not know what to expect; they were just glad to have gotten out, and individual experiences and tragedies began to spill out. Almost all of them still could not understand how old acquaintances and business associates could have turned against them almost overnight after January 30, 1933. One woman told of the night when a Brownshirt had come to the door with a small black box which, he claimed, contained the remains of her husband, demanding a delivery fee. The ashes were in her luggage and she hoped that this was not illegal. "The steamship line had promised me a refund, in dollars, for the ticket that my husband never got to use." Some men talked of actually having seen Adolf Hitler. "I was this close to him and I could have killed him! . . . Maybe somebody will." There was a constant undertone of hope that things would suddenly change radically, offering them a chance for an early return to the homeland.

Usually at that point I could no longer listen. I had been hearing such farfetched dreams for years in Paris. I would take a turn around the deck, stopping at the stern of the ship, glad that Europe was now so far beyond the horizon. Still, the talk at mealtimes was mostly of the various news items from press-service sheets that were posted every morning on a big bulletin board in the lobby: Hitler's threats against Poland and Czechoslovakia; Goebbels describing Germany as an island of peace surrounded by hostile neighbors who were oppressing the good Germans of Alsace-Lorraine and the Sudetenland; drastic changes in the German military command over the last eight months and the possibility of a Wehrmacht coup d'etat against Hitler. I wanted more news about America. And there were indeed some interesting newsreel clips during the daily film showings. On a stormy afternoon, in an almost empty rocking theater, I sat through a two-hour documentary of an American Holy Grail called *The National Baseball Hall of Fame.* One of its idols, Babe Ruth, canonized in 1936, was given the major part of the footage along with Ty Cobb, Honus Wagner, and Walter Johnson. Baseball was a sport completely unknown in Europe, and the rules of the game seemed rather mysterious. Here were many thousands of people crammed into the stadium, roaring as if in unison and dancing in the aisles as the players ran from one point to another on a diamond pattern, after Babe Ruth had hit a small ball with an ungainly-looking stick. Other movie-glimpses of America showed Hollywood stars at a place called Grauman's Chinese Theatre pressing hands and feet into slabs of wet cement. The newsreels usually ended with a funny-looking man by the name of Lew Lehr apparently describing the antics of some chimpanzees. I added "Monkeys is the cwaziest people" to my repertory of potentially useless English expressions.

The last meal on board before getting to New York was a strained and hectic affair. The waiters and stewards hovered near their tables with hawk eyes. Families engaged in fierce whispered conferences on how to satisfy these grim-faced characters. Some passengers tried to leave, nonchalantly, before the meal's end but were coldly reminded at the door that they had left no tip on the table. As the room cleared, the waiters counted the money carefully, stuffing it into their pockets without disguising their opinions about "those cheap bastards."

From the starboard side of the ship, as it moved through the Lower Bay, I had my first sight of land and houses. My map of Metropolitan New York pinpointed it as Brooklyn. Was that New York? Beyond, on the skyline and somewhat unreal because of a haze, were the towers of Manhattan. As the ship moved into the Narrows I could distinguish moving cars and the tiny figures of people strolling along the water's edge. This was June 9, 1938, an important date for me, and I wondered how long those on shore had already lived there and how they had gotten there. And then, as if a curtain had been lifted in a theater, lower Manhattan floated on the water. The fierce light of the afternoon sun reflected off these strange castles in gold, red, white, copper and turquoise hues. Windows facing to the southwest were flashing mirrors of almost blinding white light. Today these towering monoliths were not scraping any clouds. They crowded together on that small, seemingly fragile piece of land, stoically unaware of each other. Unlike the symbolic Gothic spires of my childhood, these totems violated the sky, their growth, as if stunted, coming to a seemingly abrupt end, emerging, seemingly from the surrounding water itself, with equal brusqueness. It was an image of utter self-assurance, a concept of order and logic for which no rules had as yet been written, defiant of human scale, with allusions, in stone, of impatience and cynicism toward ordained limitations.

Having seen the Statue of Liberty only from far away and in a haze, I rushed over to the port side, but that had just been cleared of all passengers. The public address system directed everyone to go to the lounges, below deck, for processing of their papers by the Immigration authorities. This foreclosed the tearful sentiment that I had expected to experience in my first encounter with the Lady of the Harbor.

I had a bit of a scare when the Immigration officer who was going through my papers called over several other people. They, in turn, read through my dossier, shook their heads, and I was told to step aside and wait until I was called. I sat tensely for about an hour with a number of other people whose examination had also come to halt. Their open expressions of fear and bewilderment had its effect on me. As it turned out, the question had arisen whether the address of Hans Augustin, my sponsor, really existed. Lafayette Street was not known to have residences of any kind. There was, in fact, only one building on that street with apartments. They were over a restaurant, and it was a historic building that had been the residence of Thomas Jefferson. Once that had been cleared up, I stepped onto the pier, where Augustin was waiting for me. He had brought along his office boy, George, with whom I was to work at the Augustin publishing office. He was also to be my mentor in the ways of America and the city and the improvement of my English.

Hans Augustin, or "J.J.," as George called him, gave me a short night-tour of Manhattan. George, who took his new role quite seriously, began my English lessons immediately. "Theater marquee," "movie house" "Dime a Dance." . . . He imitated the action as we drove around. Holding up his ten fingers, he explained, "Ten cents, you can dance with any dame. They're hoors, no good. . . . Times Square, biggest in the world, lot of bums. Bums drink cheap wine. . . . Forty-second Street; all streets go by numbers. This is Broadway." We stopped on a corner to pick up some newspapers. George showed me the head-lines. "*Daily News, Daily Mirror, The New York Times, The Herald-Tribune.* You know baseball? . . . I'll take you. The Giants, that's my team. The Yankees stink. . . . That's Fifth Avenue . . . very fancy . . . here's the Public Library . . . see those two lions? . . . biggest in the world. Look, the Empire State Building, one thousand two hundred and fifty feet . . . the biggest in the world . . . Fourteenth Street . . . that's Union Square, lots of Commies . . . talk, talk, talk . . . all day . . . always arguing. That's Fourth Avenue . . . uptown they call it Park Avenue . . . Wanamaker's . . . biggest department store in the world."

Augustin stopped him: "That's enough, George. To you everything is the biggest as long as it is in New York."

George was insulted. "Yeah, you foreigners, ya come over here and right away you know better than us who was born here." He turned to me: "Listen, don't kid around with guys who was born here." I was surprised and pleased that I could understand far more than I had expected to. "You're gonna be okay, kid. Just listen to George and do as he tells ya. You're not gonna be no greenhorn when I get through with ya. . . ."

"What's a greenhorn?"

"That's what they used to call guys like you, who just come off the boat. They used to sell 'em the Brooklyn Bridge. Don't go buying nothin' from nobody. Ask George first. I can get it for you cheaper." He slapped my back and giggled.

At J.J.'s apartment I did not even begin to unpack. I fell asleep almost immediately, and I don't remember having any dreams. I do recall a slight unease. George, before going home, had looked me up and down. "Who sold you that outfit? Geez, is that the kind of crazy stuff they wear in the old country?" So, if I dreamed at all, it was probably about that salesman in Hamburg. And that was only a hundred years ago. Wasn't it?

The very next day I was hard at work wrapping large parcels of books for mailing and delivery by hand. George loved having someone to boss around and teaching me English in the process. He also initiated me into the mysterious maze of subways and buses. The only thing that the I.R.T., B.M.T. and I.N.D. had in common with Paris' Métro was that they were underground for the most part. I was awestruck by the multitude of riders, the constant noise, the frantic rush for seats. Each stop had the almost warlike quality of a forced evacuation and the subsequent storming of the cars by victorious combatants. In the I.R.T. I had a chance to observe the "melting pot" that I had heard so much about. Since the riders faced each other along the two sides of the train, I became immediately aware of the great variety of facial characteristics that bore witness to the vast ethnic mixture in this city. I also observed that hardly any of the riders took notice of anyone else. If they were not reading, they might well look in your direction, but they seemed to be focusing on some spot beyond you over your shoulder. George nudged me. "Hey, stop staring at people." He was appalled when I offered my seat to a woman who had moved in front of me and held on to the overhead strap. "What's the matter with ya? You crazy or something?" The beneficiary of my instinctive gesture also appeared to be a bit surprised. I wondered if becoming an American would have to entail a change in my manners.

The train traveled, after a while, on elevated tracks. Craning my neck, I realized that the city had by no means ended. There were no skyscrapers here but blocks upon blocks of grimy buildings. People, many of them black, seemed to have moved their furniture onto fire escapes or were leaning out of windows. The fire escapes seemed to be quite rickety, and I was appalled to see small children playing on them, way above the street, without anyone watching them.

Lugging the packages from the station stop to their destination was physical labor that I was not used to. But walking back unencumbered by all that weight gave me a strange new kind of satisfaction. I was in America and I was working. At a candy store George treated me to a "Two Cent Plain" ". . . And put some chocolate in it . . . that's three cents more? Geez!"

J.J. Augustin, Publishers, was on the fifth floor of a building next to the Consolidated Edison Building on Irving Place and Fourteenth Street. The firm handled mostly the anthropological books and periodicals that I was already familiar with. I had come a full turn. I had set the type, had watched the printing and binding of many of these books, and now I struggled with large packages of them through subway turnstiles. A new venture for Augustin was a series of amusing state travel books, the first of which was Cartoon Guide to Arizona by Reg Manning, a well-known cartoonist for the Phoenix newspapers. It was very popular, and George and I dragged big mail sacks full of these books almost daily to the post office on Twelfth Street and Fourth Avenue.

One day, on the way back to the office, we walked into a luncheonette on the corner of Thirteenth Street. The proprietor yelled out, "Hi there, landsman."

With relief, I said, "Hey, George, this man speaks German. I won't have to go to the Automat when you're not around."

"Nah," he replied, "that ain't German, that's Yiddish."

J.J. had been planning to take an extended business trip to the Southwest and California toward the end of June. Gladys Reichard, one of my co-sponsors, had sent a message from Ganado in New Mexico, where she was doing field work on the Navaho reservation. She'd written that she thought it a good idea for me to see and meet the real native Americans before I got involved with a job and the life in New York City, so Augustin decided to take me along on his trip, as well as George as my mentor, tutor, translator and companion.

We traveled in J.J.'s Plymouth convertible, on various numbered routes through cities and states of whose existence I had not even known. Harrisburg, Pittsburgh, Columbus, Terre Haute, St. Louis, Kansas City, Joplin, Oklahoma City, Tucumcari are just a few of the places I can recall. Sometimes Augustin saw some booksellers and distributors or conferred with local cartoonists for subsequent guidebooks. For the most part, however, we were on the two-lane highway, going west, and we did not stop very long in any one place. I saw the rich rolling mountains and valleys of Pennsylvania with occasional oil derricks in pastures of peaceful cows, the mining towns and barren coal-mine tailings of West Virginia, the widely spaced, seemingly uninhabited, farm towns of Ohio, endless horizons of grain in Kansas. Strangely, though, the most lasting images were of the amusing verses on the staggered roadside signs for Burma Shave; billboards advertising Lucky Strike, Chesterfields, Sweet Caporals, Wrigley Spearmint Gum and automobiles called Graham Paige, Ford, Chevrolet, Nash and Frazier. Others exhorted us to drink Coca-Cola or Dr. Pepper. But most memorable of all for me was the yellow lettering on jet-black barnsides: MAIL POUCH.

Not too far beyond Pennsylvania, eating places on the road displayed arrows pointing to side doors marked COLORED. There were gas stations with separate toilets labeled WHITE and COLORED and dual drinking fountains as well. At one place George pulled me away: "Don't drink there. The guy'll get really mad. Can't you read no signs?"

Just outside of Santa Fe, obscured by a rise, we encountered a horse calmly standing in the middle of the road. J.J. was unable to stop in time and his radiator just caved in. The horse got back on its feet and trotted off. When the state police arrived, after we'd spent an hour or so waiting in the hot sun, J.J. complained bitterly about the presumption of the animal in blocking the road at that particular point. The trooper took us to a motel in town and cautioned J.J. that if they found a dead horse in the vicinity, the owner might demand damages, "unless the critter belongs to some Indian from around here." It took almost a week for the car to be fixed, which gave George and me a chance to splash in the motel pool every day and roam the streets of that charming old Spanish town.

Around the shady plaza and the La Fonda Hotel I saw elderly Indians, some of them wearing red ribbons in their hair. "Chiefs," George told me. They were selling silverware, turquoise necklaces and wrist-bands as well as small wooden dolls with feather headdresses, kachina dolls. One of them approached me, holding out his wares and mumbling something without raising his head. My "I don't speak English" was answered with "I wasn't speaking English." As he walked away from me, I could hear him clearly: "Damn tourist cheapskates!"

In the Spanish-style adobe-built museum I saw a large collection of kachina dolls from the Zuni and Hopi reservations, and *santos* (saints) and *retablos* carved by the people in the surrounding hills. They were the descendants of Coronado's expedition, which, marching north and east, had penetrated the continent as far as the plains of Kansas, then, not finding the promised cities of gold, had retreated back to Mexico to whence they had come. With the help of Augustin and George I managed to decipher some of the information posted about these very beautiful, but also very cruel and bloody depictions of religious themes. There were almost life-size, robed effigies of Christ with articulated arms and heads. And a ghostly skeleton with a tuft of white hair and grinning teeth, robed partially in black with marbles in the eyesockets, was seated atop a primitive wooden cart and aiming an armed crossbow. It was Donna Sebastiana, the angel of death who, during street processions, would cause the onlookers to cover their faces and turn away in order to avoid the arrow pointed at them. Other figures represented the Virgin floating on a blaze of carved sun rays; a dejected Job, his skin covered with sores and blood, seated in an open hut fashioned from a gasoline can; Saint George, his foot restraining a snakelike monster, the right arm raising a sword made from a kitchen knife. I instinctively recalled the Crucifixion panel of the Isenheim altarpiece by Grünewald wherein Christ is also covered with the sores from thorns, lashings and spikes driven through his hands and feet.

I was told that when the Franciscans left, after the Mexican-American peace treaty of 1848, they not only stripped the churches of all statuary and paintings but also deprived a devout population of spiritual guidance. The abandoned communities in those barren hills responded to their hostile environment by strengthening the sacrificial aspect of the Scriptures to the point where they engaged in an actual recreation of the Crucifixion each year. The honored man chosen to play the part of Christ in this all-too-real passion play was indeed nailed to the cross. Participants of nighttime processions did penitence by wearing crowns of thorns and self-flagellation. The *Penitentes*, as they called themselves collectively, began to fill their churches with statuary and paintings fashioned out of the roots of cottonwood trees and gesso compounds from the soil. They painted them in the colors of sun-parched skin, jet-black hair and eyes, the red of human blood and the purple of healed wounds. The order of Jesuits, who came to New Mexico when it was declared a territory of the United States, tried to modify the cruel religious rites and considered the *santos* and *retablos* unsuited for the interior of churches. I spent a great deal of time absorbing these images of stoically endured pain. These works were anonymous, the expression of a people rather than of isolated artists, and yet each one of them was highly individual, as if calling out from one soul to another. I wondered then, as I do now, if the proper creation and absorption of great art should not be based on anonymity rather than personalities. It was the Grünewald altarpiece and *Guernica* all over again, its immediacy and its universality regardless of motivating forces beneath. Parallel to these impressions and contemplations was the sudden awareness of a new breadth in the way I was thinking. This seemed to be the first time in my life that I was not guarding a free flow of perceptions and reactions in fear of an exterior threat. I no longer felt the recurring need to confine ideas within corridors of apprehension. Could it be that an invisible veil of eighteen years had vanished from my eyes and mind, lifted because it served no purpose in the spiritual space of the new world?

Basically the motivation for these *Penitente* images was alien to my thinking. The idea of a wrathful god demanding human sacrifice was as barbaric as the ethos of a people who had come to believe that the shedding of one's blood was the primary duty of a citizen. This art, however, went far beyond such dreaded clichés. For all of its anonymity I was being spoken to by individual human beings with a force that eclipsed mere dogma. I recalled something that Max had said to me on that evening, now only some six weeks ago. It was to the effect that artists who allowed their work to become the mere extension of a clergy or of an entrenched bureaucracy would have to descend to the level of unthinking illustrators. It was possible, he thought, for someone to be completely possessed by an ideological movement and find in it impetus for purely personal expression. For himself even that role was unthinkable.

The only Indians I had seen so far were the few old men selling trinkets outside the La Fonda Hotel in Santa Fe. On U.S. 66 out of Albuquerque there were roadside stands, every five miles or so, advertising pottery and jewelry: CHEAPEST PRICES. Shawled women sat with their backs to the highway, as if they did not expect anyone to stop. It was not until Gallup that I saw a larger number of America's original inhabitants. On a side street, parallel to the highway, I saw them lying in the gutters and on the sidewalks in front of shacks that were, in fact, liquor stores. The laws governing the sale of spirits to Indians were obviously being ignored. They stumbled through the street with bottles barely concealed in brown paper bags, oblivious to those who had passed out and were lying in their own vomit and blood. Here and there sat a shawled woman, huddled against some wall, waiting for her man to come out of his stupor. At one end of the street a covered truck marked NAVAHO PATROL began to throw some of these near-corpses onto the truck bed. Those drunks who managed to regain their feet were turned over to their women and tottered away. When he saw me, the driver leaned out of his truck window. "No place for you to be, white boy. Go where you belong."

Here was another first for me: the color of my skin. I had been made aware of it before in those roadside restaurants with their separate toilets and drinking fountains. Somehow it had not registered the way it did this time. I had thought of it then as a mere regional aberration. Was this really America? Certainly not. But then, it was also said that New York City was not America. Maybe there was no such thing. Could it be that the people and the landscape resembled each other? Craggy volcanic peaks, like decayed teeth, thrusting aggressively out of flat sagebrush country. Imperious cities challenging rivers and seas. Small towns, helplessly astride endless highways. Land so rich that its toilers had to battle to control it, barren fields studded with the rubble of long-gone mountains. Waters that swept entire communities into the next valley, deserts burning in the heat of the sun. Swamps with moss-covered trees that blotted out all light, snows that imprisoned humans for months on end. Deprivations and bonanzas, the seeds of myths and the mistrust of new faces. These thoughts had occurred to me near the town of Thoreau in New Mexico, where a sign by the road announced: CONTINENTAL DIVIDE. From this point on, I knew, all waters flowed westward. So vast was this land that its dramatic differences in geography and ecology resembled a string of alien nations under an endless firmament.

Nothing emphasized this awesome diversity more than when the Hubbel Brothers' station wagon took us, seemingly into the sky, onto First Mesa, the Hopi Village of Walpi. The Hubbels, an almost legendary family who ran several trading posts on the Hopi and Navaho reservations, had the consent of the Hopis to bring a small number of visitors to the annual Snake Dance. The ceremony was performed by richly painted dancers who to the insistent rhythm of drums and an almost monotone chant moved in a contracting circle toward a pit in the center of the village's plaza from which each man pulled a pair of writhing rattlesnakes. Holding the serpents aloft, one in each hand, the chant and the dance continued, punctuated by the drum and heavy bells affixed to the ankles of the stomping feet. In a double row they moved imperceptibly from one end of the plaza to the other. I found it incredible to witness these rites, the setting and the people in the same nation that had built the gigantic steel mills of Pittsburgh, Detroit's automobile industry and the sophisticated, mechanized cities of the East Coast and the Midwest. I looked at my feet and recalled that they had stood on the deck of the S.S. *Manhattan* only a few weeks ago. The spectators, most of them Hopi, stood on the roofs of the low adobe houses that bordered the plaza on three sides. Others watched from their windows and doors, or sat close to the walls. I stood with a small number of whites, and what I took to be Navahos, on the open side of the space that was also the very edge of the mesa, which behind me fell precipitously for several hundred feet. The view was breathtaking. In the distance Second Mesa, Shipolovi, and then Shongopovi rose just as suddenly out of the brownish-red land, the silhouettes of the villages blurred by the heat. As if in fear of falling, the crowd had moved closer to the dancers. The drumbeat and the dancers stopped and released the snakes, which promptly moved toward us. The people on the roofs found it very funny. It was not until we were back at a proper distance that the snakes were recovered and I found, with terror, that one or two more steps would have carried me over the cliff. The rites continued with the participants, at one point, holding the rattlers in their mouths. I did not see any of the men bitten. I was told that these snakes had indeed not been defanged, but that the dancers would chew an emetic of herbs to counteract any possible bites. After about half an hour the snakes were thrown back into the pit, and the dancing group walked, single-file, through a gap in the houses to the kiva, an underground ceremonial chamber. The interval before their reappearance was filled by four or five clownlike dancers who, by gesture and body posture, performed antics that left no doubt about their scatological nature. The delight and laughter of the people of Walpi made it obvious that the jokes, being acted out in very specific detail, had originated in the latrines of the village itself.

The ceremony continued, with the dancers returning to the plaza at regular intervals, until an orange moon began to rise through the haze of heat.

There was little time for me to digest this almost Surrealist spectacle properly, but at least I was one up on George to whom, as a big-city guy, this had also been a nerve-shattering first.

The following day we made our way in Augustin's car to Ganado on the Navaho reservation. It consisted of a Baptist mission, some homes for American Indian Bureau officials and two trading posts, one of which was owned by Lorenzo Hubbel. J.J., George and I paid a call on him and were invited by this expansive and friendly man for a Coke in his office. Sporting a large straw Stetson on the back of his head, he sat behind a big desk as he engaged in trade and one-sided banter with a group of male Navahos, whose only responses were short, gruntlike sounds accompanied by emphatic gestures of their chins toward sacks of flower, salt, sugar, beans and canned goods visible in the adjoining storeroom. Hubbel's desk was covered with stacks of beautifully handwoven blankets and piles of silver belt buckles, turquoise-studded brooches and necklaces. These were the items offered in exchange for food staples, rolls of cloth, iron skillets, tools and other necessities. The walls of the large room were hung with extraordinary blankets and saddle pads. In the corners were stacks of tightly woven, shallow wedding baskets. An almost bewildering variety of kachina dolls, some of them at least thirty-six inches tall with elaborate wooden or feather headdresses, crowded long shelves or hung in front of the blankets. Hubbel's animated features were in severe contrast to the stony faces of the Indians. The trading was conducted in what appeared to be a very leisurely manner, as if both sides had all the time in the world. If these men had come as supplicants, nothing in their bearing betrayed it. They exhibited neither anger nor elation when a final agreement had been reached. I don't know what they had gotten in exchange for their exquisite, hand-crafted wares, but they left the room with their air of dignity unchanged. I could see them through the door, receiving their goods from a clerk, loading them onto their horse-drawn wagons and driving off with their women and babies to their isolated hogans. At least, I had seen externally proud Indians, just as they had been described in the fiction of my childhood.

Gladys Reichard was not at all what I had imagined a professor of anthropology to look like. A rangy woman with a handsome, open face and slightly graying hair held in place by a beaded band, she wore dungarees, a blue work shirt and a kerchief around her neck, just like the men who had come to barter with Hubbel. She took us to where we were going to stay—in pup tents a few miles away, behind a hogan inhabited by Tom, a Navaho, and his family. Tom, whose last name I cannot remember, was an important member of his tribe, one of the few who had contact with the world outside, and a frequent member of delegations that went to Washington on tribal affairs.

Tom and his young sons spent most of their days tending their large flocks of sheep, and he had just returned from the forage and was leading his horse as we drove up. Since we were friends of Gladys Reichard, his welcome was much less taciturn than one would have expected from an Indian whose tribe members are known for being extremely taciturn toward outsiders. Before retiring we shared a meal prepared by the women of the family. It consisted of a mutton stew, ladled into earthenware pots from a large iron kettle, and corn on the cob, a very special treat because it had been brought in from the adjoining Hopi reservation with whom the Navahos were traditionally not on the best of terms. The meal was consumed with every male seated in a circle on the hard earth floor of the hogan. Afterward we sat on some benches overlooking the darkening land. There was very little talk. Tom smoked a hand-rolled cigarette; there was an occasional giggle from the youngsters, gentle noises from the tethered horses, and since there was no breeze, the windmill that drove the well had ceased its metallic clangs. The world from which I had come was more than oceans and thousands of miles away.

My growing, but still very fragile, accumulation of English grammar and vocabulary was barely put to the test. There is not much time for talking while riding on horses bareback save for a blanket, among hundreds of sheep in the company of very young Navaho boys. Like their elders, they talked hardly at all and apparently did not cherish a language other than their own. I had been hoisted, very thoughtfully, onto a very old and docile nag, who seemed to know exactly what he was supposed to do on command by the kids. Never having ridden a horse, I was terrified of sliding off, particularly when it came time to drive the sheep toward the water troughs beneath the skeletal windmills. During those on-and-off gallops the upper half of my body was often prone on the animal's back, with my arms around its neck. George did not do too much better, but he found some relief with an unending stream of curses. They were new to my vocabulary, but I was too busy hanging on to repeat them at first. After a few days of this I felt secure enough to join George and also to start giving commands to my horse as I remembered them. I made no impression on my noble steed. He had left the mark of his various bones all over my body, and I was amazed that I could walk at all and even sleep soundly. I thanked James Fenimore Cooper and Karl May for my childhood illusions about cowboys and Indians, but I wished that I could tell my almost forgotten playmates of the past what it was like to ride with real Indians over endless miles of stunted grazing land toward the next windmill on the horizon that extracted, almost painfully, the life-saving treasure of water from a hostile soil.

Now, some forty-odd years later, it seems to me that any immediate reaction to this landscape and its inhabitants should have been one of having landed on an alien planet. I probably should have found the isolated hogans and villages in the sky, built by tribes whose traditions had been formed over aeons of time, apparitions, not reality. Having just turned eighteen on the very day I was allowed to watch part of a Navaho sand-painting ceremony, I probably did not concern myself unduly with the the the means of the shift of my own past to such an unexpected present. At that time, I was probably so eager to push that past into oblivion that all of my senses recorded each visual and aural experience as if written on the blank pages of a new book.

It did not take me very long to see the stoicism and pride of these people as a final fortification against an alien culture that threatened to become visible any day now from almost all points of the horizon. Their wars had been lost, and now many of the tribes lived on land that nobody else had wanted. This impression was reinforced when we moved from Ganado to Oraibi. The Hopis had built their pueblos on the unassailable buttresses of the mesas and similar promontories rising abruptly from surrounding arid brushland. Walpi, Shipolovi, Shongopovi, Oraibi, Hotevilla, each one like a nation unto itself, suggested the ramparts of medieval castles. Old Oraibi, a butte, overlooking, as it were, its suburb New

Oraibi, is said to be the oldest existing settlement in the United States. The Hopis, generally smaller physically and more outgoing than their Navaho antagonists on the other reservation, miraculously coaxed the seemingly barren soil to provide them with a variety of staples such as corn, other vegetables and even peaches. Their summer rituals asked for the miracle of rain to give fertility to the soil, which was prudently tended between hillocks and in other natural topographic pockets below their villages.

Seeing a lone Navaho horseman moving in the distance toward his hogan at dusk or sitting with old Hopis against the wall of the trading post during the day, while the young ones were nearby at school, often provoked thoughts in this young Rhenish romantic about a time sequence that somehow did not relate to this continent; I wondered where this people had been when the Romans had conquered Teutonic tribes along the Rhine and founded Colonia Agrippina, Cologne, where some endless years ago I had played cowboys and Indians with my friends after school. I was shortly reminded that I was indeed in the United States of America and about to be introduced into the great mystery to all newcomers, the game of baseball.

One afternoon, as the large mesa of the old village cast a cooling shadow over Oraibi's equivalent of a central plaza, a bunch of Hopi boys were choosing sides for a ballgame. It seems that they were shy one man, and they gestured to me to stand at second base. All of this was done in their usual offhand, placid manner, and they obviously assumed that I would know what to do. I was lucky in the first inning. I saw no action in the field or at bat. In the second or third, however, a very slow ground ball came unmistakably in my direction. Now was the time for me to prove that I was no "greenhorn." As I scooped up the ball, I saw the batter running toward first base, and I decided that his aim was to catch me with the ball before I got to homeplate. I took off toward third, and rounding it was pleased to hear a multitude of yells from these heretofore undemonstrative youngsters. I chose not to stop at home plate. I would show them, and I continued toward first at full steam. At that point I was unceremoniously tackled by four boys and wrestled to the ground. They pried open my clutching hand and took the ball away from me. Both teams met around the pitcher's slab for a lengthy conference. Every now and then a head or two would turn in my direction with a face that registered consternation. Perhaps I had missed some of the finer points of the game. My new friends decided not to argue over rules and errors and started the game all over again with one of them playing second base for both sides.

J.J.'s next stop was to be Los Angeles, where he hoped to contract for a California cartoon guide. As a result I would experience some new spaces of the vast and unconventional mansion that was to be my home. I would stand on

America's other coast, where the nearest land mass across from that body of water was not Europe but Hawaii, or Asia or Australia.

Being a child of Dada and Surrealism, I should have been prepared for the erratic and contradictory image the United States presents to innocent eyes and minds preconditioned by a landscape locked into nationalism and ethnic cohesions. There seemed to be so much to this land that had been dictated by nature rather than by man. And wherever human beings had, indeed, made accommodations for themselves in defiance of the land, their customs and behavior, if judged by surface appearance, seemed strangely artificial. If the Hopi hamlets in the Arizona sky had given the lie to Karl May's hallucinations about Indians, the intensely numbing maelstrom called Los Angeles, on the western side of the Mojave Desert, was merely incomprehensible or, at best, illogical.

At Reg Manning's house in Phoenix I had spent the better part of the day leafing through his back-copy stacks of *Life* magazine and begun to realize even then America's scale and the unbelievable omniformity of its inhabitants. It was probably the first time that I felt a measure of discomfort. Could I ever get to know this nation well enough to be part of it? Would I be swallowed here without mastication or digestion, never to be heard of or seen again, even by myself? What kind of effort would it take to become even a drop in the bloodstream of these cities, villages, rivers, mountains, grain fields, forests, lakes, oceans, roads and streets? What about the millions of faces? Faces with a past far beyond known horizons and seas. Not that I had seen all of this multitude as yet. It was more a feeling of being in the very midst of these strangers and about to become just another one of them. Someone who, like all of them, had come with a distinct biography of his own, had crossed a fog-shrouded bridge and found himself confronted not with the simple choice of which way to turn at the next fork in the road but facing rather a bewildering abundance of paths leading beyond almost every point of the horizon. To leave things to fate, as preordained in childhood by rigid customs and social strata, suggested an invitation to defeat.

I had the strong impression that what was called for was a peculiar mixture of will and adventure: perhaps to allow one's self to drift but only in order to find that spot on the riverbank where one could grow as an individual. For that effort one would also have to be the strongest of swimmers. Brave thoughts indeed. There was a language to be completely mastered. A place to live. I could not, after all, impose myself on J.J. Augustin until some far-off dream came near to reality. Apart from my somewhat incomplete experience as a hand compositor, there was nothing I could call a craft of my own. I recalled the admonition of the train conductor on the boat-train from Paris to the effect that, in America, one could not be assured of a seat when the whistle blew by merely reserving it with one's coat.

These thoughts unreeled behind my eyes in the gelatinous heat of the Mojave Desert as I watched the peaks of ocher mountains floating above undulating waves of fever. Once in a while there was the carcass of an abandoned vehicle, half-melted strips of truck-tire treads that conjured up visions of snakes. Nothing moved. Occasionally there would be a rutted track leading from the highway toward the edge of nowhere. Could that path have been made by an unfortunate prospector hoping for another strike like the one at Sutter's Mill? This inferno would be a good place to pen in all of the black- and brown-shirted monsters, now some six thousand miles away, and let them practice their goose steps behind impenetrable barbed-wire fences.

There really was no way to understand all of these bewildering new experiences or to deal now with my anxieties. Let this phase of discovery be just that. There was simply no choice other than to let all of the images come, allow myself to be amazed, puzzled, amused and mystified.

Some of these impressions, in the form of fragmentary film clips now, added little, if anything, to my comprehension of America. There did not seem to be twenty-nine palms around the collection of shacks of that name, but there were roadside stands selling California dates, a fruit that heretofore had conjured up the mysterious Three Holy Kings and long-forgotten desert empires of the Near East. It was a discovery that was severely marred by the aftereffects of a delicious-looking concoction in a diner that had turned out to be another "first": Mexican chili. Some other initial signs of approaching civilization were snake farms with gaudy and terrifying road signs; pyramid-mountains of that rarest of childhood treats—oranges; corrugated-tin lean-tos fronted by imperious gasoline pumps and gigantic monuments of recapped tires; truck stops completely covered by a collage of gleaming hubcaps; a huge articulated effigy of a lasso-toting cowboy, one arm hopelessly broken by some wind gust, advertising an upcoming rodeo event at a place called Cherry Valley; and always the billboards.

The thought that Pasadena, Santa Monica, Anaheim, Glendale, Hollywood and Beverly Hills all amounted to one city called Los Angeles was difficult to believe from the physical evidence of endless browned scrub and grass tracts between urban clusters, with an occasional bench by the side of the road at a bus stop. Desolate roads, laid out at will like so many pieces of string, connected spots of haphazard habitation and stores that, as I was constantly told, had been built on land so wisely bought by Anna May Wong from her film earnings. "Oh yes, she is a rich woman now. Not like Coleen Moore, who went bankrupt trying to finish that crazy castle inside that canyon off Malibu Beach." That and other information came from Miriam Mallory, who, with her son Walter, lived in a trailer camp across the road from the Pacific Ocean in Santa Monica. "Oh, the trouble that that sweet Judy Garland is having with Mickey Rooney in *Love Finds*

Andy Hardy. She's crying all the time. And right after that she has to do *Babes in Arms* with him. She's only sixteen, but her hands shake like the hands of an old woman." Mrs. Mallory worked as a seamstress in the wardrobe department at MGM and, yes, she knew all the stars. Somehow she managed to have her son Walter get me into the studio's commissary for lunch. I saw no stars, or at least none that looked like any that I could recognize. "Most of them eat in their dressing rooms," Walter told me. "The bit players and extras bring their lunch from home to save money. They don't work that often these days."

The streets of the MGM lot, as well as that of Warner Brothers in Burbank, made it very plain that the magic of an Eleanor Powell showing her superb dancing legs in a *Broadway Melody* or a Jimmy Cagney and Jean Harlow, outdoing each other in respective toughness, remained inside the high walls of the very utilitarian sound stages. Actors or dancers in gaudy costumes only accented the factory-like drabness of the dream machine. And why not? It was, after all, the same contrast that I had experienced after those precious few hours in the dark. There were never any Rin-Tin-Tins when you came out of the theater.

On a stage mounted on the tailgate of a truck, in a empty parking lot, the Santa Monica Chamber of Commerce had promised an appearance of "Mickey Rooney, Clark Gable, Spencer Tracy . . . and many more" as part of a talent contest. I had failed to read the posters carefully, neglecting to notice the small print that qualified this main event with "impressions of . . ." Others may have been fooled as well. A large audience watched, with considerable reserve, as an endless succession of little curly-haired girls tap-danced laboriously across the platform, some of them not quite in synchronization with the tapping sounds that emanated from backstage. The imitations, including that of Freddie Bartholomew, were attempted by a number of very unhappy boys with frozen smiles above ridiculously large bow ties. Across the road was the Pacific Ocean, lapping at Muscle Beach, where even at this late hour strangely proportioned young men were flexing their muscles and attempting to create human pyramids around the fires. To the south I could see the lights of ferris wheels and loop-the-loop rides, and there was a strange marmalade of hurdy-gurdy sounds being brought in by the breeze. Somewhere to the east there was said to be a highly publicized restaurant built in the form of a brown derby hat, and beyond that there were orange groves. Surely none of it was really meant to make any collective sense. But this was where Wallace Beery lived. I wondered what he was doing right now.

His business concluded, J.J. Augustin was preparing to return to New York. Walter Mallory was quite sure that his Model T Ford could make it to the East Coast as well, and he suggested that I come with him to share in the driving. When I protested that I had never been behind the wheel of a car, he assured me that he would teach me on some of the long, empty stretches ahead.

I wrote about that trip in a letter to my mother that came back into my possession through Maja some forty years later:

J. J. had started out earlier and I drove back with Walter, a friend, in his car. He is a bit older than I am, and we got along very well. His car is not as good as J.J.'s. It's a very old Ford automobile that rattles loudly. In order to make good time, we drove both day and night. This was done for other good reasons as well. The battery of Walter's car may have been almost as old as the car itself. Anyway, it did not hold a charge. Stopping the motor meant that it could not be started again except with a crank, pushing it or rolling down a hill. . . .

Well, Mother, I did actually drive an automobile for the first time in my life toward the first evening somewhere in California. Don't tell me that America is not the land of opportunity. As it was getting dark, I could see that there was very little power for the headlights. Walter had moved the gears for me into third and told me to stay on the right-hand side of the road. That was a little difficult because the steering wheel had about a quarter radius of play and wobbled under my tense hands. I was not to stop for any reason and to wake Walter if I had to shift into a lower gear. (I wouldn't have known when that should have been necessary.) "The gas gauge doesn't work, but I'll wake up before the tank gets to be empty. So just keep on driving on this highway." Walter must have been very tired; he kept on sleeping and, if the speedometer was right, I was doing about fifty miles an hour (that is something like 80 kilometers per!) . . . It was awfully dark and I was always glad to see an oncoming car because it showed me where the road was going, except when I met them going over bridges, where the road was always much narrower. I don't know to this day how I avoided being side-swiped, because they certainly could not see me until the last second with our weak headlights. Those two glimmering spots may have looked to them like the eyes of the mysterious animals that seemed to inhabit the desert that night. God knows what kind of monsters I did not see and each time I imagined all kinds of things.

On the Arizona state line a uniformed guard came out of a building by the road and waved me down. Walter had said something about a fruit and plant inspection. There was no time to wake him up and I was afraid to stop. The car might stall and, after all, I was driving without a license. I slowed down a bit (my driving skills were already improving), waved right back at the surprised trooper, went right past him and speeded up again. I don't know what he did after that because the car also did not have a rear-view mirror. Of course I was nervous. I had seen a lot of gangster movies with wild car chases. . . .

When we got to Detroit, Walter decided to take the Ford apart, provide it with new piston rings, battery, rear-view mirror and whatever else might be needed to get us to New York. J. J. Augustin wanted me back there to start looking for a job. Walter's uncle lived near Dearborn in a small house, one of many lining the streets of a community inhabited by auto workers. He had been laid off by Nash and spent a lot of time on his porch commenting on the cars of his more fortunate co-workers. The industry was in trouble, he said. "They" were not building cars the way they used to. Too many people were out of work. Who, after all, would buy the cars? Where were the automobiles that really meant something, like the 12-cylinder Packard, the Essex Super-Six, the Cord or the Graham Paige? The worst thing, he repeated often, would be if we got involved in "that mess in Europe." All the jobs in Detroit would go. "I don't give a damn about Czechoslovakia or Austria. No more European wars!"

I was taken to downtown Detroit, where I had an ice cream soda in a large drugstore that proudly claimed to have invented that drink. Somehow there was more pride about that than the automobile. There was to be yet another "first" for me: my very first real hangover. Walter's relatives had gathered for a farewell party for us, and I was initiated into the mystery of whiskey. The taste, and particularly the aftereffects, seemed unusual punishment at the time.

The Ford somehow refused to respond to Walter's surgery and now, Augustin's father having died in an auto accident at a railroad crossing in Germany, J. J. wanted me back in New York before he left for Europe. We rode eastward in a Greyhound bus. Unfortunately, we only had $2.50 left between us after paying for the fare, and I remembered little of that trip, except watching the other passengers gorge themselves on sandwiches and hot dogs at the various stops.

Entering Manhattan by bus cannot conjure up the image of the weeping immigrant seeing the "land of opportunity" rising out of the waters of the Atlantic Ocean. The Jersey tidal flats in no way deserved their description of "meadows," just as the impression of Rahway, Linden, Elizabeth, Newark and Union City made it very obvious that there were no city streets paved with gold.

The bus entered the city not far from the pier where I had arrived just a few months before. Tomorrow would begin whatever reality there was to be.

Augustin assured me that I would have a job in his firm while I was searching for one and that his home would be mine until I could be on my own. This generous offer turned out to be very valuable because I would have a place to sleep and eat and could earn my keep if one thing or another did not work out—and

I often took advantage of it. The next few months, indeed, became a gray area, not of "the job" but just plain "jobs." Lots of them. I hit the streets of Manhattan from early morning. My initial point of concentration was Sixth Avenue between Forty-second and Fifty-third streets, the west side of which had a concentration of employment agencies. They were housed in decrepit low-storied buildings and listed their available jobs on bulletin boards on the street level. Moving from one knot of people to the next, I was part of a slow-moving procession up and down the avenue. There were an awful lot of people looking for work. I naturally looked for anything within the printing trade, but there was little. Certainly no one seemed to need any hand compositors. It was all Linotype, paste-up and job-press operation. I walked up a couple of flights to find out what a janitor's job (with basement room) entailed. The line in front of the desk consisted of elderly men, and when it got to be my turn, I got a split-second once-over and then: "Get outta here." I did no better as a potential steam presser, file clerk, elevator man or busboy. I was in these offices just long enough to fill out applications that bound me to pay my benefactors one week's wages, and when someone spoke to me at all, they said that I was too small, not strong enough, or "too green." "Learn how to talk good English first, kid," was about the most constructive thing I heard.

As a break from my futile wanderings I began to investigate some of the midtown environs of Sixth Avenue. The Bank of New York branch at Forty-third Street and Fifth Avenue had an imposing Old World elegance about it. I was awed by the marble floors, dark wood-paneled tellers' cages, elaborately carved desks, fireplaces, velvet ropes and sedately uniformed guards, who politely but firmly indicated to me that I did not look much like one of their depositors. The main reading room of the Public Library was an awesome sight and a strong reminder that my growing ability to read newspapers was still a long distance from reading, much less writing, in a new language. I stood transfixed in the middle of Grand Central Station after I discovered on its huge vaulted dome the constellations of the nighttime sky pinpointed by innumerable small lights. Nobody else seemed to be particularly interested in the ceiling. What did attract the attention of some, however, was the strange young man who was looking steadily up at the ceiling. They followed his gaze and, not noticing anything spectacular, gave him a curious once-over before hurrying on. It was the first railroad station I had seen in which not the locomotives, dining cars and carriages, but busy people, were the main attraction.

Rockefeller Center, which had announced the selection of its architects on the very same day as the stock market crash in 1929, was now close to completion. In the basement of the Time and Life Building, on West Forty-ninth Street, I entered the galleries of the "Temporary Quarters of the Museum of Modern Art." The initial rooms displayed a large Kandinsky, then a Miró, Picasso, Matisse, a Diego Rivera, a Delaunay and Giacometti's *The Palace at Four A.M.*, all of them familiar names or friends in a city of strangers. At the entrance to the next gallery, I stopped dead. My heart beat fast. Suddenly I faced something that I had been unconsciously looking for since I was a small child of two or three. I had recalled that image as recently as some six months ago while on my final train ride out of Germany. Here was the mysteriously missing piece of wallpaper from over my crib. It was one of those unforgettable childhood images from my cage of nightmares. Now it turned out that my father had taken it and used it, its shape unchanged. It had become a *Collage by Max Ernst,* and it was hanging in the cellar of a skyscraper in Manhattan. This was as good a place as any to come face-to-face with a small part of one's private past. . . . Nor was this to be the only relic of a never-quite-forgotten time on the same day. A Paul Klee on another wall looked very familiar. It was indeed the large watercolor that my mother had found under piles of paper in her study almost ten years ago. The modest sum for its sale had been a welcome fortune at the time. Manhattan's West Forty-ninth Street was a long way from Kaiser-Wilhelm-Ring in Cologne, where the same Paul Klee, in the absence of Maja, had shown Lou Straus-Ernst how to diaper her son properly. This lesson may well have taken place in the same room from which the piece of wallpaper was missing.

I may have taken this encounter with my own history as an omen or encouragement to become a little more daring in my search for a job. I started walking into any place that displayed a HELP WANTED sign. There weren't many, but I kept looking for them. I tried luncheonettes, delis, drugstores, and in one place, on Ninth Avenue, even a funeral parlor. In spite of the signs the jobs, strangely, had just been filled, until I hit a sign BOYS WANTED. It was outside a loading platform. In a tiny cubicle sat a very fat man with four telephones. This was the Elite Messenger Service. Mr. "Elite" waved me over to a group of youngsters sitting on a bench next to his office. "A quarter each trip. And carfare! . . . and close that door!" I had to sit on the end of the bench and moved up as the first boy in line responded to a rap from the window. When my turn came, it was: "Pickup Taft Hotel, Room 1102. Get it to 412 Woolworth Building. Hurry it up!" I had seen the Taft Hotel and found my way there easily. I don't know what was in the package, but it was heavy. The next problem was the Woolworth Building. I had seen it in photographs, but I had no idea where it was. I asked a Taft bellboy. "IRT . . . City Hall," he threw at me. Even that was not so hard until I noticed that my train doors were closing again on the platform of 125th Street. Somewhere in the Bronx I managed to get on a new discovery, a downtown train, losing a valuable nickel because I inadvertently had gone through a turnstile. I found "City Hall" on the grimy subway map and settled down for a pleasant ride until a station proclaimed: NEVINS STREET. I was well into Brooklyn. "Shoulda changed at Fourteenth Street . . . local." I followed the kind passenger's advice . . . but hadn't I been at Fourteenth Street once before? The whole voyage had already taken at least two hours. It was not until I got back to Forty-second Street that I noticed that there were two trains for each platform and one of them said LOCAL. The package was getting heavier and quite dirty from all the handling.

The very elegant receptionist on the fourth floor of the Woolworth Building muttered through clenched teeth: "Jesus Christ, where the hell have you been? . . . The hell with Elite. . . . You stink." Back at Elite, the reception was no better: "You lost me the account, you lousy jerk. I ain't gonna pay you no quarter, not a dime, and don't come back either." I realized that it had become imperative for me to get a map of New York City and study it as conscientiously as I had my Latin at the Lindenthal Real Gymnasium.

As it turned out, I did only a little better with the map than with my other agony, Latin. During the next two weeks I cleared approximately six dollars with Crosstown Rapid, Red and Blue Ambassadors and Bullet Service. I lasted almost four days at Mercury Dispatch but was somewhat relieved when I no longer had to brave Manhattan traffic on shipwrecked bicycles. This boss's valedictory was: "Four flats and three bent front wheels . . . who needs it?" There was indeed a radio at Radio Rapid, but it was turned to WNEW and was not part of the operation. My unforgivable sin there, after a few days, was some confusion on my part between a crosstown bus and the BMT shuttle that unexpectedly allowed me to discover Astoria. A promising fall-out from one of my messenger-boy acquaintances had me on the corner of Fifty-seventh Street and Lexington Avenue at 7 A.M. on Sunday mornings to deliver the Sunday *Herald Tribune* and *The New York Times* to various apartment buildings for a news dealer. My take was to be half the tips, the rest for my newfound messenger-boy boss. I didn't realize that my benefactor had assigned me mostly to those buildings where the papers were to be left with the doormen who, of course, did not dispense tips. It was a good way to get to see the inside of elegant apartment-house lobbies, and to learn at the same time more about the infinite variety of business practices in the New World. In those few instances where I could push the bell at an apartment's service door, I stood a chance for a nickel as well as to find out what the rich in America wore for breakfast. This was the first "job" in America from which I was not fired and it was also the very first one from which I resigned.

As a result of my wandering and my prior experience as an apprenticed compositor, I was able to hold a job with Kwicky Printers somewhere on Twenty-third Street. I held it, in fact, for three days, when my boss went into a fury upon finding me letter-spacing some Monotype headlines for a flyer. I told him that it would look better that way. "Who the fuck told you to waste time on the job? If I wanted an artist around, I wouldn't've hired a pisher like you."

Kings County Menu and Labels on Nostrand Avenue in Brooklyn was big enough to have a foreman. I was taken on only after I had given assurances that I was non-union. The foreman didn't like immigrants that "couldn't talk no English," but he had to be careful. "The kike that runs this place bleeds for scum like you." For some reason, though, all of my jobs kept having accidents before getting onto the press; inverted lines in the form ruined a whole press run. I was let go rather gently. "There aren't any orders coming in."

Otto Schrebinger, who owned the Superior Food Market at Eighty-second Street under the Third Avenue El, on the other hand, seemed to tolerate me because he could curse me in German and English. *"Schnell, schnell, Dummkopf. Die Sachen für Frau Schneider an der Vierundachzigsten Strasse,"* or, "So . . . you deliffered all de schtuff to Eighty-eight schtreet? Vat happened to de pound of blutwurscht und ze *Bauernbrot . . .* und vere iss de money? . . . Did ze old hag giff you zomezing?" Mr. Schrebinger decided to retrench by having the deliveries made in the afternoon when his son was off from school. I must say that I did not feel too comfortable in Yorkville. Restaurant names like Lorelei or Der Alte Ratskeller looked just a bit too familiar, even though their names were in garish neon lights. There was a bookstore on a side street that was crammed with Nazi literature and records of German martial music and *Ländlers,* those unforgettable foot-stomping country dances. Toward evening time there were clumps of men on some corners of Eighty-sixth Street debating politics in various German dialects, or they would listen attentively to a man in a brown shirt, with an American flag by his side, haranguing them about "Franklin A. Rosenfeld, Fiorello La Guardia and Herbert Lehman, Jooz, all of them!" I heard one of them trying to get a small crowd to yell in unison: "America, awake!" I could feel the blood pounding against my temples. My fists and the rest of my body grew taut like a tree trunk. A lightning bolt of hate shot up the back of my skull. Here they were again. The same slack-jawed, drooling hoarse-voiced demagogue on the street corner. Though perhaps born here, he was an intruder from a satanic other world as, undoubtedly, were a majority of his willing listeners. They had come out on a damp November evening to fill their bodies with enough hatred to feed their shriveled egos for another day. Their satisfaction was, perhaps, not as complete as that of their counterparts in the *Heimat* who, just a week ago, had succeeded in adding a new word to future encyclopedias: *Krystallnacht.* I am not so certain that I liked my violent reaction. I was filled with daydreams of physical retribution to the point of sadistic murder, emotions I had been taught to despise in others and which I had hoped to leave far behind me.

Wherever I was going to look for a job, I would have to avoid Yorkville. There was, obviously, something quixotic about my search for work. At no time had I earned nearly enough money to support myself. If it it had not been for J.J. Augustin's generosity and the job that was always available to me with his firm, I might well have gone under. My mailroom mentor George was always glad to see me coming back to Irving Place. It gave him a chance, in a good-natured way, to boss somebody around. He did not approve of most of the jobs that I had found. "How the hell can you run around the city and not speak enough English to buy yourself a sandwich?"

Actually, I thought that I was doing quite well in making myself understood. Professor Reichard had insisted that I come up to the library at Barnard College twice a week and sit around a table with three or four of her students and converse with them in English. I was acutely uncomfortable among these well-dressed and self-assured young women, who very patiently and with good cheer did their best to make me feel at ease. When I told George I was studying English at Barnard, he yelled across the office, "Hey, J.J., listen to this. This guy is going to a girl's school. He thinks he can learn English from a bunch of broads. They don't know how to talk English." He told me to stick around with him. He was going to teach me everything. He taught me a lot. Some of it I had to unlearn.

George lived with his family in a tenement on the Lower East Side. They were Russian immigrants and his stocky, bald-headed father, who could easily have been a movie extra in a horde of saber-wielding Cossacks, fought the New York climate with an ever-present bottle of vodka on the kitchen table. George introduced me to his street gang. "He don't talk so good, but he's okay." My initial impression of George, particularly the way he spoke, had reminded me of the Dead End kids. I had not realized that Leo Gorcey, Billy Hallop, Bobby Jordan and the others were indeed folk heroes. George and his friends tried to outdo one another in emulating their swagger and their sneers. As for their manner of speech, I had no way of knowing whether they were imitating Sidney Kingsley's characters or if it was the other way around. Certainly the inflection, grammar and verbiage seemed unique, and I took to it too easily and quickly. So much so that, in a relatively short time, I received the supreme accolade: "Gee, he's getting to talk just like Billy Hallop, ain't he?" J.J. Augustin didn't quite approve of my growing language prowess and urged me to pay more attention to the kinds of accents I heard on Morningside Heights than on Avenue C. But I enjoyed my gang downtown far more and managed somehow to end my trips to Barnard under the pretext of "pressure of work."

Unlike Dead End, however, there was in this neighborhood no direct juxtaposition between the poor and the rich. The streets were lined solidly with grimy tenements, and there were no "swells" to be seen. The docks on the river had all but disappeared to make way for the East River Drive then under construction. My new friends took great delight in acquainting me with their culture and the verbiage of the streets. I learned very fast and in most cases was a victim of their practical jokes more than once. One did not, for example, go into a kosher butcher shop to ask for ten pounds of "chicken manure," nor was it advisable to tell the policeman on the beat that "Officer, your fly is open." George's sister Anna put a stop to most of that foolishness. Anna, who worked as a secretary to Augustin, was, as her brother would express it, "well-stacked." George must have noticed that I became very shy in her presence and gave her more than a passing glance from afar. "You like her?" he finally asked me. I admitted that I did indeed like her but didn't trust myself to express myself properly. "Aw, for Christ sakes. Don't say nuttin' like 'liking' her. Here's what you're gonna do." He gave me very elaborate instructions. As a result I got up my courage on the corner of Fourteenth Street and Union Square to face her with: "Anna, I really don't like you. I love you. Can I screw you?" At first, her face flushed with anger, she stared at me and then at a point beyond, where George and his pals had observed the event. She roared with laughter, grabbed my shoulders and gave me a long sensuous kiss. She tore over to the gang, and, screaming, "Ya lousy creeps," beat at them indiscriminately with both fists. George hit her back. Cursing, they pummeled each other as people stopped to stare. All of this was happening while a crowd of office workers and shoppers were making their way to the subway or into S. Klein's. I wanted to go into hiding somewhere, but Anna, her revenge over, calmly hooked her arm into mine and took me to the RKO Academy to see a movie. "I'll learn ya English my way," she promised.

My fascination with movies turned out to be very useful. The combination of visual action and dialogue during those many hours of absorption in a dark theater illustrated not only the language itself but also its nuances and colloquial diversity. Almost every evening I went marquee-shopping for double features as well as bingo games, the latter a possible source of money except when the prizes turned out to be dishes. I sat through all of those B pictures, newsreels, cartoon shorts, serial episodes, and sang along with the bouncing ball on the screen. I had to endure *Peter Ibbetson,* with Gary Cooper and Ida Lupino, three times before I began to understand the rather languid plot. I accepted as perfectly normal Dick Powell's singing "You must have been a beautiful baby" to his girl in a rowboat on Central Park Lake with the musical backing of a full orchestra that was nowhere to be seen. I promised myself to try to understand the peculiarly sadistic humor of the Three Stooges and the irrational antics of the Ritz Brothers.

Columbus Circle and Union Square were the equivalent of London's Hyde Park Corner. I found the speakers in Union Square sometimes difficult to follow. Most of the rhetoric centered around "Marxian dialectics," "dictatorship of the proletariat" and, of course, "class struggle." There were always many small, and probably thoughtful, groups of very serious elderly men discussing topics that became completely elusive to me with the heated quotations from Engels, Stalin, Trotsky, Lenin, Earl Browder and Maurice Thorez. Somehow Columbus Circle offered a less demanding mixture of subject matter. The various soapboxes, for example, featured the King of the Hobos, who glorified life on the road, and an Indian swami, or at least someone dressed like one, holding forth on "reincarnation." On any given night one could hear espousals or denunciations of Christ, Gandhi, Jehovah, Norman Thomas, Abraham Lincoln, Luther Burbank, Franklin Roosevelt, Theodor Herzl. The range was wide enough to allow even for a lengthy recital of the achievements of Don Ameche. Other speakers simply brought some of their personal grievances out for an airing, such as the meanness of a given landlord or boss. On a few occasions, Crazy Hannah, as she was called by her ever-present detractors, launched into salty oratory favoring more rights for women. Undaunted by insulting catcalls, this outwardly matronly lady would rivet some innocent male with an accusing finger, demanding to know why the hell he wasn't at home helping his wife wash the dishes. "When was the last time you even talked to her, you bum?"

Columbus Circle had other attractions. On its southwest side, under a second-floor Chinese restaurant and next to the open front shop of a locksmith, stood a run-down movie house, The Circle. I finally hit the jackpot at bingo there one night. I had brought my full card up on the stage and emerged from the theater four dollars richer. As a result I indulged myself in the opulence of the "One-Dollar Chop-Suey Special." Who would dare say that this was not the land of opportunity? From my table by the window I had a regal vista of the entrance to the park and the statue of Columbus, also an immigrant. Below, to the right of the monument, were the lamplit figures of orators and listeners, and on the corner of Fifty-ninth Street, right below me, a spasm band of nine or so black youngsters attracted the attention of some pedestrians with a solid beat. I went down to listen more closely. The sound and rhythm were familiar, but the tunes themselves were not. But, no question about it, this was jazz, pure improvisation from some of the strangest instruments I had ever seen. Two kazoos, a washboard, a banjo contrived from a cigar box, two harmonicas, a gut bucket, a bass fiddle made up out of a zinc washtub and a broom handle, and one genuine guitar. The musicians were grouped in a half-circle with a hat on the sidewalk as their centerpiece. Now and then little boys jumped into a shuffle or tap dance. The tall player of the gut bucket occasionally vocalized with some scat-singing. I found the experience electrifying and could not tear myself away. Heaven knows where or when the seeds to these new flowers had been planted in my garden. Somewhat self-consciously I contributed some coins from my bingo winnings to the hat. I was still there when the band broke up after dividing the take for the night. I offered, and was allowed, to carry the washtub for the player of the instrument. Clarence, like most of the musicians, lived on the Fifty-ninth Street block west of the Circle. He didn't have a job but hoped to play a real bass somewhere professionally. Right now the nickels and dimes would have to do. We had something in common: he had ridden for Mercury Dispatch and had been fired for wrecking two bikes in two weeks. He told me that he'd had a bad time of it because his legs were too long. He wanted to know about Paris. He had heard that a lot of jazz was played there, and maybe he could go there and work. His heroes were the bass players Wellman Braud, Pops Foster and Walter Page.

From then on I went to that corner whenever I thought the December weather was mild enough for the spasm band to play. Clarence was always glad to see me, and he made it a point to talk to me during the breaks. After a while he must have felt that I was enough of a familiar figure with his friends to allow me the privilege of passing the hat for contributions to whoever had stopped to listen. Apparently that raised the take a bit because the hat was no longer a passive object on the sidewalk. The other musicians were somewhat more reserved. There were mutterings for a while about Clarence's "ofay," sometimes even "Watch that Dutch ofay." When they felt sure that I did not dip into their little collection of coins they accepted me, though still in a rather frigid manner. The spectacle of a white boy acting as collector of contributions to these music-makers seemed to astound the pedestrians, but it made them stop more readily and also, perhaps, more willing to part with some change. I got scared to death on two occasions, when we scattered in all directions from an approaching cop who threatened to take us all to the station for obstructing the sidewalk. Both times I was, by force of circumstance, the guardian of the hat with its valuable contents. I held on to it for dear life while running down the block and got grudging approbation for not having dropped a cent of it. The last time, Clarence lost the washtub when he dropped it while running and a speeding car hit it. A good part of that evening's take went into replacing it.

My Lower East Side pals were quite critical about my new association and my enthusiasm for the music. "Jazz is for them Jiggs." Their objections cut no ice with me, even though they began calling me a "nigger lover."

One night, over a late cup of coffee, Clarence asked me if I would like to hear some real jazz. There was going to be a concert at Carnegie Hall. At first I didn't quite believe that such music was played in a concert hall and, further-more, I didn't have the money for admission. "Oh, we'll get in. Just leave it to me," Clarence told me. His uncle worked on the cleaning crew for Carnegie Hall. A few weeks later, two nights away from my first Christmas Eve in America, I sat, squeezed in, on the steps of the upper mezzanine of an overcrowded Carnegie

Hall for *Spirituals to Swing*. Seats had overflowed onto the stage. Getting up there had been a furtive dash through rear doors, under the stage, past the dressing rooms and also past ushers who had turned the other way after Clarence had whispered something to them.

The names of the musicians on stage, particularly of the soloists Clarence pointed out to me, meant little to me at the time, but I was certain never to forget them. From the very opening sound that Count Basie's rhythm machine sent to the ceiling of the stately hall with "One O'Clock Jump" to James P. Johnson's almost plaintive, yet driving "Carolina Shout" and the haunting, perhaps even accusing, voices that had come from some Deep South church to sing deceptively simple spirituals, I felt as if enveloped by some spectral glove. Helen Humes sang the blues: ". . . I went up the mountain—looked down as far as I could see." Blind Sunny Terry made his harmonica talk and cry. Joe Turner shouted, "That's all right, baby, that's all right with me." And the hall was to reverberate with more presents for this Christmastime: Lester Young, Joe Jones, and Walter Page. Sidney Bechet, Tommy Ladnier, Mead Lux Lewis, Pete Ammons, people whose sounds I was never to tire of. I had the feeling of being an eavesdropper at a private event. More than a performance, each musician seemed to communicate far beyond instrument and voice. At some time, in the semidarkness of Carnegie Hall, I became aware of the fact that the color of my skin was white and the faces and hands onstage were dark. It had never occurred to me how rich the color black really was with all of its subtle tonalities. The richness of pigmentation in those strong faces suggested every possible color except white.

Despite the sign that I had seen somewhere in a restaurant on U.S. 66 about "coloreds" and the obscene dual drinking fountains side by side in that dusty and deadly silent Southern town, I had really not thought very much about the inhuman separateness of these people in this society. They, after all, did not wear necklaces of boar teeth around their necks or loincloths or apertures in the lower lips like the tribe I had seen in the Cologne zoo. They were dressed like everyone else, worked near where they lived, and walked the streets without attracting the kind of attention that people with different-color skins had caused on the continent of my childhood. Until this particular evening the histories of lynchings and segregation that I had been all too familiar with before coming here had existed only as exaggerated European notions of some dim post-colonial past. There was something in that music that was trying to reach my sensibilities. There was the fleeting thought, at some point in the night, that, hidden in the intricate structures of boogie-woogie, Kansas City, New Orleans and, yes, the blues, was the image of an architecture. I recall fantasizing the picture of a man, both hands tied, trying to build a house with his voice while sitting on a cot in his jail cell. I felt deep empathy with the only white face onstage, that of the organizer of the concert, John Hammond, who seemed awed by the artists around him, obviously honored to call them his friends.

I had come so far away from the green soccer fields of my recent youth because there were genes in me that had made me an outcast. And suddenly, on this new island of refuge, I had come face to face with the pain of the rejected, expressed through a music that I had heretofore associated only with dancing.

I tried to convey these feelings to Clarence as we stood on the corner of Fifty-ninth Street and Columbus Circle that same evening. He had already half-turned to go to his place up the block when he looked at me with an apparent lack of comprehension. "But you stood right here with my band and collected pennies for us. Didn't you notice how people looked at you? They knew you didn't belong with us, and we knew it too."

I came back often to that corner, but it was getting to be very cold that winter. I walked up the block several times. Maybe they were playing in some cellar, waiting for spring. But I never heard anything.

With thousands of others I watched the red globe drop on its spindle announcing 1939 in Times Square. A very happy drunk slapped me on the back and yelled, "Hey . . . Happy New Year. . . ." For some reason I felt compelled to thank him and pressed a nickel into his hand. Before he got lost in the crowd I heard him mumble, as if to himself, "Now what did you do that for?"

I was vaguely aware that I had done something very strange. This was certainly not a way to gain acceptance in this, to me, new world. As I looked the year 1939 in the eye, I had the sensation of treading water. The sudden realization that this celebration coincided with the onset of a profoundly different phase of my life gave that sea of noisy humans the appearance of a gigantic wave and I was not sure if I could swim through its undertow. I had probably saved my life by coming here, but my future and its purpose were still obscured by a high wall. I felt alone. It occurred to me that I had rarely experienced friends of my own age. I had known friendship in my relationships with people older than myself, and now I was really not so sure about the true nature of my prior life. There had always been the vague notion within me of an inevitable compatibility between life and work. That idealistic dream had never been substantiated by any living example. A little over a year ago my mother and I had tried to plumb the enigma of Max Ernst. To come to better terms with the complexities of that life, she had, somewhat laboriously, translated a 1932 poem by William Butler Yeats for me into German.

> *The intellect of man is forced to choose*
> *Perfection of the life, or of the work,*
> *And if it take the second must refuse*
> *A heavenly mansion, raging in the dark.*

When all that story's finished, what's the news?
In luck or out the toil has left its mark:
That old perplexity an empty purse,
Or the day's vanity, the night's remorse.

She had sent me the Yeats volume as a Christmas present. Right now it was the only book that I owned, with the exception of an English-German dictionary that I used to come closer to the meaning of the words in the verses.

Was now the time to make that choice? Or was this something that had to await the accidents of a personal history? It was as if walking in a garden of perilous choices: trample everything underfoot in a hasty search for survival and comfort or depend on the shoots of ideas to grow into viable trees. The choice was obvious.

The Wagnerian bathos of this resolve did not entirely escape me. I was, after all, neither Lohengrin abandoning Elsa by swan, nor Tannhäuser resisting the delicious temptations of Venusberg for the sake of personal purity. I remembered distinctly my ambivalent feelings about such heroic mawkishness when I was part of an awed audience in Cologne's opera house. My mother had grinned with approval when, during an intermission of *Die Zauberflöte*, I had denounced Tamino as a heel for pretending to faint while three woman actually killed the menacing dragon. Papageno was far more to my liking. His superior intelligence was in beautiful contrast to the pompous, pseudomystical world for which he supplied birds. I'd have to look a little closer at Papageno. One thing was certain: anyone engaged in the agonizing choice between "perfection of the life, or of the work" did not go around spoiling a perfectly nice New Year for an amiable drunk by pressing a nickel into his hand.

There was an enigmatic quality to my loneliness. What I was really looking for were people who were part of this country, this city, individuals who could express something more than the anger of the young blacks on the corner of Fifty-ninth Street or the likable toughs from the Lower East Side. John Hammond had given me the impression from the stage of Carnegie Hall that he and Americans like him would be an enriching human contact. Not infrequently I would look up at lighted apartment windows during an evening and wonder what would happen if I just went up there and knocked at the door.

It would have been easy in New York to have fallen into the art world that had survived from Europe. I saw no reason to turn my back on them, but they never absorbed me. The relatively small number of galleries on Fifty-seventh Street showing contemporary art had been increased by newly arrived dealers from pre-Hitler Germany. Curt Valentin had opened the Buchholtz Gallery, J.B. Neumann ran his New Art Circle and Karl Nierendorf, who had emulated his brother's activities in Cologne, operated a gallery under his own name. They ran their businesses pretty much in the same manner as they had in Europe. Their stock consisted mostly of Klee, Kandinsky, Jankel Adler, Marc Chagall, Beckmann, Emil Nolde, Picasso, Braque, Juan Gris and other examples of the school of Paris and German Expressionism. Ironically, some of the more important paintings of that period were in their possession for at least a second time. Hitler's traveling exhibition of *"Entartete Kunst"* (degenerate art), had not, finally, been burned, but brought valuable foreign currency for the Third Reich through auctions in Switzerland. Now the paintings rested again in the racks of the original dealers on New York's Fifty-seventh Street. Some of them had already found their way into the collection of the Museum of Modern Art. I don't know how well the dealers fared, though they reminded me of agile little sandpipers who miraculously elude breaking waves in their pursuit for food on the seashore. A community of interest dictated a measure of cooperation between these competitors. Many a Paul Klee was in constant shuttle from one place to the other and back until it found a buyer for a few hundred dollars. These were people who had known me since I was a baby, and I was always welcome for what seemed to be traditional coffee klatches after five o'clock in the afternoon, when immigrant artists, writers, historians and itinerant dealers dropped in to recall to each other what the world had been like before 1933. It was a time for them to complain about America's inhospitable streets that lacked outdoor cafés and the apparent void out there of a public willing to respect aesthetics. This could have been convenient company in a strange land, but their anchors were stuck in a sad past.

Max had exaggerated the paucity of contemporary art activity in New York. Long before these recently opened places there had been galleries specializing in twentieth-century painting and sculpture. Alfred Stieglitz's "291," later called "An American Place," had opened in 1909, exhibiting Georgia O'Keeffe, Louis Maurer, Marsden Hartley, Marin, Walkowitz, Dove, Francis Picabia and Charles Demuth. Constantin Brancusi and other important sculptors had been shown by Joseph Brummer in the late 1920s. By 1939 Valentine Dudensing, Pierre Matisse, Paul Rosenberg and a good number of others were actively dealing in European painting and a smattering of Americans. I recall in particular the strong and elegant pure abstractions by John Ferren and the beguiling imagery of Loren McIver. On the whole, though, Americans were relegated to a secondary role. It was left to Marion Willard, Edith Halpert, Frank Rehn, Antoinette Kraushaar and the Artist's Gallery to change the mind of an audience whose vision was rigidly tunneled toward Europe. Certainly the most interesting place at the time was Julien Levy's gallery at 15 East Fifty-seventh Street. Levy carried himself with an elegance that constantly hovered on the edge of some menacing poetry.

His smile was Mephistophelean and his voice flowed with a penetrating low timbre often intoning a world-weary wit. He had struck an early path away from the interests of a prominent family engaged in New York real estate, and it was his wish to have Alfred Stieglitz and Marcel Duchamp as his spiritual godfathers. He opened his round-walled gallery with a courageous retrospective of American photography that included Berenice Abbott, Walker Evans, Paul Strand, Charles Sheeler and Stieglitz in the late fall of 1931, and in January staged an exhibition of Surrealism with the work of Marcel Duchamp, Pablo Picasso, Max Ernst, Salvador Dali, Pierre Roy, Man Ray, Joseph Cornell and Jean Cocteau, among others. It caused a considerable stir in New York and established Julian Levy's place in the important turnaround of American taste. Although financial success, · or even equity, was long in coming, Levy made a place in America for these artists, as well as for Eugene Berman, Pavel Tchelitchev, Alberto Giacometti, René Magritte, Yves Tanguy, Giorgio de Chirico, and Alexander Calder. He had organized his first Max Ernst *"Surrealiste"* exhibition in November of 1932. No wonder Max told me that Julien's gallery was probably the only civilized place in New York and to be sure to look him up!

Somehow I managed to squeeze time out of whatever jobs I had to walk around Fifty-seventh Street. One such employment seemed ideal. I worked in the back of a butcher store on East Fifty-ninth Street from 6 A.M. to 2 P.M. trimming meat off carcasses that had been brought up from Fourteenth Street earlier. Somehow I never learned how to dress a leg of lamb or pork chops to the boss's satisfaction. I always took off far more fat than I was supposed to. Walking in and out of the icebox gave me a perpetual cold, and my hands resembled freshly ground hamburger meat from my inept handling of the sharp knives. My remaining pair of shoes was badly stained by animal blood and I must have offended my surroundings with butcher aroma while looking at a Walt Kuhn *Clown* at Marie Harriman's gallery. Delivering lunches to offices from a delicatessen in the same area was a little better until I was trusted to slice up every onion in the place before the noontime rush. I cried a lot and the smell never left my hands.

Some of the people I encountered in the galleries apparently did not mind the somewhat fragrant and fragile kid who did not hesitate to try his steadily improving English on them. I had seen a little of the work of Isamu Noguchi, George L.K. Morris, Eugene Berman and Julio de Diego, but of Louise Nevelson, Carl Holty, I. Rice Pereira, Ad Reinhardt, Charles G. Shaw, David Smith, Stephan Hirsch and Fritz Glarner I knew nothing other than that they were artists.

Carl Holty seemed to like those late-afternoon sessions at Karl Nierendorf's where he talked expansively in German. He carried himself with an air of determination and what might have been snap judgments fell from his lips with such authority that no rejoinder seemed acceptable. At the same time a humorous squint of his eyes would change to open amazement when the challenge failed to materialize. He'd had a show at Nierendorf and characterized the public reaction to it with "It looks as if nobody learned anything from the Armory show. They probably all went there because they thought they could look at dirty pictures openly." We took long walks on the sidewalks of Fifty-seventh Street, and I wish I could remember all of the advice he gave me about life in America and the word portraits he drew of artists and dealers. He took me to his studio, way uptown, where he introduced me to a very quiet but pugnacious-looking young man, Ad Reinhardt. "He's a painter," he said, adding in a stage whisper, "one of my students." He addressed Reinhardt in the same manner: "Be nice to the kid, . . . can't you see he just got off the boat?"

Holty's paintings were nonfigurative abstractions of severely disciplined colors. In my limited knowledge I could compare them only to Kandinsky and, perhaps, Herbin. I was conscious of the fact that I had heard André Breton intone mightily against the Abstraction-Creation group as "mindless circus jugglers" with whom no self-respecting Surrealist was to have anything to do. Holty had been a member of that group since 1932, and as he was proudly showing some of its publication, he said, "Well, . . . your daddy and his friends don't think too much of us . . . but let me tell you . . ." And then he was off on a verbal compilation of aesthetics, history and caricature all strung together into a marvelous harangue that ended with ". . . and the next thing you'll know, they'll be calling us fascists."

Another painter shown by Nierendorf, Julio de Diego, was given to bursts of fervor that resounded like a four-handed run from the bass up, on a grand piano. The strong lines of his face were rarely in repose, constantly changing directions from vertical to horizontal as they framed lit-coal eyes. He had a comforting habit of draping an arm around my shoulders as if to assure me that he was talking only to me. That, however, was made somewhat difficult for me by his Spanish-accented English that my ear was not yet sophisticated enough to absorb. His paintings of what appeared to be playful robot forms floating in an atmosphere that was neither air nor water were almost like his rapidly spilled words, which did not need to be understood in order to be felt.

The first time I saw Louise Nevelson, she regally swept into Karl Nierendorf's office and speared that rotund little man with a fierce, almost knightly, gesture in her visage, speaking down to him: "What do you mean by saying that you like my drawings better than my sculpture?" And regal she was indeed in her robes of rough cloth. For a moment her face was that of a stony Navaho shepherd, then it softened. ". . . oh well, half the time you people don't know what the hell you're talking about anyway. . . ." She changed the subject as if flying from one trapeze to another. Her eyes, crinkling with laughter, still kept the afterglow of fierceness . . . and then she picked up the thread somewhere along the way: "And, for Christ's sakes, stop saying behind my back that I'm more interesting than my work. . . ."

For me the best show in town was at Julien Levy. The place was far more formal than Nierendorf's or Neumann's, lacking their back-room cameraderie. The atmosphere was almost hallowed. There was a small sitting alcove and Levy, coming from his office to the front, would peer at me sitting there, not hiding his air of slight disapproval, his "Hi, Jimmy" forcing its way out of the corner of his mouth. But just as often he'd stop to ask about my job situation, or even introduce me to some people in the gallery, such as James Thrall Soby, Alfred H. Barr, Jr., John McAndrew, and Allen Porter, who had helped Julien with the gallery in one way or another. There was Gracie Allen, the comedienne, whose paintings Levy had shown in September 1938, Harpo Marx, who collected particularly Salvador Dali and Max Ernst, and Billy Rose, who seemed to be involved in some sort of venture with Levy, which turned out to be the sad and sleezy Dali sideshow of bare-breasted mermaids in a giant fishtank for the forthcoming World's Fair. The friendly dancing bear was Sandy Calder, whose circus I had enjoyed, in spite of my father's reservations, in Paris. Eugene Berman, the Neo-Romantic painter, went beyond the casual introduction and talked to me in his gentle and sensitive manner over ice cream sodas to which he treated me a few times at Tiffany's marble fountain bar. It took a while for the silent, almost gloomy, thin man in the well-worn raincoat to do more than merely sit with me in that little alcove. Joseph Cornell asked me about my childhood and about my father. Since neither one of us had the money for a soda, we took walks together in Central Park Zoo, which was only a few blocks away. He was obviously fascinated by the seals and the birds, particularly pigeons and starlings, who fed freely from what the animals behind the bars had left over. He would suddenly stop and look at a tree as if waiting for it to burst into leaf. We would huddle on a park bench in long silences, and I could swear that I was beginning to see the scene around me in slow motion. On the one occasion when I felt flush enough to treat both of us to tea in the zoo cafeteria, Cornell somehow transformed it into a kind of ceremony just by the way in which he raised his cup and the way he sat. I don't remember much about his house on Utopia Parkway in Queens, to which he took me a few times, except for his magic boxes in various stages of completion in his workroom. He held a small one out to me, on one of those occasions, but I could not bring myself to accept it. It seemed to be such a treasure to him. Some years after his death in 1972 I found that he had meticulously recorded this work as a gift to me.

Perhaps my most bizarre encounter took place in the spring of 1939. Julien was preparing an exhibition of new work by Salvador Dali. Once the great young hope of the Surrealists, Dali had been denounced by all of them for his subsequent tacit approval of Francisco Franco and the path toward slick illustration of Surrealist ideas that had brought him financial success. His wife Gala was the same woman who, when she was married to Paul Éluard, had enchanted my father into leaving Lou Straus-Ernst and me in 1922, the same woman of whom Maja had said, "You should be grateful to that witch for stealing your father from his house. He was no father, and God only knows what your mother ever saw in him." The same woman my mother had described as "this slinking, glittering creature . . . this almost noiseless, greedy female . . .

One afternoon, while I was in the gallery, Dali and his wife stepped out of the elevator. Gala Dali walked past me and then stopped, saying something to Julien about my remarkable resemblance to Max Ernst. Julien introduced us with barely concealed glee. Some seventeen years later and thousands of miles away from that bucolic setting in Tyrol, the woman with the cool smile facing me still fitted my mother's description in every respect. The impression of a predatory feline was a strong one. The deep-set eyes emphasized the presence of the skull under an alabaster skin, suggesting eerie danger. This was an unchaste Diana of the Hunt after the kill, a face and body forbidding, detached, yet in constant wait for unnamed sensualities.

The inevitable cliché: "I knew you when you were a very small baby," this time found me unprepared. The existence of this woman, after all, had changed my life drastically. I felt no particular anger but rather an intense curiosity. Somewhere there was the hint that evil might be purely instinctive rather than premeditated. I was therefore not surprised at myself when I agreed to guide Gala and Dali on a shopping trip in New York. My weak protests that my English really was not yet sufficient were smilingly dismissed by both. Dali, speaking for the first time, said something to the effect that these purchases were very important and he knew that I could help.

On the appointed day Gala showed up alone in the hotel lobby, explaining that Dali was indisposed, but she knew exactly what he wanted and we would do this tour by ourselves. It turned out to be a strangely aimless expedition. We hopped into one cab after another, with Gala always asking, "Where shall we go now?" Her response to my questions as to what she was looking for ran in the vein of: "Dali wants to be amused. Let's find something for him that is outré. The purchases finally were a cardboard Gay Nineties doll activated by strings, some medical books with illustrations of deformed limbs and torsos. In a Japanese novelty shop on West Thirty-third Street she bought some origami paper and a trick object of continuously falling rectangular planes.

We took a late lunch at the Russian Tea Room, where she ordered in her native Russian. The well-known intimacy of the Russian Tea Room must in some degree be due to its near-miniature furniture. A constant encounter of knees, thighs and shins is all but unavoidable. I liked my beef Stroganoff and the blinis with sour cream, and I tried to ignore the strong impression that what was happening under the table was more than the accident of proximity. Gala talked about the time in Tyrol when, as she said, Max and Éluard had become such close friends that they were willing to share any experience in the world. She expressed an inability to understand why my mother had refused to let Max come back to us after just a mere year's absence. If it was a test of my nineteen-year-old sophistication, I passed it, but barely. When she spoke of Dali's need to be protected and entertained, she created the image of a wondrously strange child. At this moment she was certain he was probably asleep in the other room because he had a bad cold, and she suggested that I come back with her to the hotel. Dali would not disturb us, and we could talk some more over tea. It was probably fear rather than resentment that told me how to respond to the invitation. I got up, moved the table, and walked out onto Fifty-seventh Street.

It was an exit that I was to hear about repeatedly in the years to come. Initially it was Julien Levy who told me on the following day of Gala's extreme annoyance with my behavior. Lotte Barrit, his secretary, confided to me that some of the people on Fifty-seventh Street, including Julien, had made some bets among themselves that Gala would succeed in seducing the son, just as she had the father. I mentioned it to Julien and told him that while the opportunities for female companionship were remote in my present status, I was certainly not desperate enough for this particular kind of involvement. Besides, I suggested that his speculations could only be fantasy.

Lou Straus-Ernst's response to my report of that encounter with the past was as follows:

Do you remember a few years ago as we were walking on boulevard Montparnasse and you suggested a certain restaurant for lunch? I told you then, and I emphasize it now, an ocean away, that I would never interfere with any decision you might make in your personal life. The place you wanted to go was known to me as a meeting place for homosexuals. . . . You could go there by yourself without any reproach from me. However, you may remember my saying that I would be goddamned if I went to the marketplace with you. . . . Now you tell me proudly what you did and how you handled it and you seem to have negotiated it adequately. But I am not clapping my hands in applause. Your description of the meeting with this woman, who had such a profoundly negative effect on our lives, defies my well-developed sense of savoir-faire. I hope that some of that worldly wisdom has rubbed off on you but not to the extent that it should suspend a sense of judgment altogether. . . . I am not worried about your virginity. I know that that was taken care of very nicely some years ago. . . .

Max's comment was far more succinct:

> . . . You are learning, but not fast enough. I had no hand in your upbringing, which is probably just as well. Under my tutelage you could have saved yourself a whole valuable day in your life. . . . She has become a parody of a woman. And he resembles those horrid jellies that Americans eat for dessert. . . . Stay away from Spanish olives and Russian vodka."

Julien Levy's final comment on the flap was: "You should have gone with her. You don't know what you missed. Right now she is absolutely furious and Dali is disappointed." The extend of Gala's fury was evident only a few days later, after I had followed the Dalis from Bonwit Teller to a police station. On my way to work at the delicatessen, I noticed a crowd in front of the store's windows. There was Dali cavorting furiously in one of the displays he had installed for Bonwits the day before. Objecting to modifications on some details of erotica, he was in the process of restoring the display to the original. There was some doubt, at the time, that his crash onto the Fifth Avenue sidewalk in a shower of glass had indeed been an accident. After all, there wasn't a scratch on him. To me, however, it looked far too dangerous as a means of getting publicity for his forthcoming exhibition. After Julien Levy succeeded in getting Dali released without being booked, Gala walked up to me and snarled: *"Tu est la merde. . . . monstre!"*

I had no reason to remember the perverse episode, except with amusement, until some twenty-four years later. At the opening night of the Guggenheim Museum's large Kandinsky exhibition in 1963, I very reluctantly gave in to my wife Dallas' curiosity and introduced her to the Dalis in the well of the building. I had successfully avoided them since 1939. In the course of a bit of chitchat, Gala interupted herself in midsentence: "I am very angry with you. You behaved very badly that day. We could have had such a pleasant afternoon." "Yes," her husband chimed in, "you were not nice at all. I remember it well. I was ill that day . . . I wouldn't have disturbed you."

The encounter ended on another sad note. The Dalis, having entered my car, assuming it to be a taxi, kept talking about *"ce mauvais fils de Max"* until they woke up to who was driving them to the Hotel St. Regis. Dali seemed to have heard about my recent Cultural Exchange trip to the Soviet Union. "Do they know Dali there?" It was a plaintive question. "Ah, good . . . which Dali do they know? The early or the later work?" I guessed he wanted it to be the earlier paintings, and I obliged him. "Ah, that is good. I am glad."

On the steps of the St. Regis, Gala turned back for a moment: "I am still very angry."

I suspect that Julien must have gotten a little tired of having me hang around his gallery. A full-time job would keep me out of the way. His brother interviewed me for a job running an elevator in one of the family's buildings. Not surprisingly, I was found to be unsuitable. Julien then talked to his good friend Iris Barry, the curator of the Museum of Modern Art's Film Library. Her husband, John E. (Dick) Abbott, the Film Library's director, was to interview me at 485 Madison Avenue, temporary headquarters until the projected move into the new Museum building on 11 West Fifty-third Street.

Of course, I had all kinds of optimistic visions about my possible activities in a place like that. I had, after all, written film reviews in Glückstadt for a while, knew the names of just about all of the stars and character actors in Germany and France, and had spent almost every evening in New York in a movie house. My fantasies ran to being a possible expert on German filmmaking with my own office and even a secretary. The prospects were more than promising.

Abbott, a lanky, ascetic-looking man, with small eyes behind rimless glasses, questioned me in a very businesslike manner. He seemed to take pains in giving the appearance of being a banker or a judge rather than the director of an institution concerned with the aesthetics and history of moving pictures. Where I had gotten my concept of what an executive in that field should be like escapes me now. He listened impassively to my resumé of "experience," in which I foolishly included also the writing of Surrealist poetry and my background of immersion in culture. He allowed what seemed like a full minute of silence, which had the desired effect of heightening my embarrassment. "Very good, you are hired. You start next Monday, and you report to Mike Collins, who will be your superior in the mail room. There is going to be a lot of work because we are moving into the new building next month. Collins will show you the ropes and . . . no slip-ups. The pay will be fifteen dollars a week. Actually, it's thirty every first and fifteenth of the month."

Whatever grandiose ideas I had dreamed of, if I could hold this job, it certainly beat feeding round steak and lots of fat and gristle into a meat grinder for a pound of hamburger. For some reason I felt confident enough to start looking for a place to live. I had imposed on J. J. Augustin's largesse long enough. J.J. had serious doubts about the "kind of arty crowd" I was getting involved with and assured me that I could always come back if things did not work out.

A few days after starting my job I found a furnished room on the eighth floor of an old apartment building on the corner of Eightieth Street and Broadway for

$8.50 a week. It faced an airshaft and another window of what probably was just as depressing a cubicle as mine. I could hear my neighbor's radio very clearly. Most of the time it was tuned to WNEW, which in the early evening featured Martin Block and his *Make Believe Ballroom*. Later at night there were three comedy shows: on NBC's WJZ and WEAF, also Benny Goodman for Camels or Artie Shaw for Chesterfields. I heard H. V. Kaltenborn, clipped and urgent, talking about Herr Hitler's latest threats against Poland and Memel: ". . . in the face of his prior assurances, during his rapid conquest of Czechoslovakia, that the Third Reich had no other territorial claims." Or about the news from Spain: ". . . the forces of Generalissimo Francisco Franco have taken Madrid, and that sad war is now over. He declared a return to law and order to his tortured land. Herr Hitler has already cabled his congratulations." The radio would blare long into the night, and the only refuge from the room and its oppression was below, on the street. I recall sitting on a bench on the string of islands that divided Broadway traffic. The west-side IRT pushed hot air out of a grated vent as it passed underneath, and after a while I knew the exact count between clicks of the traffic light. Now I was really independent for the first time in my life. I had a job, a place to sleep and, with some economic engineering, enough change to feed myself. It would take some rope-skipping to make it all come out even. Getting paid twice a month would work to my advantage only in February, particularly if it had twenty-eight days. After my rent there would be $13 for everything else stretched over fifteen days but . . . sometimes there would be sixteen days. . . . There was, however, a peculiar sense of satisfaction in the fact that the entire process was under my control . . . if . . . I could hold the job.

Far less reassuring were my thoughts about my mother as well as my father. Senators Borah, Wheeler and Nye felt that Europe's quarrels were not America's concern, and they found many willing ears for their arguments. It was all so sad. Why had my hero, Franklin Roosevelt, turned his back on Spain's loyalists? The Germans had tested their weapons there. I thought of Guernica happening again and again. Neither J. J. Augustin or I had been able to convince Lou Straus-Ernst to leave Europe. "Nobody in Europe believes that Hitler can win a war. If he tries anything, it will be over in no time, and I will be there when that happens. . . . One way or the other, you will be visiting me. It won't be long now."

I had written to Max, who by now was living happily with Leonora Carrington in Saint-Martin d'Ardèche near Avignon. He did not reply to my pleas to leave Europe before it was too late. Instead, he sent me photographs that showed him in the process of embellishing the walls and doorways of the sixteenth-century buildings he'd bought with grotesque cement bas-reliefs and sculpture.

Spending my evenings on the Upper West Side was rarely a positive experience. That part of Manhattan had become an enclave of German refugees. It was very unpleasant to witness the behavior of people who had fled here for the same reason that I had. Fastidiously dressed and with an air of superiority, they took their after-dinner strolls on Broadway with ill-concealed disdain on their faces, and in their voices, for the fact that this was a far cry from being Berlin's Kurfürstendamm or Cologne's Hohe Strasse. They could be clearly heard complaining in their native language about unswept sidewalks, the discourtesy of janitors, surly waiters, incompetent household help, all-too-casual postal service, noisy subways, badly sprung buses, insulting cab drivers, too many street beggars, La Guardia's love of Negroes, the unpleasant sound of Yiddish and the slovenly *Ost-Juden* (East-European Jews) who had made the "respectable ones" look bad in Germany and presented the same problem here. In stores and in front of movie houses their elbows spoke the peremptory language of an ingrained air of preeminence. It was a frustrating experience to observe, and it made the inevitable return to my cheerless cubicle all the more miserable.

Ironically, the apportionment of my pay from the Film Library for my daily needs made going to the movies a rare luxury, and as a result I had to find entertainment and information again among the soapbox orators at Columbus Circle. Their concerns were with the effects of America's continuing inflation, WPA workers resting on their shovels, refugees usurping the jobs of solid citizens, the dangers of a new pseudoreligious "moral rearmament," the waste of money on the N.Y. World's Fair and nightly assurances that "the mighty protector of the oppressed, Joseph Stalin, will crush Adolf Hitler and his gangsters if they move as much as an inch across the Polish border." Fortunately my English seemed to have improved rapidly, and I could now get more accurate and broader information from *The New York Times, The Herald-Tribune* and the many other New York newspapers that I had to dispose of at 485 Madison Avenue after the movie reviews had been clipped. Hitler's *Mein Kampf* had been published in an English translation; British as well as French diplomats and military experts were in Moscow to negotiate some sort of alliance with the Russians; Joliot-Curie had proved the possibility of splitting the atom; the British were testing large barrage balloons over London. *Life with Father* opened on Broadway, *Pins and Needles* and *Tobacco Road* were still running, and "God Bless America," sung by Kate Smith, was a hit, but *"Bei Mir Bist Du Schon"* had faded. The moving-light marquee above Columbus Circle advertised the newest-model Buick and its latest innovation: an automatic transmission.

I had discovered that the odds of winning at bingo in a movie house were astronomical. I really didn't mind having to cut down on that entertainment because now every working day was filled with cinema. Many cultural institutions were renting the Film Library's packaged 16-millimeter programs, and they had to be shipped with their proper literature; most of the other work consisted of packing and labeling everything for the move to Fifty-third Street. Cans of 35-millimeter film, prints and negatives, had to travel to and from the vaults in Flushing and DeLuxe Labs on the West Side. Every now and then I was allowed to watch a film that I had brought to the projection room at 420 Lexington Avenue for a showing. There were stills to be sorted, and I saw a lot of familiar faces. The mail I distributed throughout the office had the return addresses of major film studios from all over the world. My immediate boss was Mike Collins, a small sinewy Irishman, seemingly bouncing on the balls of his feet. His mouth was in almost constant motion, mostly muttering under his breath about some enormous inequity that had just befallen him in somebody's office. He steadied his nerves by stroking the nonexisting hair on his head with one hand while using the other one to fortify himself with a slug from a hip flask. He did enjoy his new status as a boss, though he felt that there was still too much work and that he was being exploited by those "high-faluting prima donnas" on the floor. He sent me on my first outside assignment to pick up some film at DeLuxe with the enigmatic remark: "I'm going to lose money on this." The office manager gave me five cents for a crosstown bus and 60 cents for a return cab. She declared the taxi essential because 35-millimeter film could not be carried on a public convey-ance or a passenger elevator. It was too combustible. Collins had told me to ignore the order. On my return he demanded a 40-cent cut of the anticipated profit and was furious that I had decided to obey the fire ordinance. When I told him that I was not a citizen and didn't want to break the law, he blew up even more. "Why, in god's name, did I have to get stuck with a lousy refugee?"

The most perilous episode occurred when I was sent to the screening room on 420 Lexington Avenue, where I was to separate the wicker chaises from the metal folding chairs. I was to place the wicker in the hallway for a truck pickup to John Hay Whitney's Long Island estate, where they were needed for a week-end garden party. I had not dared to ask what a "wicker" was and had, of course, made the wrong choice. Whitney was one of the major angels of the Film Library, and the office manager reprimanded me severely for having embarrassed him, his important guests and the Museum of Modern Art. There was great apprehension in the office about the size and duration of Mr. Whitney's anger. After some very anxious days I was told that I would not be fired . . . this time. Collins reiterated his opinions about refugees who "don't understand no En-glish."

I would indeed have been heartbroken if I had lost this job through some kind of stupidity. I realized after the first day that I knew precious little of film as art, thereby negating any Horatio Alger pretensions of attaining an exalted position via the servants' entrance. I was not even well-versed enough in the intricacies of office procedures really to qualify for my present job. The leeway

I was given was probably due to the fact that the Film Library did not operate under the pressure of the profit motive. It was, at the time, a very unique organization of scholars, writers and old-time movie pioneers, gathered into a group by Iris Barry to preserve and evaluate all aspects of this twentieth-century art form, just as museums concerned themselves with painting and sculpture. The diverse individuals behind their desks were far more interested in their own ideas and the goals of their still young institution than in demanding that the new office boy know his proper place.

Iris Barry's intellectual involvement with cinema had included being one of the earliest film reviewers in the British press for the London *Daily Mail* in 1925. She had come to New York, already part of London's literary establishment, with the help of Charles Laughton and Elsa Lanchester. Her ideas and expertise fitted in well with Alfred H. Barr, Jr.'s concept of a "filmotek" for the Museum of Modern Art. John Hay Whitney used his influence to get the project off the ground by inducing big studio heads and some silent-screen stars to donate reels of negatives and rare prints of classics. It was probably the very diversity of individuals assembled by Iris Barry for the project that was mainly responsible for an atmosphere of friendly cooperation, with a minimum of office politics. Each instinctively accepted the concept that his or her respective knowledge was a mosaic detail of a larger picture. They came from the young days of the industry as it emerged from the nickelodeon days of Edison and Porter, transforming itself into the inventions of Chaplin and Buster Keaton. They had worked with D. W. Griffith, Frank Capra and John Ford. As youngsters they had lived in the darknesses of the superpalaces and the neighborhood "Bijou." They hunted the negatives of lost masterpieces and they discovered forgotten pioneers.

I felt comfortable in this environment of considerate and sensitive human beings, most of whom did not consider my khaki office jacket a barrier to a kind word or a friendly gesture. I remember in particular Jay Leyda, the disciple and one-time assistant of the great Russian director Sergei Eisenstein, who was at home with Russian and Chinese film as much as he was with Herman Melville and Emily Dickinson. His acts of kindness and concern were to come my way unbidden, and yet as if he had heard a silent call for help. I felt the warmth of a friendship in the willingness of the film historian Arthur Knight to share with me his enthusiasms and knowledge of just about every phase of American culture. My boss, Mike Collins, felt that I was "too chummy with those brainy jerks" and Dick Abbott's secretary periodically communicated the director's warnings to me to "stay in your place."

For joviality there were sometimes after-hour sessions of music and remiscences with the two pianists Ted Huff and Arthur Kleiner, who accompanied the Museum's screenings of silent films, and D. W. Griffith's favorite cameraman

Billy Bitzer. Big, fat, nervous, Huff loved Chaplin and lived in that adoration. His pudgy fingers running across the piano keys evoked, beside his idol, Mabel Normand, Theda Bara and Buster Keaton. This was the sound first heard in the converted storefronts as Mack Sennett's cops upended fire hydrants in their flickering chases. When Kleiner played the score for *Broken Blossoms,* one could almost hear Lillian Gish's cries for help as she floated on the ice.

Billy Bitzer's job at the Film Library, as camera repairman, had been created for him by Iris Barry, in order to put a few dollars into the pocket of a movie pioneer who had seen several fortunes disappear. Alcohol had done a good job on him. With the air of a somewhat bloated leprechaun, he relived for us the days of *Birth of a Nation* and *Intolerance.* His animated recreation left little to imagine about the Gish sisters, Erich von Stroheim, Douglas Fairbanks, Mae Marsh, Richard Barthelmess or Lionel Barrymore. He had a rich repertory of old barroom humor and shocked the aristocratic Kleiner with his salacious version of "The One-Armed Violinist."

The soul of the Film Library, Iris Barry, set the tone of its structure with wit and decisiveness. Attractive, small and given to gentle irony, she was listened to without her ever needing to raise her voice. She also treated me as something more than a lowly employee, she was concerned enough to find out how and where I was living when I told her, she asked Alfred and Marguerite Barr to help me get out of the suffocating cell on Eightieth Street. Mrs. Barr prevailed on her cleaning woman, Mrs. Jordan, a kindly Irish widow, to rent me a room in her tenement apartment on West Sixty-fifth Street for $7 a week. Though my bed took up most of the room and the window faced a dark airshaft again, the place somehow felt different. The extra $1.50 a week made life almost luxurious and, best of all, Iris Barry lent me a small radio that became the focal point of comfortable evenings by myself. Radio was a good companion. Norman Corwin and Arch Oboler produced, at times, innovative drama; NBC had its Toscanini-led symphony. There were a lot of comedy programs, such as *Duffy's Tavern.* I listened to the antics of Bob Burns, Joe Penner, Jack Benny, Edgar Bergen and, most of all, Fred Allen. It took me a while to fathom Jerry Colonna's madness on the *Bob Hope Show.* The big bands were Benny Goodman, Artie Shaw, Harry James, Glenn Miller and Bob Crosby, most of whom had their own shows or were frequently featured by the various disk jockeys. A favorite of mine was the Chamber Music Society of Lower Basin Street, with Sidney Bechet and Dinah Shore. I had some difficulty in accepting the nature and frequency of commercials but noticed that, as one crisis after another heated up the world, the increasing interruptions for news bulletins and analysis were considered serious enough to be aired without sales pitches for toothpaste or chewing gum. Unfortunately, international sanity never was a commercially viable product.

Dreams of glory, or even advancement, in institutional culture obviously had to remain just that for me. Besides, the vast flow of memoranda and correspondence, to which I owed my job, did not exactly fit my somewhat vague concept of what the making of art was all about. There was to be, however, one burst of potential fame. I became a movie star. *The March of Time* filmed me in the process of wrapping program notes in the mail room of the new building as part of a reportage on the Film Library. I decided to blow the cost of a dinner to see myself in Radio City Music Hall. Sure enough, there I was, for a sensational few seconds, all alone on that big screen, in that awe-inspiring theater, with a multitude of tourists, eyes glued to the screen. I don't remember what main feature attraction was also screened. Obviously, those waiting in a long line at the box office had come to see me in *The March of Time*. I do recall the Rockettes and their legs. Collins was very much put out, and it didn't help when I remarked that I was probably more photogenic than he.

The fourth floor of the new Fifty-third Street building was a luxurious relief from the cramped Madison Avenue quarters. Collins was happier because the White Rose Bar was much closer. Abbott, now, was really the executive; he no longer had to share an office with his secretary, who, in turn, from her new empire, could act out all of the prerogatives of "secretary to the director." The Film Library shared its space with the Museum Library and the Department of Photography. Obviously, this was the floor of the scholars. We had class. Upstairs there were just too many busybodies.

A few weeks after all the names were on the doors, the Museum opened with a large survey exhibition, "Art in Our Time." It was preceded by galas and parties. One in particular took place a day or so before in the penthouse on the sixth floor for the Museum's trustees. Cleaning up on the following morning, I could not help but notice that each of the many empty champagne bottles had cost more than I earned in a week. There was also gossip that one of the topics under discussion had been a report by a team of efficiency experts, strangely somber men who had mysteriously wafted in and out of the offices for several weeks. It was the first time that I heard the term "pink slip."

I circumvented the fact that, as a servant, I was, of course, not invited to the opening, by staying late at the office and sneaking down to the galleries later in the evening. After all, three of my father's works were in the exhibition: *Two Children Are Threatened by a Nightingale, Woman, Old Man, and Flower*, and *Lunar Asparagus*, not to mention works by many artists who had held me on their laps. The only person who seemed to be openly annoyed by my unbidden presence was Abbott, who whispered out of the side of his mouth, "Who the hell invited you?" Allen Porter, an old friend of Julien Levy and Iris Barry, later to be assistant secretary of the Museum, winked at me and grinned as if to say,

"Don't pay any attention to him." Abbott looked very flushed, I think he was drunk. I enjoyed the evening immensely. I observed Fiorello LaGuardia, who audibly remarked that the Seurats, so far, were the only things that made any sense to him. I squeezed into the downstairs auditorium to hear Franklin Delano Roosevelt characterize the Museum, on a closed-circuit broadcast, as a "citadel of democracy." In that description he was absolutely right because class distinction in this auditorium was out. The mighty Nelson Rockefeller was there, as was one of his office boys . . . I.

The efficiency ax began to fall not long after the opening. Among the dismissed were many of the guards and janitorial staff. It was a bleak morning, to which was added further cause for consternation. The Industrial Design section of the exhibition on the main floor featured, among other objets d'art, a Buckminster Fuller–designed Pullman lavatory. Though it stood in the middle of the floor, someone, probably a visitor, had succeeded in relieving his bowels in that exhibit. There was no one to clean it up. Superintendent Ekstrom was rebuffed by the angry guards, and Charlie Fischer, the German-born permanent house painter on staff, retorted, "I'm supposed to schmear de valls in dis place. I vill not clean up nobody's schit." There was one individual who could ill afford to refuse the command to volunteer. I learned yet another trade that day.

Within a few days of the opening of "Art in Our Time," I distributed an envelope to each staff member on the fourth floor that brought smiles and surprised expressions of pleasure to them. It was a letter from Abby Rockefeller, Nelson Rockefeller and Stephen C. Clark, thanking everyone for his or her work in the past. Particular attention was paid to the success in opening the new building and the big exhibition. Each letter contained a bonus of a month's salary. When I got through with all the envelopes, I was the only one who had not received one. Maybe I had not been in the job long enough or, could it be . . . Dick Abbott was punishing me for my unauthorized appearance at the opening? I was lucky to have the job and decided not to inquire if there had been an oversight. A week or so later Allen Porter, who had successfully showed me how to knot a bow tie, noticed that I was wearing a new one and guessed aloud that this was an intelligent way to spend my bonus. When I told him that there had been none, he seemed visibly embarrassed. On a subsequent morning there was a letter for me with $60 in cash, without the written message. Porter told me: "Oh, that . . . it must have gotten lost in the shuffle." It took me a long time to discover that he and Iris Barry had put their heads together and had made a collection from the staff on the fourth floor.

I had better things to do with that windfall than to buy new bow ties; however, I did become the proud owner of three white shirts that Shulte Cigar Store was selling for 99 cents. Another One Dollar Special in that Chinese restaurant might have been in order, but I must have thought it wiser to spread my riches over a longer period of time as far as food was concerned, and I wasn't all that crazy about endless extra bowls of rice with soy sauce anyway. Furthermore I wanted to look forward to a decent string of two-week periods without a two- or three-dollar deficit.

I indulged in two modest splurges, however. For $1.75 I bought three boxes of dried-out poster paints that I found on sale in a stationery store on Sixth Avenue. The colors were green, yellow and blue. Without any preconceived notion of their eventual use to me, I reconstituted them with water and lined them up on top of my dresser. I also bought a big fat book. It was a Modern Library Giant of James T. Farrell's *Studs Lonigan* trilogy and it cost me $2.50. My curiosity had been provoked by a Columbus Circle orator who, in a rousing attack on the Roman Catholic clergy, had warned his somewhat unattentive audience that "unless you button up your flies once in a while and open up your cranium to what is really being done to you, this great country of ours will be drowned in an ocean of Studs Lonigans. Those whoring . . . and boozing . . . and foul-mouthed . . . and unwashed . . . and illiterate . . . so sanctimonious-going-to-confession . . . two-legged . . . tail-ready-between-their-legs . . . black-winged angels of seamy Chicago streets . . . growing into hypocritical, acne-pimpled louts, their minds getting filthier with each year of their life, forever to be trapped in stale beer saloons and by a marriage bed that in its creaking promises us, my friends, nothing more than an avalanche of Studs Lonigans for your children to emulate. . . . Now, I tell you . . ."

Studs Lonigan took its place next to the slim Yeats volume and the English-German dictionary that saw less and less use now. Reading became easier with each day, and my boss Collins had remarked somewhat suspiciously, "You going to some kind of night school? You talk almost as good as me now." Writing in the language of my new existence remained largely untried because there was no one to correspond with other than those whom I had left in the other part of the world.

Struggling through *Studs Lonigan*, I never had any doubt that I was reading about human beings and about situations that were real. Images from my own past were never far away as Farrell's words reconstructed twelve- and fourteen-year-old boys stripping a Negro youngster of his clothes, burning them, searing his buttocks with lighted matches, and urinating on his prone body. A humid Sunday afternoon in Washington Park is the scene of the Monitor's Jewboy Schwartz making such impressive yardage as well as a touchdown against quarterback Lonigan's Fifty-eighth Street Cardinals that the only recourse is to teach "the Kike" a lesson by beating him to death. The body and mind of Studs Lonigan absorb such images as part of the normal events of the days and nights during his twenty-nine years, as he aimlessly hangs around street corners, copes with the nuns at school, wakes up sick from rotgut, vicariously gets the better of Al Capone on the screen of an ornate movie palace or participates in a "gang shag." He is not without good dreams and hopes. He assumes that intimacy between human beings can be more than awkward fumblings in the underbrush of a park. Someday he will live in a neighborhood of sunshine and good neighbors. He anticipates indulging in the kind of generosities that will gain him unique respect from his contemporaries. It never occurs to him, as a boy or as a young man, that his soul is different or more blemished than the souls of other ordinary sinners, none of whom can help but break the same laws and inevitably trespass against higher teachings. He instinctively seems to know that God cannot punish all of them forever and he, Studs, will be among the fortunate ones.

I spent night after night with Studs Lonigan, my radio off. The news bulletins about Hitler, Daladier and Chamberlain had been raining down like confetti. Czechoslovakia was no longer. A fascist Spain had been accepted by England and France. Charles Lindbergh and Burton Wheeler talked about a new order in American relations with Europe, and there were stickers on car windows: "The Yanks are not coming." There were nights when I felt that it would be easier to bear the news in the morning. There was enough sadness in Farrell's book to make sleep difficult. As I overcame my difficulty in reading, some kind of continuity into what initially seemed rambling street dialogue, I sensed that Lonigan was doomed from the very beginning of his life. He, and I with him, kept waiting for something, yet each day passed without revelation. Mephisto followed him to church and to confession, and the Archangel held his cue stick for him in the pool hall. He must have expected that elusive radiance until his very last moment: He seemed to be choking. "Mother, it's getting dark," he called feebly.

The
Luxury of
Sadness

Hurrah for revolution and cannon come again!
The beggars have changed places, but the lash
goes on.

W. B. YEATS

AUGUST 24, 1939, promised to be humid, with a few showers, and temperatures near 90 degrees. I decided, as I did so often, to walk to work early and sit for a while on the terrace of the Central Park Zoo cafeteria with an extra cup of coffee. Someone always left a newspaper behind. That saving, plus subway fare, could pay for a bowl of cereal. And there it was, in the *Times,* the ultimate obscenity: "Von Ribbentrop's Car, Flying Swastika, Passes Beneath Red Flag at Kremlin."

It jumped out from the page before I even read the headline: GERMANY AND RUSSIA SIGN 10-YEAR NON-AGGRESSION PACT. The insanity of my time had reached the top of the mountain. It was now, as Rimbaud had phrased it in "Parade": "A paradise of violence, of grimace and madness."

My first thoughts were of death. My mother, my father, Maja, the faces kept coming. I knew then, on that very day, that if fatal harm were to come to any of them, I would never forget that the death warrants had been co-signed behind those walls facing Red Square.

The raucous barks of the nearby seals suddenly changed to offensive laughter. Inexplicably, I relived a vignette when, as an eleven-year-old, I awoke to the noise of a slamming door in the hallway, to see a young actor from a Cologne repertory theater pounding on the very door of the living room he had just stormed out of. It seems that after what had been a pleasant dinner of friends and acquaintances there had been a heated discussion about Trotsky's banishment from the Soviet Union. . . . "You can kiss my ass, you goddamned hyenas." He addressed the door as if on stage:

> ". . . *Better be with the dead,*
> *Whom we, to gain our peace, have sent to peace,*
> *Than on the torture of the mind to lie*
> *In restless ecstasy . . ."*

"How many heroes of the revolution will you 'send to peace' with your inane mouthings? You are being spoon-fed by the protectors of the proletariat. Do you really think that your consciences are clean because Rosa Luxemburg and Karl Liebknecht cannot hear you? They choked on their own blood from assassins' bullets dying for the ideas you're selling out. And don't ever tell me again that Majakowski died of a heart attack on a Moscow trolley car. It was cement-brained ideologues like you who drove him to suicide. And what about those workers' funerals you attend with your red armbands where you weep for the revenge victims of that Nazi martyr-pimp Horst Wessel. I'll see you emulating that *Schweinehund,* yet when the time comes to save your miserable necks from the insanity of your very own idols . . .

". . . But if it be a sin to covet honour, I am the most offending soul alive . . ."

He ran down the stairway, yelling from its well: "You can all kiss my ass!" *("Leckt mich am Arsch!")* The whole scene could have been Shakespeare.

That was really going back in memory, but it seemed to fit my own rage. I could not raise my fist at the trees in Central Park or the Plaza Hotel as I walked toward the Museum at Fifty-third Street. The surrender to Hitler by France and England at Munich had been depressing enough, but now the dam had broken completely. The self-proclaimed defenders of the masses, the pontificators of democratic purity, the opponents of tyranny everywhere whose *"Internationale"* had called on mankind to get ready for the last battle to achieve the rights of man, had joined the bloody hands of the "master race." They had made a pact with the very officer corps that they had allowed to train surreptitiously on Russian soil. These were the same voices that I had heard under my bedcovers from Radio Moscow eulogizing Ludwig van Beethoven for his courage when he added a funeral march to the *Eroica* upon hearing that Napoleon had declared himself emperor. That same wavelength had carried the message: "Workers of Germany, it is your duty to fight the brown-shirted enemies of the proletariat to the last man." I had seen the bodies of some, who had obeyed that call, in the sandbox of a children's playground. Would they be proud of having given their lives so five big swastika flags might fly at Moscow's airport?

But it was done now. And, perhaps, the men whose portraits had been carried in May Day parades all over the world would have just as little trouble sleeping peacefully tonight as they had before. The anger and self-pity were leaving me now, and in its place there came a strangely calming sadness. It was not maudlin, sentimental or depressing. It seemed more like the quieting acceptance of a great loss, a loss that in a peculiar way was a gain, the self-assurance that comes from having recognized the true nature of a childhood myth at an early age, the knowledge that long-sought-for wishes are not fulfilled by some abstract invention and that they have to be earned over and over again to remain in your life.

I recalled yet another small episode as a teenager. The great photographer August Sander, whose life goal was to capture a portrait of Germany, was an intimate friend of Lou Straus-Ernst. He was an excitable, tall, rangy man with bushy hair and burning eyes behind rimless glasses, who could storm through the entire apartment while expounding on some newly discovered image. A lot of his prints, including a photograph of my mother and me, sat in high stacks in Lou's study. He was making his living mostly in fulfilling commercial demands typical of German society. Lou asked the editor of a Frankfurt publishing house to come and look at Sander's work. The man had been a sometime participant in the inevitable debates around our dinner table and had never failed to be the most puritanical defender of the party line. Lou thought that he might respond to the biting frankness with which Sander had portrayed the German bureaucracy, the all-so-proper middle class and the rebellious spirit of intellectual. I watched the editor as he inspected the photographs very carefully. He had the face of an aggressive turtle, I thought. There was a long silence as his dropped pince-nez dangled from a silk ribbon. His words came in short staccato bursts: *"Ja, für mich da gibt es hier zu viel Traurigkeit."* (In my opinion there is too much sadness here.) We should not encourage it. It is a luxury that is a poison to the proletariat. We don't have time for sadness. It is a luxury that diverts us from our goals." The memory faded as I stopped in front of a fancy chocolatier, Altman and Kuhn on Fifth Avenue, and I could see my reflection in the window glass just as I had on the train from Paris to Le Havre. I had been very angry then and had found no satisfaction in the images that my rage had conjured up. But now I was indulging in "the luxury of sadness." I knew I could not afford self-pity, but this was an entirely different emotion. The luxury enabled me to face this very day with all of its contradictions. The cost for the luxury was far more bearable than for the alternatives of fury or acquiescence. On the material side I felt that even at a salary of $2 a day, there was nothing excessive about the indulgence. There was, to be sure, a distinct difference between luxury and extravagance. Undoubtedly I would not be able to avoid times of extreme anger, but, as before, the causes for such reaction would in time pass. But this tragedy, and I knew it then, would be etched in the acid of blood forever. I could even vaguely understand that pompous little man in my mother's study and his animosity toward sadness. Unlike rhetorical anger, it was a devastating weapon that carried with it the barbs of contempt.

Within a scant six days the real politik of both giants bore fruits. At the almost identical hour that the supreme Soviet ratified the treaty, German tanks, planes and shiny boots crossed into Poland. A bargain was kept; the Soviet flag flew over eastern Poland in short time. That part of the horrendous farce was over.

Perhaps Lou and Max had now changed their thinking and would abandon their hope of being able to stick it out in their Europe. It did not look as if it would be their Europe much longer. I tried to convince them in long letters and, without waiting for their answers, tried to get affidavits for them. I turned to anyone who would listen to me. When I distributed the morning mail at the Museum, I kept an eye out in every office for someone I might have missed before. I was not ignored, but the answers, invariably, were to the effect that those who were in a position to help were already overcommitted. J. J. Augustin found his efforts equally frustrated. His commitment to marry my mother failed to bring official sanction from the Immigration authorities. When Lou's and Max's answers finally came, they were somewhat more amenable to the idea while, at the same time, expressing very positive hopes that Hitler would fail miserably.

Late in November 1939, as I was separating the Museum's afternoon mail, there was a pencil-written postcard for me. It was dated October 27, and its return address was: Camp de les Milles (B.J. Rh.), Les Milles (p. Aix-en-Provence). Its message was:

Mon cher Jimmy, *

Merci de ta lettre. Je suis detenu ici. Tu pouvrais m'aider (à ma liberation) par tes excellentes relations. Fais quelque chose. Demandes aux personnes influentes.

   Je t'embrasse, ton père   Max

P.S. *(J'écrit une carte postale, car les lettres sont interdites!)*

Max, who had unsuccessfully tried to become a French citizen from the moment of his arrival in that country, had been interned in the Alpes-Maritimes, along with other individuals who were technically still German. I feared that the same thing had happened to Lou. Where Max got the impression of my *excellentes relations* was something of a mystery to me. Alfred Barr, the Museum's director, had given me a few of his warm, yet very shy, smiles when he had not been too busy to look up from whatever work he was engrossed in at his desk. In spite of his unstudied remoteness, I had felt a genuine liking for this slender,

---

*My dear Jimmy,

Thank you for your letter. I'm being detained here. You can help me (in my liberation) through your excellent connections. Do something. Ask important people.

I embrace you, your father. Max.

P.S. (I am writing a postcard because letters are prohibited.)

even fragile, walking dreamer whose eyes were never without wistful curiosity. Postcard in hand, I rushed to the fifth floor and to Barr's office. Though his door, in true symbolism of the man, was always open, few ever ventured over its threshold without considerable hesitation lest they tear him away from some deep thought. "I will call someone immediately," he said after reading the message. "The Emergency Rescue Committee is working on problems like this through Frances Perkins and Immigration. They are trying to save as many intellectuals from Europe as possible. They are helping Chagall, Masson and people like André Breton, among others, and I am sure they'll do their best to get your father without the need for all those affidavits."

A letter from Lou came a few days later from Marseilles. She had also been interned, at Gurs, a distance from Les Milles, but had been released after a few weeks. She was waiting on the coast for the release of her close friend and collaborator Fritz Neugass, in Milles. She had seen Max there on her visits to Fritz. It was depressing for Max, she wrote, even though he was there with many friends, like the Surrealist Hans Bellmer. Max seemed also quite upset about some dreadful complications with his studio in Saint-Martin d'Ardèche and the uncertainty of Leonora Carrington's whereabouts. The bottom line of the letter, however, was "Yes, I think it is time to leave here. I hope you can do something."

Not knowing where to turn and emboldened by Alfred Barr's apparent optimism concerning Max's problem, I made another trip to his office at the end of the fifth floor to ask for the committee's help. "Unfortunately," he told me a few days later, "the committee people have told me that for the time being all of their energies are centered on the more prominent intellectuals in Europe. They will send you a list of other organizations that might be able to help." I recall the concern in Barr's voice: "This is tough, Jimmy; sit down a minute. I wish I could help you right now." He gave me one of those intense Barr looks, holding his face with the fingertips of both hands. It would not have surprised me if I had seen tears in his eyes. I think that the idea of someone not being famous enough to be saved from possible death was appalling to him. I shall never forget the obvious deep concern of this great man for a nineteen-year-old mailroom boy. "They were divorced, weren't they?" I heard him say into a long silence.

An idea began to form in my head: "Oh yes, you know he was married to Marie-Berthe for about six years, and I have the document of Max's divorce from my mother. You know, those papers were probably never translated into French, as they should have been for legal reasons. Both Max and Marie-Berthe were Roman Catholics, and the first marriage might be considered not to have taken place. Max, after all, had come to France illegally and did not want to come to the mayor of some small town with a German document."

I was grabbing at straws and treading water at the same time. It was as if Barr had been waiting for the suggestion: "Do you mean that you are willing to take the risk of bringing them in as husband and wife? . . . I'll try it with the committee. It's worth it."

I don't know in what manner Barr made the proposal to the Emergency Rescue people. He merely told me that the papers were being drawn up for Max Ernst and his wife Amalia-Louise, and now we would have to wait. I dashed off separate letters to my "reunited" parents to tell them of the audacious idea. Since there was a good chance of mail censorship on the other side, the letters were long and very circumspect. But I was sure that my message would be understood. Within about a week a small package arrived for me from Europe. It had taken almost six months since my mother had mailed it for my birthday in June. Very carefully wrapped up in tissue paper was a beautiful seashell. It had been broken in transit, revealing a marvelously graceful inner structure. It looked magically Surrealist to me. On my mail delivery next day I put it on Alfred Barr's desk as a present. He thanked me and placed it on a shelf near his desk, and it was still there years later, long after I had left the Museum, when I visited him in his office.

There were often bursts of anger and private tantrums in that furnished room on Sixty-fifth Street. It was difficult to remain philosophical while listening, as on one night, to long excerpts from *Das Rheingold* on WQXR. I was sure that a small golden swastika dangled between the heaving, sweaty breasts of the Lorelei as she combed the straw that passed for her nordic hair. The rampaging Valkyrie bellowed: *"Siiieg Haihiel—Siiieg Haihiel,"* and my beautiful river Rhein was a filthy brown morass teeming with scaly, repulsive, bottle-eyed Aryan gnomes. Richard Wagner's cacophonous rutting call to racist ecstasy was the perfect melody for 60 million simultaneous masturbations in Teutonic feather beds: *Siiieg Haihiel—Siiieg Haihiel . . . ach, das ist doch so schön. . . .* I discovered that my inbred aversions to anything of a military nature were giving way to visions of myself walking into the midst of my past tormentors, machine gun blazing, and killing Hitler personally.

At the same time there were a number of individuals in the Museum's offices who made no secret of preferring someone other than "that little German" to pick up and deliver their mail and memoranda. Despite Franklin Roosevelt's announced neutrality, French, Canadian and British enlistment offices existed in New York, where I filled out lengthy application-questionnaires to alleviate my feelings of helplessness. No matter the innumerable ways in which I was murdering the entire German general staff nightly in my furnished room, I stopped short of inquiring about the French Foreign Legion. Things would have to get much worse before I was ready to emulate Gary Cooper or Boris Karloff.

The time was not without other ironies. At one of Karl Nierendorf's after-hour coffee klatches, he and J. B. Neumann discussed, with some vehemence, the fact that their friendly competitor Curt Valentin (Buchholtz Gallery) was on his way to Lausanne to bid, with Pulitzer money, it was said, on a hundred-odd *Entartete Kunst* paintings that the Germans had sent there for auction. The very idea that all of that valuable foreign exchange would flow into the Nazi war machine had created a dilemma. The ethics were "wrong." The enemy would get the money. . . . But what of the aesthetics? The least Curt could do, they felt, was to let them share in the possible bonanza by respecting their prior working relationship of sending clients to each other. They admitted to the somewhat nightmarish situation that might find them, as well as the Nazis, profiting from works of art that they themselves had sold to German museums before Hitler's sick taste had become the law. The expressed hope was that whoever was base enough to attend the auction would have the decency to refrain from bidding up the prices.

At work I encountered an unexpected minor nightmare. As part of the ongoing Museum efficiency drive, I was transferred away from the Film Library to the "enemy territory" of the fifth-floor mail room. I had never been particularly offended by Collins' barroom prejudices, but I discovered very quickly that from now on I would have to deal every working day with the rabble of the demagogic radio priest Father Coughlin. Obviously, I would not buy myself doubtful accommodation by keeping quiet in the face of ". . . You know, the Joooz killed Jesus." I would ignore being "that heathen kike." The atmosphere in this part of the Museum, quite different from the camaraderie on the floor below, also needed some getting used to. None of it proved to be too difficult because I was beginning to find something of mysterious fascination in my after-work time.

As the Museum's catalogs came from the printer to the mail room, they were usually packed with sturdy white cardboard between every fifth or tenth copy for protection. At the end of the day I would appropriate a stack from the trash can and take it home with me. I drew and doodled on them while listening to Burns and Allen, Tommy Dorsey from the Hotel Pennsylvania Ballroom, Arch Oboler, Lux Radio Theatre, Edward R. Murrow or William Shirer. I began trying out my revitalized poster colors. The color range was limited, but I found that one could achieve an almost endless variation of green with the addition of blue and yellow. The blue, by itself, would have to pass for black. The first consistent images that emerged were dancing figures constructed out of elongated, green, of course, leaves. The repertoire of my ballet seemed endless, and I was surprised by the ease with which I could handle my precious materials. I branched out into fauna and flora landscapes animated by my dancing figures in battle with giant insects and the strange bestiary that had followed me across the Atlantic from

Grünewald's altarpiece in Colmar. Granted, the images tended to be a bit crowded with that abundance of green, yellow and blue. Discovering India ink helped a little. Going back to my room at night became something to look forward to, and immodesty got the better of me. I took some of my "works" to West Fifty-third Street to show them, with some trepidation, to individuals who had shown more than perfunctory civility toward an office boy.

Stanton Catlin, a recent Ph.D. from the Fogg Museum, who had recently joined the Exhibition Department, lined the "Dancers" up on his desk and, after keeping them for a while, found some very encouraging things to say. Jay Leyda pulled a five-dollar bill out of his wallet and commanded me to "get some of the other colors." Victor D'Amico, head of the Department of Education, presented me with a set of oil colors and some brushes that had been sent to him as manufacturer's samples. He kept adding to my supply steadily. I had discovered the riches of the Forty-second Street Public Library after intimidating bouts with its card system and consulted *The Materials of the Artist* by Max Doerner. I opened it to the chapter heading "Painting in Oils," which starts: "It is recommended that the painter grind his own colors. . . ." I could just see myself trying to do that in my 8-by-10-foot chamber. I read as far as: "The brushes must be well-cleaned after the work is finished," without having understood anything and decided that, since I had been in many studios and seen enough artists at work, I would do better to find out for myself.

The oil paints initially presented several problems. Instead of unattainable canvas I found that 20 cents could buy all of the scraps of Masonite and plywood that I could carry from a lumberyard on Sixty-seventh Street. In the process of experimenting with the painting process, my relatively unventilated room became a smelly haze of turpentine, linseed oil and Damar varnish. The chair served as an easel, forcing me to work sitting on the bed, surrounded by my precious paints, brushes and rags. An understanding landlady supplied me with an old sheet to protect the pillow and covers. The slow-drying paintings made dressing in the morning a gymnastic adventure as I navigated past them on a newspaper-covered floor. How the good Mrs. Jordan managed to change my linens without disaster seemed a miracle. The satisfaction of looking at an evening's work before going to sleep was sometimes enough to make gloomy radio news such as the Russian invasion of Finland almost bearable. One by one I discovered stones that I could place in the structure of a personal world. Perhaps it was not "a seat where gods might dwell," but it was mine. Nor was the door to the room a barrier to the unexpected. Jay Leyda knocked on it one evening. He wanted to see what I was doing. There was no room for him to sit or even to move in. He turned, standing in one spot on the paper-strewn floor in order to see the various paintings in progress. He had just stopped in on his way to somewhere, he said, to offer me the use of his apartment on weekends, when he and his dancer wife were away. As a result, on many a Friday night I would bundle up my materials and work well into late Sunday night in the Leydas' sunny and spacious place over-looking the East River in the upper nineties.

These weekends became my "working vacations." I cooked my own meals, walked along the river and, on good days, painted on the roof of the low building. I don't think that working in the open had any effect on the imagery of the paintings except for a more disciplined use of color. But getting back to Sixty-fifth Street with the wet work was a problem. I'd wait until late at night, when the buses were fairly empty and I could spread the panels around where I was sitting. I remember a drunk staring at my impromptu one-man show for many blocks before stumbling out at his stop, shaking his head as if to exorcise some of my Hieronymus Bosch monsters and Giovanni Bracelli dancers.

One of my pleasanter duties at the Museum was filling in for the fourth-floor receptionist during lunchtime twice a week. The elevator opposite the desk serviced several sections in addition to the Film Library. Beaumont Newhall, a tall professorial type who headed Photography; Bernard Karpell, the librarian whose rimless glasses seemed to emphasize an ever-present friendly twinkle; the Dance Archive's Paul Magriel, mustachioed with a barely concealed ebullience, and their co-workers would stop by to look over my shoulder at what I was doing without being too critical. It was an hour during which I could draw and cut away, with a single-edge razor blade, at spare linoleum tiles that I had found in a storeroom and from which I would print impressions on onion-skin paper at home. There was no switchboard to man, and often I could direct visitors to a given office without stopping my work. When someone complained about my preoccupation, Allen Porter said (so I heard), ". . . that should be a perfectly normal activity in a Museum of Modern Art."

One noontime at the desk, a man and a woman startled me with: "Perhaps it's you we're looking for. Are you Jimmy Ernst?" I was stunned by the idea of two strangers walking out of an elevator in New York looking for me, and merely managed to nod my head. The young woman was small and had a haircut similar to mine. She walked with a pronounced limp and apparently needed to squint to see properly. In doing so, her head moved forward like that of an inquisitive colt. The slender man's reddish-blond curls hinted at an austerely contained halo, his eyes would be vigilant even in repose and his mien suggested a fearless familiarity with dreams.

Jane and Paul Bowles had heard of me through Julien Levy. We chatted, a bit awkwardly, about common friends and acquaintances, particularly those of the pre-war Paris days. They had spent some interesting hours with my father and "just wanted to see what his son is like." When they were ready to leave,

Jane Bowles, pressing the elevator button, turned back. "Are you ever free in the evening?" Falling over my words, I assured them that I was indeed, including tonight. She wrote down an address. "Why don't you come on down after you get through here." And they walked into the elevator.

The place was a garden apartment on West Eleventh Street in a row of houses not unlike some I had seen in the Southern states. The evening unfolded like a play in which it is difficult to distinguish between an audience and the actors. The characters walked onstage as if casually dropping in on the backroom of some obscure bistro known only to them. The degree of familiarity seemed to vary, but the conversations, as the place filled, gave the impression of continuing after some indefinable, but not very long, interval. Invisible spotlights picked out a minor character here, and then swung to one who obviously had a major part, the dialogue revolving around one or the other. The tone of the confidences, opinions and repartees never exceeded a restrained low-decibel range, even when the voices were barbed or cutting. Much of the talk, in wit or somberness, went past me because of the tempo or its unfamiliarity to my ears. But I had an instinctive recall of this aura from the little world around Lou Straus-Ernst. These friends, not all of them young, but all involved in some aspect of the performing or creative arts, were finding each other, like spokes of a wheel radiating from a center. This center was a shelter from the aesthetic and moral dicta of a society deaf or blind to innovation and afraid of deviations from imagined norms. It was also an energizer, a core of reassurance that no one need be alone in dissent or diversity. I recognized the casually woven thread of community and liked its texture. What might have looked like a mere patchwork cloth was in reality a colorful fabric with much unexpected luster.

Without really knowing whether I was welcome, I returned to Eleventh Street regularly, as if I belonged. Something was always going on. Sometimes the scene changed to John LaTouche's recently rented duplex on Minetta Lane. He could now afford it because he'd had his first success as a lyricist with *Ballad for Americans*. The Eleventh Street place belonged to Mary Oliver, a rather odd figure even in this many-faceted assembly. She was a fortyish lady with a slightly vacant face under blond Colee Moore bangs and a perpetual smile, who was never seen without a tall glass filled to the rim with a liquid that was definitely not water.

Some of these floating social evenings seemed to have as their tradition John LaTouche's endless quest to come up with adequate translations of Bertolt Brecht's German lyrics for Kurt Weill's *Threepenny Opera*. Sometimes ignored, but never for long, Touche, impish in size and face, would plunk himself down at the piano and play Weill's music, trying to find fitting counterparts to Brecht's sardonic German original. All of this was delivered in a falsetto frog-voice that certainly caught the sarcastic flavor of the songs but hardly ever came close to the bite of the words. At the end of his experimentation he invariably sat back, compressing his lips into a thin-lined smile that reached from ear to ear, and waited for applause and approbation. Instead he'd become the object of critical, good-natured banter. Jane Bowles, for example, predicted that she would come across Touche, twenty years hence, sitting at some sailor's dive in Rabat still wrestling with Polly Peachum's love song. Elsie Huston, a stunningly beautiful singer who at the time was performing at Tony's on Fifty-second Street, caricatured LaTouche by singing that very song in an obviously improvised Portuguese version. Marianne Oswald, a bizarre-looking, red-haired, ex-Berlin chanteuse, tried it in French, changing over abruptly to "Surabaya Johnny" from her repertoire. I didn't dare, as yet, to get into the spirit of the ongoing satires, but I had a feeling that there really was something about Brecht's jargon that defied translation.

LaTouche persisted in his dream project for many years. He conceded defeat only in the late forties. Even a superb Duke Ellington score could not sustain an inadequate book and lyrics for *Beggar's Holiday*, a lavish Broadway musical that bore hardly any resemblance to the original *Threepenny Opera*. I saw it at the Shubert in New Haven and I witnessed LaTouche's futile struggle with innumerable collaborators and play-doctors. The show never made it to New York. It continues to challenge lyricists to this day, some with better luck.

My initial guide through the endless nuances within that new to me and always surprising little enclave was a man of small physical stature. Acting alternately like an elfish puck or a stern philosopher, he seemed completely self-assured in his acknowledged role of father figure. This position could just as easily have gone to the courtly and admired avant-garde composers Aaron Copland or Edgard Varèse. But the chosen annotator and disciplining seraph was Frederick Kiesler, who took me under his wing and proceeded to fill me in, with a good measure of waspishness, on the unfolding polychrome of characters and situations. In the process I got a capsule history of his own provenance.

I had heard his name dropped on a few occasions in the Department of Architecture at the Museum of Modern Art, and not always in very flattering terms. He felt cheated by fate and maligned by some of his European fellow architects, whom he accused of having been instrumental in denying him his rightful place on the American scene. "They sailed in on the fame of overblown *Geschrei* (ado) over the Bauhaus. And now they use their exalted chairs at Harvard and Yale to dominate architecture in America. They build and they scheme and they scheme and they build. They copy each other in arrogance and they say, 'Kiesler . . . what has he built lately?' My problem was that I came to New York from Austria too early. All my projects went down the drain with the Depression. Had I waited, like Mies or Gropius or Breuer, I would not have needed to redesign the display windows for Saks Fifth Avenue or create the interior of the Eight Street Playhouse to pay the rent or eat. I was too far ahead of everybody when I invented a wraparound projection screen for the sure-to-come wide-angle-lens movies. 'Never,' they said." He felt comfortable, but hardly fulfilled as director of scenic design at Julliard and with his lectures at Columbia University. "But I will get to build my Endless House yet. A totally new concept: That will be the new architecture! Their Machine for Living? It's an aberration . . . an inhuman coercion, forcing everyone to live and work in boxes that differ from prisons only because there are no visible bars behind those merciless sheets of glass."

I got these little lectures and character sketches at irregular intervals in a precise, slightly nasal, Viennese-tinged English, an admonishing finger raised to make a point, lips pursed as an exclamation mark of reproach or witticism, his commanding presence and mien erasing any thoughts of his diminutive size. And they took place not only on the evenings at Eleventh Street or Minetta Lane but also when I was taken along, in somewhat the manner of a mascot, on frequent expeditions to nightclubs to hear Marianne Oswald, Elsie Huston or Mabel Mercer. To Jimmy Daniel's place in Harlem or Café Society Downtown in the Village we went, to hear Billie Holiday, Teddy Wilson, Mead Lux Lewis and a pudgy new comedian, Zero Mostel. At Mecca-Temple one night, I think it was a rally for Spanish Refugee Relief, I heard for the first time Touche's "Ballad for Americans" in concert, and Kiesler explained: "Touche is having a problem with that. He hates the idea of it being treated as a patriotic hymn. He can't convince people that it was meant to be a satire on Americanism. He's had trouble of that kind with a lot of his work. It always seems just to miss. I always thought he should have chosen Paul Bowles to write the music for "Ballad." You know, Paul is a fine composer but he also has a very analytical, almost surgical, literary mind." In this manner I received bits of biographies about new friends, some of which were more intimate than I needed to hear.

Kiesler drew a group portrait for me: "Virgil Thomson decided that we should call ourselves the 'Little People.' Isn't it peculiar that most of us are not very tall? Genius and talent is hardly ever given to tall people. With the exception of maybe Aaron Copland and Oliver Smith, everyone here is little . . . you are little." I didn't ask if that meant that I had talent or if I, indeed, could consider myself as belonging to the Little People. I had my answer on that same evening. Sitting together on the piano bench, Jane Bowles and LaTouche, embracing each other, were openly crying. They explained their sudden sadness: "Now that Jimmy is with us, we're not the youngest Little People anymore."

Knowing that there was now a place for me in a community of spirited individuals, who had accepted me without precondition or trial, lifted from me yet another layer of my isolation. I made time for it by sleeping less, painting well into the early morning hours, sometimes arriving at the Museum with pigment still on my hands. These fugitive hours meant more, even, than being with friends, and I remember them less for what I actually produced than for an equally fugitive sense of fulfillment, wanderings, however short, in the direction of a possible discovery voyage. Intangible as the satisfaction was, I remember a very similar feeling of waking up as a eight-year-old in my room on Emma Strasse and imagining life existing in that bizarre skyscraper I had constructed from building blocks, which had mysteriously withstood slammed doors and other perils of a boy's room for over two weeks. I recall it as an experience of being at home with myself. In the privacy of Mrs. Jordan's furnished room I felt no constraint to indulge in the most outrageous vanities and comparisons whenever I seemed to be getting close to understanding the reason for the strange light in the eyes of the great artists around me. I kept remembering the tipsy sailor-poet Joachim Ringelnatz declaiming William Blake's line: "No bird soars too high, if he soars with his own wings."

Frederick Kiesler, in particular, took a special interest in my painting and my job and introduced me to other young artists. He and his petite, charming but sharp-witted wife, Steffi, made me feel welcome in their penthouse on Seventh Avenue and Fourteenth Street. My impression of the little man ran counter to the opinion expressed by his detractors that he was dissipating his gifts with his too-wide-range interest in architecture, painting and sculpture, literature and theater. I was fascinated by the way he was able to connect all of these elements as a philosophical base for his greatest love: architecture. But I could also see that this breadth of thinking made difficulties for him in a profession that functioned in a very materialistic atmosphere. As he was showing me his scale model of the Endless House and the drawings for it, Steffi interrupted her husband's lecture: "This boy doesn't get enough to eat. He's too thin. From now on you come with us to Pappas' on Sunday evenings." This was to be my weekly "square meal" at the comfortable restaurant near Eighth Avenue, and I was closely watched and had to clean my plate.

It had never occurred to me to live my existence in accordance with Bertolt Brecht's cynical dictum: *"Erst kommt das Fressen . . . dann kommt die Kultur"* (First comes the gorging . . . then comes culture). I had simplified the economics for feeding my body, after a number of tiresome experiments in out-of-the-way diners, cafeterias and hamburger joints, and found that Hash 'n' Eggs was the American flag: the same everywhere. Studies in quaint sociology were a time-consuming by-product of the drab adventures and, besides, I was now a very busy young man. It was now below my dignity to go to the automat because I had quickly forgotten that the English language had once been a problem for me.

When I heard "Hiya, landsman" or *"gehackte leber"* in a delicatessen, I knew it to be hybrid Yiddish and not German. I was punished for some of my culinary eccentricities, however. I had asked the counterman in the drugstore down the block from the Museum if he could change my daily sandwich of American cheese on rye to camembert on rye instead. He complied after I promised to come in every day to eat it. Much to my regret he must have ordered at least a year's supply of the rapidly ripening cheese, and I noticed that my lunchtime neighbors on the high stools were beginning to give me ample elbow room as the months wore on. Only occasionally did I dare to break my promise and went to eat lunch in one of the little French restaurants on West Fifty-sixth Street, where I avoided the relatively high menu prices by ordering ". . . *votre merveilleuse soupe à l'oignon,"* then explaining to the waiter, who probably could not even speak French, that *"je n'ai pas beaucoup de faim."* My only real extravagance was purely visual. Almost every evening, after having dragged three or four big mail sacks through heavy traffic to the post office, I found myself mesmerized by the grandiose display of desserts in the Broadway window of Lindy's Restaurant. Someday—I could almost hear myself thinking it—"I'm going to have a piece of that unbelievable black-cherry cheesecake."

The thrust generated by the 1913 Armory show in changing America's attitude of indifference, if not hostility, toward modern art got a further potent impetus from Alfred H. Barr's "Picasso, Forty Years of His Art." I don't know if this evolution in taste ran parallel to the country's ebbing political isolationism as a mere coincidence. Whatever the public's predisposition toward Picasso and his generation of innovators may have been, this exhibition was the first for the Museum of Modern Art, and for the United States, that had block-long waiting lines every day. Visiting hours were extended to 9 P.M., resulting in a financial boon for me. I was asked to help out at the main-floor information desk on certain nights and entire weekends. I took it as confirmation that my proficiency in English was found trustworthy enough to have me sell tickets, catalogs and reproductions as well as giving general information. Concurrent with the Picasso show the Museum was holding a "Russian Film Festival" in the downstairs auditorium, and a lot of people from the movie industry came in. I was properly impressed by the fact that Burgess Meredith asked me, "What's so different about Russian movies? . . . You mean they don't have a chase in the seventh reel?"

During the run of the exhibition I was swimming in money from the extra job, which had about doubled my monthly wages, and I decided to find out what Broadway theater was all about. Ted Huff, that gentle soul, became my guide. He had ways of getting cut-rate tickets for even the cheapest seats. The first play was *Outward Bound*, with Laurette Taylor. On that particular night the ingenue was played by her understudy, Diana Barrymore. Having been on a trans-Atlantic steamer not that long ago, I could easily be moved by the drama of wandering souls on a voyage to a mysterious destination. I believe that the male lead was played by Kent Smith. Olsen and Johnson's *Hellzapoppin* would have come across loud and clear even if I had gotten off the boat from Europe on that very same night. I loved its spectacular irreverence and the breathtaking speed with which the hilarious sight gags followed one upon the other. The show's opening newsreel of a frenzied Hitler and a posturing Mussolini screaming to their masses in Yiddish was probably the only time I ever laughed at them. As long as the money held out, I managed to hear Walter Huston sing "September Song" in Kurt Weill's *Knickerbocker Holiday,* experienced the bittersweet gentleness of Julie Haydon and Eddie Dowling in William Saroyan's *The Time of Your Life* and watched Tallulah Bankhead turning the forbidding spaces of a Southern mansion into a terrifying yet bloodless battlefield in *The Little Foxes.* James Barton's Jeeter Lester of *Tobacco Road,* an apparent Broadway must for some years, seemed just a bit too grotesque for my, as yet, limited knowledge of America. A few times Huff initiated me into the ways of mingling with an intermission crowd and thus catching the last act of ". . . performances you have to see." It would have been nice to walk the streets of New York afterward with an arm around a girl's waist or, perhaps, just across her shoulders. The latter, of course, presupposed that she be my size or smaller, but at present I had no choices at all.

I was now reunited with *Guernica* in the same building where I worked and I must have gone to see it just about every day, if only for a few minutes. The war in Spain was over. The agony of its people was now a memory that Picasso would never let us forget. Brave soldiers had fought in vain under invisible flags of perdition. The protectors of the humanist faith had timidly abandoned and betrayed them. *Guernica* pointed an accusing finger not only at monstrous flying machines overhead but also at my very own hero, Franklin Roosevelt. And the calmly accepted tragedy now was that it had all been just a rehearsal for the science-fiction obscenities in the skies over Poland. There was just one remaining, though gloomy, satisfaction: the artist's eye would continue to stare at us long after all of the temporizing justifications as well as the mountains of documents and photographs had faded into the commonplace. Would Spain ever be free enough to be the deserving home for *Guernica?*

With its circulating exhibitions reaching far across the land, catalogs of unequaled scholarly excellence, a rapidly rising membership and the growing popularity of the Museum as one of New York's major tourist attractions, the brave band of original dreamers was beginning to find itself facing pressure from contending power-factions within the board of trustees and the office administrators. Successful cultural institutions inevitably encounter the ledger-scanners who are convinced that their way of "marketing the product" will keep those attendance figures high. "You just have your ideas and let us decide if it will go."

There was probably no question that the fast-growing institution needed to strengthen its administrative side, but most of the changes implied further intrusions into the exercise of scholarly independence. Dick Abbott had been appointed "to relieve" Alfred Barr of some major responsibilities. The choice of exhibitions showed the influence of Nelson Rockefeller as United States Coordinator of Latin American Affairs. Some firings and changes seemed capricious or part of empire-building by some newly arrived power figure. "Better and Better" really meant "Bigger and Bigger," in spite of the efficiency experts. I could not help but sense the tensions in the curatorial departments as I made my daily mail routes through the building and I admired these intelligent and sensitive people as they stood their ground successfully more often than not.

As it stood, I had some problems of my own, though they were of a more petty nature. Often I was not blameless when I was called down for some breach of office etiquette or for expressing opinions that were none of an office boy's business. I was just too interested in what the Museum did, especially if it touched on some ideas that I had been brought up with. I can imagine the reaction of some curatorial assistant when he heard "that kid" make a slighting remark about the paintings of Candido Portinari as they were being hung. They were really pretty bad. Sometimes I was accused of snooping. "No, Miss West, I did not read that confidential memo about the Mexican show. I was just thinking aloud that it seemed a logical thing to come next." There was also no doubt that I could have been more efficient in my job. On my rounds through the building I might suddenly forget my errand in front of a Matisse or watch a specialist working on the repair of Max Ernst's *Lunar Asparagus* or *Two Children Frightened by a Nightingale.* As Europe's war brought more and more artists from Paris to New York, it must have been distracting to Museum officials to see me joyously embraced by Yves Tanguy in the elevator, Léger interrupting an office conference to pat me on the head—"I've known him since he was a little boy"— or André Masson shouting across a room, *"Voilà, le petit fils de Max."* I renewed my acquaintance with Luis Buñuel, who had found a much-needed job through the good influence of Iris Barry. There didn't seem to be anything for him to do, and I saw him the first time sitting in apparent brooding depression with nothing on his desk other than an unstretched 1936 portrait of him by Dali. Sometimes he braved the smell of my Camembert lunch at the drugstore and told me marvelous stories about the making of *L'Âge d'Or* and *Chien Andalu.*

I carefully tried to keep distractions to a minimum, though, if my curiosity hadn't gotten the better of me once in a while, I might have missed cameos like Charles Laughton acting out his raptures over Picasso's *Girl Before a Mirror* when it was hanging just inside the entrance of the Museum. In front of the same painting I witnessed another memorable performance by a portly young man, a WPA art teacher who regularly brought groups of black elementary school children on tours of the Museum. His gesticulating arms seemed too short for his body, his eyes were loosely basted ebony buttons and his nostrils flared dramatically over an elastic mouth in a bread-dough-white face. I had seen him performing as a comic at Café Society Downtown. Zero Mostel now had the undivided attention of his very young audience as he pointed at the large painting.

"All right, there . . . pay attention and *shut up!* This here is Picasso. He's Spanish . . . but he don't live there . . . he doesn't like that lousy dictator Franco . . . who does? Upstairs there's a big painting about a whole village of poor farmers being killed by German bombers. Can you imagine what that feels like? But he knows about women too. This picture is called *Girl Before a Mirror* . . . ever seen anything like it? . . . Shut up . . . you're not supposed to watch your sister undressed, you're too young. Your old man shoulda hit you in the head. . . . Anyway . . . this is a girl in front of a mirror. But listen, is that a girl, or isn't that a girl? Christ . . . that's a woman . . . and what a woman . . . *zoftig!* Waddaya mean, it don't look like no woman? . . . This one is all woman, you gotta believe me. Look at her. Look what she's got. . . . More than one of everything. See that *tokus?* She's got two of em. One of them is more like a *tushy* . . . that's ass, you jerk. Naa . . . he didn't forget the *pupik* . . . there it is and here again. You wouldn't know a *brust* if you fell over it, but you know tits, right? But Picasso's girl's got four of them. Why shouldn't she? That's the way he saw her, and he has a right as a citizen of the world to see anything the way he wants to. . . . Everybody sing with me, 'America, America. . . .' That's enough . . . shut up. . . . All right, let's go . . . and see the swinish bombers."

At first there were some nervous discussions on how to tame the wild man, but since there were no complaints from delighted visitors, the news of his presence, whenever, in the galleries circulated swiftly, and many staff members took time off from their work to catch him in the act. Not all of his appearances ended in laughter. He took his young charges to watch Clemente Orozco at work on his fresco *Dive Bomber and Tank* during the "Twenty Centuries of Mexican Art" exhibition. Mostel, aware of Orozco's strong right-wing political stance, encouraged his kids to pepper the painter with some sassy remarks and questions. An exasperated Orozco wheeled abruptly toward his small tormentors. The motion dislodged his artificial arm from the smock pocket, and the wooden hand, as if on its own, landed painfully on a startled black face.

I could not imagine what it was about me, in that lowest of jobs, that caused the top office brass to pay such troublemaking attention to me. For forty-odd years now I have puzzled over what transgression of mine could possibly have provoked an episode that for all of its apparent triteness was a frightening throwback to my childhood helplessness in the face of brown-shirted hostility. I underwent an hour-long interrogation in the controller's office by a panel of Museum personnel executives. The charge: I had tried to sell to my mail-room boss four 10-cent stamps that I had obviously stolen from petty cash to begin with. An amateur philatelist among my inquisitors was convinced that I must have been stealing for a long time because each stamp was of a different series. My explanation that I bought 10-cent stamps for my letters to Europe whenever I had a spare dime and that I had been short of money for dinner, cut no ice whatsoever. During the painful exposition of all my failings I had the slightly reassuring impression that there was someone at the Museum who had taken the trouble to protect me. Therefore the effort to find good cause to fire me. It ended in a depressing standoff. Charges could not be proved. I would not lose the job now. A few months later I did not receive a promised three-dollar increase.

Frederick Kiesler's active interest in my painting as well as my well-being resulted in a rich lode of new friends for me. From very early on he had seen the great artistic potential of the young Chilean painter Matta Echaurren. I had seen Matta's work in the back room of Julien Levy's gallery and been strongly affected by his explosive imagery. He was taking his Surrealism into a world first suggested by the painters Yves Tanguy and André Masson. It was a biomorphic universe that probed into an inner world of organic matter and forms, beyond recognizable representation. The one-time student of Le Corbusier had created pulsating invented forms that coexisted with, and became part of, subtle linear implosions. A growing number of young American artists found much of their own thinking reflected in the imagery of infinity that they saw in Matta's paintings and drawings. Having preceded the other Surrealists to New York at the same time as Tanguy, this youngest member of the Paris group differed from them by engaging in interested companionship within the New York art community as he found it. Small, brilliant and intense, he treated me as an equal from the very beginning. He was not at all above giving technical or aethetic counsel to young or aspiring artists who, like me, were more interested in the act of painting than in often perplexing theories. Many of the artists he came in contact with were not aware that Matta's nonfigurative work was considered something of a deviation by some of the Surrealists, an indication that the arteries of that adventurous movement were showing signs of hardening. If modern art on this side of the Atlantic were ever to develop a characteristic all of its own, new light was discernible in the direction of what the Abstract painters in America had already been doing and in the utilization of imagery arrived at through manual gesture alone. The steps were halting and immature, but if and when the fuse was ignited, Matta would be one of those who had lighted the match.

Paris' café-life was a natural garden for the bloom of ideas and casual encounter of like-minded individuals. New York had to rely on meeting places less accessible and slower in becoming known. One of these places was Francis Lee's loft on East Tenth Street. He was a photographer with hopes of making experimental films. Compared to his friends, his daily existence was a bit more secure, though even he had recurring problems of meeting the monthly $18 rent on a space that, for most of us, could only be dreamed of. Jerome Kamrowski lived in a Village basement, Peter Busa in some small rooms on Fourteenth Street, and William Baziotes, who was on the WPA easel project, lived in a tiny tenement apartment on Thirteenth Street with his wife Ethel, around the corner from Kiesler. The loft was thus the center of most social activities. On any given evening people might casually drop by and suddenly a communal meal was underway under the supervision of Ethel Baziotes and Lee's girl friend Lydia.

Loft-living in 1940 was a constant adventure with the authorities and Consolidated Edison. Habitation for domestic purposes was against the law, and a small cache of money was always held in reserve for capricious inspectors from the Fire and Building Department. They usually got their $2 take in nickels and dimes, contributed, by tacit understanding, by anyone who came to visit. When the pot overflowed, the surplus was invested in more spaghetti, tomatoes, garlic or wine. The cooking facilities were hidden by ingenious trapdoors, and whenever a gumshoe from the city inquired about the profusion of beds and couches, he was told that these were for the models to rest on. Some rest, some models! Most of the electric and gas meters in these places had been "improved" with clever devices—jumpers—that bypassed them. Some tenants, like Francis Lee, were delinquent in their bills, and the jumper was absolutely essential to them.

One night was not atypical. Gene Varda, a collagist from San Francisco, was the guest of honor and about ten of us, including Louise Nevelson, Kamrowski, Busa, the Baziotes, Lee and the writer Harry Roskolenko were digging into a huge bowl of pasta when there was a sharp rap at the door. The signal device on the stairs had failed to ring the bell. "Con Edison! . . . Open up . . . meter inspection!" It was incredible. At 10 P.M.? But Francis knew the drill. Without explanation to us, he yelled: "Just a minute . . . I gotta get dressed!" He raced for the meter and disconnected the jumper. The inspector played his flashlight over the eating group around the table in a darkness relieved only by some light from a gigantic roof-top billboard on the corner that was dominated by the lace-covered breasts of Rita Hayworth. Even after the inspector departed, having made sure that the seal on the meter had not been tampered with, we continued to enjoy our meal without electricity. The guy usually stuck around on the street for a while to watch the windows for illegal use of Con Ed's services. We collected some money, and I was delegated to rush up to Fourteenth Street to buy candles. I found them in a Mom-and-Pop candy store. They had Hebrew letters on the glass.

It was not a tightly bound circle. At one time or another Kiesler might drop in with a large entourage of visitors from Europe or California. David Smith, Willem de Kooning, Arshile Gorky, Esteban Frances, David Hare, John Graham or Harold Rosenberg might be there a few times and then not be seen again for a long time. Louise Nevelson, who had a loft across the street, was there quite often, "but she did not seem very impressed by any awed talk about "biomorphic space" or quotations from André Breton's latest discourse. Louise obviously had her own ideas and professed impatience only with a world that denied her the material means of getting at her work. "I don't want to get anyone angry," she confided to me, "but I'd just as soon wait to see if some of those pronouncements make it across the ocean in the bottom of a ship. And once they get here, they might not have any meaning for me." There was also some talk about another skeptic, Jackson Pollock, whom I never saw at Francis Lee's, but a few times at Matta's place. The atmosphere there was somewhat different, the talk more concentrated on Surrealism and the need, perhaps, to initiate a young move away from its literary dos and don'ts. Neither Busa, Kamrowski, Baziotes nor I felt inclined to become part of a palace revolution while the palace itself was such a vague edifice to us. There was no question of our admiration for Matta and the liberating nature of his paintings, but we had also talked to Gorky and, not least of all, to Stanley William Hayter, and had observed them as individuals not at all prepared to become engaged in any kind of new orthodoxy. Bill Hayter, who had no peer among graphic artists, had brought his Atelier 17 from Paris to the New School of Social Research. A man of decisive mind with the countenance of a wise hawk, he could be relied upon to make short rift of too much theory by tersely reminding us that one could "try it . . . but it doesn't have to be eaten whole hog. . . . There are an awful lot of people around with indigestion."

I felt most comfortable with Ethel and Bill Baziotes. I could talk to them easily and, from the very beginning, there was no doubt that both, but particularly Ethel, felt very protective of me. It was almost impossible to imagine them apart from each other. Just to watch them walk on a street, dressed like a proud working couple on a gray Sunday stroll, made it unmistakable that they were "one bone and one flesh," bonded for life and perhaps beyond. Ethel's Byzantine-icon face rarely lost its serenity other than her eyes widening in astonishment or her delicate lips pursing as if to prepare the Madonna for a broad smile. If her laughter was decorous, Bill's usually somber and quizzical mien, that of a truck driver intent on the road, transformed itself into a simultaneous stretching of all facial muscles to the sound of bellringing laughter. He seemed a curious mixture interchangeable of earthiness and sophistication. He held his head as if the collar of his shirt were starched and high. His rugged face would not have been out of place in the Greek village of his ancestors. His friends could not avoid comparing him to a somewhat smaller Humphrey Bogart, a hat securely on his head, a cigarette dangling from the side of his mouth, one hand, as though always ready, defiantly protecting itself in the overcoat pocket. What did not fit that image was a slightly bulbous nose and the inevitable umbrella he seemed to hold at the ready against any kind of weather, even indoors. It was entirely believable that, as a youth in Reading, Pennsylvania, he had been a lookout against revenuers and rival gangsters for Dutch Schultz's trucks, and that he had hitchhiked the long road to Philadelphia to look at *Une Semaine de Bonté*, Max Ernst's collage novel. In New York he had worked his way through the National Academy of Art as a student of Leon Kroll, whom he admired but whom he could also imitate to devastating effect. Bill was an outrageously inventive raconteur whose stories, nevertheless, could not ever be discounted by his friends because they always contained a substantial kernel of truth. I, for one, believed all of them, always, and retold them with great glee.

He also had a way of talking about painting that avoided the extremely complicated verbiage of literary high priests. On a Saturday round of Fifty-seventh Street galleries we had run into the Social-Realist painter Sol Wilson, who had declared all nonrepresentational art totally inconsequential to the social and economic needs of the day. "You guys can do anything you want to do, but you'll never contribute anything for the masses of humanity. You are talking to a few aesthetes who themselves don't know what time it is. I paint people . . . hungry people or working people . . . my pictures are of the people and for the people. . . ." Over a cup of coffee we didn't focus on Wilson's particular point of view, which was all too familiar, but Bill tried to put his finger on the larger issue of "meaningful art." That, he felt, could occur only within groups who shared a totally common experience. Or in a time, perhaps like the Renaissance, when the artist's subject matter ran fairly parallel to a predominant belief.

"I could see where a small city became isolated by a worldwide catastrophe. They'd try to stay alive, feed themselves and rebuild their homes. At some point they'd pin up on some standing walls all of the drawings and other pictures made on pieces of paper or scratched into tablets since they'd been living in their lean-tos. I bet they would understand every scrap they looked at. That was something they had all lived through, including the dreams. But let some couple or a youngster go to the top of those hills in the forbidden zone to look at another horizon and fantasize on a future life; they'd come back with images that were strange to the rest of the people . . . until they, too, took the risk of looking . . . over there."

And we did look "over there." Matta's as yet unfinished painting *The Earth Is a Man* was precisely what it implied—cosmic nebula in breathing bursts of detonation and implosion. It was a visceral interior as vast as any imaginable universe. With a surgical curiosity bordering on mania, Matta had invaded one of Yves Tanguy's enigmatic flesh machines and had discovered a cosmic totality that was, indeed, both man and earth.

At his Fourteenth-Street studio we saw Bill Hayter's large canvases on which the brush had taken over for the severe discipline of the engraver's burin. Though still linear, the field of vision had become a battle scene in an, as yet, unseen empire of energy.

Arshile Gorky allowed a glimpse, now and then, of his deliberate struggles to let his own eyes direct the hands of Picasso. The heavy brushed surface and the ponderous outlines of forms were giving way to a more spontaneous flow of color and structure. It seemed immaterial to him that there was now more than a mere suggestion of Miró in his morphology. He seemed to be moving toward gestures similar to Matta's. The unmistakable passion inherent in the paintings of that period, such as *In the Garden* and *Garden in Sochi,* and the drawings, impressed me as being painfully personal. Gorky could laugh from beneath his drooping mustache but it rarely dispelled the melancholia of his dark eyes. His gaunt body was accented by a slight stoop that seemed less intended to accommodate smaller friends than it was a stalking in permanent search. At times he puzzled us with an air of hauteur that may have been just shyness. We suspected that he must have retained his heavy accent deliberately, for reasons that escaped us. He had, after all, arrived from Armenia in 1920, at the age of fourteen. The speculation of why he had emulated Aleksei Maksimovich Peshkov in adapting the name Gorki, with a slight variation, led nowhere except the suggestion that its translation as "bitter" may have seemed appropriate to him. Negative voices sought to dismiss him as a mere emulator who would always remain "a few steps behind." To be on top of such an aesthetic pecking order was a career goal for some even then, but Bill Baziotes dismissed these quite properly as "culture pimps." For all of Gorky's image as a "loner," he commanded our deep respect, and we identified with him.

Baziotes, whom I knew best, was living example of an American, who, unlike his European counterparts, had become an artist without growing up in the shadow of Greek, Roman, Gothic or Baroque edifices. His landscape, and that of other Americans, was silhouetted by coal-mine lift-cages, oil derricks and grain silos, skyscrapers, New England church spires and water towers. The land ebbed and flowed into endless plains delineated by mighty rivers, infinite forests and wilderness. With all that, Bill was exploring the interior of yet another landscape in his small room. He was giving life to dreams and to intuitive suppositions of what lay hidden in the secret and locked rooms of nature. His were visions alluding to recognizable imagery that transformed themselves into mythological apparitions from a pantheon of gnomes, serpents and birds. Spontaneous and thorny meanderings of the brush clustered into a clearly intended sensuality. Soft pink of flesh swam into vision as the fragment of a nude obliquely observed in a mirror. His Venus, as he once told me, was at her most glowing and erotic "when I watch her straightening the bedcovers after making love."

Day by day I was getting richer. To find myself in a growing circle of individuals whose eyes were looking in the same direction as mine meant far more than a release from loneliness. We friends were all *objets trouvés,* parts of a growing collage that took on a life of its own regardless of origin. Our fathers were laborers, storekeepers, miners, farmers, artisans or artists. The fact that mine was an idol gave rise to a very natural curiosity, but I had the unmistakable impression that, to my friends at least, inheritance of status or genes was an alien consideration. The newcomer in their midst was a kid on his own in a big city who, just like they, was interested in ideas rather than material success. In perfect keeping with my new life, I had an existence that owed little to my past. These were *my* friends and, if the future was to allow it, that was the way I'd introduce them to my parents.

I cannot imagine a young artist in the privacy of his work-space indulging in an extravagance of modesty. He must believe that he is "on the right track" or even on the very brink of deserving discovery. Unlike some young painters I did not even have much difficulty in learning to control my tools. It was as if I had observed and retained far more in the studios of Ernst and others than I realized. Though not unaware of the multiple influences evident in everything I painted, I felt justified in seeing a strong growth of original imagery asserting itself. In fact, there were frequent occasions when I had visions of the cultural magi, well on their way to my door at dawn to discover the newborn masterpiece of that night. Alas, in the morning light, and even more so a few days later, I had to admit, but only to myself, that my talent was still being held captive by Surrealist ghosts. It was about time for me to dismantle other walls that I had erected as a child against art and artists. I remembered a young sculptor friend of my mother who had opened my twelve-year-old eyes to amazing things while on a walk through woods and meadows. A small lizard whose protective coloring made him almost invisible, a black-and-green beetle with antennae resembling the horns of a mature stage. We counted the number of wing-beats, between soarings, of a large black bird. For the first time I saw the delicate vein filigree of a long-dead oak leaf and the majestic arrangement of seed pods crowning a wild wheat stalk. I had probably pushed that memory into the dark because the artist, Arno Breker, had subsequently become an early adherent of the Nazis and been rewarded by Hitler and Albert Speer with numerous architectural and sculpture commissions. Dismissing the source as far less important than the experience, I realized that it was unproductive to follow the dictates of any preconceived philosophy of painting. In the final analysis it all started with the eyes, and what all artists seemed to have in common was an intense visual curiosity as a precursor to any subjective idea.

The artistic climate in America appeared to me to be relatively free of bitterly contending groups or movements. The ideological or stylistic variants that did exist were fortunately not dominated by aesthetic autocrats. Not yet, at least. Fortunately, contention did exist, but in a context far different from Europe. There was more than a mere vestige of hostility, in or out of the arts, to anything modern. Even the 1913 Armory Show in New York was to these minds the carrier of a spreading plague. Some artists, caught totally by political ideology, echoed the line that any nonrepresentational art was either an attack on the people or the work of charlatans. There were distinct differences even among the relatively small number of avant-gardists of these early 1940s. From my own observations, however, a group like the American Abstract Artists, though obviously intent on certain formal concepts, were not totally resistant to other ideas. Kiesler had taken me to the opening of their exhibition at the Riverside Museum, where it was my impression that their range of expression was not in the least as parochial as that of similar groups in Europe. There were more than subtle differences among Josef Albers, Carl Holty, Ilya Boltowsky, George McNeil and David Smith. I was particularly taken by Balcolm Greene's *Ancient Form.* If there was any conformity to a prescribed concept, it was certainly not in evidence with individuals like Ibram Lassaw, Byron Browne, Ad Reinhardt, Vaclav Vytlacil, Fritz Glarner, Gertrude Greene or Giorgio Cavalon. Of all of them John Ferren was probably the best-known. His elegant and dynamic work, still somewhat under the influence of the French Abstractionist Jean Helion, had been exhibited at the Pierre Matisse Gallery. Though the work of some of these Abstract painters was already in various collections and had been seen in some museums and smaller galleries in New York, acceptance of them was severely limited by the meager scope of what "art world" there was. After the opening there was a communal dinner around a very large table in a first-story Italian restaurant on upper Broadway. I sat next to Balcolm Greene, who invited me to come to his studio. Greene did not fit Kiesler's image of "little people as geniuses." Even seated, I had to crane my neck to talk to him. Kiesler conceded that there might be a few exceptions to his rule.

The talk around the table was less about art itself than the ways and means of stretching the modest WPA stipend that enabled many of these artists to pursue their calling instead of relying on charity. The Works Project Administration had been one of several agencies established by the New Deal as an alternative to the dole for the unemployed. Franklin Roosevelt was said to feel that the contribution of artists, writers, composers and other creative individuals was of the same importance to the troubled nation as were roads, public parks, post offices and land reclamation. Conservative elements in Congress and the press had constantly blown out of all proportion the programs' inevitable abuses and inefficiencies. The idea that artists deserved the attention of their government during a national crisis as much as day laborers was the subject of derision in almost the same measure as the ever-present photograph of the public works ditchdigger caught leaning on his shovel. But the idea was already transforming the drabness of public housing projects, post offices, federal buildings, airports and schools with murals and sculpture. The imagination of the sculptor transformed children's playgrounds, parks, courthouses and other public buildings. But artists were worried now since Roosevelt, to curb the criticism, had combined all of these agencies under one bureau and some investigators and supervisors felt emboldened to impose their personal tastes, of content and quality, on individual artists. It was not unusual for a painter to be called into a disciplinary meeting, under the threat of suspension, because someone had fancied the hidden image of a hammer and sickle, or a red flag, in an Abstract painting.

Baziotes had told me a great deal about his own experiences as a painter on the WPA project. Standing in line on Fridays with colleagues like Louise Nevelson and Stuart Davis for a paycheck of $23.86 meant another week of adequate food and shelter. To show me what was going on, he borrowed a friend's car and we visited the sites of some mural projects around New York for a whole day. The Newark Airport Gorky murals had been installed in 1937. These heroic aerodynamic Abstractions impressed me as a very individual absorption of Miró, Helion and Léger. In the Aviation Building of the Flushing World's Fair his silhouetted shapes were less ponderous and, in some instances, soared as if liberated from the two-dimensional wall. We drove over to the nearby Marine Terminal of La Guardia Airport, where James Brooks was beginning to evoke a powerful collection of Abstract aero-industrial forms in that domelike building. Jim, a warm and thoughtful individual, seemed almost too shy in the face of his work, and yet one could sense a well-controlled intensity as he talked to us. Philip Guston was finishing a mural for the Queensbridge Housing Project community center. There was an air of melancholia in both the man and the images. The somewhat stylized figures in a dense urban environment suggested some of the later work of De Chirico in the stoical acceptance of their individual isolation.

Guston's own face, particularly around the eyes, could have come out of a Romanesque mosaic. He expressed anxiety and impatience with the work in progress. His face could light up in a wide smile, but then only as if the sun knew that it was about to lose a battle with the clouds. . . . This was the artist in America, a dinghy on a rough sea.

My own first "mural" commission came as a result of John LaTouche's complaints that his enormous bathroom in his little house on Minetta Lane in Greenwich Village was "just too damned depressing." Having just begun to collaborate with Touche on what was eventually to be the musical *Cabin in the Sky*, Vernon Duke suggested, "Why don't you let Jimmy do a mural on those dreadful walls?" "Mural" was an inhibiting word after what Bill Baziotes had shown me. This was no place for either profundity or cake-icing humor. I would have to pretend that the place belonged to me and decide what I would want to look at while taking a long bath. In true theater style Touche created a "Jimmy Beautification Society" to collect the necessary funds for the Duco automobile enamel, brushes, turpentine and rags that I had decided to use for my project. The contributors to the fund included anyone who attended the housewarming party, and that included Teddy Griffis, Touche's fiancée, Bob Faulkner, his companion and roommate, Aaron Copland, Oliver Smith, Paul and Jane Bowles, Julien Levy, Virgil Thomson and Frederick Kiesler. The work proceeded over a series of long weekends. Friday nights I usually had the place to myself because "everybody" in New York went to Constance Askew's salon on the East Side. I had been taken there once by LaTouche, but Mrs. Askew, wife of the prominent art dealer, Kirk, had indicated to him that I was not yet quite ready for the company of Nancy Cunard, Noel Coward or whoever else happened to be in town. I did have the pleasure of being filled in by Touche, when he and friends finally got home late at night, on the scene in general, the witticisms and the intellectual cat fights. It was obvious, for example, that it would have been wrong for me to have been there when Dick Abbott, now executive director of the Museum of Modern Art, and my boss, had flailed in helpless drunkenness on the carpet, loudly rejecting any assistance to put him back on his feet. Or when a talented understudy tried to make sure that her star would not be able to make it onto the stage for the next performance by escorting the alcoholic lady to a cab and then was overheard directing the driver to take his fare to a hotel in Albany.

As the "mural" took shape, it became very clear to me that the images and spaces in this *oeuvre* diverged radically from the biomorphic ideas of Matta, Gorky and Baziotes (that extraterrestrial biology) that I was trying to approach in my "more serious" work. The flora and fauna that grew from inside the bathtub onto the walls, around mirrors, dived into the toilet bowl, plunged through the towel racks and obscured the medicine cabinet owed much of their visual life to the day when I had stormed into my father's studio after experiencing the *Guernica* for the first time. Given a good number of technical inadequacies, convenient simplifications and the inexperience of a rookie, these were the carnivorous plants and insects from Max's 1937 *La Nymphe Echo,* the floating ogres of the same year's *L'Ange du Foyer* and the long-beaked birds, with feline bodies, from yet earlier paintings. The fact that I had carried these images hidden within me and the autonomous way in which they discharged themselves from agnostic hands, were enough for me to let them run their course.

If I had planned to have this creation witnessed by a very select audience only, I could not have chosen a better place for it. LaTouche had established a salon of his own, which drew heavily on the same groups that attended the Askew soirees but also attracted younger aspirants like Truman Capote, Tennessee Williams, Leonard Bernstein, and Judy Holliday. These social events usually took place when I was working on those walls, and since automobile enamel gets viscous very quickly, I did not take time out to join the parties, but kept going. At one point or another, someone like Pavel Tchelitchew or the writer Charles Henry Ford would drift in, or Julien Levy, Virgil Thomson, Kurt Kasznar, Maurice Grosser, Oliver Smith, Eugene Berman, Sylvia Marlowe with Leonid, e. e. cummings or Gypsy Rose Lee. I never knew if they wanted to see the "W.C. Beautification" or merely make use of the utilities. I literally had to "play it by ear," with resulting stage bits like "My dear, you'll have to leave me alone for a minute. This lady has to pee! . . ." declaimed by an imposingly beautiful woman in a gigantic flowered hat, Stella Adler.

My modesty was not well served when *Look* magazine decided that the mural would make a most exciting background for LaTouche at work by moving his desk into the bathroom. There was Touche, sitting on the hidden toilet, pen in hand, contemplating a globe dominated by a semi-draped bird creature . . . probably on the verge of solving the translation riddle of Brecht's *"Soldaten wohnen auf den Kanonen . . ."* (Soldiers live on the cannons) *"Ja, da kann man sich doch nicht nur hinlegen. . . ."* (Yes, it is not enough to just lie down) Or when a *World-Telegram* reporter cut off LaTouche's protest—that the Republican party's plan of using "Ballad for Americans" at their upcoming convention was a misreading of that song's real character—with a categorical "Listen, kid, I know a Fourth of July flag waver when I hear one" shortly amended his opinion: ". . . After seeing that bathroom, though . . . I don't know what to believe."

A useful but not very welcome reaction came from Julien Levy: "I wish you hadn't asked me that, Jimmy, but I think it's dreadful. If you really feel that you have to paint, you shouldn't have to ask for a standing ovation before you have done anything worth looking at." Leo Lehrman, far more kindly, responded to my impertinence with a very broad, but diabolical, smile, which I should not have arbitrarily interpreted as benign approval.

On the positive side there was a remuneration for the work in the form of a $50 credit at Brentano's, one of the lesser corporate assets of Teddy Griffis' father Stanton.

Less satisfying was a situation that I had created through my notion that I was hopelessly infatuated with Jane Bowles. The cause may well have been my innocent misreading of her sexual preference. I was not totally bereft of romantic reality, however. At one of Francis Lee's loft parties I had met a Brunhilde type, Helga, who was very willing to explore quite thoroughly the heterosexual possibilities of her libido. There was also Bettina, an art history student of promising Mediterranean temperament that would assert itself, alas, only after a meal at Longchamps. It made me very uncomfortable to see the waiter's face after I told him that I was not hungry and ordered dinner for "the lady only." Jane Bowles was warm, often delightfully fey and, in spite of her gamin quality, extremely feminine. When she looked at Elsie Huston or Mary Oliver with that soulful expression, I readily ascribed it to her astigmatism but forgot to do so when those eyes looked at me in the same way. On the few occasions when she allowed me to sit at her feet, next to her writing table, she might, somewhat absentmindedly, stroke my hair while working on her manuscript. That was all there was to it, but if I chose to interpret these gestures as more than genuine affection, I had only my romantic nature to blame.

The "mural commission" finished, my prior weekend excursions to Jay Leyda's place by long bus trips had changed, via West Side I.R.T., to Bill and Ethel Baziotes' new apartment on 104th Street and Broadway. Bill painted in one of the bedrooms, and he offered me the use of their living room on Saturdays and Sundays. I brought my little radio and, for the first time, worked happily on a well-mended outdoor watercolor easel belonging to Bill until dinnertime. Ethel served lovingly prepared meals, often featuring my favorite, knockwurst and sauerkraut. At the table we'd discuss the news that I'd heard on the air. After the fall of Paris my feelings of anxiety and helplessness about the fate of my mother and father had become almost obsessive, and Sunday was always the proverbial time for ominous rumors out of Europe. But I was still able to join in the gossip about Fifty-seventh Street and what we'd seen during the week. Once in a while Bill would talk about the grim street scenes at the height of the Depression, when the only defense by unemployed protesters had been the marbles with which they tried to upset the horses of mounted policemen in front of the general post office. Sunday night came to an end with a double feature somewhere on upper Broadway.

The fact that I worked at the Museum of Modern Art did not bother any of my friends, even though they were very critical of its favoritism toward European, and now also Latin American, art. Its permanent collection of American avant-garde work was growing only slowly. What there was of it owed its presence to the embattled prescience of Alfred Barr and Dorothy Miller. There were, after all, other, earlier neglected Americans deserving prior consideration. The Museum owned four superb Edward Hoppers, for example. His haunting *House by the Railroad* had been chosen as one of the large color reproductions for the front desk, where its sales were second only to Picasso's *Woman in White*. Some of the other Americans were Maurice Prendergast, John Marin, Charles Sheeler, Charles Demuth, Charles Burchfield, Alexander Calder, John Flanagan, Walt Kuhn and Loren McIver. There was doubt at the time that the growing institution was ready to look at the experiments of younger Americans more than peripherally. In the opinion of these artists, the Museum had stepped backward in opening its doors to Botticelli's *Birth of Venus* and a rich treasure of other Italian early masterpieces. There had been a thinly veiled promotion tie-up with a new newspaper, *PM*, under the heading "The Artist as Reporter" and, in succession, a large show of Mexican art and the uninspiring presentation of the Brazilian painter Portinari. The latter two exhibitions made it clear that the Museum was going to be an arm of the Coordinator of Latin American Affairs, Nelson Rockefeller. Shortly after "Italian Masters" closed, I had the embarrassing experience of having to walk through a picket line in which I discovered many of the faces of new acquaintances and friends from the "American Abstract Artists." They were protesting, with handbills, the Museum's "three-ring" atmosphere and questioned its judgment, wondering how far afield "Art in Our Time" could be stretched. One of the participants, Ad Reinhardt, sensing my dilemma of not wanting to cross any picket line, ever, temporarily halted his milling colleagues, and I was encouraged to go through with a round of applause.

More major figures of Europe's intellectual world decided to continue their work in a safer America and in New York in particular. Immigration was at that time a responsibility of the Department of Labor under Frances Perkins, who from early on realized that individuals like Jacques Lipchitz, Marc Chagall, Ossip Zadkine, Walter Gropius, Mies Van der Rohe, Franz Werfel, Kurt Seligmann, Marcel Breuer, Fernand Léger, Piet Mondrian, André Breton, Max Ernst and many others—not only in the arts—were a treasure to be saved from the madness abroad.

It was not an easy matter for Secretary Perkins, considering the many perverse provisions and interpretations of immigration statutes, most of them basically hostile to individuals whose attitudes about sex, marriage, patriotism and politics were well known to be at variance with the mores of the day. With the help of Varian Fry, Frank Kingdon, Alfred and Margaret Barr, Eleanor Roosevelt, Leo Cherne, and many others in the arts, academics and sciences, and, not least of all, Secretary Perkins' then son-in-law, the sculptor David Hare, America became the host and beneficiary of some of the finest minds of the twentieth century. For many the process was to be tortuously difficult. Franz Werfel had made his way across the Pyrenees on foot; others were to come by way of Cuba, Chile or Brazil. While I was sitting at the bar of Fifty-second Street's Famous Door with a young and intense French cinema addict, Henri Langlois, listening to Count Basie, Max Ernst was waiting in relative comfort to get out of Marseilles, and Lou Straus-Ernst was writing her thinly disguised memoirs somewhere along that coast, and as I was to find out years later from the writer Kay Boyle, supplementing her daily needs by occasionally joining a refugee soup line.

Among the immigrants in New York was a twenty-eight-year-old English painter, Gordon Onslow-Ford. A product of upper-crust British schools, including the Royal Naval College, he had served as a lieutenant in the Mediterranean and Atlantic fleets before deciding, in 1937, to become a painter. In Paris he had become a close friend of Matta and been formally accepted by André Breton into the Surrealist group. Baziotes and I agreed during many speculations about him that Onslow-Ford was, indeed, the very image one expected to come out of this background—handsome, suave and well-spoken. But he was far more than that: inspiring, generous, without a hint of condescension toward the small group of artists who formed a circle of friends and listeners around him after Matta introduced him to us when he lectured on Surrealism at the New School for Social Research. His thoughts, though delivered with some formality, never closed the door on those of us who were aware of our intent but unaccustomed to the serpentine interpretations of them.

Onslow-Ford looked to the future of painting with a particular emphasis on the events in Matta's canvases that left the narrow scope of figuration behind for a world of as-yet-unseen realities. His work, devoid of Old World elegances, had biomorphic elements moving in and through strata of an unearthly landscape. It was a step beyond Breton's Surrealism and, indeed, beyond the Freudian dream catalog. To some of us it seemed to say for the first time, "Why not?" rather than, "It has to be." When he and Howard Putzel (an early enthusiast of avant-garde art) organized exhibitions at the New School, we had, in spite of ourselves, become something of a group.

In the course of these shows in a modest space, artists like Boris Margo, André Racz, Jerome Kamrowski, Robert Motherwell, Leon Kelly, Baziotes and I hung on the same walls as Miró, Masson, Tanguy, Matta, Gorky, Ford and Hayter as if we really belonged there. I often wondered why I, a child of Dada, breast- and bottle-fed on Surrealism and taken by the hand through a maze of manifestos in the ateliers and sidewalk cafés of Paris and Cologne, had remained so uncomprehending of all those words and theories. I had grown up among those thinkers and makers, had witnessed and digested their verbal and visual ideas. But maybe, even at an early age, I felt discomfort in observing so much compliance to external didactics by supposedly free spirits. Perhaps it was my memory of seeing the Weimar Republic, with all of its well-meant reforms, its humanistic aims, failing in the streets of Cologne, while its intellectual leaders tried to outshine one another with semantic exercises in our living rooms. I was aware that this was not a mere choice between dream and reality. The man on the bread line was just as angry at not being able to work as Max Ernst was when he saw treasured friends being bent by political or aesthetic wills. My own instinctive reservations about compliance and dogma may well have been fostered by the knowledge of my father's running nonconformity, as an artist and as a man, even within his own circle.

Onslow-Ford talked not so much to us as with us. What we heard was less of the "how" of imagery than the "why." We were not getting the "last word from Europe" but rather the possibility for a further horizon that implied individualism. At some point, and that was tacitly understood, we would be going our own ways. There is no such thing as a collective idea.

When André Breton arrived in New York, it became quite evident that he preferred not to see any splinter groups even remotely connected with Surrealism. He had doubts that the young Americans qualified as bona fide members of *his* movement. He made no secret of his suspicion that Abstract art was about to invade the Surrealist precincts. The established artists were urged to withold their support. *Automatism should not become the vehicle for counterrevolutionary abstraction.* Though he later modified this absolute, it was now a useful argument for the retention of Surrealism's leadership in his wiser hands. I don't believe that Onslow-Ford ever had such grandiose designs. Still, this "correction" took place while he was in Mexico on a visit with the painter Wolfgang Paalen. As a result the "youth movement" was scattered, leading, in some cases, to premature independence of its "members."

My annual vacation of six paid days did not allow for any "grand tour." For the previous summer, 1940, I had, with the help of Ted Huff as co-signer, floated an onerous loan of $25 from the Household Finance Company to join Julien Levy's secretary, Lotte Barrit, and her mother at a hotel called Châlet Indien in Boyceville, in the Catskills. It was a place favored by German-Jewish refugees and was really a glorified boardinghouse that announced itself from the road with a large Catskill version of a garish totem pole. Unfortunately, some of the guests spent a lot of their time comparing this spa with the elegant grand hotels of a fugitive past. I enjoyed all of it—the regular meals, the swimming pool and hikes with the two ladies, and left my mark behind in the form of a large painting on the wall of the communal playroom. It was a somewhat grim house-paint composition of planetary elements modestly entitled *La Deuxième Creation du Monde*, with Darius Milhaud in mind.

My 1941 dim vacation prospects were magically solved when a returned expatriate writer, who had joined John LaTouche's social and intellectual scene, offered to let me join him and his family at a cottage they had rented in Amagansett, on the eastern tip of Long Island. He would even stake me to the train fare. It made me very happy that I would be spending my birthday near the water. We took a 5 A.M. fisherman's special on a Sunday, missed our stop and had to make our way, mostly on foot, all the way back from Montauk. The cottage was a converted lobster boat that had been washed onto Promised Land on Napeague Bay by a hurricane.

My benefactor and his very beautiful wife and small baby showed me my room, which was the awning-covered stern of the boat. "The nights can get quite cold here. Don't hesitate to get warm in the cabin," he said on the same day as he stepped onto a return train to New York. "I'll be here again next Sunday to bring you back home." It was a glorious week for me, swimming, sunning, and taking an evening's walk past the Elm Tree Inn where, to my astonishment, I recognized a group of conservatively dressed men, out on their own stroll, as the loyalist Spanish government in exile. On the day my vacation was to end, the wife of my peripatetic host whispered to me, "It's perfectly all right. You can kiss me, you know." On the long train ride back, her husband seemed extremely preoccupied and almost hostile. He barely talked to me. I kept wondering what kind of faux pas I could possibly have committed.

It took John LaTouche to clear up the matter after some prodding. It seems that as a result of a "misplaced sense of propriety" I had failed to enrich my vacation to an undreamed-of extent. When I told Touche that none of the nights had been cold enough for me to seek refuge in the cabin, he laughed and burst out: "Jimmy, you missed the whole point. You think you were nice, but you were nice in an unexpected way. I'm not surprised that he is furious with you, and she's probably mad at him because she has you tagged as one of his other diversions."

Barely back at work in the Museum mail room after my brief holiday, I received two pieces of news in one day. The first one, in the morning, was my boss telling me with ill-concealed satisfaction that, although I would not now be fired, I could expect no increase in wages or other benefits ever. If I wanted to stay, I would have to be aware of that condition. I might have been an annoying pebble in the ongoing hostilities between the "dreamers" and the "realists." The other one, in the afternoon, was a cable from Lisbon that "Max Ernst and party" would arrive on tomorrow's Pan Am clipper in New York. I had absolutely no idea what the words "and party" meant.

In keeping with the "no quarter for Jimmy" policy, it took a no-nonsense Alfred Barr memo to the "business side" to get me the day off. He did not know what "Max Ernst and party" meant either, but it definitely did not include Lou Straus-Ernst. The audacious idea of bringing my parents out together had fizzled badly. In part, Lou herself had contributed to the failure. Barr had just gotten some of the background information on what, for me, was ominous news. I was startled to learn that my desperate plan appeared still to have had a chance of working until the spring of 1941, when the International Emergency Rescue Committee consulted none other than Eleanor Roosevelt on the matter. Varian Fry, in a cable from Marseilles, advised New York: "ELEANOR RIGHT ABOUT LOU ERNST UNABLE POSE AS STILL MAX'S WIFE." This was after Hiram Bingham, U.S. Vice Consul at Marseilles, interviewed Max and Lou for the purpose of granting them an American visa. My suggestion, and slim hope, that their German divorce decree be considered invalid on a technicality, turned out to be unacceptable to the consulate. Max immediately offered to remarry her, but Lou, in front of the Consul, rejected the idea: "But Max, you know that this is nonsense. We have led separate lives for a long time now and neither one of us has ever resorted to sham. I am sure that Jimmy will get me out. After all, he got us both this far. I don't like charades. . . . A life for a marriage license? . . . And who knows, maybe none of this will be necessary after all. I'm an optimist." Later, in Varian Fry's office, she repeated the same sentiments, obviously unaware of the committee's then current policy to concentrate its energies on saving the lives of the more prominent personalities first. She may also not have known how nearly impossible it was at the time to find another affidavit in America to add to the one from J. J. Augustin. I just had to believe that time would not run out while I searched for it.

Gordon and Jaqueline Onslow-Ford came with me, on that fourteenth of July, to the La Guardia Marine Air Terminal. Part of the scaffolding for Jim Brook's mural was still in place, but there was enough to see for me to imagine receiving my father and proudly pointing to the work of "one of my colleagues in America." We watched the clipper taxiing to the pier and unloading. I thought I spied Max from the distance, but whoever it was emerged surrounded by a bunch of children. Inside I waited for the doors from Customs Inspection to open for my father. When it did, it was for a strange man, two women and at least six children.

One of the women, I guessed her to be about forty, came toward me, her body and walk suggesting considerable hesitation. Her legs seemed absurdly thin even for her fragile, angular figure. Her face was strangely childlike, but it expressed something I imagined the ugly duckling must have felt the first time it saw its reflection in the water. All the features of that face seemed to be intent on wanting to draw attention away from an unnaturally bulbous nose. The anxiety-ridden eyes were warm and almost pleading, and the bony hands, at a loss where to go, moved like ends of broken windmills around an undisciplined coiffure of dark hair. There was something about her that wanted me to reach out to her, even before she spoke. "You must be Jimmy. Max was very impatient on the plane. He talked about you all the way over. I am Peggy Guggenheim. . . . Over there is Laurence Vail, he was my husband. And that is his wife Kay Boyle, my daughter Pegeen and my son Sinbad . . . the other children are theirs . . . we had a dreadful flight. . . . There is some kind of trouble about Max's passport inside. Maybe they'll let you in there and you can help." Who was this woman? I was stunned. Was this what "Max Ernst and party" meant? I tried to recall what I knew of this name, Peggy Guggenheim. I had heard some idle talk about this heiress and art patron at the Museum as well as in cocktail chatter at LaTouche parties, and now I also recalled Alfred Barr's telling me that Max and some of the other Surrealists still in Marseilles had been helped by Peggy Guggenheim while she herself was waiting for transportation to the States. At the time I'd been too preoccupied about the fate of my mother to pay attention.

I'd half expected Leonora to walk off the plane with Max, but now here was yet another new face, and this one with a legendary name. I should have been used by now to sudden changes of women and plans in my father's life. What had happened so quickly in Marseilles or Lisbon? I couldn't get the answer right now. I had to go and see what was happening in the Immigration Room.

The frosted glass door was opened reluctantly, and after I identified myself, I was admitted to a rather funereal scene. My father, surrounded by note-taking reporters, looked awfully scared and seemed to respond to the questions only with stammers. Three men stood apart, studying his open passport on a table without touching it. I headed for them first. "That your father? . . . Yeah, his visa and everything are all in order . . . but we can't let him in. . . . How come, after all these years in France, he comes over here with a German passport?" I told them that during all that time he had vainly tried to become a French citizen. The French wouldn't have any of it, and it was probably the only document he could get. "Well, we can't make the decision here. We've got to put him on Ellis Island. Maybe they'll be able to figure it out. He's going to have a hearing over there. . . . When? . . . Could be soon. There isn't much action there anymore, and the commissioners have to be gotten together. Can't tell if they'll let him in."

I had never seen Max so shaken. I embraced him, suddenly feeling that it was up to me alone to give him some assurance. The reporters abandoned their reluctant subject and crowded around me instead. What was it that lawyers told about their accused clients to the newspapers? "It's just a technicality." All I could say was "This is a great artist. The Germans have burned his paintings in public. They would shoot him if they could get hold of him. That German official in Vichy, France, who gave him the passport will probably lose his job." And then I remembered something else that I had read: "That is all I have to say to you, gentlemen. . . . My answer to everything else is: No comment." I never had a chance to see if my handling of the situation had impressed the great man, my father. Flanked by the three officials, he was being walked toward a car outside the rear of the room. "It's too late to get him over to the island tonight," I heard one of them say. "We'll put him up at the Belmont Plaza until tomorrow morning." It occurred to me that the only words Max had spoken to me were in English: "Hello, Jimmy, how are you?"

The three days of waiting for a decision from Ellis Island were disturbingly calm. Ellis Island . . . The term alone conjured up fantasies induced by many accounts, real and fictional, of that strange place, promising ultimate freedom or threatening dismal banishment. Was this a gate that was meant to open or to close? I was not too worried about Max's finding himself in those historically sad surroundings. He had a unique way of extracting sardonic humor and novel insights from just about any unexpected situation. My fear was of an imminent decision for his future, over which so few, certainly not I, had any measure of control. My own childhood fears of anything or anybody in an official function, such as police or similar authorities, had been too deeply inbred to abate with the climate of my new life. But the situation was in the hands of people I trusted, people in a position of power. I had not forgotten the effectiveness of the American steam-ship agent in Hamburg.

In fact, Peggy called me several times at the Museum during that waiting period. She had, indeed, collected influential support to vouch for Max when the time came. She repeatedly told me not to worry. Nelson Rockefeller, John Hay Whitney, American Smelting and Refining, the Borough President of Manhattan, Edward M. Warburg, people from the Morgan Bank, Lehman Brothers and Eleanor Roosevelt would all be represented. With the knowledge that such important names were involved in my own affairs, I went about my Museum chores with an undeniable sense of smugness. Maybe I was imagining it, but the attitude of the "unfriendlies" toward me seemed to have changed almost overnight. Some actually thanked me for putting the mail on their desk. The connection between Peggy Guggenheim and Max Ernst had obviously been gossiped about, and my phone calls from her were no secret in the offices. I think that Alfred Barr was enjoying the byplay too. At one point he looked up at me from his desk and broke into a wide grin, uncharacteristically winking one eye.

I was holding the fort in the mail room during lunch time on July 17 when Elizabeth Litchfield, Barr's secretary, called: "There is a very important letter from Mr. Barr that has to be delivered to Ellis Island immediately." I told her that I was alone in the mail room and not allowed to leave. Without being unfriendly, she said, "I'd prefer someone more reliable anyway. You always get lost on the subways, and South Ferry is tricky to get to. I'll try to get a messenger service." She was unsuccessful and called back: "I'll have to take a chance with you. God help me. Never mind the office rules. Get going . . . and please pay attention to where you are going. Mr. Barr will have my head if that letter doesn't get there in time."

I was not going to louse up this one and miraculously made the ferry without a long wait. It was the first time that I had been on the waters of New York Harbor since June 1938, and the significance that I was approaching the Statue of Liberty from the opposite direction this time was not lost on me.

The uniformed guard at the Ellis Island dock looked at the address on the envelope. "Take it to that building over there. . . . Sign your name in the book." I told him that I was just a messenger delivering a letter. "You gotta sign your name and purpose of visit." I complied. He looked at the name, then at me, then at another list. "You say you're a messenger? . . . You any relative of this applicant here, Maximilian Maria Ernst? . . . Some fancy name. . . . Hey, Bud, take over for me while I take care of this. . . . Follow me, Ernst."

I held Barr's letter in my outstretched hand as I followed him through the doors of an old building. "But, officer, I'm just supposed to deliver this letter."

On one side of what was obviously a waiting room were about fifteen or twenty people. They all looked very important with elegant briefcases, in clothes that character actors would wear when portraying high-powered lawyers in a movie. I saw Peggy, along with Ernest Lundeen, the American Smelting and Refining executive who had met her at the plane. Julien Levy was there, as well as a number of people I had seen a few times emerging from board meetings at the Museum, a couple of city officials and a congressman whom I recognized from newspaper photographs. I got a few curious glances from them and a look of astonishment from Peggy as I walked toward the door of the hearing room that the guard held open for me. "You been holding up proceedings here, kid. They been waiting for you. Sit over there in front of the commissioners' bench."

It was an austere, grimy cavern of a room. A stenographer, ready for work, sat on one side of the dais and a clerk on the other. A door in back of me creaked open. I turned to see a fragile, white-haired figure in a rumpled raincoat seating himself on a wooden bench against the back wall. Max squinted because the light was in his eyes. "Oh, it's you, Jimmy, how are you? Did they send you to get me out of here?" The emphasis was on the word "you."

Three robed gentlemen filed into the room and took their places above me on the bench . . . the commissioners. The clerk addressed me: "Please rise, place your hand on the book and swear that you will state the truth, and nothing but the truth, to the best of your ability, so help you God." I repeated as I was told, still holding the letter in my hand, which I had to transfer to the other to touch the Bible. Then came: "State your full name, place, date of birth and present address. . . . Be seated."

The commissioners took over: "Do you recognize the applicant in the rear of the room? State his name and your relationship to him."

"Sir, his name is Max Ernst; I mean Maximilian Maria Ernst, and he is my father . . . but, sir, I was just supposed to deliver this letter here. There are others who—"

"Let us decide what is appropriate in these proceedings. Do you hold gainful employment, and what is your salary? Are you willing to support the applicant and house him?"

"Sir, I work at the Museum of Modern Art, and I am paid thirty dollars twice a month. I live at 51 West Sixty-fifth Street. Of course I am willing to support my father . . . but my father has a lot of friends. Maybe you should read this letter I was supposed to deliver—"

"Never mind that. We're interested in you, not his friends. Can you accommodate the applicant in your quarters?"

"Well, sir, my quarters is a furnished room. The bed is a little bigger than a single and I am sure that my landlady, that's a Mrs. Jordan, wouldn't object. He is welcome to share my room, if he wants to."

"You ever been in any trouble? Police record? Anything like that? You're under oath. Are you a citizen of the United States of America?"

"Sir, I have no police record or any other kind of trouble. I have been in this country for only thirty-six months, but I have taken out my first papers. . . . Do you want this letter?"

"Young man, once more: Are you willing to assume full responsibility for the welfare of this applicant toward the end that he should not, ever, become a burden to the state and that you vouch him to be of good moral character?"

"Yes, sir, I do."

"So help you God?"

"So help me God."

I heard only the rustling of papers in the room and a slight cough from my father, while the commissioners conferred. Then:

"I recommend that applicant Maximilian Maria Ernst be released in the custody of his son, James U. Ernst, who appeared before this board on this day, July 17, 1941, in his behalf. . . . The motion is unanimously carried."

"Thank you, gentlemen. What should I do with this letter?"

In the waiting room Peggy rushed up to me. "When are they going to hold this hearing? All these important people have been waiting for a long time." A guard, in back of me, answered, quite formally, in my place: "The hearing has been held and is concluded. The applicant has been granted admission to the United States in the custody of his son. He is getting his belongings now. The next ferry for Manhattan leaves in about twenty minutes." There was a stunned silence as quizzical eyes sized up a very awed young man, still holding an envelope in his hand. "Well, well, Max is in your custody." Peggy looked happy. "Will you let me share the custody with you?"

On the ferry a few people came over to shake my hand and congratulate me, one even going so far as to pat me on the head. "This is great. The American system really works, doesn't it? Even that cripple in the White House can't change that." But for the most part, I noticed a lot of grim lawyer demeanors that expressed obvious annoyance at the waste of the better part of a day only to be upstaged by some kid. I didn't particularly mind still not being able to talk to Max. He and Peggy were surrounded by well-wishers with buttoned-on faces of fawning triumph, though half of them didn't know who the hell Max Ernst was, except that he was somehow connected to a Guggenheim. The painter William Gropper, who had also testified for some immigrant friend that day, introduced himself to me, hoping to meet Max, but quickly realized my embarrassment at not being able to do anything about it. It gave me an opportunity, however, to watch the action and the actors on the ferry with some detachment. The women in my father's life had invariably been physically attractive and sensuous. This alliance did not fit that image at all. I knew that Leonora Carrington was on her way to America somewhere out on the Atlantic. In spirit or appearance Peggy could not possibly compete with her. Yet I had sensed almost immediately, from admittedly scant evidence, that this shy and ungainly woman felt herself to be a part of Max's life now. Somehow I hoped that my father might have changed and that, for him, there was more in this relationship than possible exigencies of the moment. Peggy and I shared a cab from South Ferry to the Belmont Plaza, Max and the rest of the crowd having driven off in a parade of dark limousines. Peggy tried to maintain her poise at this insensitive slight with rapid intakes of breaths and a simultaneous twitching of her head. Tentatively touching my hand, she remarked that I must be very pleased to see Max again after a long separation. "He talks about you all the time . . . he should be very happy, the way things have worked out. . . . Has he said anything about me to you? . . . He can be so sweet, you know. . . . Has he said anything about us at all? After all, this is something new in his life, and he shouldn't want you to be surprised. . . . Am I asking too many questions, and you're thinking, Who's she?

I really think he needs me. . . . He is so beautiful, isn't he? . . . And wait until you see his new paintings. . . . He can be such a baby. . . . On the clipper, do you know what he did? He had a terrible row with Pegeen, my daughter, because he was afraid that she would get the last berth and he'd have to sleep sitting up. She shared mine and Max was so happy . . . it was a terrible flight. Max hates Kay. They fought all the way . . . Pegeen and Sinbad are my children with Laurence. He and Kay have had them for a while, and I think Kay has turned them against me. She is very strong . . . destructive. . . . Now, I'll have them back. . . . I think Kay is leaving Laurence. I think she has turned them against Max too. . . . Maybe you can help me; I want them to like Max. . . . I'm sorry, this must be difficult for you. I'm talking too much. Somehow, I feel that I can . . . I don't know why . . . Forgive me."

It was a bit much to absorb. I was bewildered and touched. Sophisticated and mature people were not supposed to be so insecure. I had thought that to be my province. Self-pity was an adversary who was never far away from me. My ego had assumed that the effects of years lean of love and abundant in threat would abate within a reasonable passage of time. Was it true—I just wouldn't believe the wisdom around the kitchen table—that the rich could be very sad people too? Was Peggy telling me something of herself? A lifetime of uncertainty concerning the motives of anyone within the vicinity of her feelings? Should I invent an answer, now, that would put a temporary dressing on the abrasion? I didn't have that small power and thought it best, perforce, to talk only about my own immediate concerns.

"I wish I had some answers right now, but I don't even have any questions. There hasn't been a minute yet for Max and me to talk at all. I have talked to everybody else, and so has he. I don't know when the time will come, but it will. But even then I won't know anything about his private life. There was never any reason why he should have told me about his choices in life. Most of the time the surprises were pleasant. I don't know if I can help you, but if I can, I will."

The scene at the Belmont Plaza was no different from the one on the ferry. Some of the faces had changed. Tanguy and his wife Kay Sage, Howard Putzel, Matta, Bernard Reis and his wife Becky (friend and accountant to many artists), Nicolas Callas and others were beaming at each other as Breton joined Max in holding court. Peggy grabbed my arm when Breton asked no one in particular about Leonora Carrington and when her ship was expected to arrive. Max mumbled something to the effect that she had married "that Mexican diplomat" and turned the conversation to something else. Howard Putzel, an old friend of Peggy who resembled a well-worn teddy bear, gave her the news that her collection had arrived but would take time to clear customs. She was very pleased but also concerned that she might have to pay duty on some Surrealist or Cubist works that the American authorities might not consider works of art. I decided that I'd had enough for one day and began to edge toward the door. Just then Breton had decided to express himself on "the strange behavior of Paul Éluard," suggesting obliquely that he might be a collaborator with the Germans in Paris. Max's face became an iron mask. "I won't listen to this. Éluard is a great man. Perhaps his apologies for Stalin disturb some of us, but his poetry is the blood of our bodies . . . he is my close friend and brother. He could have come here, like we did. Be safe. But he stayed. Say these things against him to his face. I can't stop you from writing them, but don't whisper behind his back."

He stalked away and pushed me ahead of him into the bedroom. He slammed the door with the word *merde,* turned to me and then said in German, "How shall we talk, German, French or English?" I answered him in English that I would probably talk to him in that language. He would do it also, he said, but once in a while he would need some German or French until he became more fluent. "The way you live, those terrible stories out there on Ellis Island, is that really true?" I reminded him that I had been under oath and had been scared, in fact, that the truth might cause difficulties for his admission to the country. "Well, I would have ruled the same way if I had been sitting up there. You behaved like a solid citizen. I'm just glad that I don't have to share your 'quarters,' wherever you're living now. . . . Look, take this and quit your job. You'll find something better. Until you do, I am going to help you. I have to go back in there now. Breton has had enough time to think of a good apology that won't sound like one."

I had never seen a hundred-dollar bill. I stuck it in my pocket, afraid to touch it because I was not sure that I should have taken it. I was standing by the elevators when Peggy came down the corridor, looking for me. "Max told me. Don't worry; it is his money. I've been buying paintings from him. . . . Putzel just told me about the collection getting here. I am going to need help. There'll be a lot of running around, record-keeping, letters and cataloging . . . maybe you'll be my secretary. I think we'll get along. . . . Twenty-five dollars a week would make things easier for you, don't you think?" I promised her to think it over and let her know tomorrow. "Oh, and Jimmy! . . ." I had to hold the elevator door open. "Thank you for what you did at the hearing. Max said that you were marvelous. I want him to be very happy. You've helped already." She took my face in her hands and kissed me.

Walking up Lexington Avenue and across the Park, I protected the unfamiliar piece of currency with my hand in my pocket against any eventuality. I was very tempted to take it out so I could see whose portrait was on it. I knew I was close to making a positive decision about tomorrow when I indulged in a fantasy about taking a taxi home and then seeing the driver's face as I handed him a hundred-dollar bill.

I saw Kiesler and talked it over with him and then, late at night, I went to Bill Baziotes to ask his advice. They both urged me to go ahead. Kiesler was not worried about my learning on the job. "And besides," he said, "you might be very helpful to your friends. There are all kinds of people who would like to dominate that woman." Steffi, his wife, felt that it was about time that I ate better regularly. Baziotes was fascinated by the idea. "Geez, you sure as hell won't be bored in that crowd. You been here longer than a lot of them. Tell 'em a thing or two; this isn't Paris."

I probably didn't think too much about my function and the consequences thereof in stepping back into a world that I had left. Nothing that I had done so far, outside of my painting, had been with any thought of a future. It would be more like landing on the West Side docks, three years ago, perfectly willing to let things happen to me and dealing with them as they occurred. The Museum of Modern Art job gave every indication of becoming progressively more uncomfortable. But I must have had some apprehension about the possible course of Max Ernst's future relationship with Peggy Guggenheim. The cameos of the last few days kept recalling, in particular, the painful anguish I had witnessed as Marie-Berthe saw Max drifting away from her.

She had, apparently, not survived the separation as well as my mother had earlier. The last I had heard of her was that she was no longer collecting stray animals from the streets of Paris. She was shepherding a very ill Chaim Soutine from one remote area of France to another. Soutine, Lithuanian Jew and "decadent modern" painter, was a likely victim of Paris' conquerors. In fact, he was to die in her arms. Up until now I had been an uneasy spectator of the vagaries of my father's personal life. This time I might be so close to the scene as to risk unreasoning involvement. There was really no one to give me any advice, including my mother, whose whereabouts I did not know at the moment and who, in all probability, would have left the decision up to me anyway.

The 99-cent Shulte Cigar Store shirts now cost $1.05. I wore a new one and also my "special-occasions" bow tie the next morning for work. Mrs. Jordan had washed and ironed my chino office-boy jacket that bore my name. I started on my rounds of delivering the incoming mail. When I placed the director's mail on Elizabeth Litchfield's desk I pointed to the envelope on top. "Here is the letter you gave me yesterday. I didn't deliver it. I tried, but nobody wanted it. I really tried." She had a marvelously pealing laugh, and this time it rang out like a fire alarm. "We heard all about it. Mr. Barr says you were the man of the hour, and the rest of the crowd got an idea what Ellis Island looks like."

Barr stuck his head in the door and grinned. "Some people called me last night; they complained that I had sent them on a wild-goose chase."

I orchestrated my final delivery in the office of one of my erstwhile stolen-stamps tormentors and told her that I was quitting my job. "I think we were a bit rash about that stamp business," she told me with a straight face. "Besides, your work has improved since then and we can talk about a promotion and a little more money. Take some time off and see your father get settled. Maybe you'll reconsider." Things certainly had changed dramatically overnight and I enjoyed telling her that I had a better offer. If yesterday's empathy had been with Peggy's predicament, I became aware of Max's possible dilemma with this parting shot: "Is it Miss Guggenheim who is taking care of your father's affairs?"

After one last annoyance—a suspicious bank teller who scrutinized me carefully before changing the hundred-dollar bill into smaller denominations— I headed straight to my drugstore on the corner. With feigned casualness, I threw five dollars on the marble counter. "Here, throw that overripe Camembert away." My new job was waiting for me at the Belmont Plaza.

To celebrate Max's arrival, Julien Levy had decided to treat us to a typical New York dinner that night at Lindy's Restaurant. The Ernst party was seated close to the window, and I looked a few times to see if there was anyone rubbing his nose against the glass on the side street, admiring the display of fabulous desserts. It was a sumptuous and long meal. Sometime between the matzo-ball soup and the cheese blintzes, Peggy delegated her new secretary to "thank the two gentlemen at the table over there. They were so sweet and helpful to me when I was waiting for Max's hearing on Ellis Island yesterday. They took turns holding my hand and patting my head. One of them lent me his handkerchief."

My first major assignment in my new responsibility got me some startled, if not frightened, looks. "Waddaya talkin' about, kid? . . . Ellis Island? Ya crazy or sump'n'? Not us!!!! Me and Sam wuz at de track all day yestiddy. Yeah, all day." Before Julien had a chance to ask for the check I ordered my long-dreamed-of black-cherry cheesecake. It came floating toward me like the castle in the *Wizard of Oz*. There was a haze about it, it shimmered and it moved, even after the waiter had placed it in front of me. Something was wrong. All I can remember is one of the bookies pointing with his thumb. "Turlette's over dere, kid."

Some Desperate Dances

Here error is all in the not done,
All in the diffidence that faltered.

EZRA POUND

T HE July 14 Pan-Am clipper had unloaded an unexpected dimension to my existence. Trying to sort out my impressions and reactions was like letting fine sand trail through my fingers. Someone had appeared within my new, yet still fragile, independence, someone to whom I had ties the exact nature of which was still puzzling to me. I was not sure of the effect my father's arrival would have on my evolving personal universe. The woman who, at least for now, seemed to be part of his life, was also something unique in my experience. No one before had ever asked, so openly and instantaneously, for my trust and amity. I had certainly no reason to expect this from an individual who, because of her station in life, was used to having any mortal wish fulfilled without the asking. At least those were the fantasies engendered by the fascination of the European press with the lives of American heiresses. Peggy Guggenheim's name had been part of just about every conversation at John LaTouche's by expatriates recently returned from Paris, and I had also heard the name in the offices at the Museum. The gossip was about eccentric behavior, lavish living, the collecting of artists and their work and the capricious stipends in support of avant-garde writers. This "dollar princess," it was said, though not as rich as some of her kind, was the "Barbara Hutton of Bohemia." That image was very inconsistent with my first impression of this woman, whose lack of affectation, whose shyness suggested a painful past. At the same time there were kinetic flashes of brilliance, charm and a warmth that seemed to be in constant doubt of being reciprocated. It must have been the anticipation of such rejection that caused her abruptly changing moods, penetrating retorts and caustic snap judgments, but never at the cost of her femininity.

I had never succeeded in being totally objective about the women in my father's life. They had all been beautiful and never dull, and I was not unaware of the difficulties so many of them had experienced as a burden of their love for him. Peggy Guggenheim certainly did not fit the first part of that image. Meeting her, under circumstances now familiar to me, brought back my previous images from all of the other chapters of my father's personal life that I had witnessed from a child's periphery. These little worlds had always left distinct feelings of discomfort in me, because of my inability to absorb with equanimity the elusively changing portraits of the father, of someone's lover, and of Max Ernst the genius-stranger.

These reservations were far too vague for me not to accept Peggy's offer. I was anxious to support myself with something potentially more meaningful than dragging mail sacks to the post office. The gallery of personalities in my new daily work was indeed a distinct change. It was like stepping into a meadow of graceful grasses and flowering thickets that hid constant surprises, as well as deceptively elegant marshlands on which one could lose one's footing. It had an ecology somewhat alien to America and it did not take me long to recognize its flora and fauna as being transplants from Lou Straus-Ernst's living room or Max Ernst's atelier. I thought I had left behind that atmosphere charged by intellectual contention, obscure political dicta, personal vanities and ideological rivalries that simultaneously bred and strangled whirlwinds of ideas while monsters walked the streets. Now this community was reassembling in a more affluent and secure part of the globe, and at least some of the individuals seemed unaware that things could never be the same again. I was watching some of them, on whose knees I had been bounced as a child, as they acted out imagined roles of life-giving ambassadors to a culturally deprived nation. If they expected that a pebble thrown into the American pond could create more than mere ripples, they largely ignored the possibility that in this new land many a wave expired without trace on a flat beach of fashion. Now I saw them again, as part of my new job, drawn as if by a magnet to the intellectual hospitality of Peggy Guggenheim, Max Ernst, André Breton and Marcel Duchamp.

But now I was no longer a child, and I could not help but compare them to the sad emigrés of Paris who equated the braid and epaulets of their doorman's uniforms with what they had worn as favorites of the Czar's court. I could also understand now how gestures of generosity had ballooned into the kind of gossip I had heard about Peggy. Written and phoned appeals for assistance regarding one project or another were the order of the day, and I was now the funnel through which they had to pass. This was particularly discomforting when it concerned someone's personal needs and I was blamed when help was not forthcoming. The same applied to my function in the area of social matters and appointments. Plainly, I had no experience to deal with such problems in a wise manner. Fortunately I found a sage guide in Marcel Duchamp, who, beloved by Peggy, was much on the scene. He became a paternal friend whose even-tempered counsel helped me avoid many potential disasters and acted as an explainer of the scene around me. Most typical may have been his remark after he observed me on the receiving end of one of André Breton's outbursts for some imagined slight: "I have only known him to do that to individuals he wants to impress. . . . Don't worry about it, unless you had your heart set on becoming a properly certified Surrealist within the next few weeks."

Peggy and I spent a lot of time inspecting the condition of her collection of twentieth-century art at a warehouse after its miraculously safe trans-Atlantic voyage. It consisted of approximately 150 paintings, drawings and sculpture, pieces ranging from Cubism to Abstraction to Surrealism. Among Peggy's personal effects was an elaborate Calder sculpture created especially to serve as the headboard for a double bed, innumerable earrings, bracelets and necklaces from the hands of as many painters and sculptors, plus many rare books on modern art. She proudly showed me her nine superb Paul Klees but regretted that she had failed to buy a good Cubist Picasso and something by him of his more recent period. There was also a need for a more typical early De Chirico. The collection was particularly strong in the pioneering works of the Russian Suprematists Kasimir Malevich, Aleksandr Rodchenko and Eliezer Lissitzky, the Dutch Neo-Plastic art of Georges Vantongerloo and Theo van Doesburg, large charcoal drawings by Piet Mondrian and the path-breaking Abstractions of Kandinsky and Jean Helion. Peggy had never pretended that she alone made choices for the collection. She had neglected the Surrealists simply because there had been no one to whom she could turn for advice, until she met Duchamp, Breton and Ernst. She had tried to get a late Picasso just a few days before the occupation of Paris, but the master, wanting to show his contempt for an "American heiress," had insulted her by concentrating all of his attention on some other studio visitors, "some dreadful Italian aristocrats," and then, addressing her in the servile manner of a department-store floor walker, had asked, "Now, what can I do for you madame? Are you sure that you are in the right department? Lingerie is on the next floor." She had walked out

The need now was to find a place in which to house the collection. Our search for that location was made difficult by almost daily developing "crises" between Peggy and Max, caused by real or imagined slights. "He's been gone all day, I don't know where he goes. . . . Yesterday he gave me one of his books and inscribed it "To Peggy Guggenheim from Max Ernst" . . . I don't really think he loves me."

Her insecurity came to a head when Leonora Carrington arrived in New York by boat with a large body of Max's work in her care. The outbreak of the war had ended her idyllic life with Max in a small town near Ardèche. The separation had become permanent after a series of traumatic misfortunes had befallen Leonora, culminating in her commitment to a Spanish insane asylum through the long arm of her powerful British family. During this tragic detention she came to believe that she was indeed possessed by madness. Finally, upon reaching Lisbon, she found Max, who had gone there with Peggy to await the clipper flight to New York. Some horrendous confrontations between them may have been the motive behind her marriage to a Mexican diplomat. I don't recall ever again seeing such a strange mixture of desolation and euphoria in my father's face when he returned from his first meeting with Leonora in New York. One moment he was the man I remembered from Paris—alive, glowing, witty and at peace—and then I saw in his face the dreadful nightmare that so often comes with waking. Each day that he saw her, and it was often, ended the same way. I hoped never to experience such pain myself, and I was at a loss of how to help him.

Peggy, as if fearing another calamity in her life, made the impetuous decision to look for a place in America other than New York where a showplace for her collection would be welcomed. It was decided that while searching for a location, our caravan—Max, Peggy, her daughter Pegeen and I—was to have its base at the Santa Monica house of Peggy's sister, Hazel McKinley. Our quest began with a violently uncomfortable prop-plane flight to San Francisco and ended some four weeks later with a transcontinental return trip to New York in an elegant long, gray convertible.

My recollections from the Guggenheim-Ernst foray to the West Coast have a character not dissimilar to the severe lurches and bumps of the aircraft from New York, during which, symbolically perhaps, Max was the only passenger not to get airsick. The cameos and fragments of the entire period are still a jumbled mosaic, the pieces of which refuse to stay in place because I was so preoccupied watching a staccato of twists, eccentricities, and combat in the bewildering relationships between Max and Peggy, Peggy and her daughter Pegeen, Pegeen and Max, and finally all three of them with me as a kind of sounding board, battering ram, and totally inept arbitrator. Sixteen-year-old Pegeen, very pretty and very confused after having spent much of her childhood with her father Lawrence Vail and his wife Kay Boyle, engaged in tearful hostilities with Peggy, as well as with Max, in apparent retaliation for her peripatetic life in Europe and the uncertain prospect of a future with a mother whose emotional insecurity she sensed only too well. These ever-recurring scenes were my only punctuation for a kaleidoscope of impressions and images that started in a San Francisco hotel and continued when our happy little family just about took total possession of the Santa Monica house of Peggy's sister. Hazel McKinley graciously assigned me her painting studio as my living space while Max staked out the large enclosed porch as his place of work. Max and Peggy's room had the McKinley framed family crest over their bed. The wording, "Not Too Much," was repeatedly discussed during meals and cocktails, and not always amusingly at that. Max severely reprimanded me for not cleaning Hazel's brushes properly and using up all of her stretched canvases. We went on almost daily expeditions along the coast in search of an Ernst-Guggenheim home-plus-museum. Charles Laughton's residence on Pacific Palisades would have done nicely, but it was in danger of sliding onto the highway some three hundred feet below. The price of $40,000 for an entire canyon opening onto Malibu Beach that contained an unfinished sixty-room castle begun by a now deceased silent-movie queen was unsuccessfully met with a counteroffer of about half that sum. We also considered a bowling alley, a couple of fake-adobe churches and the original home of Ramón Novarro, whose vast garage looked like a possibility for the collection. Peggy sent me on an errand to downtown Los Angeles to investigate California's marriage procedures. Man Ray and his future wife Juliette, having come for cocktails, joined Max and Peggy in first insulting and then pointedly ignoring another guest, the prominent American painter George Biddle, because of his published criticism of modern art. At that same party Hazel, at first, would not allow some other invited guests into the house because "they brought with them a house guest and he's Japanese." It was the great sculptor Isamu Noguchi. . . . Hazel's husband Charles complained that he might not get his pilot's license if we did not stop using his car for house hunting; he could not get to his plane. Peggy bought a silver-gray Buick convertible with the automatic shift I had seen advertised in lights during those Columbus Circle nights. I coached Max for hours from a driver's manual for his test. He learned so well that he felt encouraged to make some fun of the mean-spirited test inspector's question with "The parallel white lines at street intersections are for the protection of pederastians." Charles Everrett (Chick) Austin, the elegant and flamboyant director of the Wadsworth Athenaeum, who among other brilliant accomplishments had staged the world premiere of Virgil Thomson's *Four Saints in Three Acts* in Hartford, breezed in for a visit and left with a new acquisition for his museum. It was, to everybody's outrage, a Jimmy Ernst, not one of the marvelous works from Max's temporary studio on the porch. It is an embarrassingly bad painting, and my attempts over the years to swap it for a more recent and better work were resolved by the museum's promise to keep it in storage for the donation of a replacement. It also took me three years to collect the agreed-on $50 for it.

We took Pegeen to Ciro's for dinner in the hope that she would see famous movie stars there, but the only celebrity that night was a tiny, corpulent baldheaded movie mogul who had just been indicted in the Bioff and Brown studio labor scandals, dancing with a glossy thin starlet at least three times his height. Peggy bought Pegeen a ticket for a supposedly star-studded charity ball at the Ambassador. She wanted a fur cape for the occasion and we took her to a very elegant store in Beverly Hills, where Pegeen loudly protested to the saleslady that she wanted "rabbit, not mink."

Peggy decided that California was not ready to house her museum, and Max rolled up his eyes with relief. In every state through which we passed on the car trip back to New York, I was sent to inquire about marriage-license possibilities.

And after each inquiry there were at least two days of icy silence between Max and Peggy.

On a late afternoon we got out of the car to watch a gigantic rattlesnake crossing U.S. 66 just outside of Flagstaff, Arizona. As Max looked up at nearby San Francisco Peak, he blanched visibly, his face muscles tightened. The mountain's green treeline abruptly gave way to a band of bright-red rock beneath a peak cap of sun-created pure magenta. He was staring at the very same fantastic landscape that he had repeatedly painted in Ardèche, France, not very long ago, without knowing of its actual existence. . . . That one look was to change the future of his life in America. At a tourist trading post in Grand Canyon, he and I found ourselves in the usually closed attic of the building surrounded by a sea of ancient Hopi and Zuni kachina dolls. The recently hired manager, a merchandising expert from Chicago's Marshal Fields, followed us up the steps, yelling to someone over his shoulder: "We've got to get rid of all that junk, we need the room for new goods." Max bought just about every one of the kachinas for $5 each, $7 for the larger Zuni dolls.

In every city, such as New Orleans or Houston, where we stayed for any time at all the four of us went through elaborate room changes for the benefit of whoever was interviewing Max and Peggy for the local press. Peggy said that she did not want people to know that she was "living in sin with Max. Max thinks that he's solved the problem by signing the hotel register: 'Max Ernst and party.' " And finally there is a gasoline station somewhere around Savannah, Georgia, where the cameo-recollections of that trip stop. Walking with me in some field browned by summer heat, Peggy turned to me. "Max tells me that you have had trouble getting another affidavit for your mother. My advisers in New York have told me that I cannot give any more. But I think I can get around that. Would you accept help from me?" I am pretty sure I cried when I kissed her.

Peggy and Max's temporary home in New York was the hotel Great Northern on Fifty-seventh Street. This is where I had my "office," a little corner of the Ernst-Guggenheim two-room suite, which became a daily salon for visiting museum people, continuing Breton-run séances of the Surrealists, sales talks by real estate brokers with offers of houses and apartments, settlements of domestic catastrophies involving Pegeen, her brother Sinbad, their father Laurence Vail and his departing wife Kay Boyle, and the ever-present overstretched rubber band that signified the relationship between the principals of that roiled household, Max Ernst and Peggy Guggenheim. Both of them, however, regardless of the tension, took care not to pull me in his or her direction during their disputes. As a result I learned the enviable role of acting the unbiased messenger when communication, for whatever mundane reasons, was essential. From that position it was even possible to walk the dangerous line of arbitrator. Though I knew that there were some very simple things to be observed in the proper usage of words, I would never again remind Peggy that she had an appointment with her coiffeur to have her roots touched up or satisfy her curiosity about what I might have observed of Max's domestic behavior with prior women in his life. And Max knew that he could trust me never to reveal where he might be while away from the hotel. I'd also learned that it was wise to call the suite from the hotel desk before going to work in my "office" because I knew that the couch in the sitting room saw considerable use as a refuge from nocturnal disagreements.

During the day as I worked doing the correspondence, the cataloging, the social calendar-keeping, I was frequently interrupted by demands for my opinion on any given subject that arose in the room. And often I wished I were elsewhere. As when André Breton was taken to task, during a translation session into English of his latest manifesto in that room, for not again merely implying but stating outright that Paul Éluard was at the time collaborating with the Germans in Paris. Matta tried to involve me in that one, but Max saved me by threatening to walk out if Breton persisted. No one quarreled with Breton's attack on Salvador Dali, whom he renamed Avida Dollars. The group's anger with the one-time young genius had probably less to do with the material success of his vapidly illustrative Surrealism than with his almost perverse public support of Franco and everything that it symbolized. I witnessed a hauntingly sad visual echo of the De Chirico-Ernst encounter in Paris some twelve years earlier. On a New York street, Max and I came face to face with a supplicant Dali proffering his hand to a former friend. He stood there, his hand still stretched out, as Max, hissing *ce chien couchant*, pulled me with him to the opposite sidewalk. On other issues there was far less cohesion. One got the impression that a Movement was transforming itself into a School via new dicta and limitations. There were some, of the older generation, who wanted to dampen the rising star of Matta and his enthusiasts by deploring "the pernicious inroads of Abstract form and space into 'our' revolution." Again it was Max who reminded everyone that "orthodoxy is a poison to any revolution."

After that it was a relief to spend the evening in the Tenth Street lofts with my friends, who were full of curiosity about their heroes uptown. I was glad that I was not the only messenger with news from Olympus. David Hare, the marvelous young sculptor and photographer, as one of the few Americans with unlimited access to the "masters," managed to tame down my sometimes unbalanced feature stories. It was after taking potluck with Baziotes, Bill Hayter, Jerome Kamrowski, Boris Margo and Arshile Gorky that I would go home to my new little apartment on East Fifty-eighth Street, which I had inherited from a lovely young woman now living in another city. And there, having washed away the

European residue of the day, I'd paint well into the early morning hours. The influence of Gordon Onslow-Ford, by then unfortunately far away on the West Coast, and my other friends began to loosen the imagery on my canvases. Though I was still swimming in the undersea biomorphology so strongly suggested by Matta and now by Gorky as well I found my eyes and hands responding increasingly to the stimulus of the linear energy-storms that Stanley William Hayter, the great graphic pioneer, was creating in his Fourteenth Street studio. "He has no equal as an engraver or an etcher . . . but why does he also want to paint?" was the reaction I heard all around me in my uptown world, and I was too timid to disagree with Peggy, Breton or Ernst. I am quite sure that I did not fully understand or appreciate the prophetic quality of these powerful paintings at the time, but I do remember that where others saw "rawness," "lack of discipline," or "chaos," I felt a sense of "immediacy" and "action on the canvas." If anyone can be said to have bridged the gap between the orthodoxy of a dying Surrealism and the about-to-be-born art of the School of New York, it was this artist. Hayter had taken the Surrealistic tool of automatism a giant step away from its dependence on Freudian interpretation toward the idea, long cherished by artists, that a work of art be self-subsistent, released from the demands of all-too-limiting cross-references. His approach to this problem was perhaps a bit early in the day for the younger Americans, me included, who were under the spell of other innovations. When the idea became a major factor in American painting in later years, Hayter's important contribution to the evolution of the School of New York was inconvenient to the chorus of historians who wanted to characterize the movement as a purely American creation. Matta was to be treated in a similar manner.

My brave struggles with all of these exhilarating, often conflicting, ideas and influences that I allowed myself to swirl in, had a somewhat more spacious battleground in my new two-room apartment than at Mrs. Jordan's rooming house. Since I could obviously produce more paintings there, I also indulged in the illusion of all young artists that I was successful in making "a major statement." Quite apart from such pretensions I do recall that strange sense of well-being when the dawn became strong enough to overpower the makeshift lighting system and the noises in the street below signaled the end of an intense night of working alone and having as witnesses of that five-minute-eight-hours all kinds of images that, for better or worse, were extensions of myself. "The painter's brush consumes his dreams," Yeats had written, but here I had proof that something more than "dreams" were in place. It was a glimpse of a new dimension in my young life. Perhaps this was to be the core of my home, wherever that might be.

Remembering Max and Peggy's disapproving frowns after Chick Austin's indelicate purchase of my *Vagrant Fugue* in Santa Monica, I was careful not to mention my painting in their company. But Max asked me one day about it and suggested dropping by to see what was happening. He looked at everything I had done, for several hours, without saying too much. I was apprehensive that he might leave with an encouraging, but paternal, pat on the back with maybe something about "talent" thrown in. Instead he asked me if I had thought of painting on a larger scale. A few days later several enormous stretched linen canvases were delivered to my place, with a note from Max that he had opened an account for me at Leo Robinson's Art Supplies and to order whatever else I needed, including "better paints and brushes. They don't hurt, you know."

I still continued for at least one day of the weekend to paint in Bill Baziotes' 104th Street living room on the easel he had set up for me there. Older than I by about eight years, Bill had indeed assumed the role of an older brother. I was fascinated by the world, so different from mine, that had brought him to painting, and I felt privileged by his willingness to let me share his America with him. These long Sundays were always very special. While Bill worked in the silence of the back room, I liked the aural distraction of the radio, particularly the afternoon concerts of the New York Philharmonic, while Ethel in the kitchen carefully transformed modest staples into elegant early-evening meals to which I could now occasionally contribute a bottle of wine.

It was on just such a Sunday that I became aware that the music had been interrupted for a news bulletin. I heard only part of it at first, and even when it was summarized in repeat I was too stunned by its implications to comprehend it completely. Baziotes was in the final stages of a subtly menacing, but seductive painting, *Accordion of Flesh*, when I walked in on him with the news that Japanese bombers had attacked the fleet in Hawaii. He had been in the process of drawing a delicate line, but now his brush began to slash a skein of electric impulses around a pink-sepia torso in a yellow rectangular recess. "That's it, Jesus Christ, that's it. We've got us a war." He stepped back to look at the painting, decided to change something on the torso and kept on working.

I went back to my own painting, without the radio now, and may have even finished it. But it might as well have been a blank screen for the running splashes of images and remembered omens that now crowded into the space behind my eyes. For the better part of my twenty-one years I had watched scattered malignancies grow and assemble themselves into a festering monster. Fed by the collective clairvoyance of wishful thinking, it now dared us to kill it by force. There it was: force, killing, death. Words I so dreaded during childhood and adolescence when even the sight of a uniform, any uniform, had provoked the image of evil. The credo of pacifism from those days, within just a few minutes, had unbelievably been shattered by this new insanity. There was no running away, fate had not allowed these historical knots to be dissolved of their own volition. The enormity of the event forced me to seek out that part of the danger that was of immediate personal concern. My mother was trapped. That cynical piece of paper—the Hitler-Stalin Pact—signed in a palace that flew the flags of the swastika as well as the hammer and sickle, looked more and more like a warrant of death.

There had, in fact, been a letter from her just a few days ago, its postmark reading "Manosque, Alpes Maritime." It had taken a long time to travel from that little mountain village, and now I had the new fear that it might be the last one for a long time to come, if not forever.

It was a typical "Lou letter." Cheerful in the face of daily uncertainty, finding even in adverse experiences good omens for our future together "over there where you are." She felt reasonably secure in this little mountain village, where she was under the protection of the great poet and writer Jean Giono. "Even if the Germans ever came to Vichy, the peasants here revere this poet of their work and land so much that they would hide me from them. The police commissioner told me quietly: 'Stay close to the town. Don't let yourself be seen elsewhere. You'll be safe from the CGQJ *(Commissaire-général aux questions juives)*, (Commissioner General for the Jewish Question) as far as I am concerned.' Just a few friends know that I am here and, of course, the American Consul in Marseilles. I'm in good hands."

Optimistic as all of this sounded, I was too well aware that my mother lived a mere breath away from the Vichy authorities, who were only too ready to cooperate with their German masters. And I remembered only too well the slogan "*À bas les Juifs*" (Down with the Jews) on the walls and sidewalks of Paris. Officially nothing was known in America about the fate of dissidents and Jews once the Nazis got hold of them. Both *The New York Times* and the *Herald-Tribune* ran occasional quotes from foreign sources and refugee specialists about outrages and extermination camps, but they were usually labeled "mere speculation" when a government voice was heard at all. I could not believe that Washington would keep silent if it knew, and the figure of ONE MILLION VICTIMS on the banners at a Madison Square Garden protest rally seemed an impossible one. Still, I had been jostled by Brownshirts in those streets, I had seen the faces of these "respectable burghers" during the long hours in the railroad carriages. There had been times when I had literally smelled the hatred that emanated from the compatriots of Goethe, Bach and Rilke. And now the time had finally come when goose-stepping boots and screaming Stukas might vanish into the pages of an insane chapter in history. But with this expectation there rose in me a new darkness to fear. It was a wordless cloud that warned of a consequential cost for this wish-fulfillment. December 8 was a somber day for me at the Triplex.

This Triplex was the magnificent apartment that Peggy had found on Fifty-first Street, overlooking the East River. Max had a magnificent studio on the top floor, and Peggy's entire collection filled the house, waiting for a suitable museum-gallery in Manhattan. My "office" was in the two-story-high ballroom-sized living room under Miró's large *Seated Woman*, Léger's *Men in the Town* and Kandinsky's *Landscape with a Red Spot.* To the left of my desk stood Brancusi's *Bird in Space*, which I polished every morning as part of my chores, and on the coffee table behind me lay Giacometti's *Woman with a Cut Throat.*

That morning we listened to Franklin Roosevelt's speech, after which I put my foot down when Max wanted to go up to his studio to work and Peggy wanted me to write some letters for her. I told them of my anxieties about Lou's need for some action from this side on her American visa. The flow of papers from the Jewish agency HIAS to Washington to Marseilles had been considerable, without tangible results, and nobody could be sure how much longer Vichy France would remain unoccupied. Peggy called her people on Wall Street to make sure that there would be no financial problems about transportation and other costs, and urged American Smelting and Refining to try for some influence with the State Department. My father's discomfort was plain to observe. He was, after all, safe. Though he must have known that I could not fault him for his efforts to make the original plan work, he reconstructed the events of that time and expressed regret at not having been more insistent that Lou remarry him. He knew of Giono and reassured me that his protection and influence was good reason for hope.

Under the circumstances I found the social and cultural activities in and around the Triplex not quite so diverting as I might have. The events in the Pacific, as in Europe and Africa, were sobering reminders that the "Free World" could not roll back the fanaticism of the Axis powers by the wishful thinking of a society that knew of the terrors of modern war merely through its press. I had, like everyone else of my age registered for the draft and, while waiting somewhat stoically for that call, tried my best to become absorbed in the kind of life that the people around me felt was important to them.

Peggy tried to convince herself that, with Max happily working in the house, domestic and personal problems might give way to a tranquillity that had eluded her throughout her lifetime. She established a truce in her tempestuous relations with her daughter Pegeen, who was thrilled to have a room of her own in the Triplex. The paintings and sculptures looked magnificent in their setting, and Max presided over all social functions, including the meals, seated in an enormous high-backed throne-chair, a one-time theatrical prop—unless, of course, he spent the day and evening away from the house on what he discreetly described to me as "a treasure hunt." Not infrequently he might bring visitors to show them his paintings or the collection. By seeming coincidence Peggy was always absent from the house, and the visitors usually were young, attractive and female. I found it very awkward to be discreet and often wished that my place of work were more secluded.

There was a constant flow of more formal visitors, usually for tea or drinks. Elsa Schiaparelli came to ask for Peggy's support in organizing a charity exhibition of Surrealism for the French Relief Societies at the Whitelaw Reid mansion. She blandly denied any knowledge that her shop on the Place Vendôme was catering to high German officers and their mistresses. "After all, I am not there and I can't control what my salesgirls do from day to day." I was surprised that Max and Peggy seemed satisfied with that explanation.

The first one of the later much fought over Guggenheim-Ernst Apso Terriers was a "gift" from one of the high-society literati in return for a small Max Ernst oil that his wife had successfully managed to steal during cocktails, even though the strange proportions of her long skirt had not escaped anyone's notice when she left. When, on another occasion, Gypsy Rose Lee and William Saroyan happened to drop in on the same afternoon, their respective egos created a schizoid-social problem, with court being held by each of them separately, one on the top floor, the other downstairs. A more interesting, and potentially more explosive event was a photo session that lasted from lunch way past dinner. In conjunction with an exhibition at the Pierre Matisse Gallery, some group pictures of New York's "artists in exile" were taken. The result was a much-published assembly of twentieth-century masters not unlike a standard high school graduation photograph. The faces are somber and self-important, with the exception of that of the class joker, Max Ernst, up front and center, which wears a distinct smirk, as if in secret judgment on the rest of the gang Max had to endure. Grouped from left to right are Matta, André Breton, Ossip Zadkine, Piet Mondrian, Yves Tanguy, André Masson, Ernst, Amédée Ozenfant, Pavel Tchelitchew, Jacques Lipchitz, Marc Chagall, Kurt Seligmann, Fernand Léger and Eugene Berman. Present as a mere observer "because I have stopped being an artist and now only play chess," Marcel Duchamp watched the ballet of jockeying for position that took place between each photographic take. He was right, a similar assembly just a few years back, in Paris, might have ended in an early fistfight. I had heard it all before: "Léger, a proletarian? Ha, he's nothing more than a petit-bourgeois horse-meat butcher." . . . . "Berman is just a small-time decorator, and he paints too." ". . . Tchelitchew's pornography isn't even interesting." . . . "Lipchitz has three left hands, and he can't make sculpture with any one of them." . . . "Chagall would cover his grandmother with cerulean-blue paint if he could sell her for dollars." . . . Unfortunately I was not so familiar with the objects of the derision to know their opinions of the Surrealists. All hostilities were in abeyance. There was no clue from any face or pair of eyes. Almost everybody managed to look past the other, even when conversing politely. But it was clear that there were at least two individuals, Mondrian and Ozenfant, who commanded some kind of grudging respect. They were "loners" in that crowd of prima donnas, not only by virtue of the uniqueness of their respective work, but also as individuals known for their singular lack of intellectual prejudice. . . . As for me, I was a bit embarrassed by masters, whom I had reasons to look up to, behaving like Hollywood starlets for the sake of a camera.

An incident of considerably less decorum punctuated a cocktail party that had filled the entire Triplex with just about "everybody" from New York's art and literary world. A friendship between the poet Charles Henry Ford and the writer Nicolas Callas came to a violent end in the entrance foyer, the walls of which were filled with the smaller paintings of Ernst and Kandinsky from the collection. I have rarely seen so much blood and gore in a relatively short span of time. All of the doorways were crammed with spectators, who watched not only the flailing arms, legs and fists, but also my wild dashes in and out the fight's arena in a effort to get at least some of the paintings out of harm's way. After Callas was taken to the kitchen to treat his bloodied face and Ford had been told to go home, Alfred Barr, in a most scholarly manner, asked me to explain why I had removed only the Kandinskys and not the Ernsts. I was astounded by his question and at a complete loss for an answer and mumbled something about blood being more visible on the Kandinsky surfaces.

It was a different crowd that came for an evening, at the invitation of André Breton, for a screening of *From the Tsar to Lenin*. They were a somber lot, and most of them had obviously seen the documentary about the Russian Revolution many times before. Max Eastman, their apparent patriarch, spent his time in conference around the kitchen table at the back of the house, once in a while peering through the window curtains at a number of men in trenchcoats who were engaged in a long leisurely stroll up and down the front of the house, in a steady rain.

I decided early not to spend too much of my free time at the Triplex, particularly not around dinner time. If I wanted to know what had happened there, I'd hear it soon enough on the following morning from Peggy herself or had to listen to it in recriminatory summation at the breakfast table from her, my father and Pegeen. It was a tiresome recital of petty quarrels that often ended in smashed dinner plates, slammed doors and someone rushing out into the night. Friends, old and new, found themselves, often willingly, part of small or large games of sex-provocation that often resulted in some strange pairings. It didn't seem at all logical then that I should be the lightning rod or mediator of these morning-after tempests that might continue for several days. It was a bit much for a son, adopted or otherwise, because it was enough in my daily routine to catch hailstones from friends, artists, collectors, dealers and just plain social climbers who felt that Peggy's secretary was a far safer target than the lady herself. Once in a while I blew my cool with Peggy. "Will you please tell Julien Levy to stop blaming me for Max's leaving his gallery for Valentine Dudensing?" . . . And more hailstones from home. "No, I did not give Pegeen permission to open a charge account at Bergdorf Goodman." . . . "My dear, it was you who gave that little creep from Helena Rubinstein that Herbin painting just to get rid of him. I wouldn't have let him into the house in the first place." . . . "What your son Sinbad does with a girl in this house is none of my business. Don't ask me if I think he's a homosexual and then get mad at me when I tell you that I have proof to the contrary." . . . . "We can't send a bill to Gypsy Rose Lee. Max gave her that painting. . . . I don't know if she paid him for it in *that* way." . . . "I'm not going back to that butcher again and tell him that you think he overcharged you for four lamb chops last week." . . . "The next time the Baroness Rebay calls, I'm going to put you on, whether you like it or not. Yesterday she screamed at me in German that if 'that dreadful Guggenheim girl' calls her an evil Nazi witch again behind her back, she will use her Washington influence to have Max deported from America."

It must have been after one of those sessions that I laughed into an imaginary mirror. "You jerk, if you hadn't loused up on the subway that day, you could have worked yourself up at the Elite Messenger Service. Someday you could have become the dispatcher with all of those telephones on that loading platform and listen to WNEW all day long."

The Baroness Hilla Rebay was indeed something of an ogre and an embarrassment in the Guggenheim family firmament. This imperious caricature of German aristocracy—"Och, I saw dat Chimmy Ernst ven he vas chust a schmall baby in Köln, his mutter vas a nice Chewish girl"—seemed to be in total control of Peggy's Uncle Solomon, not only as the director of his Museum of Non-Objective Art but also as the mistress of the Guggenheim household at the Hotel Plaza. Her prerogatives extended from pouring tea at the apartment to cramming the East Fifty-fifth Street Museum with the dreadful Kandinsky imitations of her "discovery," the talentless Rudolf Bauer, who, as a result, lived in baronial splendor on the Jersey shore. The baroness, as self-proclaimed protectress of Uncle Solomon's collection as "the only valid art," had tried to prevent Peggy from using the Guggenheim name for her museum-gallery in London, which had been under the directorship of Herbert Read, because it would be "propagating mediocrity, if not trash." Through the grapevine of some of my downtown artist friends, who held menial jobs at the "Rebay" museum, it was no secret to us that she was now interfering with Peggy's New York plans by threatening likely real estate firms if they cooperated with us in the search for a gallery location anywhere in midtown Manhattan.

A place was finally found on the top floor of 130 West Fifty-seventh Street. I hoped that a good and practical designer would supervise the conversion of the double loft into a viable exhibition space, but I was apprehensive about the myriad "advisers" around Peggy, who might create a physical and emotional mess. Other things still had to precede that phase. Peggy felt that Art of This Century could not open without the existence of an elaborate, well-documented and illustrated catalog. The very name of the projected gallery dramatized the obvious gaps in her collection, which she then proceeded to fill with some impatience and some resulting errors. She managed to buy a 1911 Cubist Picasso and a 1914 De Chirico. The Picasso had a two-inch tear somewhere in the upper half, and rather than spend a lot of money on repair, Peggy prevailed on Max to patch it instead. Alfred Barr came for tea to look at the De Chirico and ever so gently informed her that the Museum had the identical painting with a verified date. Peggy had been victimized in a situation not uncommon in the case of that once great painter, who for material reasons had not been above "recreating" his earlier work and by mis-dating it had actually perpetrated a "fake."

The collection was more appropriately enriched by a Malevich—Barr traded it for a Max Ernst—a Marcel Duchamp, an excellent Ozenfant, a fine example by the American Abstract pioneer John Ferren, as well as works by Charles Howard, Yves Tanguy, André Breton, Henry Moore, Victor Brauner, Wolfgang Paalen, Oscar Dominguez, Leonor Fini, Matta and Leonora Carrington.

The richest lode, however, came from Max's aerie in the Triplex. It was as if the most amazing allegorical images were giving birth to themselves. The painter's personal history and obsessions were coming to life in a running tandem race between dreams and desires, the past and the future. Growing out of an intricate web of sponges, corals, rocks, botanical afterlife and ruins of timeless civilizations were feathery brides with heads of stately owls. Leonora Carrington's horse pranced onstage in gleaming armor. Leonora herself could be detected again and again among carnivorous foliage or standing alone in the prophetic after-war landscape *Europe After the Rain.* Here and there might be a forlorn figure, resembling Pegeen, and every so often there appeared the menace of a female ogre, failing in her effort to be seductive. It was painful for Peggy to recognize herself thusly and, during quiet moments in our work together, when she plaintively asked to be told that she was mistaken, I simply had to evade the question.

A number of these extraordinary paintings went into Peggy's collection as part of a straightforward exchange arrangement under which Max's share of household expenses and his personal bills, a healthy share of which were owed to Julius Carlebach's treasure shop of primitive art on Third Avenue, were totaled up against a fair market price for the new paintings. It was a measure of Max's pride that he always insisted on a contribution from his side that far exceeded his obligations. What Peggy received in value, more often than not, just about covered all of the establishment's running costs. It was unfortunately part of my job to keep the records and to participate in the embarrassing, strangely formal, bimonthly negotiations to settle accounts between my father and the woman with whom he was living. He must have been aware of my squirming during those long silent periods when Peggy studiously pored over the minutiae of detailed figures, sometimes coming up with a small discrepancy or a forgotten outlay. After each of these sessions he went out of his way to relieve my obvious distress. "I have never been much of a father to you, but it seems that I am teaching you things in spite of that. None of this is as strange as it may look to you now. I don't want to owe anything to anyone, and Peggy has to do it that way . . . it came with mother's milk . . . Try to remember it if you ever get rich."

Once in a while he went further in his concern for me. Differences in value favorable to Max resulted in his receiving works from the collection that Peggy felt were disposable. "Here, this is for you," he'd say to me, "she doesn't pay you enough for some of the things you have to do. It's my contribution to your salary."

For reasons of their own, neither Max nor Peggy wanted me to use the facts of this arrangement whenever I was confronted by the leers and gossip of cocktail parties or the press that equated my father with the fortune-hunting blondes of Tommy Manville or Barbara Hutton's endless parade of impoverished aristocratic husbands. I managed to bar some offending people from the Triplex, but I was frustrated in trying to stop the talk.

A major part of my daily work now consisted of giving shape to the catalog for Art of This Century. For the first time my apprentice years at Augustin's printing plant in Glückstadt came into proper play. Though the actual production of the book would be handled by John Ferren's wife Inez, I felt very much at ease with the procedures of typography, half-tone reproduction and bookbinding. What was new for me was doing the research for biographical material, essays and photographs. Peggy had not kept very good records, but to my personal delight I adapted quickly to the search for sources and material. I also became aware very early of the fact that Art of This Century would present very pitiful evidence of painting and sculpture in America. The potent voices with access to Peggy's ear on aesthetic questions were largely the Surrealists. Their interest in some of my American friends was conditioned almost entirely by the measure of creative compliance that might be evident in the work. Admission of Onslow-Ford, Gorky, Esteban Frances, Jerome Kamrowski and Baziotes to the circle seemed possible but was held in abeyance. Painters like Stuart Davis, Carl Holty, Balcomb Greene and many others were considered "enemies," while such names as Jackson Pollock, Mark Rothko, Willem de Kooning and Bradley Walker Tomlin were met with incomprehension when they were mentioned by Matta, Howard Putzel or me. Putzel, Peggy's old friend who had dreamed of the job that was now mine, was particularly forceful in his advocacy of the still hidden group of artists in New York. We did succeed in having Peggy add to her exhibition plans a show of "new painting" at least once a year. She thought it would be nice to have "a sort of *salon du printemps,* where I don't have to buy if it doesn't fit."

The bitter European battles of the "isms" had indeed survived their trans-Atlantic crossings. I did not see how they could continue in the very climate of this refuge and I saw the first truce in the spring of 1942 at the imposing dining table of the Triplex.

"Mondrian is a very nice man. *Mais, mon Dieu,* what can one say for these cold Abstract arrangements that are the very denial of *la peinture?"* Max, presiding in his throne-chair, Breton, Marcel Duchamp and Yves Tanguy were waiting for the courtly gentleman Mondrian to join them for lunch as he completed a viewing of the collection with Peggy. They could not repress some patronizing chuckles when they saw him pointing at the large Miró while asking who had painted it. When he repeated it with a Kandinsky and the Juan Gris, they appeared certain that this would be an easy pigeon for them. I was not at all happy with what might happen to that kindly, quiet man who had so graciously invited me into his apartment the year before, when I was on a mere errand to him for the Museum of Modern Art. He had seemed so delighted when I identified the phonograph record he was playing at the time as Pete Johnson and Albert Ammons on a 12-inch Blue Note. I had taken up his invitation to come again, and we had spent hours listening to and discussing our mutual enthusiasms for jazz, and boogie-woogie in particular. I had heard Max himself express some reservations about the continuing aesthetic separatism practiced by the Surrealists, and I could not imagine Yves Tanguy, that irrepressively charming painter of strangely unpopulated, horizonless, interior landscapes, being part of a bullying session. But still, there they sat, ready to pounce as Mondrian chose the extreme end of the table to face them as he characteristically stroked his chin.

As I had expected, it all went on very politely through the soup and salad and entrée, but with the coffee came Breton's long, leading question: "Of course, my dear Mondrian, we all respect your aim at a form of painting that seeks to cleanse the vision absolutely of the irrational and that, of course, means dreams as well as reality. We would be very interested to hear your opinion of other painting, let us say Surrealism, which seeks to elaborate these elements rather than erase them."

There was no immediate answer and Duchamp added, "What, for example, do you think of the work of our friend Yves Tanguy here?"

The reply, after more thoughtful chin stroking, came firmly, but calmly, "I enjoy conversational games as much as you do, but I shall not indulge in them. I have seen Tanguy's exhibition at Pierre Matisse several times and found it very beautiful but also very puzzling. Yves' work is much too Abstract for me."

There was a sputter from Breton: "Too Abstract? For you?

"My dear Breton, you seem to have a very fixed idea about Abstraction. I certainly do not fit into your concept of it and I don't mean to play with words when I say that I consider my way of painting to be a deep involvement with reality. I may well be mistaken in my feeling that Tanguy's paintings are getting too cold for me and too Abstract, and I also have no doubt that when he reaches his destination, as I expect to reach mine, we will both discover that we are still living on the same planet . . . together. In art the same elevator goes either to the basement or to the penthouse."

Tanguy jumped up and embraced Mondrian. "*Ça, on faut accepter, cher maître, tout à fait.*" (That, dear master, we must accept without qualification.) His giggle infected Ernst and Duchamp, and even Breton seemed to accept the good-natured put-down with elegant grace.

With all due respect for the five men, whose names are inscribed in the cultural history of our time, I could not help but feel that I had just watched them shooting marbles or jumping hopscotch. Had they indeed discussed principles . . . a credo? Or was it just like any other game played with artificial gaiety at a kid's birthday party? I had watched these toy balloons of theory dance in the smoke of European cafés and living rooms during an entire young lifetime, and although I could discern their relevance to a given work, I could never accept the notion that any one of them should ever prevail over the others. This air-borne plethora of doctrine had impressed its fragility on me, not only by the short life span of much of it but also because the apparent fiats conflicted with an early remembered admonition in *Much Ado About Nothing:* "Let every eye negotiate for itself/And trust no agent." On the other hand, it probably was not fair to expect constant profundity from any of the highly creative individuals whose daily presence was a commonplace for me. Furthermore, having known so many of them since childhood, I should not have been surprised by their foibles and their peculiar gift of making difficulties for themselves and everyone around them.

The ferment of constant scenes and tension that accompanied the labor pains of Art of This Century has an important place in my cage of nightmares. André Breton and Howard Putzel had persuaded Peggy that Frederick Kiesler was the ideal individual to create the physical setting for her gallery-museum. That made me very happy because it meant an opportunity for this extraordinary man to realize just a few of the dreams that had been preempted by men of far lesser talents. His plans for the project were indeed breathtaking in their ingenuity and elegant simplicity. The anticipated costs appeared to be extremely modest to everyone except Peggy, who thought them astronomical. "I am one of the poor Guggenheims. If my father had trusted his brothers and not left the firm forty years ago, I wouldn't have to think about such things as money." But she decided to treat this man's work in the same manner she had treated the many poets and painters who were on a regular generous stipend from her. And that meant: No interference. I saw this attitude as a source of terrible troubles to come, because I was convinced that Kiesler had kept his cost projection unrealistically low out of fear that the entire project might be shelved. I deliberately immersed myself in my other work so as to stay away from the site, where a crew of carpenters and plasterers were beginning to convert two dingy lofts into what did indeed become a spectacular and innovative showplace. I loved Kiesler and did not want to be a party to the nightmares that were just below the surface of Peggy's "Yes this time, but not a penny more!"

But it blew up anyway, in the manner of time-spaced pre-set fireworks. It was idiotic of me to believe that I could escape the falling debris by ducking, and my treasured friendship with Kiesler was never to be the same again. As the work progressed and the bills began to come in for an electric eye to activate the Klee carousel, the latest, most expensive light-fixtures, oak for the floors instead of pine, linen, and not cotton, cloth for the undulating walls of the abstract gallery, Kiesler saw his dream disappear in Peggy's mounting fury. He came to me and demanded that I hide some of the bills from her for a while and let them trickle out later. When it was obvious to him that I could not possibly cooperate, Peggy began to come back to the Triplex with Kiesler's outlandish tales of my perfidy. He accused me of a secret effort to sabotage the entire project. In his opinion, I deserved instant dismissal from my job. I never revealed to her the real reasons for these attacks, because I knew that it would be the end of Kiesler's job and more chaos.

Art of This Century was important, but it also became clear to me that, at some point, I needed to breathe a different air. I was not going to stay in the "family business." I was certain that life in America had its healthy slice of neurotic intrigue but it would have a long way to go before it could match the continent that had a patent, I felt, on it. I could coexist with these present living reminders of my alien past but, unlike them, I had not come to this land in search of mere shelter. Granted, I had led this new life for a mere four years, and I was proud of many of the things that I had brought with me, but I had been ready to open my baggage immediately upon arrival to learn how much of it could survive a new climate. Secure as I was right now, stimulated by my surroundings, I would have to put a distance between myself and the complications of that other world. Living within the perimeter of my father's daily existence had already forced me into making judgments about his life-style that could be catastrophic to our need of getting closer to each other. It was with all of this in mind that I gently dissuaded Peggy from continuing discussions with her lawyers, without my prior knowledge, of legally adopting me as her son. This was not, she assured me, an attempt to tie Max closer to her, nor would my relationship to my mother be in any way disturbed.

Peggy's repeated, somewhat jocular, complaint since Pearl Harbor—"I don't like the idea of living in sin with an enemy alien"—had taken on a more serious coloration for Max. He had become more conscious of the specific nature of that status when I went with him to the General Post Office to have him registered, photographed and fingerprinted. Other restrictive realities, such as the requirement of special travel permits for any trip and the rule against possessing a radio with a short-wave band at the Triplex, finally resulted in Peggy's becoming Mrs. Max Ernst number three somewhere in Maryland as part of an ostensible visit to Washington, D.C., and her cousin Harold Loeb (the model for the Robert Cohn character in Hemingway's *The Sun Also Rises*). This still did not free Max from any of the restrictions, but Peggy reasoned that it somewhat softened the meaning of "enemy" . . . ". . . which is more than one can say about my Uncle Solomon's dreadful Nazi-Baroness."

It seemed a good time for them to make the marriage more than a formality by going to Cape Cod for two months that summer. The catalog was almost ready for publication, having been enriched with essays by André Breton and Piet Mondrian. Work at the gallery proceeded under a general truce between Kiesler and Peggy, with me picking up loose ends by working part of my time at the Triplex while they were away. I looked forward to more time for painting and an abatement of daily strife. Before they left, it seemed that Peggy was prepared to tolerate Max's "treasure hunts" as an inevitably continuing by-product of the new marriage.

"I think Max is going gaga over some crazy girl again. I can tell from the look in eyes . . . of course that goes away once he's had them. . . . Do you know he's had the preposterous idea of renting another studio near Wellfleet for some female who, he claims, wants to paint his portrait? . . . I have seen her around a few times. She's very pretty and lively . . . probably would turn out too lively for him . . . I think. . . . The poor dear . . . he was so surprised and hurt when I put my foot down on that situation. . . . Told me that she's the best portrait painter in America. . . ."

It was not an interest in portraiture that was to add to my life someone who was "very pretty and lively," but far more than that. Yet, within a short time it was I who was sitting for that portrait. It shows me against a street background, the most prominent feature of which is a progressive row of assertive street lamps.

Elenor was an about-to-be divorced young woman, who as a Morris Kantor student at the Art Students Legue had enrolled her gigantic Briard as a student when that animal was barred from accompanying her to class. I had learned of this and other colorful details from some of my Tenth Street friends, and a subsequent party at one of the lofts did the rest. . . . The thought that I might be stepping on territory that my father wanted to claim never occurred to me. . . . Or did it?

It was to be more than the fugitive infatuation of a lonely young man with a responsive woman of more maturity than he. That early summer I prepared my first meal, ever, for someone other than just me in a place that I had the right to call my own. I had just become twenty-two years old, and the gifts I received were just about everything I had imagined Marlene Dietrich to have promised "Johnny" on the night of his birthday. And, just like the lyrics on that well-worn shellac-disc, there were to be a lot of *Geburtstage* (birthdays) unmarked in the calendar. But the relationship between Elenor and me went beyond celebration to grow into a mutual dependence for which there were to be no regrets even when it ended some years later. By the time Max and Peggy returned from Cape Cod, I had inaugurated the filling of a longed-for need in my life, that of sharing it.

Their return was unexpectedly early with the help of the FBI, who made Max very brusquely aware of the fact that his travel permit had not allowed him to move with Peggy from the rental in Wellfleet into Matta's house in Province-town. The Federal Attorney in Boston, having in his youth been an employee of the Guggenheims, smoothed the way for them so they could immediately return to New York without a penalty. It obviously was more than uncomfortable for Max to have been interrogated for several days by the agents about the presence of a short-wave radio in Matta's house and their suspicions that he might have been a party to supplying fuel for German submarines offshore. "I kept telling them," he repeated, "that I don't paint with diesel oil." From then on he was very leery of a radio in anyone's house, lest it have a short-wave band.

When I told her, Peggy was more than just delighted with the developments in my personal life. "It's your declaration of independence from Max. I'm sure that no one, but no one has ever done this to him. I can't wait to see his face when he finds out." The denouement came at a cocktail party in Kiesler's penthouse, a few days later. Max spotted Elenor and me across the room. His initial stare was one of stunned disbelief, but then his face broke into a wide grin and he wagged his finger at me in the manner of the parent toward the disobedi-ent kid after he's made it through the deepest part of the pool. That was it; the matter was never raised again.

A birthday letter from my mother had taken four months to travel. The mutilation of the envelope by various censors gave ominous testimony to a growing atmosphere of danger that was, however, completely absent in its written content:

> . . . My most important present by the time I turned twenty-two was that I did not have to spend days—or nights—always alone, and it is my wish that you will have the same fortune. If you are so lucky, I hope that it is someone who will give you things that only women in love are capable of. . . . I have had several messages from the Consulate in Marseilles telling me each time that the visa "is being processed" or "we should have it in a few days," but so far there has been nothing concrete. But my bags are ready and I know how fortunate I am compared to those who have no place to go and nobody anywhere waiting for them. . . . People here are terribly frightened, but you know me. I have a ship named *Optimist,* on which I may have gotten a bit wet at times, but I know it cannot sink. . . . Maybe things won't go as smoothly as we want them to, the worst that can happen is that we won't hear from each other for a while. By now we should both be used to uncertainty. . . . Jean Giono is a generous, ever-helpful, worldly human being. No wonder the peasants here love him so. Nothing bad can happen to me as long as I have him for a friend. . . . The other day I went for a long walk into the mountains. It was a crazy idea, I was told, and the mistral was indeed quite icy. But I wanted to see what was on the other side of those mountains. The same heights I had so often faced in my uncertain life-travels before and that had threatened to throw me back many times. I believe I can say that I never lost hope of finding still another path that would lead me over the top. The fact is, that I carry as part of my baggage something that gives me wings—always an urge that drives me to look in anticipation of the yet-unseen. It is an appetite for adventure and an eternal curiosity, the inexhaustible precious lot of the nomad. . . . when we are back together again, it will be fun to compare notes on our respective mountain-climbs. . . .

The letters I wrote to my mother were also full of optimism. They were mostly about my American life's relatively small circle of the arts. I was certainly not disinterested or unaffected by the behavior or events portrayed in a press that was audaciously alive and irreverent of authority. For all of my good feeling about this society, there were some disturbing, often heartbreaking, contradictions in its ever-changing makeup that I found myself incapable of comprehending after only four years of observance. How could I possibly explain to Lou Straus-Ernst what I myself had seen in the slums of Harlem and on the Indian reservations of the Southwest? How could a people look the other way in the face of segregation and lynchings and then dance to the music of the victims? I had seen the Mexican farm workers of the California fields within sight of castlelike villas. What about the corrupt fiefdoms of local politicians, big and small, all over the nation? Who were the large masses that obeyed Frank Hague, Tom Pendergast, and Ed Crump, or listened enthusiastically to Father Coughlin and Martin Dies? Less macabre, but still unexplainable, was the nationwide panic induced by Orson Welles' radio version of *War of the Worlds*. And on the human side, how could I possibly write to her that Fiorello La Guardia held the same position in New York that Konrad Adenauer had held in Cologne? How could you possibly describe a La Guardia or place a Harold Ickes into the context of this many-faced society? All of that in a vast country that had eagles, vultures, pelicans and red cardinals, but not a single nightingale; where there were also bears and pumas, coyotes, rattlesnakes, scorpions, sharks, barracudas and a langouste with enormous claws, called lobster. Someday I would have a better picture of it, but I realized, with some excitement, that I would have to learn for the rest of my life and still have surprises to expect.

In confining my letter writing to the life immediately around me I hoped to abate the fears and reservations about this extraordinary country that I had heard from Lou Straus-Ernst and her intellectual peers. The best way I could do that was to report on what I had been able to achieve, given such a short time, in what I had to call an environment of hope. I had produced a cloth-bound 156-page book, the catalog for Art of This Century, for which I had gathered most of the material, worked out the layout, but ironically, not been involved in the selection of the typefaces. My copy was inscribed: "To Jimmy in gratitude for all he has done, from Peggy." One of my paintings, *The Flying Dutchman*, was hanging in the Marian Willard Gallery on Fifty-seventh Street. The sculptor David Smith had recommended it to Marian Willard after he saw it at Bill Baziotes' place. Max had also looked at it. "Well," he said, "nobody will be able to say that you paint like your father. . . . You see what a difference good paints can make?" I decided that had to be a compliment.

Of course I told her all about Elenor and how important she was in my life, but I also wrote to her with pride about the number of people who had remarked on the fluency of my English and the absence of an accent. There was nothing to be ashamed of in having an accent over here, I told her, but that was the way I wanted it. To me the language was a symbol of my new life. I not only wanted to speak it, but also to think, see, dream and even be silent in it.

I intended to write to her about the Schiaparelli-sponsored exhibition, "First Papers of Surrealism" at the Whitelaw-Reid Mansion, because, though its title suggested symbolic application for American citizenship, it gave the unfortunate impression of European elitism talking down to its current provider and host. Alfred H. Barr's "Fantastic Art, Dada and Surrealism" at the Museum of Modern Art had introduced many of the artists now on view to a broader public in 1936, and they were indeed represented by excellent examples. Still, there was about this new exhibition the unmistakable aura not of an alive movement but rather that of a closed circle of licensed practitioners. The gesture toward Surrealist protagonists working in America was meager and justified, in terms of quality, only by the inclusion of works by David Hare and William Baziotes. Fine painters like Kamrowski, Gorky, Tanning, Margo, Stamos, Kelly or any of the known artists from the California group were absent. Perhaps their work might not have measured up to the elegance or inventiveness of the represented masters, but they would still have added a missing element and certainly would have outshone some selected sycophants who were barely beyond their tenth painting or recipients of nepotism, like me. The low point of the entire affair was the fact that most of the festive opening crowd seemed to be not at all embarrassed at having to enter the exhibition past a life-size bust of Marshal Pétain. Some of us, the younger people, led by Matta, protested and asked for our elders' influence in having the offending bust removed. We were told not to rock the boat; besides, "You are not important enough."

Here was that same phrase again—"not important enough"—that was keeping my mother in that crowded waiting room on the other side of the Atlantic. But things were looking up. The most recent news was that the issuance of a visa had been cabled to the American Consulate in Marseilles. It was now up to some minor official under that selfsame Marshal Pétain to issue her the automatic French exit visa and for Spain to grant the equally available transit to Lisbon. Hopefully there was no need for another letter from me.

Art of This Century opened a week later, on the night of October 20, for the benefit of the American Red Cross. I felt no immodesty in my satisfaction at several aspects of its immediate success. The opening night crowd had been huge, the subsequent press coverage nationwide and favorable, catalog sales were brisk and daily attendance was consistently large—all of these things had been my area of responsibility and I now had additional reasons to feel secure in my ability to take on tasks completely new to me.

Admittedly the real success of Art of This Century was its collection of paintings and sculpture and Kiesler's genius at transforming two dilapidated lofts into a magic environment of constant surprises. Unfortunately his warfare with Peggy had reached a new peak when the final construction costs came in. I didn't think they were all that outrageous, considering what he had achieved with a modest amount at a time when most of the materials needed were severely restricted and, as a result, prices inflated. The final straw seemed to have been Kiesler's insistence with Peggy on having some control over the opening invitations. Among the "banished" was to have been my Elenor, because it was her evil influence over me that had caused all of his setbacks.

The considerable acclaim for the museum-gallery must have eclipsed some of Peggy's prior notoriety. Not infrequently she recognized some visitor who seemed a bit alien in these environs: "My God, I think that is a relative. . . ." Periodically I came to face various members of New York's fabled Jewish aristocracy, and Peggy's family's view of the cousin or niece had always been somewhat less than charitable. The whispered names were Loeb, Straus, Gimbel, Seligman and, of course, Guggenheim, one of whom at least, Aunt Irene, had braved the possible wrath of her husband's friend, the Baroness. We served her a ceremonial tea on our littered worktable next to the entrance to the gallery. She was a gracious and elegant lady who mistakenly thanked Peggy profusely for giving her the catalog, after which Peggy demanded the pre-publication price of $2.75 for it. I had to run out to make change of a twenty-dollar bill. Aunt Irene did not take the book with her. She feared that her chauffeur would undoubtedly report her transgressional visit to the Baroness and the catalog would merely add to the unpleasantness.

In direct contrast to this and other manifestations of frugality, Peggy handed me a signed blank check one cold snowy morning: "Don't you have a decent winter coat? Go out and buy one right now." I went to a low-priced men's chain store, Crawford's and, already wearing the selected coat, I filled in the proper amount on the check. The salesman looked at the signature. "And your name, I suppose, is Rockefeller?" I gave him the phone number at Art of This Century to check for himself. "Don't give me that cockamamy kind of con. Who do I know I'm talking to? That trick don't work no more." I called Peggy myself and after a few minutes the phone rang. It was Ernest Lundeen from American Smelting and Refining on Wall Street. I could hear portions as he yelled at the blanching salesman: ". . . You don't want to wait for a call from the president of your lousy chain and get fired, do you? Give the kid that goddamned overcoat." "I knew I shoulda called in sick this morning," the man said as he made out the sales slip. ". . . If you belong to that fancy crowd, why the hell didn't you go to Saks Fifth Avenue? . . . Twenty-one dollars fifty cents. . . . Jeeeesus! God protect me from the carriage trade."

Not long into Art of This Century, overriding all protest, which I knew better than to join, Peggy decided to combat the running costs by charging a 25-cent admission "to anyone . . . including relatives. . . ." The coins were to be deposited in a Spanish tambourine by the entrance. It did not take much time for indigent artists and students to discover that I could wave them in during

Peggy's regular two-hour lunch period. Twenty-five cents, after all, could buy a decent lunch at the Automat down the street. The freebies stopped a few weeks later when, after a scant hour, Peggy suddenly reappeared and counted the quarters in the tambourine. "This is two dollars seventy-five cents short. . . . I know you didn't take it; you've let people in without paying. I've been down in the lobby, watching the elevator dial. . . . and I've counted the trips to the sixth floor . . . eleven people didn't pay." She was not moved by my explanation and insisted that I, tambourine in hand, make the proper collection in the galleries. In my embarrassment I surreptitiously made up the difference from my own pocket, but she wasn't fooled, noting the mysterious presence of two one-dollar bills. The incident passed without another word, and I had to rely on a deal with the elevator man to know when the coast was clear downstairs.

Working at the gallery insulated me somewhat from the continuing tremors at the Triplex, and it was ironic that a decision in which I had a hand was about to result in a growing cloud of destructive proportions. Following an earlier suggestion of Marcel Duchamp, Peggy and I began preparations for a January exhibition of women painters, thirty-one of whom were finally chosen through recommendations of Breton, Duchamp, James Sweeney, James Soby and Max. A letter to Georgia O'Keeffe resulted in a visit by that formidable lady to the gallery with a small entourage, during which she stonily faced an awed Peggy down with "I am not a woman painter." Peggy would not trust the individual ladies to make their own choices of works to be shown and, without a second thought, I concurred with her suggestion that Max was ideally suited to make the final selections in the various studios. There was no doubt that he enjoyed the assignment tremendously and, with some of the painters, found it necessary to make additional visits. "Max is very, very happy," Peggy remarked several times during that period. "It will be a very exciting show." That turned out to be something of an understatement. The lives of all concerned were about to undergo some very profound changes in the coming few months. As I watched the enfeebled marriage in the Triplex unraveling almost stitch by stitch, I saw a tragic Peggy attempting to salvage it with a succession of utterly destructive responses, while, at the same time, realizing my father's desperate need to escape his partially self-made emotional deprivation, I could not help making comparisons. Was this the way it had happened in 1922? Granted there was a world of difference between my mother and Peggy in almost every respect. Moreover, in the case of Lou, the painful break came to a woman who was unprepared for it, while Peggy seemed to have lived all of her relationships in fearful anticipation of yet another failure.

Into the midst of this period of personal anguish fell a blow of terrible proportions. In response to the Allied invasion of North Africa, Hitler ordered

German troops to occupy Vichy-France. Another door of the trap had fallen shut, this time with the help of some little clerk, proudly wearing the Légion d'honneur on his shabby coat lapel, on whose desk an application for an exit visa had been buried for over a month.

In my wretched numbness I could see myself staring at the monstrous wall that grew even as I tried to understand its height. Penetrating through its pernicious stone and mortar was one persistent image: the expression of disbelief on my mother's face when the earth opened up and swallowed the safe path in front of her. It had been so close. Just a few more steps to the other side of the mountain. Why deny her that? And who had failed her?

The answer to the last part of that question would remain pointed at me. Though it was a futile effort, I had to imagine that any one of innumerable actions taken just a few hours earlier, a phone call, perhaps, or a letter, might well have made the difference. If ever I had thought that one could win at a game of chess with the bureaucracy of evil, I had now been taught the lesson that my mother and I belonged to the millions of expendable pawns on a board of inhuman size. We were inconsequential victims, spiderwebs disposed of by the flick of a finger.

Here was yet another example of that tribal instinct that causes murder and conquest in the name of whatever sanctity is convenient.

I had to grasp at straws to hope that the sense of betrayal had not totally destroyed my mother's self-confidence and optimism. I simply had to believe that the protective mantle provided by the good people of the village of Manosque and their honored poet Giono would be sufficient for continued safety. I even convinced myself that the distance to the Swiss border from that village was not forbiddingly great.

The shock of my mother's mortal danger caused a cold light to shine on the present situation of my own daily life. Finding myself in the center of a seesaw between my father and Peggy did not contribute to anyone's balance, particularly not my own. It was far too grandiose for me to assume that I might yet be able to defuse an explosion between these two people for whom I cared deeply. Nor could I detach myself sufficiently to concentrate on my work alone, ignore the endless combats of alienation and the provocative games of deliberately unconcealed infidelities. I did not like the role of traffic cop, trying to prevent embarrassing encounters at cocktail parties and art openings. There was nothing I could do to prevent the consequences of Peggy's desperate personal gambles, such as taking away the key to the Triplex from Max and then hysterically calling me in the middle of the night to help her find him. Nor did I have the remotest right to question Max's search for his own tranquillity, which he seemed to have found with the artist Dorothea Tanning, whose superb self-portrait *Birthday* he had chosen for Peggy's exhibition entitled "Women-Painters." In fact, during some agitated moods, Peggy had berated me for suggesting Max as the selector for the show in the first place.

It was all so sad. Max confided to me at the time that, in his depression over the loss of Leonora, he had made a terrible mistake during the Marseilles-Lisbon interlude in allowing Peggy to believe that he loved her. Now he did not know how to end it without hurting her. For the rest of her life, Peggy was obsessed with the question: "Max must have loved me at one time. Didn't he?" When I saw her for the last time, bedridden at her cold Venice palace in 1979, she asked it of me on every one of the evenings I spent with her. I am glad that I was less than frank with her, because she died not many weeks later.

As the tensions increasingly manifested themselves even at Art of This Century, I found my presence there more and more untenable, in spite of Peggy's pleas that there was no reason to let any of it spoil our personal and working relationship. The solution came in a draft-board notice that ordered me to report for my physical in January of 1943. I used the four-week waiting time to break in my replacement as Peggy's secretary and finished a series of paintings in Elenor's apartment in an ancient building on Central Park South.

On a pre-dawn subway ride from the draft board to Grand Central Palace I tried to gauge the moods in the gray faces of the other sleep-stunned young men who had been led through the turnstiles with me by a sergeant right out of *The Big Parade.* I was really trying to look at myself. Where was that little pacifist who had resolutely turned his back on those Sunday-morning military parades on the Kaiser-Wilhelm-Ring? What had happened to his inbred fear of uniforms, his rejection of any toy reminiscent of war? The bad dreams of childhood were real now. There was a war, and my stake in it was real. The collective insanity that had brought me across an ocean had not collapsed of its own implausibility. It not only threatened my new world here but it might already have destroyed the life that had given life to me. The only regret I remember was that of separation from Elenor. There was nothing casual about my feelings. I loved her. She stood at the gate of life for me, the first individual willing to walk with me for my own sake.

I walked out of Grand Central Palace some five hours later with very mixed feelings. Most of the physical had been routine, until a psychiatrist began to interrogate me about one entry I had made on the lengthy questionnaire. I had thought it perfectly normal to designate Elenor as the recipient of my worldly goods, whatever there was of them. The doctor wanted to know more about my family relationships and in turn called in a number of his colleagues, who grilled me endlessly, collectively, or in relays, for hours about my fears, my hates, my dreams and every clinical aspect of my sex life. I finally got stubborn. I was going to war, like everyone else, and my personal life was strictly a private matter. In the process I must have given the experts a psychological profile worthy of comparison with Dr. Freud's darker case histories. I remember clearly the hostile stare of a beribboned colonel as he pounded my stack of papers with the large stamp: REJECTED.

That night, at Carney's Bar around the corner from the Art Students' League, I got very drunk in the company of Elenor's friends from the Morris Kantor class. I felt awful, and even worse the next morning. I didn't realize that drinking was also something one had to learn to do properly.

Suddenly it was the almost forgotten question, again: "What are you going to be when you grow up?" But this time it was not the idle chatter of some stranger with the kid who is passing the cookies at a tea party. My answer then might have been that I wanted to be the romantic lead in a movie with Dolly Haas, or be Archbishop of Cologne or play left-wing forward on the national soccer team. Those fantasies had come to an end when good burghers, and even relatives, began saluting each other at home and in the streets with the raised right arm, with me eventually winding up in a part of the world where the greeting was invariably by first name, even by people who hardly knew one another.

I had now been alive for twenty-three years and had traveled on whatever roads of survival and accommodation had been open to me. None of it had done me any harm, even when the scenery had been depressing. I was confident now that I could support myself with my hands or my mind, or both, without asking anyone for help. To look for the goal of a profession, however, was strangely absent from my thinking, because I had seen enough to know that painting and becoming a professional painter were poles apart. There was no question that I would paint, but to be an artist was not necessarily achieved through carefully predetermined career steps. Of course, many a good artist had been the apprentice of a master or studied at an academy. I, on the other hand, had lived and breathed that atmosphere all of my life. My hostility to it had been the artificial manufacture of a rebellious youngster, and I knew that I had really never closed my eyes or mind to any of it. My unexpected reaction to Picasso's *Guernica* had proved that to me. I was not at all afraid to make a slightly mystical connection with the fact that the great painting had followed me to America, and if the wish of its master, that it find a home in a free Spain, were to come about, it would be a symbol of a nightmare's ending. But it was a painting that had done that and not necessarily the man. That would have to apply to me as well; whatever I did, it would have to exist as something beyond me. It might be a very long time before I could call myself an artist, and I would have to do it under the conditions that existed for me now.

I had a little money saved up and had given up my small apartment to live with Elenor. Before finding another job, I was going to help Elenor with a dream she had—to start an art gallery. Instead of riding an elevator to the elegant environs of Art of This Century every weekday morning, I was now learning the uses of unfamiliar tools to spruce up a run-down first-floor loft on West Fifty-sixth Street. While Elenor was in Reno, waiting for her divorce, I built storage racks, patched and painted walls, sanded floors and nearly electrocuted myself trying to improve the lighting.

Opening an art gallery may have been a foolish thing to try in an America at war, and the news from the global fronts for the most part was not good. But though New York was now darker at night because of a somewhat casual "brown-out," its life had not gone underground as it had been forced to in London. The signs of crisis were restricted to dimmed automobile lights, gasoline rationing-stickers, some food and clothing items in short supply, but there were no lines in front of stores and a matter-of-fact calm prevailed during the periodic tests of air-raid sirens. The hostilities came into proximate focus only with the news that German saboteurs had landed on the beach at Amagansett, the tragic burning of the liner *Normandy* in New York and the number of young men in uniform on the streets. Their presence was a constant reminder of my own unearned safety: no amount of rationalization eased my own feelings of guilt and discom-fort. I was, after all, not even qualified to drive an ambulance, as I found out when I tried to volunteer for any number of services.

There was little material incentive for the promotion and selling of art. Affluent New Yorkers were not emulating their London counterparts who had bought up any available good art as an inflation hedge with the declaration of war. There were more places now exhibiting contemporary painting and sculp-ture, but the scene was dominated by the work of the better-known Europeans now safely in America. Still, Elenor felt it worth the gamble of her very limited means to make her Norlyst Gallery at least self-supporting. With the promise of the loan of works from most of the more established Americans, there should be a chance of doing something with and for struggling individuals whose efforts had not, yet come to any public attention at all. The opening group show of the gallery, in March 1943, ran its somewhat undisciplined stylistic course in just about every interesting direction we could find. And, like other inexperienced hosts, we had second thoughts about unintentional omissions. None of the fifty artists were familiar beyond a very small world, few of them, indeed, had a name of more than minor prominence at the time. I should not have been surprised by the various hidden pockets of artist-generations that I had been ignorant of, so many individuals, quietly persisting in their personal ways in attics, kitchens and basement corners of a noisy but inattentive city. The wonder of it all was, how did they manage to do it? Once the pictures were hung, it was a revelation how well they got along with each other in spite of their often contradictory styles. Milton Avery's sophisticated candor seemed in no way hostile to the deep Slavic romanticism of Nicholas Vasilieff. Joseph Cornell's *Soap Bubble Set* and George Constant's *Tiger* could have found room within the same ageless dream. The lumber-structured *Napoleon* from the amazing hands of Louise Nevelson could very well have sat at the very table that held Sarah Berman's almost primitively painted *White Coffeepot*. Baziotes' haunting *Leonardo's Butterfly* and Mark Rothko's *Oedipus* were the twin singers of forgotten airs. Crowded as these walls seemed with their disparate windows from the lives of Adolph Gottlieb, John Ferren, Boris Margo, Robert Motherwell, Gabor Peterdi, Virginia Admiral and Charles Seliger, they became the silent voices of just as many visions, and they all created their own light. Far from being ignored, the public interest and the press reaction affirmed Elenor's contention that there was need for such a venture and that there was nothing wrong in breaking an unwritten rule that frowned on the juxtaposition of widely differing styles and expressions on the same walls.

One artist whose work was not hanging at Norlyst was Jackson Pollock. I had gone to see him at his Eighth Street studio and it seems that I was not very convincing in allaying his doubts about contributing to a new gallery. When he came to check on it himself he may not have been sober and a frightened Elenor asked him to leave. I did see two of the paintings from my Eighth Street visit again when Peggy asked me a month later to help her out for a few days with her first "Spring Salon." The first of the jurors to arrive for selection was Piet Mondrian. We were waiting for the others—Barr, Duchamp, Ernst, Soby and Sweeney, while placing all of the submitted work around the walls. Peggy joined Mondrian, who stood rooted in front of the Pollocks. "Pretty awful, isn't it? That's not painting, is it?" When Mondrian did not respond, she walked away. Twenty minutes later he was still studying the same paintings, his right hand thoughtfully stroking his chin. Peggy talked to him again: "There is absolutely no discipline at all. This young man has serious problems . . . and painting is one of them. I don't think he's going to be included . . . and that is embarrassing because Putzel and Matta think very highly of him."

Mondrian continued to stare at the Pollocks, but then turned to her. "Peggy, I don't know. I have a feeling that this may be the most exciting painting that I have seen in a long, long time, here or in Europe."

Peggy was astounded. "But, Mondrian, this is not the kind of work I expected you to admire."

"I did not use the word 'admire,' Peggy . . . not yet, anyway, and I don't know if I ever can . . . Just because it points in the opposite direction of my paintings . . . my writings . . . is no reason to declare it invalid. Everybody assumes that I am interested only in what I do in my own work. . . . There are so many things in life and in art that can and should be respected . . . yes, admired . . . I don't know enough about this painter to think of him as 'great.' But I do know that I was forced to stop and look. Where you see 'lack of discipline,' I get an impression of tremendous energy. It will have to go somewhere, to be sure. . . . Right now I am very excited."

I knew of Peggy's willingness to listen. I had never perceived her as "imperiously all-knowing," and I was not surprised at all when she brought each of the now present jurors over to the work. "I want you to see something very exciting. It's by someone called Pollock."

Norlyst was definitely "Off-Fifty-seventh Street," as far as the more prestigious dealers east of Fifth Avenue were concerned. Julien Levy called it a "bargain basement with some nice native souvenirs for the Grand Concourse clientele." He exiled Gabor Peterdi, the magnificent printmaker and painter, from his gallery when Peterdi refused to bow to an ultimatum never to show with Norlyst again. Other characterizations were: "Where did they dig up all of those Sunday painters? Must be rejects from Major Bowe's *Amateur Hour*. Or: "Who would want to walk one flight up to a dump like that?"

Karl Nierendorf was more benign. "I don't care if you show those Nevelson sculptures. There is nothing to them . . . refugees from a lumber yard. I'm interested only in her drawings . . . and there isn't much you can say for them either." We took him up on that a few months later, when Nevelson was the star of Norlyst's "C*I*R*C*U*S," with twenty-four of her extraordinary inventions. Erstwhile bedsteads, doors, bureau-drawers, carved lintels, chair-backs and, indeed, lumber scraps, had become a *Ferocious Bull, The Trapeze Artist, The Juggler, Balancing Seals*, a whole menagerie of animals and *The Crowd Outside* —each piece a majestic conception the live scale of which had retained the dignity of the creature or the loneliness of the clown child. This unique assembly was surrounded by nineteenth-century circus posters of Steinlen, Toulouse-Lautrec, Chéret and Bonnard, and anonymous broadsheets of colorful tigers, elephants, horses and human cannonballs that Elenor had discovered in the studio of one of her artists. The floor was covered with a three-inch layer of marbles. Though it was not called a "happening" then, it was just that. With the positive exception of Emily Genauer in the *World-Telegram*, the reception was again very mixed. Edward Alden Jewell in the Sunday *New York Times* referred to Nevelson's simultaneous show of drawings at the Nierendorf Gallery as "her more serious work" and dismissed the sculpture at Norlyst with, "As for the floor, that is strewn with a strange conglomeration of 'sculptural' forms. . . . Might also mark the onset of the 'Silly Season.' " But something must have nagged at him, because, in an unprecedented second review five days later, he was far less derisive, though still closing on a negative note: "These very queer objects are chiefly of wood roughly hammered together and often equipped with assorted gadgets calculated to assist in creating a bizarre soupcon of verisimilitude."

If there was general concensus that Norlyst was no threat to the establishment, my abilities as a carpenter, wall painter and floor scraper had also not been adequate to create the usual hallowed tasteful sanctum, with the result that toward the end of the day it became the hangout for an increasing number of artists whose working schedules seemed to require a breathing spell. Somebody would bring some wine, and it was time to worship with gripes, gossip and group aesthetics. There were the "old" and the "young," "Masters," nevertheless, masters all, out of sheer politeness, but some, obviously, more "equal" than others, judging by the way they were treated or listened to. Joseph Stella, now in the last years of his life, held informal court in the manner of a family-don, his game leg extending from the chair as he recalled the events leading up to the 1913 Armory show and the selection of "outsiders" like him, Edward Hopper, Charles Sheeler, Stuart Davis and William Zorach for that epoch-making New York event. And the story would improve each time around. Milton Avery might come around once in a while, taciturn, but always friendly and respectful of others. "Just curious to see what's going on." Boris Margo, the Russian-born American Surrealist, used the forum to complain repeatedly about Max Ernst's injustice to him in dismissing Margo's pre-Ernst use of the decalcomania technique as only a clever pre-dating-the-work trick. Max, in fact, had been quite annoyed with me for supporting Margo on this matter. Mark Rothko and Adolph Gottlieb were regular drop-ins. They were very close at the time as friends and as collaborators in a programmatic post-Surrealist style of painting that relied heavily on archaic myth imagery. Of the two, Mark was by far the more approachable. A large, dignified man with the sorrowing face of a doubter in the temple, he could exude a very personal compassion that would suddenly wane as when a cloud shuts off the sun. But even in those momentary seclusions there was never the absence of kindness. His humor, often self-deprecating, implied at the same time an almost biblical self-assurance. He became a friend whose unobtrusive guidance grew into as strong a supportive branch as that of Baziotes' on the still immature tree of my life as a painter.

The world of these artists contrasted sharply with what I had observed around St. Germain-des-Prés and all the legendary little side streets near the river Seine. Each one of these individuals seemed to do his or her work and his thinking in the absence of the social ease, so comforting for a few hours of the day, of Paris' Left Bank. Instead of the intellectual skirmishes and battles of "isms" at Deux Magots and the occasional baleful stare from the *citoyen d'honneur*, these painters and sculptors were surrounded by a dominion of indifference as well as the prevalent posture of cynicism that "knows the price of everything and the value of nothing." In spite of this twilight existence of subtle inattention, they had their internal differences and contentions, so perhaps absence of literary high-priests to fan embers into brush fires was just as well. Political commitment was evident and there were groups, as well as individuals, whose work followed ideological lines quite closely, but no unofficial ambassadors clever in the uses of dialectical materialism, like Ilya Ehrenburg, were sent to prowl the American equivalent of the rue du Bac in search of intellectual window dressing for Stalin. Maybe the territory was not deemed worthy of attention. Not inconspicuous was a certain amount of flag waving that championed solid regionalists like Thomas Hart Benton. That side seemed to insist that artists of this land should feed on nothing but local corn, confusing in the process "art in America" with "American art." I did not feel that the people I knew saw themselves as the potential flag bearers of an indigenous national art. This, indeed, was not a community ready to exchange diversity for any self-limiting chauvinism.

As I shared my time and walked the streets of New York with this growing circle of varied friends, my sense of participation grew as well. I was gradually leaving my place as merely an awed observer. Their language was straight; but I was still used to more circuitous reasonings. I could not become part of this landscape overnight, though its inhabitants very clearly were ready to accept me. This was evident from the open manner in which they interested themselves in my work. Few of them were given to shallow flattery; I was as welcome in their studios as they were to come and see what I was doing in the room I was using as a studio in Elenor's apartment. So I had to believe that the kind of attention and criticism they brought to my work was not mere politesse. They did not hesitate to acknowledge their awareness of my special problem in having a great painter as a father. I recall Mark Rothko saying to me, "You know, it isn't as if your father was some kind of politician, a big shot, who was 'bringing you into the business.' You'll have to do it all by yourself . . . if this is really what you need to do . . . and then you'll be judged by what you've done. . . . At least, I hope so."

Bill Baziotes, who was there, added, "Hell, if you think about it, everybody who paints or writes has 'fathers.' I have lots of them, just like you. You're in trouble only if you can't outgrow them. Sure, it's more immediate for you and tougher . . . I don't envy you."

Both of them were helping me pick a group of paintings for a showing at the gallery. They and other friends had agreed with me that accepting Peggy's offer for such an exhibition at Art of This Century would certainly have created a well-deserved impression of nepotism. Peggy filled the time-slot instead with the work of the young painter Charles Seliger, who had first shown at Norlyst. With the self-assurance and impatience typical of a twenty-three-year-old added to the voices of encouragement, it never occurred to me that putting a whole room of my paintings on public view anywhere might be a bit too precipitous, and nothing really happened to bring my young expectations down. A lot of people saw the exhibition and a number of things were sold to good collectors, including *The Flying Dutchman*, which went to the Museum of Modern Art, though they asked me for a ten-dollar reduction from the asked-for price of $85. Every critic in New York reviewed the show, and by choosing to ignore the fact that they were, for the most part, rather kind, I lived with the glorious illusion that I had scored a critical success. I readily accepted the nice things they said about my "deftness of technique" and "dreamlike fantasies, or that my work was "profoundly felt" or had "much imagination, . . ." I also chose to interpret as a compliment Edward Alden Jewell's line in the *The New York Times* about *The Flying Dutchman:* "Jimmy Ernst may well have laid to rest the myth of the ancient mariner." Mention of my parental heritage was blessedly perfunctory in its rare instances, and the only embarrassing note was Emily Genauer's opinion in the *World-Telegram:* "But he has a way with color that Max Ernst never touched." My father's reaction to this was predictably one of amusement tinged with sarcasm, and his congratulations on my "debut" were probably a similar mixture, with an emphasis on the latter: "I would have given anything for such reviews when I first started showing." Sometime around then I also met the already legendary American painter Stuart Davis for the first time. "Well, kid," he said, "you're launched. Now you're gonna find out if you can swim. Don't let the bastards drown you." It was that remark that made me aware of a secret self-admission that had registered only faintly when I first saw so many of my paintings, all in a row, in a public place. These images, I thought, made up in surface deception what they lacked in personal depth. I must have known while working on them that there was much mental shorthand in them. Now, looking at them in a new environment, I, like any other outside observer, saw the legerdemain for what it was. To use Davis' analogy, I had conveniently mistaken the ocean for a pond. It was not a despairing admission of failure, but rather the recognition that I had entered into a landscape with no horizon.

It was then that the unfathomable connection between eye and hand began to confront me with an emerging image that, at first, suggested a mistake but somehow resisted correction by reappearing in canvas after canvas, until it had grown or created a space around itself defying human logic, that said clearly: "I think differently from you." It was a message I learned not to ignore. When it worked, the experience was really that of a strange dialogue between myself and the painting, one moving in and out of the other.

The most sinister result of that long winter that had fallen on me with the German occupation of southern France was total silence. Whatever I had heard or read, since that day, did nothing to lighten the opacity of that imperious curtain. It provided endless breeding space for suppositions in which there was no dividing line between hope and despair. Could it be that, just now, as I was waiting for a light to change on a street corner, there was a long-dreaded knock on Lou Straus-Ernst's door some four thousand miles away; or was she out there walking a mountain path? As I was having my second cup of coffee and reading the art page of the Sunday *Herald-Tribune* was she perhaps listening to the clicks of rails on some train ride to an unknown destination; or had she just finished her own Sunday treat, lunch at a peasant bistro? How many moments, seconds, minutes of apprehensive speculation would fill the infinite void of not knowing? It was a selfish nightmare; I had to accept the possibility that it might last forever.

Compared to the dark ruminations I had of my mother's present existence, the pain experienced by both my father and Peggy in untangling themselves from their mutual entrapment struck me as a sad but minor drama, from which I had done well to create some distance. There would be scars, but they were both, after all, still capable of redirecting their lives.

Max Ernst had saved himself from the brink of personal disaster, inevitable in a continuation of this totally incompatible marriage. He had retrieved a happiness, perhaps even a euphoria, that I had observed in him only once before, during his life with Leonora Carrington. Whenever I saw him and Dorothea Tanning together at their Fifty-eighth Street apartment or elsewhere, there was a strong sense that they belonged together. I could understand the feeling because of my own love for Elenor.

It was a bleak time for Peggy. She had been living in dread anticipation of this, yet another, failure. She berated herself for many past acts of irrational behavior and particularly for the childish impulse that had brought about the final break. She had resorted to the installation of a powerful short-wave radio, its prohibition for German aliens thus giving Max the welcome option to stay away for good. At the time I did not know that she was also writing a very spiteful autobiography. She would not let me talk her out of trying to retain the civil-liberties lawyer Morris Ernst. That great advocate, who had successfully sued for the American publication of Joyce's *Ulysses*, wanted no part in the play on names and told her that he did not handle divorce cases. Removed as I was from the immediate scene, I still got involved in skirmishes over pet dogs, books, trinkets and paintings improperly possessed by one or the other party, and I can only imagine what life would have been like if I had stuck around.

Art of This Century did not remain unaffected by the change in Peggy's life. She felt betrayed not just in her personal life but cooled perceptively toward the Surrealists as a whole. The trend of her exhibitions moved decidedly in the direction of painters like Pollock, Rothko, Still, Baziotes and Motherwell. She became particularly active in promoting and selling Jackson Pollock, though with mixed initial results. She was not alone in her perception that something very new and vital was emerging in America's art, and particularly in New York. Her new interests were paralleled by the open minds and eyes of scholars like Alfred Barr, Dorothy Miller, Lloyd Goodrich and James Johnson Sweeney, to mention just a few. A growing number of art dealers were walking in the direction first pioneered by Alfred Stieglitz in risking their fragile enterprises with the possibility of a new vision. There was still a lot of sleep, but New York was waking up.

With Norlyst Gallery well underway, I landed a well-paying job in a small advertising agency with the help of Gabor Peterdi, which had him as its prime asset as an artist. The position even had a title: production manager. I quickly discovered that my graphic apprenticeship at J. J. Augustin in Glückstadt, Germany, served me well in theory but left a great deal to be desired when it came actually to producing ads and direct-mail pieces. There was not much need for excellence in typography and little time to allow for what I thought were the proper standards for printing and photoengraving. The graphic "arts" were a means rather than an end here. Instead I roamed across Manhattan and Brooklyn by telephone, bus and subway, haggling with printers, typographers, binders, direct-mailhouses and engravers, pressuring them for speedy delivery, laboriously counting and collating paper sheets and fearing physical violence from truckers who insisted that delivery was "to the sidewalk only." I learned quickly but not well. I doubted that I would ever be tough enough to "make it" in business. Whenever I got into trouble, it was Peterdi's intervention that saved the job for me. Indeed he saved me from eventually being fired by recommending me as an assistant to the art director in the advertising department of Warner Brothers' home office on West Forty-fourth Street.

The art director, Tony Gablik, was a volatile dynamo whose Hungarian accent increased with the volume of his not infrequent rages. And he had ample reasons. He commanded a "bull pen" of about twenty-five highly paid retouchers, letterers, illustrators and paste-up men, who, though they admired this impatient and tremendously gifted man, conducted a continual warfare with him. Since it was my responsibility to convey Gablik's orders to his rather independent staff and see to it that they were properly executed, I was viewed by the men with some suspicion until I became the subject of Gablik's wrath one day. The outburst found me standing in the middle of the bull pen, waiting through the apoplexy to hear what he really wanted me to get for him. The instructions never came. Instead he hit his forehead with a loud smack, screaming: "Iss dere no vone what can read my mind?" That bit became a minor classic of the Gablik-legend in the industry for a while, and my relationship with the men was cemented. Of course, he had his quieter days, when he patiently worked me into his way of doing things. He was, in fact, quite forbearing in the face of my first test, the pressbook of ads for *Shine on, Harvest Moon,* with Ann Sheridan and Dennis Morgan. I knew next to nothing about marking up the innumerable pieces of artwork for their proper placement by the engraver, and the first batches of blueprint proofs were a total disaster. But by the time we got to my first Humphrey Bogart picture, *Passage to Marseilles,* I had things pretty well in hand. Gablik was a very good Abstract painter himself, and he loved talking about art, complaining, though, that he needed more time for it. I had small concern with that. I was young, happy to have a job for adequate self-support, and the eighthour day was a minor burden as long as I liked what I had to do. On slow days nobody seemed to mind if I occupied myself with drawings, collages or gouaches at my desk. The nights and weekends were for my separate life as a painter.

Without any deliberate effort I found the content of my paintings shifting toward a more pronounced Abstraction. I don't know whether I did this as an act of growing rebellion against the overly literate dicta that had seemed such an essential part of the artistic world in which I grew up. I was no longer reluctant to let a painting become just an act in itself, without resort to some mysterious personal biomorphy. This did not mean that I was free enough to let the act speak entirely for itself or that, on the other hand, I had banished all thought of biographic cross-reference. For example, certain totally nonfigurative passages on a canvas became strongly reminiscent of the Gothic church-architecture and stained-glass windows of my youth. There was no orderly progress from one discovery to the next, but still, every now and then, something would occur that I instinctively recognized as something worthwhile keeping. Nor was I working in a vacuum. The eminent Philadelphia painter Franklin Watkins had thought enough of one of the newer paintings to invite it for the next Pennsylvania Academy Annual. Another one had been chosen for the Pasadena Art Institute Annual, where it won a medal. Paintings were reproduced in art journals, and *Time* magazine and the critics treated my second exhibition in New York with considerably less condescension than the prior one. However, I again had depressing after-the-fact reservations about the way all of the work had really looked. I could not know then that such doubts persist through one's lifetime. "Well, that's not a bad reaction to have," Max told me in one of the rare talks we had about my work, "as long as you think you know how to do it better for the next time. Second thoughts are not as good as first ones. But don't worry, the critics will get nastier as you get better. Look at me."

He had spent the summer with Dorothea in Great River, Long Island, and in the garage near the water, sprouting like uninhibited mushrooms, grew a series of plaster sculptures. They were miraculous inventions that reached back to his early suns and moons; out of his petrified forests had emerged the creatures that he had suspected of being there all along. Their ominous wit made them the siblings of his beloved Hopi kachinas, NorthWest Coast potlatch-objects and the ancestor-icons of New Ireland in the Pacific. He did not belittle them when he said to me that making sculpture was a good way of relaxing between paintings. It was in Great River that I listened with him to radio bulletins about the Allied landings in the south of France not too long after D-Day in Normandy. The long global nightmare might be moving toward an end. "You'll see," he said, "we're going to find Lou. The Nazis probably never bothered with a small place like Manosque. . . . That was completely silly . . . a remarriage would have been just a formality. . . . I have to believe in her optimism . . . we'll know, pretty soon now." Somehow I was no longer sure that I really still wanted to know. The pall of silence had been in place with such apparent finality that I feared what was hidden beyond it.

On April 12, 1945, Franklin D. Roosevelt died in Warm Springs, Georgia, and two days later American and British soldiers marched the good burghers of Belsen and Buchenwald to a spot within the visible horizon of their obscure towns. They indignantly denied any knowledge of what they were shown. They would have objected to the smell alone, they were heard to say.

Just a few weeks later, work in the Art Department on the ad campaign for the Joan Crawford movie *Mildred Pierce* was halted by a phone call. In relays, floor by floor, the entire personnel of Warner Brothers filed into the upstairs screening room to be shown the collective film footage of something unspeakable that the various newsreel companies were about to release to the general public.

No one, not even Hieronymus Bosch or Goya, had ever dared to imagine such a panorama of nauseating horror: The mountains of cadavers; the gigantic open lime pits with an occasional arm, leg or head protruding through inadequate dirt covering, suggesting the volume of rotting flesh beneath; the sight of the gas chambers and the open maws of ovens with ashes and remnants seemingly still hot from the fires. As the cameras moved through the barracks, from some of the many-tiered stacks of cots containing spasmodically moving skeletons, here and there an arm suddenly reached out blindly. And then there were the chimneys, those obscene ducts of human smoke. I could feel the blood rushing through my head and neck in fear of recognizing the face I hoped not to see even among what remained of the living.

I will never know why I followed everyone down the several flights of stairs back to our floor. No one talked about what they had seen. Neither did I.

Somehow I never asked myself on that day why I was sitting at my desk working the caliphers to measure the type sizes in the credits to make sure that Miss Crawford's contractual percentage of the title was correct. I remember checking if the photo retoucher had indeed done away with the suggestion of a smile on Jack Carson's face. *Mildred Pierce* after all, was not being advertised as a comedy.

Perhaps it had been someone other than me up there earlier in the screening room. Of course, I had seen it. I had seen the piles of clothes and shoes all in neat piles ready for sorting. Shoes of all sizes—for men, for women, for children . . . What else? Mountains of teeth, sequestered glittering gold fillings .. . . had I really seen that? . . . My mother had been so proud of the good dental work by her close friend Dr. Jacobs and his discreet way with gold inlays.

That night I went home to Elenor, as usual. We ate in a bar around the corner with some friends. Of course, I told them what I had seen. I couldn't believe that it was my voice talking about some newsreels. Why wasn't I screaming? How could it be that I painted all of that night and the next? . . . And on the weekend? I took Elenor's briard into the park every morning, as usual, and maybe I stayed a little longer, not realizing that I was looking through a tree rather than at it. Perhaps nothing had really changed. The silence, existing parallel with me, was still there. The corpses on that standard 36mm film were "everybody else."

On May 8 the front-page photographs were of the crowds in Times Square on the previous evening, celebrating final victory in Europe. Elenor and I had been there, but I could not find either of us in the picture. That is what happens in crowd pictures. Had I really, foolishly, tried to put some distance between myself and those newsreels, grabbing at the straw that "these corpses were other people"?

A stack of inquiring letters was waiting in my desk for the resumption of postal services. Now was the time to mail them, hoping that some of the houses were still standing and the names on the mailboxes not new and strange. I was not sure at all that I wanted to know the truth.

More documents, more photographs and new names now came daily across the Atlantic, defying in scale and in horror anything one might have imagined about the plagues of the Middle Ages. Dachau, Malthausen, Treblinka and Auschwitz. Carnage factories all, run with awesome organizational skill.

Early that summer I felt that I must see my father for a few days in Amagansett. For a number of years that lovely village in East Hampton Township had been a summer retreat for many of the European artists. The painter Lucia Wilcox had made her house a gathering place for friends like Breton, Ernst, Duchamp,

Léger, Matta, David Hare and Motherwell, where they shared the potluck of her Syrian cuisine, played chess and engaged in severely regimented intellectual party games on the beach, much to the annoyance of the local Bonackers. I was not interested in games this time. Max and I walked the beach by ourselves and I told him why I had come. A friend of J. J. Augustin had been with the United States Mediterranian invasion forces. He had made his way to Manosque and was told there that Lou Straus-Ernst had been "taken away . . . maybe in September 1943." No one wanted to say which police force had executed the order, " . . . but it was not anyone from here." That meant it was probably Vichy, on German orders. Her destination was assumed to have been Paris, and from there everything pointed to ". . . trains going east." Max put an arm across my shoulders and we walked in silence. I saw tears in his eyes, and I realized that this was something I had not been able to do, cry. Standing on a dune, we looked down on a group of people sitting in a solemn, almost ritual, circle. "I don't believe it"—he almost whispered it—"they are still playing Breton's inane game of Verité . . . a cadre, a palace guard, playing at 'Surrealist revolution' . . . I'm sorry you saw this today."

I took the train back to New York and I doubt that I thought too much, or even too harshly, about that little world on the beach, except to know that I did not belong to it. I was far too preoccupied with my own conflict between logic and disbelief. Was it really possible that the German Wehrmacht, fighting on three fronts, had been willing, or even capable, of sparing the needed rolling stock to feed gas chambers and ovens in a place thousands of kilometers east of Paris? Unless, of course, the dictates of functional efficiency demanded that the long trains not return to the Fatherland devoid of freight. There had been a change in my reasoning. I seemed to be temporizing less in terms of hope than in tenuous logistics. The answers to the latter were all too clear. Still, along with every mortal on earth, truster, doubter or heretic, I remained standing in line looking for the possibility of miracles.

The door of that time was only slightly ajar. Some unfelt wind might occasionally make it click but it did not slam it shut. It was a period of waiting for something other than me to make the decision: open it wide or close it forever. The images that I can remember from those days, nights and months must have been swept up by that same wind. What remains of them is like notes scattered and retrieved without specific relation to their import.

I can still see the neat small bullet hole in the windowpane of the ground floor cold-water flat facing West Twenty-first Street, where I lived since something had come undone in my life with Elenor. It seemed better this way, though we would still see each other. The raised kitchen tub was filled with coal for the stove to keep the place warm at night. I had to use the baths and showers of friends, but that was a small inconvenience compared to painting with ice-cold hands.

"Well, I don't care if you think it is terrible. I am not going to change one comma in it. Your father can consider himself fortunate that I am not more explicit." Peggy had taken me back to her little office during an Art of This Century opening and asked me to read the Max Ernst chapter of her manuscript, which was to be published by the Dial Press the following year. I was appalled by its devastating pettiness and I could not believe that she could let such vindictiveness stand. Barely avoiding vulgarity, it seemed almost an act of self-flagellation in its frequent failure of rational thinking. It was tailor-made for the scandal press and it would hurt her almost as much as the intended subject of destruction, my father.

"How dare you say to me, 'You can't do that, Peggy'? How can you possibly defend him? Oh, I see it now, you are against me too . . . probably always were. And why? What kind of a father has he been to you?" . . . Peggy and I did not see each other for a long time after that.

Max gave me a small new painting, *Moon over Sedona*. It was very beautiful. "That's for helping me and being a good nurse to Dorothea." She had been very ill, and I had spelled my father in taking care of her, giving him a chance to go out for a few hours on some evenings. Quite often we talked for a while, after he had come home to their apartment on East Fifty-eighth Street, and the atmosphere of opening up to each other with our problems was not unlike that night, seven years ago, in the empty apartment on rue Jacob. He was very concerned about Dorothea's illness and depressed by a growing hostility and studied indifference toward him in New York. The source of that climate was obviously Peggy's manuscript, the contents of which was almost general knowledge, though the publication date was still some time off. Some supposed friends, sensing "a shift in power," were revealed as the sycophants they had been from the very outset. To the obsequious talents in the exercise of negative power the gossip was a life-giving feed bag. There was no mistaking the tactile air of isolation around Max Ernst. "The climate in Arizona will be better for Dorothea's health, and maybe they will leave us in peace there."

The view from my windows had changed. Instead of Chelsea it was now Fifty-eighth Street on one side and portions of the Queensboro Bridge on the other. Dorothea and Max had arranged for me to sublet their place when they moved to Arizona's Oak Creek Canyon in the spring of 1946. They were pursued even there by the scandal sheets and newsmagazines with stories elaborated from Peggy's now published book. The New York art world, museums, galleries and all, treated the couple as "non-persons." Their answer to these humiliations was their marriage, in a double ceremony with Man Ray and Juliette, in California in 1947. So severe was their hand-to-mouth existence that Max, for the first time in his life, accepted a little help from me in the form of an occasional money order from my own modest salary, with the promise that I not allude to it in my letters lest Dorothea learn about it.

On the day I moved into the apartment, Max came upstairs again from the packed car: "I forgot to tell you. That bunch of small plasters in the corner over there. The chess-set, you know . . . please throw them away . . . I didn't get to that. Throw them down the incinerator shaft next to the kitchen." It was a superb set he had made for himself when he could not find one to his liking to buy. I obeyed him before doing anything else. It was only when I heard the last rook hitting the bin five floors below that I asked myself whether I should have been as dutiful a son as all that.

Many of the letters that I had sent to Europe began to trickle back: "Undeliverable," "Not known at address"; none of the rest was answered. Others came to me from distant relatives on the Ernst side, total strangers to me. I was startled by one because it asked me for books, "particularly anything about atomic energy," others were pleas for help—anything, food, clothing, money—with photographs from better times to serve as introductions, raising the immediate question: Had they been Nazis? I looked at those faces, clean, proper and smiling, not for any family resemblance, but to fathom the possibility that some of them might well have been killers. What was it that bothered me vaguely about the term "collective guilt"? Would I ever be able to walk among these people and point an accusing finger into the face of just anyone at random: "You, you, you . . . and you"?

The nightmare was over. Day after day, for more than a year now, page after dreadful page of new history was being accumulated into an anthology of evil written in the blood that had been the dream and glory of the Third Reich. So poisoned had the soil become that the land was no longer entitled to any good memories. Corpses had risen in all of their stink and anonymity to force their murderers to eat the fine print in the encyclopedia of humiliation and shame. It was as if some specter had carefully cataloged every one of the curses by still-to-be-counted victims so that none would be forgotten.

It should have been a time of satisfaction, if not triumph. If that was the experience of others, I found myself unable to share in it. And how I had waited and dreamed for it to happen. I had walked to school in the very streets from which had flowed this unbelievable hatred. Bred by empty stomachs and vacuous minds, a disease, cloaked in Wagnerian pomp, had matured into a global pestilence that was bound to have left dormant contagion anyplace under the sun. For instance, the word "concentration camp" had not been used in the forced detention of the Japanese on America's West Coast, but what else, after all, had it been?

I felt no exaltation in the knowledge that my own maledictions on that boat-train to Le Havre eight years before had been fulfilled.

I know how close I myself came to justifying whatever retaliatory excesses I could think of when all illusions of hope for my mother's fate had come to an end: Fritz Neugass, Lou Straus-Ernst's closest companion from the 1933 days in the rue Touiller until his 1941 escape to New York, had obtained information from the newly formed Centre de documentation juive contemporaine in Paris: After her arrest in Manosque, my mother had survived in a Paris detention camp until she was sent on one of the last trains east to Auschwitz.

The few pieces of paper, ghastly documentation, are now in my possession.

A total of seventy-seven freight trains left Drancy and Compiègne for Auschwitz, carrying in all 73,853 human beings, beginning March 27, 1942. The last one departed on July 31, 1944.

Under the letter "E" on the list of 1100 "certified" Jews in the next-to-last train, Convoi 76, appears the name Ernst, Louise, born February 12, 1893, Cologne. Departure June 30, 1944. How much longer would it be before the acts of the judges would become as barbaric as those of the lawbreakers before them?

I cannot put in order the time-blurred thoughts that followed in the wake of that final truth. I remember a similar coldness possessing me some twenty-nine years later and then only for a moment. And that was when I saw curtains, forgotten in haste, in the blind windows of a house, bricked up on the inside, that had become an obscene part of the Berlin Wall.

Time and again I have been frozen by the thought of the obsessive perversion symbolized by Convoi 76 leaving a railhead momentarily expected to fall to the advancing Allies. I have never been able to imagine what it must have been like to exist in Drancy. To hear the clocklike departure of trains, with the knowledge of their final destination probably no longer a secret. Was it really true that the new arrivals heard final encouragement to disrobe for a cleansing "shower" from fellow Jews, who wore the same prison stripes as the musicians seated to one side? Why is it that we accommodate thoughts on someone's death without the flashes of what might have been seen in the last terrifying seconds before the ultimate void?

My nightmares, sleeping or awake, are of nozzle-studded ceilings and a gently descending spray of mist.

The only mental shield that I have against the image of a string quartet performing Haydn at the entrance to the gas chambers is the desperate hope that death might have come before, in a filthy freight car. The raw chill is really the dominant recollection.

The bleakness of finality erased with cruel indifference all that remained of my past. The continent on which I had lived for close to eighteen years was now populated by shadows, mere silhouettes bound to fade with the rising of a moon.

Far more disturbing than the loss of all ties to my past was my stunned discovery of having carried an undetected scar within me for many years. The many faces of mourning had been incomprehensible enough when I was a child, but dry-eyed stoicism in the wake of tragedy had always remained a total mystery to me, even now, when I experienced it myself. Had the antitoxin that had inured me to the malignancy of a multimillion marching boots also taken from me the ability to weep at the death of my mother?

Whatever I felt now awoke in me again the resentful confusion I recalled after Lou Straus-Ernst's answer to an early, innocent question: "Yes, the Jews do not feel that their God has singled them out for wrathful punishment. On the contrary, they are convinced that he has chosen them for severe testing so that they may prove their faith in his infinite wisdom, justice and love. . . . I can't blame you for having your doubts. Yes, I also think that five thousand years is an awfully long time to wait for benevolence. I don't know when the trials will end. I don't have the answer."

No human ear has heard as yet the voices from the "congregation of the dead" to know their judgment. No contrition of the killers who caused the chimneys to belch their smoke could now possibly equal my guilt for still being alive. Was this the continuance of the supreme arrangement? Another test?

One shred of consolation, however, sought a place amid my impotent anger. This extraordinary woman had left me a final gift. She had provided a humanist armor that enabled me to find a world of my own making, the existence of which she had sensed to be on the other side of her mountain.

I had carried this gift with me when my boat docked at a New York pier on June 9, 1938. It had spared me that melancholy combat with the past so debilitating to the expatriate in asylum. Her murder, finally, was terminal evidence that I never belonged to what I had left behind. I felt no pain in the realization that I had been prepared for the future by living my youth in exile.

Yesterday Is a Far-off Shore

I saw the ghost of children at their games
Racing beyond their childhood in the shade.

STANLEY KUNITZ

E ARLY in May of 1975 a small item in *The New York Times* reported that Max Ernst was recovering from a recent stroke in Paris. "According to friends," his condition was improving. I was bewildered that I learned about it only through a newspaper. I had noticed for some time that the circle around my aging father had been less than communicative with me, but I wondered what anyone could expect to gain by keeping me in ignorance. Suffice it to say that this was to be the tawdry prologue to a long-running episode that belongs to the tales of avarice by the Brothers Grimm.

It was demeaning for me to have to explain my visit to my father's bedside as coincidental with the planning of some forthcoming exhibitions of my own work in Europe and, most of all, to see Max's large show at the Grand Palais.

Walking through that exhibition a few days before its official opening was a voyage into what André Breton has called this "most magnificently haunted brain." Some of the apparitions from the journal of an obsessed life were still leaning against bare walls. Others, already fixed in place, were startling windows onto a forbidden world. The *Capricorn*, Max Ernst's sculpture masterpiece, was in place. The giant magician-king, grasping his scepter-staff of a petrified serpent, was ready to hold silent audience. He and his fish-tailed consort had grown out of the red rock of Arizona's Oak Creek Canyon in the troubled times of 1948, where his artist-creator had lived, virtually ignored, if not shunned, by hypocritic aesthetes, scholars and merchants in New York , with the woman he loved. I had worked, for several periods, in that little shack-studio, adjacent to *Capricorn*, after he had returned to Paris. Some of his most marvelous paintings had come out of that flimsy roost against the mountain. In some left-behind magazines I read such condescending "critiques" as ". . . the once-Surrealist, who now speaks a language no longer pertinent to the ethos of the Twentieth Century." Near the top of a pile of photographs was a picture of me, age seven or eight, in a remembered knitted knee-pants suit, a cap in one hand and the other holding on to a child's bench. Propped up against the back wall, as a windbreak, was the almost life-size 1930 collage-painting *Loplop Présente une Jeune Fille.*" A Hopi ceremonial mask hung from a nail on the window-sash overlooking Sedona, and outside were old pieces of left-over concrete that had fashioned *Capricorn* and the innumerable gargoyles on the house that he had built with his own hands on land bought with Dorothea's savings. I still do not know for whom these vestiges of an entranced existence, lived in poverty, isolation and perseverance by an enigmatic man and master, had the most telling impact: the son or the young artist?

I saw him, partially paralyzed, in that quiet silvery room on the rue de Lille on successive afternoons for a little over a week. But I did not see him alone until one Sunday, most of which I spent experiencing Paris at its best, filling in the time before I could visit him. The young street entertainers were out in force at Notre Dame, Parc Luxembourg and boulevard Saint-Germain, just as their predecessors on sunny weekends had been when I had strolled the Left Bank with my mother some forty years ago. I sat in Notre Dame Cathedral, afternoon light streaming through the rose windows, listening to the music of Mozart by a superb string ensemble until it was time to go to the rue de Lille. Walking through the streets of Paris, where giant exhibition-posters and banners with my father's name were prominently displayed everywhere, reminded me of how much my life had diverged from his, even in our respective choices of places we call home. Max Ernst had come to America fascinated by its resemblance to an as yet incompletely cut crystal. Some of the newer facets, as they emerged at the time, however, magnified officious attitudes that he had no choice but to consider as hostile to his way of life and thinking. He had been humiliated enough in gaining his American citizenship in the face of roadblocks from a sanctimonious bureaucracy, only to have it threatened again later in the mid-fifties by the narrow-minded small print of some xenophobic federal statute. The matter could have been resolved, but he chose, as he told me, not to "run or beg anymore." France's offer of citizenship, ignoring its own restrictive chauvinism, became America's loss. It eased the way for him to live the rest of his life where he felt he belonged. My choice of home, on the other hand, hinged less on the inconsistencies and failures of this far-from-perfect society. The reaction, for example, to such later shameful blots as My Lai, Kent State, the criminality of its elected leaders and the ebbs and tides of jingoism I saw as reminders that these excesses are not taken for granted. My father felt the need for a civilized ambience; I saw myself as part of a civilization that still had many ways to grow.

Going up the stairs to his room, I felt no regret at not having belonged to my father's immediate world, but there was a sadness that our lives, though parallel in many ways, had not been able to touch more often. And now time was running out. Perhaps he had not tried to advise me, but had rather warned me about himself, when he once said to me, "Don't work too hard on discovering yourself, you may not like what you find."

Sitting on a chair by his bed, I had to marvel at his seeming absence of resentment against his body's imprisonment by stroke. He could not read or watch television. He just lay there, and I had to believe that the area behind his eyes was peopled by the biomorphy of his invented creatures. When he spoke they tended to intrude by blending with his recall of what was real and what was imagined. The infrequent slips in tenses had a logic all of their own, and it was not out of tolerance that I did not correct them. This was the first time that I was in the room alone with him, and he seemed to prefer to speak German, something that some of the tight circle around him had objected to when they were present on my previous visits, as if we might be discussing matters of any concern to them.

I read to him Harold Rosenberg's superlative *The New Yorker* article about the Max Ernst retrospective at the Guggenheim of some months ago. He was pleased. "Yes, yes, that young woman, Diane Waldman, did the catalog . . . wonderful . . . but they tell me that the show at the Grand Palais here is even better. . . ."

He continued, switching from one topic to another: "Did you see your *Capricorn* there? It just sat there in Sedona, and when somebody finally did want to do something with it, I told them to come to you. I wrote it down somewhere. All those pieces from there belong to you. I hope you made some money from it. . . .

"Rosenberg is a friend of yours, isn't he? Whatever made me think that he didn't like me very much? . . . That nice white-haired painter . . . De Kooning . . . doesn't he live near you? What's the name of that place near the ocean where we used to go in the summer? . . . And Rothko . . . do you like him? . . . Do you see him? He is always so serious . . . even when he smiles. Sad . . . is he always so sad? Do you see a lot of the friends from what they call the School of New York? Are you still one of them? Are they as famous as you are, over there? Everybody in America is famous." I did not tell him that Rothko had committed suicide five years before, and I simply did not consider it appropriate to ask him where the note about the Sedona sculpture was. It was not the first time that he had mentioned it. I could not get myself to find out now if I might have been mistaken when I did not question the authorization that a young sculptor once presented, many years ago, as he proceeded to make rubber molds from *Capricorn* at the site. Instead I changed the subject. I pointed to one of his early paintings on the wall, relating to him for the first time my childhood memory of Anton Raederscheidt and the two artist-fathers' painting over each other's work. Maybe that was the painting that had the naked Mrs. Raederscheidt underneath? He was amused for just a moment. "Raedersheidt painting over one of my pictures, what a nerve! You know that swine wound up doing a portrait of Hermann Göring? . . . You know, you weren't a very interesting baby, but you smiled a lot . . . except when you screamed with nightmares . . . even when awake. There was something about that piece of wallpaper I had torn off, and you yelled that it was a dragon with claws and wings and it was going to eat you if you fell asleep. . . . you have babies, don't you? . . . Is Dallas with you on this trip, or is it all business?"

He always asked about "your little family," about my daughter Amy Louise and the boy Eric Max. "Does he want to paint too? Why did you have to give him that name? Makes it a bit difficult, doesn't it? Oh, yes, Amy. That was a good idea, Amy Louise; she looks like Lou, you know. We enjoyed her when she spent the summer with us . . . showed us some of that Lou independence, but never nasty. Just like her grandmother. Lou is really a remarkable woman . . . how is she? Does she live with you over there in America? Who is she married to now? Your grandfather Jacob thought it was the end of the world when we got married. You know, I really wanted to come back to Cologne. I never thought that this business with Gala would last very long . . . those Russian histrionics were too much for Éluard and me. Look what she did to poor Dali . . . is he still around? . . . No wonder he fell in love with Franco. . . . Lou is the only woman, except Leonora, I ever thought of going back to. She was probably right. It was better for me to stay away. A wandering father is difficult to explain to a young son. . . .You want to know a little family secret? It's the kind a brewmaster passes on to his son in the business. Everybody always wants to know who and what Loplop is, and they write marvelous stories about him. Well, when you were still much too small to sit on one without help, some idiot gave you a present of a wooden rocking horse instead of buying one of my paintings. It was a dreadful bore to hold you on it and to sing to you: *"Gallopp . . . gallopp . . . gallopp . . . gallopp."* You loved your Loplop. I hated it. You'd wake up during the night and scream that you wanted your Loplop. When I made up that creature-device as the presenter of smaller things in a larger composition, Paul Éluard said it needed a name and I remembered your damned Loplop. Never mind that mine was more of a bird than a horse. Whenever I was asked, I told them all kinds of stories— but never that it was your *Schaukelpferd.* I guess I had too much fun to see how much of a myth they could invent themselves. Yes, Loplop is your rocking horse."

The nurse came in, a young Englishwoman, to take his temperature and pulse "Oh, is that Dorothea . . . it's Lou . . . no, no, it's my beautiful niece Heike." And then I saw something that I had envied him for since early boyhood. His face transformed itself into a glow, his eyes sparkled and he flirted with the young blonde, making small talk, causing her to blush. I had never been able to do this, but I had observed it in my son Eric when he was interested in a girl.

I had been there for a long time and I kissed him good-bye. He called me back as I opened the door. "You know there are a lot of people around me now who know what is good for me. I'm glad we could be alone. Lots of conferences

. . . papers to be signed. They tell me what's in them. I can sign when they hold my hand. I'm sure it has nothing to do with you. Don't worry about it. As I moved toward the door, I heard him say, "Are you coming back tomorrow? . . . And remember: I love you, Jimmy."

He must have wondered why I never came back to see him. A telephone call informed me that further visits would suggest the nearness of death to him. I walked past the place a few times and, looking up at the windows of the apartment, I kept hearing those final, almost whispered, words again. I wondered why it had taken him fifty-five years to say them.

Rather than return immediately to the United States, I decided to travel east and walk the streets of Cologne for a couple of days. I had been back a few times —for an exhibition, some lectures and Max's seventy-fifth birthday celebration. This time I wanted to look at it again just by myself. The city had been rebuilt pretty much the way it had looked when I was a boy. There were some older residences still showing the marks of bullets and shell fragments. A street here and there had been gently straightened, some of the Arno Breker-adorned Nazi architecture had been blended in, but the trolley tracks were still there, as was the Kaiser-Wilhelm-Ring, and the prison I had looked out at from my first elementary schoolroom looked cleaned up but the same. Stollwerk chocolates were sold in the same location in just as elegant a store as the one that had been flattened by the British along with everything around the cathedral. During the nightmare of the past, a goodly number of Jews were said to have passed through the mighty Dom's portals into its awesome interior, there to begin a long and mysterious voyage to a safe haven, oceans away, with the help of Cologne's saintly Cardinal Frings. Some of the names on the residential doorbells were still there, as were the river Rhine and the Pressa Building across the way in Deutz. Most of the changes would have come with intervening years anyway, and I could almost see myself trudging to the dairy store in 1926 to get the milk blue with water. I had once belonged to this place and, dressed up as an American Indian, roamed the streets at Carnival time. I had lived here once, but in this late May of 1975 I was seeing it with the eyes of a stranger who cannot understand why everything is so familiar and who at first disbelieves the many fragments of his younger life as he encounters them in unlikely corners of a place he must have loved once. Not the least of those ghosts were the childhood anxieties that threatened to outlast long voyages and years. Somewhere here that image that was to confront me so often in my life must have appeared for the first time: the open palm of a hand thrust in my face, pushing me back and commanding me never to come any closer. Suddenly the poliphony of Cologne's church bells transformed themselves, in memory, to Tristan Tzara's "Glockenspiel of Hell."

I took the train ride to Brühl again, as I had as a youngster for my weekend visits to grandfather Philipp. Three men in the compartment, about my age, noticing my *International Herald-Tribune*, struck up a conversation in halting English with me. I answered them in my German, which by now had acquired an American accent, and I had to convince them that I had been born in Cologne. Soon enough they began to express their discomfort with having to live with the shame of Hitler's crimes against people like me. This was followed by the inevitable turn of conversation that began with "You know, if Eisenhower had not held the Americans back in Aachen, the Nazis wouldn't have had the additional time to arrest more Jews in Cologne. And since you've had your wars in Korea and Vietnam, you have done some horrible things yourselves. Now, it's not just us anymore."

I had heard this one just once too often. I forgot my carefully reasoned conviction that to mark any people or nation with the tarring brush of collective guilt is unjust. "Look, yours is not the only society gone berserk with killing minorities who have offended some trumped-up sense of value. The excuses never add up to restitution or atonement, and then you find that you only feel better when you point the finger away from you. It happens all over the world, all of the time. But you, your fathers and your children will have to get used to the idea that you did these things better and more efficiently than anyone else. In that sense you are indeed the experts, the masters." I decided not to walk through Brühl, the town of some pleasant memories and the birthplace of Max Ernst. I waited for the next train back.

On the way to the airport in Paris I tried rue de Lille once more, but was not admitted. The nurse had her orders.

Out of the plane window I saw the French coast disappear below. I was unaware of it at that moment, but I had traveled this same route for the first time thirty-seven years earlier, to the very day, but by boat. In 1938 I had opened the door on the far shore. Now I knew that it had been the door to home.

POSTSCRIPT: CELL # 12—
MAY 1944—LOU ERNST

 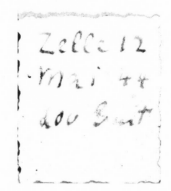

This identification photograph was taken in the Drancy concentration camp near Paris a few weeks, if not days, before Lou Straus-Ernst was put on Transport 76 for shipment to Auschwitz with over a thousand others. Her garb is concentration camp stripes and a dramatic loss of weight after one year's detention is evident. The back bears in her handwriting the number of her cell, the date, and her name. As a further evidence that this photo was part of some kind of grisly passport imposed by camp and transportation authorities, the lower left of the original still shows the faint impression of an official rubberstamp—probably German.

I found this final document waiting for me on a visit to a major Max Ernst exhibition at the Fondation Maeght in St. Paul de Vence in late September 1983 when the galleys of this book had already been bound. It had been sent there for forwarding by Charles K. Fiedler, one of the group of political and Jewish refugees that had lived under the protection of the great poet Jean Giono in Manosque (Alpes Maritimes) during the war. Fiedler, a young German architect, was the shepherd of Giono's farm animals and he met Lou in her capacity as translator into German of Giono's writings. In a subsequent Paris meeting the eighty-year-old Fiedler told me: "Your mother was one of the most loving, most intelligent, women I have ever known. Though I was ten years younger than she, I count the few years of our friendship as unforgettable in my life. I am proud to tell you, her son, that we knew each other in a biblical sense. One of Lou's sister-inmates, an Auschwitz survivor, not only sent me the Drancy photograph, but also provided me with the very final image I have of her. It has haunted me for thirty-five years and I often wish I had never heard of it. She remembered Lou as a woman totally exhausted, half lying down, half leaning against a wall, warming herself in the last rays of a dying sun."

INDEX